Mark Tutton
Locative Expressions in English and French

Applications of Cognitive Linguistics

Editors
Gitte Kristiansen
Francisco J. Ruiz de Mendoza Ibáñez

Honorary editor
René Dirven

Volume 28

Mark Tutton

Locative Expressions in English and French

A Multimodal Approach

DE GRUYTER
MOUTON

ISBN 978-3-11-063504-1
e-ISBN (PDF) 978-3-11-035486-7
e-ISBN (EPUB) 978-3-11-039410-8
ISSN 1861-4078

Library of Congress Cataloging-in-Publication Data
A CIP catalog record for this book has been applied for at the Library of Congress.

Bibliographic information published by the Deutsche Nationalbibliothek
The Deutsche Nationalbibliothek lists this publication in the Deutsche Nationalbibliografie;
detailed bibliographic data are available on the Internet at http://dnb.dnb.de.

© 2018 Walter de Gruyter GmbH, Berlin/Boston
This volume is text- and page-identical with the hardback published in 2016.
Printing and binding: CPI books GmbH, Leck

♾ Printed on acid-free paper
Printed in Germany

www.degruyter.com

To Alexis Tabensky and Maarten Lemmens,
for their tremendous hard work and encouragement.

Foreword

This book is a revised version of my PhD thesis, which was written under the joint supervision of Dr Alexis Tabensky and Professor Maarten Lemmens. I have immense gratitude for the enormous investment that both Alexis and Maarten made in my work. In my first year of candidature, Alexis spent hours with me every week making sure that I had done the necessary groundwork and teaching me the intricacies of gesture analysis. She taught me the value of writing clearly and held me accountable for every word I asked her to read. I was particularly lucky to find this same dedication in Maarten Lemmens. Maarten spent hours at a time discussing my research with me, whether I was in France or Australia. He consistently provided critical feedback and has unfailingly encouraged and supported me, ever since he supervised my Master's thesis. Both Maarten and Alexis worked tirelessly throughout my PhD years to ensure that I produced work that reflected the best of my ability. I am pleased to dedicate this book to them.

I am also grateful to those who helped me at different stages of the research reported in the current work, particularly Marianne Gullberg, Asli Özyürek, and Cornelia Müller. I benefited greatly from a brief stay at the Max Planck Institute for Psycholinguistics, Nijmegen, in 2007, and would like to thank Marianne Gullberg for hosting me. I also acknowledge Bettina Boss and Hugues Peters for their support during my PhD candidature and for their feedback on my work. As members of my PhD examining committee, Gale Stam, Maya Hickmann and Sotaro Kita also provided me with valuable comments and advice, for which I am very grateful.

Part of the research reported in this book has appeared, in some form or another, in the following publications. I would like to thanks the publishers for their permission to reuse this material.

Tutton, Mark. 2014. Gestures and location in English. In Cornelia Müller, Alan Cienki, Ellen Fricke, Silva Ladewig, David McNeill & Jana Bressem (eds.), *Body – Language – Communication: An International Handbook on Multimodality in Human Interaction. Volume 2.* (Handbooks of Linguistics and Communication Science 38.2), 1677–1686. Berlin, Boston: De Gruyter Mouton.

Tutton, Mark. 2013. 'Describing adjacency along the lateral axis: the complementary roles of speech and gesture.' In Carita Paradis, Jean Hudson & Ulf Magnusson (eds.), *The construal of spatial meaning: windows into conceptual space*, 98–117. Oxford: Oxford University Press.

Tutton, Mark. 2013. A new approach to analysing static locative expressions. *Language and Cognition* 5(1). 25–60.

Tutton, Mark. 2012. When and why the lexical Ground is a gestural Figure. *Gesture* 12(3). 361–386.

Tutton, Mark. 2011. How Speakers Gesture When Encoding Location with English *on* and French *sur*. *Journal of Pragmatics* 43. 3431–3454.

Tutton, Mark. 2007. A speech/gesture interface: encoding static, locative relationships in verbal discourse. In Robyn Loughnane, Cara Penry Williams & Jana Verhoeven (eds.), *In Between Wor(l)ds: Transformation and Translation*, 223–234. Melbourne: School of Languages, University of Melbourne.

As far as financial matters are concerned, I would like to thank the Australian government for funding my PhD scholarship (Australian Postgraduate Award). The French government also allocated me travel assistance as part of my study program, and I gratefully acknowledge this. Both the University of New South Wales and Université Lille 3 provided me with additional financial and technical support. Special thanks go to Simon Trevaks at UNSW for his technical expertise with Photoshop, and to Peta Dzubiel for drawing the stimulus pictures used in my experiments.

It would be remiss not to thank my family, who have been a tremendous support to me, and my friends. I particularly think of Judith Holler here, who not only encouraged me during my PhD, but also offered me a postdoctoral role at the University of Manchester. Many wonderful things have come from my time in Manchester and so much of this is due to Judith. Thanks are also due to Gaëlle Ferré, who very generously lent me her laptop on many occasions while I prepared the final version of this book.

Finally, I would like to acknowledge Gitte Kristiansen, editor of the *Applications of Cognitive Linguistics* book series, Birgit Sievert and Angelika Hermann, my contacts at De Gruyter Mouton, and an anonymous reviewer for their vital roles in seeing the present work published as a book. I always intended for my PhD thesis to be published as a book, to be read as a coherent whole that brings together a whole range of observations on the topic of static locative expressions. Their work has helped make this a reality.

Table of Contents

Foreword —— VII

1　Introduction —— 1
1.1　　Previous research into how speakers express static locative relationships —— 2
1.2　　The place of our study in the literature on space and gesture —— 4
1.3　　The value of a comparative English/French study —— 5
1.4　　Structure of the book —— 6
1.5　　Further precisions —— 8

2　Language, gesture, and locative expressions: a background —— 10
2.1　　An overview of the spatial domain —— 10
2.1.1　Basic concepts in static locative relationships —— 11
2.1.2　Separating static locative relationships from dynamic motion events —— 12
2.1.3　The lexical encoding of static locative relationships in English and French —— 13
2.1.4　The different types of static locative relationships —— 16
2.1.5　Direction and frames of reference —— 18
2.1.6　Perspective and viewpoint —— 22
2.1.7　Deixis and origo —— 25
2.1.8　The different sub-types of locative relationships —— 26
2.1.9　Summary —— 28
2.2　　Gesture —— 29
2.2.1　The different types of gesture —— 30
2.2.2　Gesticulations —— 33
2.2.2.1　Iconicity in gesture —— 34
2.2.2.2　Metaphoric gestures —— 36
2.2.2.3　Pointing gestures —— 36
2.2.2.4　Beats —— 37
2.2.2.5　Cohesives —— 38
2.2.2.5.1　The gesticulations of interest in the current research —— 38
2.2.3　The relationship of speech and gesture —— 38
2.2.3.1　An overview of the literature —— 38
2.2.3.2　The view taken in the current study —— 41
2.3　　Gesture and the expression of spatial information: what we know —— 42

2.3.1	Gesture and spatial conceptualisation —— 42	
2.3.2	The relationship between lexically-encoded and gesturally-expressed spatial information —— 43	
2.3.3	The role of gesture in communicating object size and relative position —— 44	
2.3.4	Gesture and the expression of static locative information: hypotheses —— 45	
3	**Methodology —— 48**	
3.1	Background to the experiment —— 48	
3.2	Pilot study —— 49	
3.3	The revised study —— 51	
3.3.1	Theoretical considerations —— 51	
3.3.2	The use of two pictures —— 51	
3.3.3	Experimental setup —— 54	
3.3.4	Further precisions concerning experimental procedure —— 56	
3.4	Recruitment of participants —— 57	
3.5	Editing and transcription of data —— 58	
3.6	Structure of data analysis —— 66	
3.7	Presentation of examples in the analysis —— 66	
4	**Defining and separating static locative expressions in oral discourse —— 68**	
4.1	Defining static locative expressions —— 68	
4.1.1	Functional versus grammatical concerns in defining static locative expressions —— 71	
4.1.2	Static locative expressions and the clarification of directional information —— 74	
4.2	Segmenting static locative relations in oral discourse —— 75	
4.2.1	Differences in lexical and gestural Figures and Grounds —— 78	
4.2.2	Primary locative expressions and secondary locative expressions —— 81	
4.2.3	Overall locative expressions —— 83	
4.3	Summary —— 85	
5	**Describing location along the frontal axis —— 87**	
5.1	The frontal axis —— 87	
5.2	Lounge room scene – English descriptions —— 89	
5.2.1	The use of front-encoding items —— 91	

5.2.1.1	The role of gesture in clarifying frontal direction —— 92	
5.2.1.2	A different origo and Ground in speech and gesture —— 96	
5.2.1.3	Different perspectives in speech and gesture —— 98	
5.2.1.4	Gestural representations of foregrounds —— 100	
5.2.2	The use of back-encoding items —— 101	
5.2.3	The use of directionally non-specific items —— 102	
5.2.3.1	The use of gesture with directionally non-specific items —— 107	
5.3	Lounge room scene – French descriptions —— 108	
5.3.1	The use of front-encoding items —— 109	
5.3.1.1	Gestural representations of foregrounds —— 110	
5.3.1.2	How speakers use 'devant' and 'en face de' —— 111	
5.3.2	The use of back-encoding items —— 115	
5.3.3	The use of directionally non-specific items —— 116	
5.4	Street scene – English descriptions —— 119	
5.4.1	The use of front-encoding items —— 122	
5.4.2	The use of back-encoding items —— 127	
5.4.3	The use of directionally non-specific items —— 128	
5.4.4	The use of sequence-encoding items —— 132	
5.4.5	The overall use of gesture with directionally non-specific and sequence-encoding items —— 135	
5.5	Street scene – French descriptions —— 139	
5.5.1	The use of front-encoding items —— 141	
5.5.2	The use of back-encoding items —— 147	
5.5.3	The use of directionally non-specific items —— 147	
5.5.4	The use of sequence-encoding items —— 149	
5.5.5	The overall use of gesture with directionally non-specific and sequence-encoding items —— 153	
5.6	Comparison and discussion —— 156	
5.6.1	Comparison of lounge room and street scene descriptions in English —— 156	
5.6.2	Comparison of lounge room and street scene descriptions in French —— 157	
5.6.3	Comparison of English and French descriptions of the lounge room scene —— 159	
5.6.4	Comparison of English and French descriptions of the street scene —— 160	
6	**Describing location along the lateral axis —— 164**	
6.1	The lateral axis —— 164	

6.2	Lounge room scene – English descriptions —— 167	
6.2.1	Encoding location with 'next to' —— 170	
6.2.2	Why speakers use 'next to' to encode adjacency —— 175	
6.2.3	'Between', the lateral axis and gesture —— 177	
6.2.4	The use of 'then' to encode location along the lateral axis —— 179	
6.2.5	The use of gesture with semantically-similar lexical items —— 180	
6.2.6	Gesture and the use of other directionally non-specific spatial items —— 182	
6.2.7	The use of left-encoding items —— 183	
6.2.8	The use of right-encoding items —— 185	
6.3	Lounge room scene – French descriptions —— 186	
6.3.1	Encoding location with 'à côté' and 'à côté de' —— 188	
6.3.2	Establishing the Ground's location in gesture space when using 'à côté de' —— 192	
6.3.3	'Entre', the lateral axis and gesture —— 194	
6.3.4	The use of gesture with sequence-encoding items —— 196	
6.3.5	The use of gesture with directionally non-specific and sequence-encoding items —— 198	
6.3.6	The use of left-encoding items —— 199	
6.3.7	The use of right-encoding items —— 201	
6.4	Street scene – English descriptions —— 202	
6.4.1	The use of directionally non-specific items —— 204	
6.4.1.1	'Outside (of)' —— 204	
6.4.1.2	'Opposite' —— 206	
6.4.1.3	'Next to' —— 208	
6.4.1.4	Expressing directional information relating to directionally non-specific items —— 209	
6.4.2	The use of left-encoding items —— 210	
6.4.3	The use of right-encoding items —— 212	
6.5	Street scene – French descriptions —— 214	
6.5.1	The use of directionally non-specific items —— 215	
6.5.1.1	Expressing directional information relating to directionally non-specific items —— 218	
6.5.2	The use of left-encoding items —— 219	
6.5.3	The use of right-encoding items —— 221	
6.6	Comparison and discussion —— 221	
6.6.1	Comparison of lounge room and street scene descriptions in English —— 221	

6.6.2	Comparison of lounge room and street scene descriptions in French —— 223	
6.6.3	Comparison of English and French descriptions of the lounge room scene —— 225	
6.6.4	Comparison of English and French descriptions of the street scene —— 228	
7	**How speakers gesture when encoding location with *on* and *sur* —— 231**	
7.1	A basic overview of topological relationships —— 231	
7.2	Using *on* and *sur* to encode location —— 233	
7.3	Identifying representational gestures for *on* —— 235	
7.3.1	Gestures relating to *on* in descriptions of the lounge room scene —— 237	
7.3.2	Gestures relating to *on* in descriptions of the street scene —— 244	
7.4	Identifying representational gestures for *sur* —— 248	
7.4.1	Gestures relating to *sur* in descriptions of the lounge room scene —— 249	
7.4.2	Gestures relating to *sur* in descriptions of the street scene —— 252	
7.5	Comparative discussion of English and French results —— 256	
7.5.1	Ground-encoding complements of *on* and *sur*: lounge room scene —— 256	
7.5.2	Alternative strategies to using *on* and *sur* —— 258	
7.5.3	Ground-encoding complements of *sur* and *on*: street scene —— 261	
7.6	General discussion and summary —— 262	
8	**Further findings, and the theoretical application of our results —— 266**	
8.1	Summary of our approach to analysing static locative relationships —— 266	
8.2	Referencing different spatial axes in speech and gesture —— 267	
8.2.1	Different spatial axes in speech and gesture: lounge room scene —— 268	
8.2.2	Different spatial axes in speech and gesture: street scene —— 271	
8.2.3	Discussion —— 274	
8.3	A different Figure in speech and in gesture —— 275	
8.3.1	Establishing the location of the lexical Ground —— 275	
8.3.2	Establishing the location of the lexical Ground when speakers use direction-encoding items —— 280	
8.3.3	Why speakers mark the location of the lexical Ground in gesture space —— 281	

8.4	Positioning our findings within Cognitive Grammar —— 285
8.4.1	Adjusting the phonological pole of symbolic assemblies —— 288

9 Conclusion —— 295
- 9.1 The framework of our investigation, and main findings —— 296
- 9.1.1 Laying the foundations —— 296
- 9.1.2 Methodology —— 297
- 9.1.3 Defining and separating static locative expressions in oral discourse —— 297
- 9.1.4 Describing location along the frontal axis —— 298
- 9.1.5 Describing location along the lateral axis —— 300
- 9.1.6 How speakers gesture when encoding location with *on* and *sur* —— 301
- 9.1.7 Other ways in which gesture expresses unlexicalised locative information —— 302
- 9.2 Overall conclusions —— 303
- 9.3 Theoretical implications of results —— 304
- 9.4 Future research —— 305

Appendix A —— 307

Appendix B —— 309

Appendix C —— 311

Appendix D —— 315

Appendix E —— 317

Appendix F —— 319

References —— 321

Index —— 329

1 Introduction

Expressing the locations of objects is one of the most crucial and recurrent communicative tasks that we perform in our daily lives. From describing a pen's location *next to* a telephone to stating that there is a bus stop just *after* the traffic lights, we must learn how to master communicating location across all different types of spatial settings. This book examines how speakers of English and French express locative information in speech and in gesture. More specifically, we examine *static locative relationships*: that is, relationships in which the object(s) being located (the 'Figure', following Talmy 2000), as well as the object(s) in relation to which this localisation occurs (the 'Ground', Talmy 2000), are at fixed points in space (Hendriks et al. 2004).

(1)   the book is next to the sofa

In example (1) *the book* is the Figure, and the Ground is *the sofa*. The nature of the locative relationship that holds between the two objects is encoded by the spatial item *next to*.

In what follows, we focus on how speakers express the nature of static locative relationships, such as that encoded by *next to* in example (1). We argue that both speech and gesture play pivotal roles in this process. Our research reveals that gestures express key directional information concerning the Figure's location, and that this information relates to the locative relationship lexicalised in speech. We therefore show that speech and gesture are interconnected modalities which can express different, yet complementary, aspects of a scene or event (McNeill 1992, 2005; Kendon 2004). Our research also reveals that the objects which a speaker conceptualises as a Figure or Ground cannot be known through the analysis of speech alone. This is because speakers recurrently establish the location of the lexical Ground in their gesture space: these objects are therefore simultaneously 'gestural Figures'. The expression of location in oral discourse works on the levels of both speech and gesture, and the information in the two modalities combines to present complete, overall depictions of locative configurations. The upshot of this twofold. Firstly, gestures allow us a much clearer insight into how speakers conceptualise locative relationships. For example, as mentioned above, an object may appear as Figure in gesture only. Therefore, to know something as basic as the Figure of a locative utterance requires us to attend to a speaker's gestures as well as to their speech. Secondly, listeners stand to benefit by attending to speakers' gestures, which can contain salient, unlexicalised locative information. This suggests that the gestures used in locative utterances have the potential to be communicatively important vehicles of information transfer.

1.1 Previous research into how speakers express static locative relationships

To date, the most extensive cross-linguistic research into how speakers encode static location has been undertaken by researchers at the Max Planck Institute for Psycholinguistics, Nijmegen. Researchers at the Institute sought to identify a 'basic locative construction' (BLC) for a variety of the world's languages. A basic locative construction is defined as a response to a 'where' question, such as 'Where is the book?' In order to elicit data, researchers presented informants with picture-based stimuli which depicted basic 'topological' locative relationships, such as those encoded by *in*, *on*, *under*, and *near*. The results brought to light the various grammatical classes used by different languages to encode locative semantics, as well as the different semantic features of locative relationships that achieve lexical expression. For instance, speakers of certain languages, including Dutch and German, use posture-encoding verbs in basic locative constructions. This is shown by the following example from German.

(2) *das buch*   *liegt*   *auf dem tisch*
    the book   lies/is lying on the table

The inflected form of the verb *liegen* in this example not only encodes static location, but also the manner in which the book occupies its location. In contrast, English typically uses the copula verb *be* (Levinson 1992: 29), which is neutral with regard to the semantic features of posture and position (see example 1). Similarly, French speakers use *être* ('be') or the generic locative verb *se trouver* ('be found'), neither of which encodes posture nor position (see Borillo 1998). A special edition of the journal *Linguistics* has been dedicated to the topic of locative verbs (see Ameka and Levinson 2007) and provides a detailed cross-linguistic investigation.

The concept of a basic locative construction has therefore been fruitful for uncovering the different ways in which location is encoded in a broad cross-linguistic perspective. However, our work concerns only English and French. Furthermore, we aim to uncover the variety of ways in which speakers of these two languages express location in oral discourse. Hence, while our discussion of location will include examples of basic locative constructions, it will not be limited to them.

As far as other research into the encoding of static location is concerned, an ongoing research project by Lemmens (2005) also investigates locative verbs across a range of European languages, including English and French. Research into the expression of location that does not specifically focus on locative verbs includes work by Kopecka (2004) on French and Polish, and by Grinevald (2006) on Amerindian languages. Both these studies use the basic locative construction, described above, as an investigative tool. As far as English and French are concerned, Hickmann and Hendriks (2006) have investigated how speakers lexically encode 'specific' (i.e. fine-grained) semantic information relating to motion and location. Moving away from spoken languages, Perniss (2007) has analysed how location is encoded in German Sign Language (DGS), Özyürek, Zwitserlood and Perniss (2010) have investigated the expression of location in Turkish Sign Language (TID), while Eberle (2013) has looked at the expression of location – focusing mostly on relations that would be encoded by *on* and *in* in English – in five signed languages: Catalan Sign Language (CSC), Estonian Sign Language (ESO), Nigerian Sign Language (NSI), Thai Sign Language (TSQ), and Australian Sign Language (ASQ).

It is also important here to mention a doctoral dissertation by Arik (2009), which examines how motion and location is expressed by a range of signed and spoken languages. The sign languages investigated were Turkish Sign Language, Croatian Sign Language, American Sign Language and Austrian Sign Language, while the spoken languages were Turkish, Croatian, and English. Arik's aim was to test a hypothesis, the 'Crossmodal Spatial Language Hypothesis', "which claims that the features from spatial input are not necessarily mapped on the spatial descriptions regardless of modality and language" (xviii). That is, as far as static location is concerned, he hypothesized that not all features of a locative configuration, such as object orientation and the distance or proximity between objects, would be encoded by speakers in their locative expressions. This was expected to hold regardless of whether the language was signed or spoken. For spoken languages he considered both speech and co-speech gestures, in order to more correctly determine the features of locative configurations which speakers took into account. The cross-linguistic analysis confirmed his 'Crossmodal Spatial Language Hypothesis'. Moreover, results showed that gestures could express locative information using a different frame of reference (qv. Chapter 2) to that encoded in speech. His study, however, differs greatly to our own, as we discuss below.

1.2 The place of our study in the literature on space and gesture

Our investigation differs from those mentioned above in several key ways. Firstly, we are not concerned with the role of the verb in locative expressions. This is because our work is focused on the *nature* of the locative relationship that exists between the object(s) being located (the 'Figure') and the object(s) in relation to which this occurs (the 'Ground'). This information is typically (but not exclusively) encoded by prepositions in both languages: for example, *on/sur*, *between/entre*, *next to/à côté de*, etc. Secondly, we present gesture as a crucial component of utterance structure (cf. Kendon 2004). Hence, we consider how speakers use *both* speech and gesture to express the nature of locative relationships. This multimodal approach has not been adopted in any of the studies mentioned above, apart from that of Arik (2009). However, Arik's work differs crucially to ours in three key ways. Firstly, his is a large study that focuses on seven languages and spans three semantic domains: motion, location, and time. As far as location is concerned, he only briefly considers gesture in his analysis: it is not the subject of an extensive examination. Secondly, Arik does not attempt to identify the role of gesture in expressing locative information. Gestures are examined in order to evaluate the 'Crossmodal Spatial Language Hypothesis' mentioned above. Thirdly, he does not investigate the ways in which speech and gesture combine to present different, complementary aspects of locative relationships. We therefore believe that our study is the first to examine in depth how speakers use gesture to express locative information. This new approach to the topic has necessary consequences for how we understand and separate locative expressions in oral discourse. We eschew the common, grammatically-based system of separating locative expressions on the basis of phrases or clauses in favour of an approach which is more receptive to the informational contribution of gesture (qv. Chapter 4). Hence, we propose a new system for the analysis of static locative expressions which is open to the contributions of *both* speech and gesture.

As stated above, the nature of locative relationships is commonly encoded by prepositions in English and in French. Numerous studies have provided detailed semantic accounts of individual members of this grammatical class (see, for example, Bennet 1975 and Tyler and Evans 2003 for English; Vandeloise 1986 and Franckel and Paillard 2007 for French). However, none of these studies has considered whether speakers use gesture to express additional information relating to prepositional semantics. By taking a multi-modal approach, we show that our understanding of how speakers use prepositions requires the joint consideration of both speech and gesture. Speech and gesture are semantically coordinated (McNeill 1992), such that the consideration of one modality necessitates the consideration of the other. Therefore, our work may also be taken as a new contribution to the existing literature on spatial prepositions.

1.3 The value of a comparative English/French study

Having established that the purpose of our study is to identify how speakers express the nature of locative relationships in both speech and gesture, the question remains as to why a comparative study is being undertaken. Our answer to this is two-fold. Firstly, comparative linguistic studies shed light on the different lexical encoding possibilities available to speakers of different languages. Hence, we are interested to see whether English and French possess a similar range of lexical spatial items that encode the nature of static locative relationships. In order to achieve as detailed an analysis as possible, we concentrate on how speakers encode location along the two horizontal axes: the frontal axis, which runs front to back; and the lateral axis, which runs from left to right. Furthermore, we examine how this occurs when speakers describe location in two different spatial settings: a small internal space (a lounge room scene), and a larger external space (a street scene). This reflects the fact that spatial language changes as a function of the scale of space under consideration (Lautenshütz et al. 2007). We therefore ask the following questions: do English and French speakers make use of a similar range of lexical items to encode location, and do these items change when speakers describe location in different spaces?

Secondly, a comparative study allows an investigation of whether English and French speakers express the same information in gesture when they use semantically similar spatial items (i.e. *next to* and *à côté de*). Do both groups of speakers use gesture to express unlexicalised spatial information relating to the lexically-encoded relationship? If so, what is the nature of this information, and is it the same across the two linguistic groups? What does this similarity, or difference, tell us about the role of gesture in expressing locative information? We work from the basis of the following three hypotheses.

– Speakers will use representational gestures (qv. Chapter 2) when describing locative configurations. This follows on from findings which show that speakers use such gestures when describing dynamic motion events (e.g. Kita and Özyürek 2003; McNeill 2000b). It is also based on Krauss, Chen and Chawla's

(1996) finding that preventing speakers from gesturing reduces speech fluency when speakers express spatial information.

– Speakers' gestures will express salient, unlexicalised locative information. This is based on earlier research which shows that not all aspects of a spatial event receive form in speech: some emerge in gesture only (Alibali 2005; Arik 2009; Emmorey and Casey 2001; McNeill 2000b). As such, gesture provides us with an ideal means of access into spatial cognition (Alibali, 2005; Hostetter, Alibali and Kita, 2007; Levinson, 2003b).

– The use of lexical spatial items with similar semantics in English and French will result in the expression of the same locative information in gesture by speakers of the two languages. This highlights the tight interrelationship of speech and gesture in the expression of semantic information (McNeill 1992, 2005; Kita and Özyürek 2003).

1.4 Structure of the book

In this section we outline how our study is structured and present a brief overview of the contents of each chapter.

Chapter 2 presents the theoretical background that underpins our study. The first part of this chapter targets the spatial domain and identifies concepts that are pivotal to static locative expressions: these include Figure, Ground, Path, origo, perspective and viewpoint. We take particular inspiration from Talmy's cognitive-semantic analysis of motion events; indeed, the impact of his stratification of this conceptual domain will become increasingly clear as the book progresses. We subsequently turn our attention to gesture and identify the different sub-types of gestural activity documented in the literature. We establish that our focus will be on what McNeill (1992, 2005) terms 'gesticulations': that is, the spontaneous movements of the hands which do not have a stable, independent meaning when considered out of the context in which they occur. We then draw the domains of spatial language and gesture together by considering previous research into how speakers gesture when expressing spatial information.

Chapter 3 presents the methodology behind our experimental tasks. We begin by presenting our pilot study and discuss how the outcome of this study influenced our approach to undertaking the main experiments. We explain how participants were recruited, how and where the experiments were filmed, and our subsequent approach to analysing the data.

Chapter 4 addresses the methodological concern of how static locative expressions should be defined and separated in oral discourse. It draws on our experimental data to show the inadequacy of past approaches to these questions, and highlights the need for an analytical framework which takes into account both speech and gesture. We therefore present a new system that is capable of understanding static locative expressions as multimodal constructions.

Chapter 5 concerns how speakers express location along the frontal axis. The frontal axis, otherwise known as the 'sagittal' axis in the literature (e.g. Brown 2007; Kita 2009), extends through the regions understood as an object's 'front' and 'back'. Our analysis targets English and French separately, and dedicates individual sections to how speakers describe the two visual stimuli. In this way, we are able to compare the English and French data for descriptions of the lounge room scene, and the English and French data for descriptions of the street scene. We also provide an analysis of the similarities and differences noted in the descriptions of the two scenes within each language group.

Chapter 6 examines how speakers express location along the lateral axis. This axis connects the spatial regions understood as an object's 'right' and 'left'. We apply the same structural approach to our analysis as that adopted for the frontal axis. One of our major results is that, in descriptions of the lounge room scene, English and French speakers very frequently recruited spatial items which did not encode either left or right directional information. This information, however, was present in their gestures. We interpreted this finding as evidence of a complementary relationship between the two modalities in the expression of location.

Chapter 7 explores how speakers use gesture when encoding location with the topological prepositions *on* and *sur*. This contrasts to the two previous chapters on the frontal and lateral axes, which targeted how speakers express directional information. The aim of Chapter 7 is to examine the type of information which speakers express in gesture when the Figure and Ground share a common location in space, and when the lexical item (i.e. *on* and *sur*) encodes a relationship of contact and/or functional support (cf. Herskovits 1986; Vandeloise 1986; Coventry and Garrod 2004). Our findings suggest that gesture's role in the expression of location is tightly related to the expression of directional information.

Chapter 8 presents a qualitative analysis of two ways in which gesture expresses unlexicalised locative information, before moving on to a discussion of how our results might be accommodated within the framework of Cognitive Grammar. As far as the two ways in which speakers express unlexicalised locative information is concerned, the first of these is speakers' presentation of one or several strands of directional information in gesture alone; the second is the use of gesture to express the lexical Ground's location. On the basis of the latter finding, we argue that lexical Grounds can simultaneously be 'gestural Figures', and therefore that Figure and Ground roles can vary cross-modally. Concerning the second half of this chapter, we discuss the compatability of our findings with the Cognitive Grammar approach, and suggest a modification of the symbolic assembly (the key unit of analysis in this framework) in order to accommodate the inclusion of representational gestures as part of symbolic language behaviour.

Chapter 9 concludes our research by highlighting the major findings of our study. We articulate what these findings suggest about how speakers of English and French conceptualise and communicate the nature of static locative relationships. Drawing on these results, we identify several key questions to be investigated in future research on the topic.

1.5 Further precisions

This book is an exploratory study into the different ways in which speakers of English and French express the nature of locative relationships. We aim to show the many manifestations of locative expressions, and to compare tendencies across the two languages. As part of this cross-linguistic approach, we provide frequencies for the occurrences of many spatial items and the gestures which relate to them: this allows for easier comparison both intra- and interlinguistically. This quantitative aspect of our study is particularly evident in the chapters on the frontal and the lateral axes. Nevertheless, it should also be pointed out that our overall approach is qualitative in nature: the aim of the book is to bring to light the variety of ways in which speech and gesture combine to create locative expressions. It is the job of a future research project to take the findings reported here and make them the subject of a larger, quantitatively-driven study that may determine statistical significance.

We use the term 'spatial linguistic item' to refer to any phrase which encodes locative information. This includes a whole range of items, from simple prepositions such as *on/sur* to adjectives such as *right/droite*. This allows us to identify a comprehensive range of lexical items used to encode locative relationships. Moreover, it enables us to avoid the pitfalls of debating the definition of grammatical categories, such as what constitutes an adverb or a preposition[12]. This sort of debate, however illuminating, is not of interest in the current work.

---

[1] See Huddleston and Pullum (2005) for an interesting discussion of this question.

2 Language, gesture, and locative expressions: a background

This chapter introduces the key spatial concepts at the core of our study, and identifies the interest in gesture as far as the expression of locative information is concerned. The chapter is divided into three parts. The first part introduces the spatial domain, paying particular attention to how static locative relationships are understood in the literature. This discussion also introduces spatial concepts which are pivotal to understanding static locative configurations, such as *frames of reference, perspective, viewpoint,* and *origo*. The second part of the chapter introduces the domain of gesture studies and specifies the types of gestures which are of interest in the current study. Finally, the third part of the chapter brings gesture and the spatial domain together by examining previous research into how speakers gesture when describing spatial information. This then sets the stage for the empirical investigation that follows.

Many of the examples in this chapter come from our own data. Each of these is followed by a tag, such as (EngDesc3). 'EngDesc' specifies that the example comes from the English language data, while 'FrenDesc' specifies that it belongs to the French data set. The number which follows each of these labels allows us to identify the particular participant who uttered the expression.

2.1 An overview of the spatial domain

What are static locative expressions? How is locative information grammatically encoded in English and French, and are there differences between the two languages as far as this is concerned? Proposing a workable definition of static locative expressions is more challenging than it initially seems. As far as the current study is concerned, these expressions are understood within the context of oral discourse. An appropriate definition should therefore consider experimental data in order to account for the full variety of ways in which speakers encode static location. Furthermore, our definition should also bear in mind the need to separate locative expressions for subsequent data analysis. These interrelated concerns of defining, and separating, static locative expressions are treated in Chapter 4. For the moment however, it will suffice to explain what we mean when we talk about *static location*. We follow Hendriks, Watorek and Giuliano (2004) in understanding this as the relationships between immobile objects in space. The following example encodes a simple static locative configuration.

(3)   *the tablecloth is on the table* (EngDesc1)

The tablecloth is located in relation to the table, both of which are conceptualised as immobile entities joined in a relationship of topological contact (*on*). The particular spatial concepts which underpin the expression of static locative relationships are the concern of what follows.

2.1.1   Basic concepts in static locative relationships

An ideal starting point for our investigation into static locative relationships is the research of Leonard Talmy. Talmy's conceptual framework for spatial semantics, along with his work on how such information is encoded cross-linguistically, has fuelled intense discussion and been used as a springboard for countless further theoretical and practical investigations (i.e. Kopecka and Pourcel 2005; Lemmens 2005; Slobin 2006; to name just a few). The first point to note is that Talmy considers static locative relationships as a type of Motion event. That is, "we treat a situation containing motion and the continuation of a stationary location alike as a **Motion event** (with a capital M)." (Talmy 2000: 25). The object being located is known as the *Figure*, and is described as "the salient moving or stationary object in a Motion event whose path or site is the relevant issue" (Talmy 2000: 153). The Figure's location is determined in relation to the *Ground*: "the reference object in a Motion event, with respect to which the Figure's path/site is characterized" (Talmy 2000: 154). The *Path* is "the variety of paths followed or sites occupied by the Figure object in a Motion event" (Talmy 2000). In other words, the Path is the nature of the locative relationship which exists between the Figure and the Ground. The fourth central component of a Motion event is what Talmy terms 'Motion' itself: this encodes the existence of the event. These four concepts are highlighted in the following example.

(4)   *the tablecloth*   *is*   *on*   *the table*
      Figure   Motion   Path   Ground

In example (4) *the tablecloth* is the Figure since it is the object whose location is at issue. *The table* is the reference object, and hence Ground. Linking the two syntactically are the copula verb *is*, which encodes Motion, and the preposition *on*, which lexicalises Path.

2.1.2 Separating static locative relationships from dynamic motion events

Talmy's approach to Motion events, which incorporates both dynamic motion events and static locative relationships, reflects the interconnectivity of the dynamic and static sub-domains of space. This interconnectivity is highlighted by Vandeloise (2006: 140), who reveals the deceptively dynamic nature of static location: "immobility is always the result of an equilibrium between two opposite forces." While this suggests the dynamic nature of all locative configurations, it is nevertheless necessary (as will soon become apparent) to separate *static* locative configurations from those which feature a Figure in motion. Hendriks et al. (2004) posit such a division by separating locative relationships into three categories: 'static general localisation'[2], 'dynamic general localisation'[3] and 'change of localisation'[4] events, each of which is explained below.

– Static general localisation
(5)   *Reskio est au bord du lac*
       Reskio is at the edge of the lake

– Dynamic general localisation
(6)   *Reskio fait du patinage sur le lac*
       Reskio skies/is skiing on the lake

– Change of localisation
(7)   *la petite fille sort de l'eau*
       the little girl comes out/is coming out of the water

(Examples from Hendriks et al. 2004).

---

[2] This is a translation from the original French "localisation générale statique". Translation: MT.
[3] This is a translation from the original French "localisation générale dynamique". Translation: MT.
[4] This is a translation from the original French "changement de localisation". Translation: MT.

Example (5) is the only one in which the Figure is presented as a stationary entity. Here, the Figure (*Reskio*) is located in relation to the edge of the lake, and the locative relationship which holds between the Figure and Ground is presented as stable and unchanging: this is encoded by the inflected form of the verb *être* ('be'). Example (6) is similar to (5) in that the Figure remains within the boundaries of the Ground entity. The crucial difference however, is the Figure's constant motion within these boundaries. This leads us to example (7), in which a boundary-crossing event does take place. The *little girl* is in the process of leaving one location (*the water*) to arrive in another (*out of the water*). Only locative relationships that fall under the category of 'static general localisation' will be investigated in the present work. Hence, any use of the term *locative expression* should be taken to mean *static locative expression*, unless stated otherwise.

Expressions of static general localisation, as well as those which belong to the other two categories of localisation shown above, fall under the umbrella of Motion events in Talmy's (2000) framework. This, however, turns out to be a problematic inclusion, as the following section reveals.

2.1.3 The lexical encoding of static locative relationships in English and French

In recent years, there has been much interest in how languages encode dynamic motion events. Much of this interest has been fuelled by Talmy's (1991, 2000) hugely influential verb-framed/satellite-framed typology, which categorises languages as a function of how they lexicalise the 'core schema' of a Motion event. The core schema "is generally the Path alone in some languages, such as English." (Talmy 2000: 227). When a language conflates Path with Motion in the verb, the language is said to be a *verb-framed* language. When this conflation occurs in a satellite, understood as "any constituent other than a noun-phrase or prepositional-phrase complement that is in a sister relation to the verb root" (Talmy 2000: 102), it is termed a *satellite-framed* language. As far as dynamic motion events are concerned, English is a satellite-framed language while French is a verb-framed one.

(8)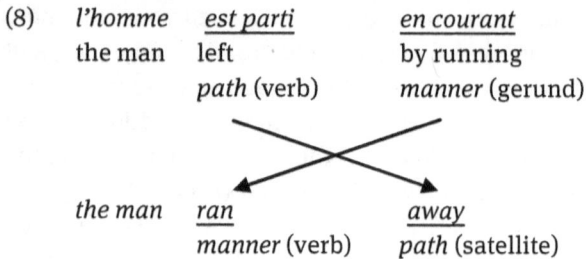

In example (8) the core schema of Path is lexicalised by the verb *partir* in French and the satellite *away* in English. Recent research, however, has indicated that the simple verb-framed/satellite-framed dichotomy is inadequate to fully account for how languages encode dynamic motion events. Kopecka (2004, 2006), for instance, shows that French not only encodes Path in verbs, but also in bound affixes which behave as satellites. She provides the example of the bound, path-encoding morpheme *em-* in verbs like *embouteiller* ('to bottle'), which affixes to the nominal root *bouteille* ('bottle'). In other work, Slobin (1997) points out that when a dynamic motion event does not involve boundary-crossing, verb-framed languages can encode manner of motion, as opposed to the core schema of Path, in the verb. This observation is echoed by Kopecka and Pourcel (2005) in their work on French. Hence, in an expression such as *il danse dans le salon* ('he dances/is dancing in the room'), Path is encoded by the preposition *dans* ('in'), while the lexical verb conflates Motion with manner of movement. Slobin calls further attention to the shortcomings of the verb-framed/satellite-framed dichotomy by proposing the third category of *equipollently-framed languages* (Slobin 2004: 9; Slobin 2006). These languages, such as Mandarin Chinese, lexicalise both Manner and Path components in verbal morphemes, thus distinguishing them from verb- and satellite-framed categories. Beavers et al. (2010) go further by arguing that languages cannot be expected to fit into a two- or even three-way typology, given the range of lexical, morphological and syntactic combinatorial possibilities that exist cross-linguistically. Furthermore, these same researchers convincingly show that purported typological differences can exist intra-linguistically, which further weakens the case for a narrow typological account. This links back to earlier work by Svorou (1986), who had already made the point that Path information (termed 'expressions of location' in her work) can be encoded by both open- and closed-class elements within a single language.

Although the goal of the present book is not to investigate how languages encode dynamic motion events, it is important to realise that Talmy (2000) considers these events in the same category as static locative relationships: they are both 'Motion' events. Hence, English and French should differ typologically as far as the encoding of static locative relationships is concerned. That is, French should encode the nature of the locative relationship (the 'Path') in the verb, while English should encode it in a satellite. This is not the case, however. Example (9) below reuses an example from Talmy (2000: 55) to make this point.

(9) the ball was in the box for three hours

There is no satellite in this locative expression. Rather, it is the preposition *in* which encodes the semantic component of Path, and prepositions are not satellites: recall that Talmy defines satellites as "any constituent *other than a noun-phrase or prepositional-phrase complement* that is in a sister relation to the verb root" (Talmy 2000: 102, our emphasis). The problem of separating satellites and prepositions is discussed by Beavers et al. (2010), who recommend an inclusion of prepositions within the category of satellites. Also important is the fact that French does not lexicalise Path in the lexical verb, which is what we would expect of a verb-framed language.

(10) la balle   est   dans la boîte
      the ball   is   in the box

In example (10), Path is encoded by the preposition *dans* ('in'). This is not an isolated case, because French habitually uses prepositions to encode the nature of static locative relationships (Borillo 1998: v). Hence, as pointed out by Lemmens and Slobin (2008), both verb-framed and satellite-framed languages use spatial prepositions to encode the Path component of locative relationships.

Including the sub-domain of static locative relationships in Talmy's Motion-event typology is therefore problematic. In fact, English and French show important similarities in their encoding of static location. Figure and Ground objects are typically lexicalised by nouns in English (Landau 2003); the same is also true of French (Borillo 1998: 15). The existence of the locative relationship itself, or 'Motion' in Talmy's terminology, is generally encoded by a stative verb in both languages (see Hendriks et al. 2004; Levinson and Amecka 2007): this is the copula *be* in English and *être* in French. Manner of location may also be expressed in English and French verbs, although the frequency with which this occurs is greater in English than it is in French (Lemmens 2005). As far as the encoding of Path is concerned, the closed grammatical class of spatial prepositions plays a pivotal role in the two languages (Borillo 1998; Herskovits 1986; Vandeloise 1986; Landau and Jackendoff 1993). Hence, there are important similarities between English and French in the encoding of static locative relationships.

2.1.4 The different types of static locative relationships

So far then, we have established that static location concerns the fixed locations of entities in space. We have also shown that the consideration of static locative relationships as a type of Motion event in Talmy's typology is problematic. Furthermore, there is similarity in how English and French grammatically encode these relationships. The latter observation is bolstered by research undertaken at the Max Planck Institute for Psycholinguistics. This research investigated how basic locative relationships are encoded cross-linguistically. To this end, researchers sought to determine a 'basic locative construction' (BLC; see MPI Annual report 1998) for each language studied. Basic locative constructions[5] are responses to 'where' questions, such as "where is the ball?" The typical answer in English and French is a syntactically simple construction comprised of two noun phrases (NP's), a preposition and a copula verb linking the subject noun phrase with the prepositional phrase. This is shown in the example below.

(11) the ball   is   on   the sofa
      la balle   est   sur   le canapé
      NP   Copula   Prep   NP

The research revealed that languages could be divided into three categories on the basis of these basic locative constructions: 'general verb languages', 'postural verb languages' and 'multi-verb languages'. Both English and French fall into the first category since responses to 'where' questions generally involve the use of the copulas *be* and *être* (e.g. example 11). Verbs which encode Manner of location (i.e. *hang* and *lie*) are not obligatory, although their use is somewhat more frequent in English than in French (Lemmens 2005).

Further research into French and English locative verbs is currently underway (see Lemmens 2005) and will not be of interest here. Instead, we will con-

---

[5] On the other hand, existential constructions such as "there is a ball on the sofa" do not constitute responses to 'where' questions, and are therefore not considered basic locative constructions (see Grinevald 2006). Note also that the verb used in such existential constructions is different in English and in French: while English retains the copula *be*, French uses the verb *avoir* ('have') (Grinevald 2006).

centrate on the different ways in which speakers express the nature of static locative relationships (i.e. the 'Path') in speech and in gesture. This firstly requires identifying the different types of static locative relationships. Levinson (1996) suggests that there are two broad categories into which these may be divided: those which use coordinate systems, and those which do not. Levinson's categorical division patterns out as follows.

(i) Descriptions where no coordinate system is required
– Prototype deixis
– Contiguity: topological relations
– Named locations

(ii) Descriptions where coordinate systems or "frames of reference" are used
– Horizontal spatial relations. These require the use of one of the three following frames of reference: *absolute*, *intrinsic* or *relative*
– Vertical spatial relations

The work which follows will focus, in large part, on a sub-type of Levinson's second category: horizontal spatial relations. Given the space restrictions of the current investigation, vertical spatial relations will be considered only briefly. As far as non-coordinate relationships are concerned, our study will look at the topological relationships encoded by the English preposition *on* and the French preposition *sur*[6]. A discussion of prototype deixis[7] will arise in the study, but will not be a focal point. Named locations will not be of interest because they do not allow us to investigate how speakers express the semantic feature of Path.

The following four sections introduce concepts which are pivotal to understanding how speakers express horizontal and vertical spatial relations: these are direction, frames of reference, perspective, viewpoint, and origo. Alongside the discussion of origo is a presentation of spatial deictic items. The discussion then turns to a presentation of how researchers understand topological relationships in the literature.

---

6 See section 2.1.8 for a discussion of topological spatial relations.
7 See section 2.1.7 for a discussion of spatial deixis.

2.1.5 Direction and frames of reference

According to Landau (2003: 19; original emphasis), "when we represent an object's location, we do so in terms of a **set of orthogonal axes** with its **origin** centred on the **Reference object**." This 'reference object' is the 'Ground' in the terminology that we have adopted. As far as 'orthogonal axes' are concerned, we understand these as the three spatial axes: *the vertical axis*, which connects an object's top and bottom; *the frontal axis*, which runs from the object's front to back; and *the lateral axis*, which connects left and right. Hence, one of these axes (the vertical axis) is vertical in nature, while the other two (the lateral and frontal axes) exist in the horizontal plane. A clear example of all three axes is provided by the human body. We have a frontal axis which is defined by our front and back, a lateral axis which joins our left and right sides, and a vertical axis which runs from the top of our head to the bottom of our feet. These three axes provide spatial parameters for how we understand location. Crucially, each axis is defined by a set of two directions: these comprise the axis's 'endpoints' (Ashley and Carlson 2007: 1022). Taking these endpoints separately allows us to break down the three spatial axes into 'six half-line axes' (Herskovits 1986: 157).

– Up axis (i.e. *above*; *au-dessus de*)
– Down axis (i.e. *below*; *sous*)
– Front axis (i.e. *in front of*; *devant*)
– Back axis (i.e. *behind*; *derrière*)
– Right axis (i.e. *to the right of*; *à droite de*)
– Left axis (i.e. *to the left of*; *à gauche de*)

In our study, we will examine how speakers express location within the framework of the three larger spatial axes: that is, the frontal, lateral, and vertical axes. However, we will consider that each of these axes is defined by two directions: these are the endpoints which define the six half-line axes. Therefore, we understand direction in terms of up, down, front, back, right, and left. Both English and French have lexical items which encode these specific directions: an example from each language has been provided for the half-line axes shown above. In contrast, they also have spatial items which can generalise across multiple directions: for example, *towards* and *vers*, which are applicable for any direction; and *next to* and *à côté de*, which are commonly associated with the lateral axis (and hence both left and right directions). We can therefore divide spatial items into two major categories on the basis of this distinction: those which are 'directionally specific' (i.e. which reference one of the six directions mentioned above), and those which are 'directionally non-specific' (i.e. which can apply to more than one of the six directions). Chapters 5 and 6 in our book investigate how speakers express location along the frontal and lateral axes. In these chapters, we categorise lexical spatial items according to whether or not they encode a specific direction along an axis. As such, the distinction between 'directionally-specific' and 'directionally non-specific' items will be important to our work.

Now, expressing direction along a spatial axis requires the use of a system that provides spatial cues for appropriate navigation. Levinson (1996, 2003b) calls these systems *frames of reference* and divides them into three categories[8]: 'absolute', 'intrinsic' and 'relative'. When a speaker uses an *intrinsic frame of reference*, "the figure object is located with respect to what are often called *intrinsic* or *inherent* features of the ground object" (Levinson 1996: 366; original emphasis). Levinson points out that the very notion of spatial properties as *intrinsic* is a slippery issue, since many such properties are not so much intrinsic as culturally assigned: for example, the *front* of a television is determined by how we typically view televisions (Levinson 1996: 366). Moreover, as far as visual artefacts like pictures are concerned, spatial properties such as *foregrounds* and *backgrounds* crucially depend on an external point of origin ('origo') in relation to which distance is established. Hence, foregrounds and backgrounds are attributed on the basis of the perceived distance between a viewer and different sections of a visual scene. While we may consider such properties as intrinsic to visual representations, they are really the conventionalised products of the egocentric relative frame of reference[9]. In contrast, the example below provides a clearer example of an intrinsic frame of reference.

(12) devant la cheminée   il y a un tapis (FrenDesc6)
      in front of the fireplace   there is a rug

In example (12) the rug is located in relation to the front of the fireplace. Since fireplaces have intrinsic fronts (i.e. the side in which we place wood and start a

---

8 Equivalents of these three frames of reference are found elsewhere in the literature. For instance, they appear as 'environment-centred', 'object-centred' and 'viewer-centred' reference frames in Carlson-Radvansky and Irwin (1993). For a detailed discussion of frames of reference in the literature, see Watson (2006).
9 This is developed from Lemmens (personal communication), who suggested that prepositional forms such as *in the foreground/background of* rely on conventionalised relative frames of reference.

fire), an intrinsic frame of reference underpins this particular use of *devant* ('in front of').

A *relative frame of reference* involves the presence of an observer who attributes spatial properties to the Ground. The following sentence provides an example of this.

(13) *et juste devant ce tapis*   *i' y a un os* (FrenDesc11)
and just in front of this rug   there's a bone

Rugs, in contrast to fireplaces, do not possess intrinsic 'fronts' or 'backs'. How then can the Figure (*the bone*) be located *in front of* one? In situations such as these, the Ground is attributed spatial properties by an unlexicalised observer. In the current example, this is an implicit human observer. As far as English is concerned, Levinson suggests that the attribution of a 'front' likely results from the 180-degree rotation of the observer's intrinsic front onto the Ground entity (Levinson 1996: 369-371; Levinson 2003: 87). French also uses this mirror-like reflection of frontal properties when speakers encode location using a relative frame of reference (Borillo 1998). Note, however, that the attribution of left and right properties does not entail this same 180-degree rotation. Hence, the *left* and *right* of the rug would align with my own left and right sides as I view it. Therefore, while left and right remain constant, front and back do not. This is known as 'mirror order' (Herskovits 1986). The image below shows how this occurs in relation to a tree. Trees have intrinsic orientation in the vertical plane, but do not possess intrinsic front/back or left/right properties (Hill 1982). For the moment, let us consider the diagram on the right half of the image[10].

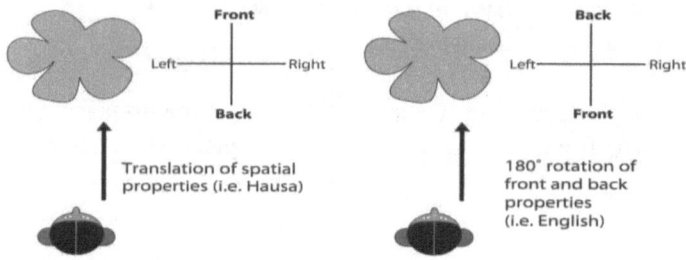

Fig. 1: Assigning front/back spatial properties under translation and 180° rotation

---

[10] Thank you to Simon Trevaks for creating this image following my specifications. It is based on those in Levinson (2003b).

In normal circumstances, the oriented speaker of English or French would map their front onto the side of the tree opposite them. Hence, if they were to describe an object *in front of* the tree, this object would be located in the area between the speaker and the tree (cf. Hill 1982). In contrast, the back of the tree would be the least proximate side to the oriented speaker, behind the conceptualised 'front'. These attributed spatial properties are shown on the linear axes drawn next to the tree. Not all languages behave in this way. For example, Hausa uses a system in which speakers graft their coordinate axes directly onto the Ground object without any rotation (Hill 1982). This means that the 'front' of the tree in the example above would be facing in the same direction as the speaker, and its 'left' and 'right' would also align with the speaker's own left and right sides (cf. Levinson 2003b: 86-88). Levinson (2003b) refers to this process as the 'translation' of spatial properties. This is shown in the diagram on the left of Image 2.1 above.

Now, while speakers of Hausa most typically assign front and back properties in such a way, Levinson (2003b: 88) points out that "Hausa also allows a less-favoured English-like interpretation of the 'front'/'back' terms." This is important to note, because our study shows that English speakers sometimes use translation, as opposed to the 180-degree rotation of frontal properties. Crucially, this may only be evident to an addressee if the speaker's gestures are taken into account. We discuss this phenomenon in Chapter 5.

Finally, *absolute frames of reference* use environmental cues to provide directional information. These cues are "fixed angles extrinsic to the objects whose spatial relation is being described" (Brown and Levinson 2000: 167). They include, for instance, the cardinal directions 'north', 'south', 'east' and 'west'. Such directions act as environment-centred cues that establish the direction of a Figure in relation to a Ground, as in the following example.

(14)   *Gosford is north of Sydney*

Here, the cardinal direction *north* provides an environmentally-based cue which localises Gosford in relation to Sydney. Absolute frames of reference are used in English and French to localise landmarks in large-scale space: for example, towns, cities or geographical regions. In contrast, neither language uses the absolute frame of reference in smaller scale space: for example, to localise a sofa or a table in a lounge room. This runs counter to many non-European languages that do use absolute frames of reference across different scales of space (Brown and Levinson 2000; Levinson 2003b). The experiments at the heart of our study do not concern large-scale spaces, such as cities. As such, speakers should exclusively use intrinsic and relative frames of reference when encoding location along the horizontal axes.

As shown in section 2.1.4, Levinson's categorisation of static spatial relationships distinguishes between those that concern the vertical axis, and those that relate to the two horizontal axes. The reason for this distinction is as follows. Although the vertical axis makes use of frames of reference (Levinson 2003b; Carlson-Radvansky and Irwin 1993), all three frames of reference tend to align. Hence, an object which is above the intrinsic 'top' of an object is also likely to be above it in the absolute sense (gravity being the environmental cue) and the relative sense (from my viewpoint) (Levinson 2003b: 75). This makes it difficult to know which particular frame of reference underpins the speaker's expression of vertical direction. Given that the current work focuses primarily on the horizontal axes, this will not be a major concern in what follows.

2.1.6 Perspective and viewpoint

Two further concepts which require explanation are *perspective* and *viewpoint*. These terms are sometimes used interchangeably in the literature, and researchers have different understandings of what they mean. In what follows, we will explain how we understand *perspective*, before moving on to an explanation of *viewpoint*.

When speakers view a visual image and are asked to describe the locative relationships in the represented scene, they have two possibilities: to encode location from an imagined point within this scene itself, or from one external to it. In her work on German Sign Language (DGS), Perniss (2007) calls these broadly different points of observation *character* and *observer* perspective. These speaker-internal (character) and speaker-external (observer) perspectives of spatial scenes are noted in the literature on direction-giving, appearing under the titles of *route perspective* and *survey perspective* (see Emmorey, Tversky and Taylor 2000). When a route perspective is used, "the viewer is conceived of as immersed in an environment" (Emmorey, Tversky and Taylor: 159). In contrast, a survey perspective entails that "the viewer is conceived of as outside an environment, looking at it as an object" (Emmorey, Tversky and Taylor: 159). One example of survey perspective would be if a speaker adopted a bird's-eye view of a spatial scene, and gesturally depicted locative relationships on a low, horizontal plane in front of them (cf. Emmorey, Tversky and Taylor 2000). In contrast, a speaker using a route perspective may make full use of their surrounding space to convey location. Hence, the use of different perspectives may entail different uses of gesture space. Different perspectives may also occur in speech and in gesture (Fricke 2003): this is explored in Chapter 5.

The representation of spatial information also depends on the *viewpoint* (Perniss 2007) that a speaker adopts. Viewpoint is the "vantage point" (Perniss 2007) from which a scene is viewed. A speaker may be external to a represented scene (hence using an observer perspective), yet still be able to represent direction from different viewpoints. Imagine two speakers who are seated opposite each other. One speaker describes an object's location in the following way.

(15)   *next to the bone on the right there's a ball* (EngDesc10)

As the speaker says this, they gesture out to their right. However, this is a gesture *to the left* from the addressee's viewpoint, because the addressee is seated opposite them. Hence, the speaker has the choice of representing direction as they see it (*speaker viewpoint*), or as the addressee would see it if looking at the picture (*addressee viewpoint*).

The selection of a viewpoint is also important when expressing direction along the frontal axis. Hence, if I were describing the location of the rug below, I might say that it is *in front of* the fireplace.

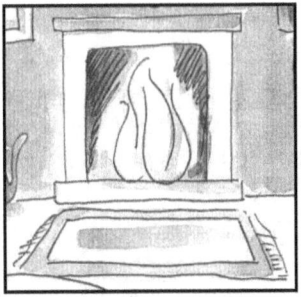

The gestural expression of this information using speaker viewpoint would involve moving my hand from out in front of me, and in towards my own location: this is because the rug is closer to the foreground of the picture (and thus seemingly to my own location) than the fireplace is. However, if I wished to express direction from the viewpoint of my addressee (who is sitting opposite), I would need to gesture *forward and out* from my location: this is because I would need to represent the relationship as though the addressee were looking at me and seeing the picture itself.

As far as the expression of directional information is concerned, our study concentrates on how speakers express location along the frontal and the lateral axes. We will therefore be interested in whether speakers represent this information in gesture using speaker or addressee viewpoint. As explained above, the use of each of these viewpoints has different implications for how speakers represent direction along these two spatial axes.

The concern of perspective will also be addressed in what follows, but will not be a focal point of our work. Speakers normally describe the stimulus scenes from the default position of external observer and signal in speech when they adopt an imagined location within the picture itself. This allows us to readily distinguish between the use of an observer or character perspective in speech. As far as gesture is concerned, the hand orientation used in iconic depictions of Figure and Ground objects can indicate perspective (Brown 2007; qv. Chapter 5). At other times however, hand form may not allow us to distinguish between the use of an observer or character perspective. On these occasions, if the directional information which a speaker expresses in gesture is consistent with the perspective adopted in speech, we will consider that the gesture uses this same perspective. Discrepancies in the representation of direction may signal double perspectives cross-modally (qv. Chapter 5). It is difficult to assess perspective in gesture as a function of how speakers use their frontal gesture space. In contrast to Emmorey, Tversky and Taylor (2000), we did not present our subjects with maps, but rather with visual representations of three-dimensional spaces. Hence, even when speakers used observer perspective, they did not take a 'bird's eye' view of the space. Rather, they made productive use of the large gesture space before them, recreating the spatial relationships as though they were looking out into the visually represented scene itself.

Finally, it should be pointed out that McNeill (1992) uses the concept of 'viewpoint' in his work, but that his approach differs to the one adopted in our study. McNeill proposes that when speakers describe an event they may assume the role of a character implicated in the event itself (*character viewpoint*), or that of an observer viewing the event (*observer viewpoint*). This is a useful interpretation of viewpoint as far as the analysis of motion events is concerned, and indeed motion events provide the basis for many of McNeill's examples. For example, if I were to describe a man running down the street, I might embody the agent in motion by activating my arms in such a way as to reflect the activity of running. However, this approach to viewpoint does not fit as well when speakers describe the fixed locations of objects in space: this is because speakers are less likely to take on the viewpoint of an inanimate object, such as a sofa, than they are an animate agent in motion (such as a person running). Hence, while we acknowledge McNeill's (1992) approach to the concept, it is more fitting for our study to adopt the approaches to viewpoint and perspective outlined by Perniss (2007).

2.1.7 Deixis and origo

Returning to Levinson's categorisation of static spatial relationships as outlined in section 2.1.4, another way in which speakers establish location is through the use of "prototype deixis". Levinson (1996: 360) defines deixis as "the way parameters of the speech event enter into the interpretation of linguistic expressions". One of the most influential theories of deixis is that proposed by Bühler (1982). Bühler identified three domains in which deixis plays a major semantic role: these are the domains of person, place and time (Bühler 1982: 10). As far as space is concerned, the key deictic items in English and French are *here/ici* and *there/là*. These items draw attention to features of the utterance context that provide pivotal information concerning the Figure's location.

(16) *il y a un os..   qui se trouve là* (with a pointing gesture) (FrenDesc10)
       there is a bone..   which is found there

In example (16), the deictic term *là* calls attention to contextual features that allow for the Figure's location to be understood. These features are the pointing gesture and the speaker's own location in space. It is in relation to this location that the pointing gesture acquires locative meaning. The speaker fulfils the role of (unlexicalised) Ground, as well as what Bühler terms the *origo* (Bühler 1982). An origo is the point of origin for a coordinate system (Fricke 2003: 71); it is the oriented entity in relation to which direction is understood. Hence, the direction of the speaker's gesture is understood in relation to their intrinsic frontal orientation. Understanding this directional information enables the location of the bone to be communicated.

An origo underpins every expression of direction; it is not a concept that is exclusive to the use of deictic adverbs like *here/ici* and *there/la*. Consider the following example which uses the prepositional expression *to the left* to encode directional information.

(17) *next to the table to the left is a little dog* (EngDesc1)

Tables are objects that do not have intrinsic left/right distinctions. Hence, the dog's location *to the left* of the table in example (17) requires an observer to map this lateral distinction onto the Ground. This observer constitutes the directional point of origin, and hence origo, of the relationship. Since the table does not possess an intrinsic left property, we also know that the speaker must be using a 'relative frame of reference'. Finally, as far as the idea of direction is concerned, note that the speaker uses what we have termed a 'directionally-specific' item, *to the left*, to encode this information.

The role of the origo is also pivotal when an intrinsic frame of reference is used. Hence, if the dog was to the left of *me* instead of to the left of the *table*, I would constitute the origo, as well as the Ground, of the directional relationship. This is because the encoded direction *to the left* is understood in relation to my intrinsic lateral properties.

2.1.8 The different sub-types of locative relationships

Frames of reference, perspective, viewpoint and origo are all key concepts when speakers communicate directional information. However, speakers may characterise locative configurations by encoding other kinds of semantic information instead.

(18) it's **near** a table and chairs (EngDesc7)
(19) a bird is **on** the branch of a tree (EngDesc9)

Examples (18) and (19) encode locative relationships which are non-directional in nature. In (18) the preposition *near* encodes a relationship of proximity, while the use of *on* in (19) encodes the Figure's contact with the Ground. Levinson (2003a) categorises such distance- and contact-encoding relationships under the heading of *topological* relations. He defines these as "relations of contact or propinquity (like English *on, at, in, near*), which, following Piaget and Inhelder (1956), have been taken to be the simplest kind of spatial relation." This same view of topological relations is taken by Coventry and Garrod (2004) and Hörberg (2007). Borillo (1992, 1998), in contrast, understands topological relations in a somewhat different manner. In her view, these are relationships in which the Figure and the Ground occupy the same portion of space, either partially or completely. This includes relationships in which the Figure is 'carried' by the Ground (i.e. the tablecloth is *on* the table), or in which the Figure is included in part of the space occupied by the Ground (i.e. the tablecloth is *in* the box). She states that there are basically three such prepositions in French: *à* ('at', 'in', 'on'), *sur* ('on'), and *dans* ('in'). There are also two additional prepositions, *en* ('in') and *chez* ('at the house of'), which relate to *dans*. As far as English is concerned, Borillo's approach to topological relationships would allow for Levinson's *on*, *at*, and *in*, but not *near*. The other category which Borillo proposes is that of *projective* relationships. These are configurations in which the Figure is exterior to the location occupied by the Ground: for example, the relationship encoded by the preposition *near*[11]. Borillo's dichotomy therefore works by distinguishing between relationships in which the Figure and the Ground occupy (at least partially) a common portion of space, and those in which they do not. She labels the former type of relationship *localisation interne* ('internal localisation'), the latter *localisation externe* ('external localisation') (Borillo 1992).

An important concern in our data analysis is to distinguish between different types of static locative relationships. How should this be achieved? One way is to start with the idea of direction. Any object, such as we perceive it in three-dimensional space, must occupy a location along the frontal, lateral and vertical axes. Hence, spatial items and phrases may initially be divided according to whether or not they encode a particular direction along a spatial axis: we have termed these 'directionally-specific items'. As stated in section 2.1.5, we understand direction as the six endpoints of the three spatial axes.

But what of items that do not encode such direction? We could divide these into topological and projective sub-categories, following Borillo (1992, 1998). Hence, we would have topological items that encode a shared Figure/Ground location (i.e. *in*, *on*, and *at* for English; and *dans*, *sur*, and *à* for French), and projective items that encode the Figure at a separate location to the Ground (i.e. *next to/à côté de*, *between/entre*). Observing this distinction is potentially productive, because the direction of the Figure to the Ground may well be more salient when speakers use projective items than when they use topological ones. For example, a Figure which is *next to* a Ground is necessarily located in a certain direction away from it. However, this is not true for a Figure which is *in* a Ground, because the two objects share a common portion of space.

---

11 In contrast, other researchers use the term *projective* to describe relationships in which the Figure is not only external to the Ground, but also located in a certain direction to it (Coventry and Garrod 2004; Hörberg 2007). Kemmerer and Tranel (2000) broaden this to include relationships in which the Figure is located in relation to one of the Ground's spatial axes, thus admitting prepositions such as *beside* (which references a horizontal axis, but not a particular horizontal direction).

We therefore have a system which builds on Borillo's (1992, 1998) approach to spatial relations. That is, we have topological items (i.e. *on* and *sur*), projective items (i.e. *next to* and *à côté de*), and direction-encoding items (i.e. *to the left of* and *à gauche de*).

A final point worthy of mention is that topological items may introduce directionally-specific noun phrases: this allows the Figure's location to be encoded within a particular sub-region of the Ground[12].

(20)   *on the right-hand side the first shop is a café* (EngDesc5)

In example (20), the topological preposition *on* introduces the direction-encoding noun phrase *the right-hand side*. This phrase may be analysed in two ways: either as an undivided whole (*on the right hand side*), or as a segmented combination (*on* + *the right hand side*). Now, our chapter on the lateral axis (see Chapter 6) is concerned with how speakers encode left and right directional information. With this in mind, it matters little whether we itemize the phrase as *on the right-hand side* or simply *the right-hand side*. In such instances we simply keep the whole phrase as a single unit (i.e. *on the right-hand side*).

2.1.9   Summary

In the sections above we presented the concepts which are pivotal to understanding how speakers express static locative relationships. Firstly, we stated that we understand static location as the relationship between immobile objects in space (Hendriks et al. 2004). We then showed that such relationships cannot easily be incorporated within the framework of Motion events in Talmy's (2000) verb-framed/satellite-framed typology. We looked at Levinson's (1996) approach to categorising static location, and identified that our concern would be with how speakers encode location along the frontal and lateral axes, as well as with how they encode a particular type of topological relation (lexicalised by the prepositions *on* and *sur*). We stipulated that we understand direction in terms of the endpoints which characterise each of the three spatial axes: that is, *up*, *down*, *front*, *back*, *left*, and *right*. We describe items that encode just one of these directions as 'directionally-specific' (i.e. *in front of/devant*), and those that refer to more than one as 'directionally non-specific' (i.e. *towards/vers*). Speak-

---

[12]   See Borillo (1992, 1998) for a discussion of nouns in French that encode a sub-region of the Ground.

ers must use a frame of reference when expressing directional information. Participants in our study should make greatest use of the *intrinsic* and the *relative* frames of reference. Direction must also be established in relation to an *origo*, or point of origin. When a relative frame of reference is used, this is an entity that is different to the Ground. Speakers will also express directional information using a particular viewpoint. This is important, given that the participants in our study will be seated opposite each other (qv. Chapter 3). Hence, a gestural expression of direction along the frontal and lateral axes will necessarily change depending on whether a speaker expresses location from their own viewpoint or from that of their addressee. Moreover, speakers may also express location from an imagined scene-internal location (character perspective), or from a scene-external one (observer perspective). Once again, this may impact on their gestural representations of directional information.

Finally, we showed that the concern of direction is ideal for classifying lexical spatial items. We will therefore use the directional endpoints of each spatial axis to categorise spatial items in our chapters on the frontal and the lateral axes. For example, *in front of* will be classified as a 'front-encoding' item, while *behind* will be a 'back-encoding' item. As far as the lateral axis is concerned, *to the left* will be a 'left-encoding' item, and *to the right* a 'right-encoding' one. All other spatial items used to encode location along the frontal and lateral axes which do not encode a specific direction will be categorised as 'directionally non-specific' items: for example, *next to* and *à côté de*. Note, however, that we will not include occurrences of simple topological prepositions, such as *on* and *sur*, in this category. Instead, we deal with topological prepositions separately in Chapter 7.

2.2 Gesture

What is gesture? The task of defining this term is deceptively simple, and it can be difficult to draw the line between what constitutes a gesture and what does not (Kendon 1997). One key feature of gesture is its meaningful role in communication. This allows us to exclude as gestures any movements which respond purely to physical, bodily need. Gullberg (2006: 104) identifies such movements as *functional actions* (such as raising a cup to one's mouth to drink), *symptomatic movements* (such as scratching), and *posture*. As pointed out by Efron (1972: 89) in his pioneering study on gesture, "one is never confronted with a purely physical movement in gesture, but always with gestural movement, i.e., *meaningful* movement". This idea of meaningful movement is echoed by Goldin-Meadow (2003: 500), who suggests that, "In order for a manual movement to be considered a gesture, it must be produced with the intent to communicate." These two statements suggest that gestures are meaningful movements because they help to realise the speaker's communicative aim. This is neatly summed up by Gullberg (2006: 104), who considers gestures to be "symbolic movements relating to ongoing talk and to the expressive effort or intention (what you are trying to say)."

In terms of physical realisation, gestures are commonly executed by a speaker's hands and arms, although other parts of the body, such as the head and even the feet (Rodrigues 2007), may be used. Gestures also show considerable variability in terms of the types of information they present and how they present it. The following section provides a brief overview of the different kinds of gesture, before targeting and further exploring the types that will be of interest in the current study.

2.2.1 The different types of gesture

In his 1992 book *Hand and Mind*, David McNeill proposed an ordering of gesture types that he labelled 'Kendon's continuum'. This was inspired by a paper written by Adam Kendon (1988) which explored "the different ways in which gesture can be used as a component of an utterance" (Kendon 2004: 104). The gestures along this continuum were ordered according to two criteria: their relationship with speech (i.e. whether the gesture can 'stand alone' or whether it depends on the presence of speech), and their presence or absence of linguistic properties (i.e. whether the gesture has fixed signification, and whether the gesture can combine with other gestures to form a larger utterance). McNeill (2005) subsequently showed that one continuum was insufficient to arrange gesture types, because the ordering which results depends on the variable under consideration. For example, ordering along the continuum changes when the variable is degree of conventionality (i.e. whether or not the gesture type adheres to a standard of form), or when the variable is the gesture's relationship to speech (i.e. whether it is produced with or without speech). He therefore revised his initial approach by proposing multiple continua instead, with each continuum ordering gesture types according to different variables. Discussing the nature of each of these continua is not essential to the present study. However, presenting the different gesture types that comprise them is ideal for understanding the various manifestations of gestural activity. These different kinds of gesture – signs, pantomime, emblems, speech-linked gestures and gesticulation – are presented below. In addition, we have included a brief discussion of pragmatic gestures, which cannot be integrated satisfactorily into any of the gesture types proposed for the continua.

– Signs
The gestures with the most language-like properties are the signs of sign languages. Sign languages are "the natural languages of the deaf" (Perniss 2007: 1) and are similar to spoken languages in that they are subject to rules of morphology, phonology and syntax (Perniss 2007: 2). Hence, signs have standards of form, fixed signification (like lexemes), and can be combined to form larger utterances. In spite of these similarities with spoken languages, sign languages do not involve the use of speech and rely on visual accessibility to the signer.

– Emblems
When many people think of gesture, they think of signs such as nodding one's head or the thumbs-up sign. These types of gestures are part of the communicative repertoire of hearing subjects and may or may not be used in concert with speech (McNeill 1992, 2005). An important characteristic of these gestures is their fixed signification. For instance, in many Western societies the thumbs-up sign means "ok", and nodding the head is a sign of agreement or approbation. Such gestures are therefore fully contained packages of meaning that may be executed without any accompanying speech. In this respect, they share a similarity with the signs of sign language. These gestures are known in the literature under various terms, including 'emblems' (Ekman and Friesen in Kendon 1994), 'quotable gestures' (Kendon 1994) and 'lexical gestures' (Poggi 2004: 73). For the sake of consistency, we will retain Ekman and Friesen's term 'emblems' in what follows. A detailed survey of many emblems and their significations across the European continent is provided in Morris et al. (1977).

– Pantomime
Pantomime is the use of gesture to create a narrative in the absence of speech (McNeill 2005). Pantomime can also refer to the use of gesture to represent objects and actions without any accompanying speech. This is exploited in games such as 'Pictionary' and 'charades', in which players create imagistic representations of items and actions using the visual-spatial modality alone.

– Speech-linked gestures
Speech-linked gestures fill a grammatical role by substituting for a word or phrase in speech. They combine with the lexical content that precedes and/or follows the gesture to create overall utterance meaning. For example, if I were

asked how I felt about my unpleasant neighbour Mary I might say, "She's a bit [gesture]", with the gesture being a particularly unpleasant contortion of my face. This gesture would fill the grammatical role of adjective, and so complete the utterance structure.

– Gesticulations
Adam Kendon (1980) proposed the term 'gesticulation' to refer to the movements made by individuals as part of the "process of utterance" (p.207). These movements are the creations of individual speakers and do not have fixed form-meaning pairings. Hence, the same gesture form can mean different things, depending on the content of the co-occurring speech. One example of a gesticulation would be if I were to outline a rectangular shape with my index fingers while describing a rug. The referent of the gesture (i.e. the rug) would be understandable thanks to its concurrent encoding in speech. In another context however, this same rectangular gesture could represent another object entirely – a box or a table, for instance. As pointed out by McNeill (2005: 5), "Gesticulation is motion that embodies a meaning relatable to the accompanying speech." Hence, gesticulations necessarily occur with speech and do not substitute for it in an act of communication. They are also the most frequently occurring type of gesture (McNeill 2005: 5).

– Pragmatic gestures
So-called 'pragmatic gestures' (Streeck in Müller 2004; Kendon 2004) are more difficult to describe. They are not true 'gesticulations' because they do not contribute to the referential content of an utterance (Kendon 2004: 158). Rather, they fulfil functions such as indicating the speaker's attitude towards what is being said, or conveying a particular type of speech act. Kendon (2004) identifies three main functions of pragmatic gestures: 'modal', 'performative' and 'parsing' functions. Exploring each of these three sub-types is not crucial to the current investigation. However, providing an example of one of them will help to clarify what we mean by 'pragmatic' gestures. An ideal example is the palm up open hand (PUOH) gesture, which has been described in detail by Müller (2004). This is an example of a 'performative' pragmatic gesture, because it provides information about how the content of speech should be received by the addressee. In terms of form, it consists of an upturned open palm, with fingers at least minimally extended. The picture below shows a speaker performing a PUOH gesture.

(21) Example of a PUOH gesture (EngDesc6)

The PUOH gesture borrows from the concrete act of presenting on the open palm. Within the context of interactive discourse, speakers use this gesture to proffer "an abstract discursive object as an inspectable one – an object which is concrete, manipulable, and visible, and it invites participants to take on a shared perspective on this object." (Müller 2004: 233). Hence, the speaker shows that the content of the accompanying speech should be received in a particular way: as an object for discussion in the speakers' interaction.

As far as the present study is concerned, the focus firmly rests on gesticulations. Gesticulations are of interest because they provide a vehicle for the expression of locative information alongside the use of lexical spatial items. This opens up the possibility that speakers express locative information multimodally. For instance, do speakers express information in gesture that is not present in the co-occurring speech? If so, what is the relationship between the strands of meaning presented in the two modalities? The following section presents a more detailed examination of gesticulations, and highlights the specific types that are of interest in the current research.

2.2.2 Gesticulations

As described above, gesticulations are the spontaneous movements that accompany speech as part of a communicative act. McNeill (1992, 2005) identifies five major types of gesticulations: iconic gestures, metaphoric gestures, deictic ('pointing') gestures, beats, and cohesives. These are not mutually exclusive types, and a single gesture may borrow features from multiple categories. For example, a gesture may have a form that is iconic for the object it represents, while simultaneously pointing at a location in space: it would therefore be both iconic and deictic in nature. With this is mind, McNeill (2005) points out that it is more prudent to talk of gesture *dimensions* than *categories*. This more accurately reflects the complex semiotic properties of gesture.

2.2.2.1 Iconicity in gesture

If a linguistic sign is iconic there is "a resemblance between form and meaning" (Perniss 2007: 21). Linguistic iconicity is present in devices like onomatopoeia, where the vocal realisation of a word reflects the sound it signifies: the lexeme 'moo' to designate the noise made by a cow, for example. Such examples of symmetrical form/meaning pairings are rare in spoken language, as linguistic signs are characteristically unmotivated (de Saussure [1916] 1995): that is, "the connection which links the signifier and the signified is arbitrary" (de Saussure 1995: 100; translation MT). In contrast, non-arbitrary form-meaning mappings form the core of a major type of gesture, so-called 'iconic' gestures (McNeill 1992), which "present images of concrete entities and/or actions" (McNeill 2005: 39). These entities and actions are referenced in the co-occurring speech. Therefore, just as an iconic linguistic sign has a relationship of identity to the thing it signifies, an iconic gesture also identifies with the thing signified by the linguistic sign. The gesture's perceived iconicity depends on the presence of the linguistic sign. It should be stressed that the referent of an iconic gesture is not the entity or the action designated by the linguistic sign: rather, it is the *concept* of this entity or action which is given kinesic form (Kendon 1981: 34). As pointed out by Müller (2007), gestural representation is conceptualisation: it implies taking a perspective towards objects and events. Actions and entities are conceptualised by speakers within contextual parameters, and the resulting iconic gesture reflects salient characteristics at the time of speaking. An example of an iconic gesture from our data is shown below.

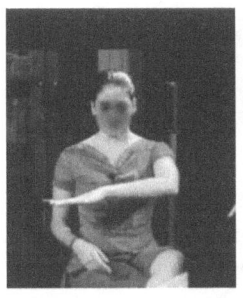 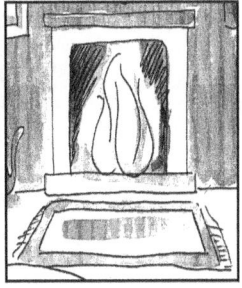

(22) *so here's the rug* (EngDesc3)

In example (22) the speaker uses her left hand, which is held flat with its palm facing down, to iconically represent the rug shown in the picture excerpt above. Speakers also use gestures to represent the semantic content of speech even when this content does not concern a physical referent or action. This is the case, for example, of gestural depictions of lexically encoded directional information.

1   2   3

(23) *to the right of the dog* (EngDesc4)

In the gesture shown above the speaker conveys the lateral direction encoded by the prepositional phrase *to the right*. Her right hand rises from its initial position (stills 1-2), and moves out to the right. Notice how the speaker uses speaker viewpoint in this example, expressing direction to her right (and thus to our left, as we see her). Interestingly, the speaker's head also tilts to the right, thus reinforcing the directional information. Given the close association of the label *iconic gesture* with concrete entities and actions, it is better to avoid its use when describing gestures that express locative information. Therefore, we will use the label *representational spatial gestures* for gestures that represent lexically-encoded locative information.

2.2.2.2 Metaphoric gestures

Abstract concepts may be represented in gesture as physical objects. McNeill (1992, 2005) terms these representations *metaphoric* gestures. The physical object depicted in gesture acts as a vehicle through which the lexically-encoded abstract concept achieves concrete form. There is iconicity because the gesture is an iconic representation of a physical object, and there is metaphoricity because the abstract concept is represented in terms of a concrete object. An example would be if I represented the idea of 'happiness' by making a box-like gesture with my two open hands. In such an instance, the abstract concept would achieve kinesic form through the manual representation of a concrete object (i.e. a box).

McNeill (2005) also points out that speakers can use space in a metaphorical fashion. To use the 'happiness' example once more, a speaker might divide their gesture space to reflect the contrasting states of 'happiness' and 'sadness'. They might associate the front-right area of gesture space with 'happiness', and the front-left area with 'sadness'. Subsequent reference to these concepts in the speaker's discourse might entail the use of gesture to refer to these respective portions of space.

2.2.2.3 Pointing gestures

Pointing gestures purposefully draw attention to a particular portion of space. Also known as *deictic* gestures in the literature, they are described by Kendon (2004: 200) as "indicating an object, a location, or a direction, which is discovered by projecting a straight line from the furthest point of the body part that has been extended outward, into the space that extends beyond the speaker." Pointing gestures can be realised with different parts of the body, including the hands, the fingers, the head and the speaker's gaze (Calbris 2004: 153). The parts of the body engaged in the act of pointing vary cross-culturally: for instance, the lips are used in Laotian (Enfield 2001).

In his 2005 book, McNeill considers pointing under the heading of deictic gestures (p.39). However, he also includes under this same heading non-pointing gestures that establish a referent's location in relation to an origo (pp. 39-40). Hence, pointing gestures are not housed in a category of their own. While this may be understandable on a semantic level (that is, both pointing and non-pointing gestures have deictic properties as far as establishing location is concerned), it nevertheless ignores key semiotic properties of pointing gestures. As McNeill (2005: 12) states, pointing "has a form that is standardized within a given culture". This stands in contrast to non-pointing examples of gestural locative deixis – such as McNeill's (2005: 40) 'bends it way back' example. Furthermore, the form that a pointing gesture takes may have other implications. For example, Kendon and Versante (2003) show that the use of the thumb to point in Neapolitan suggests that the location pointed to is not as important as a location marked by an index finger point. This shows that the form which the pointing hand or finger adopts is not arbitrary. It is therefore better to separate pointing gestures from general deictic phenomena in gesture. As a reflection of this we will use the term *pointing gesture* instead of *deictic gesture* in our work.

There are two types of pointing gestures. The first singles out concrete objects in the speaker's environment. Kendon (1996) refers to pointing of this kind as *actual object pointing*; the second involves pointing at a location where no object is visibly present (see Kita 2000: 162; Kita 2003: 4). Such *abstract pointing* (McNeill 1992) designates the location of an abstract entity in space. An example of this would be if I wished to visually highlight the difference between 'quotable gestures' and 'pragmatic gestures'. I might use my extended right index finger to point to the right-hand area of gesture space while uttering "quotable gestures", before pointing straight across to the left-hand area while uttering "pragmatic gestures". In doing so, my gestures would create a symbolic division of space, metaphorically reflecting the separate identities of the two gesture types.

2.2.2.4 Beats

Beats (McNeill 1992), or 'baton' gestures (Efron 1972; Ekman and Friesen 1981) as they are also known in the literature, mark the accompanying speech content as contextually salient. Their function is to highlight the importance of the co-occurring information in speech to the speaker's overall discourse (McNeill 1992: 15). In terms of form, beats resemble "beating musical time" (McNeill 1992: 15) and are rapid movements of the hand or finger up and down, or backwards and forwards.

2.2.2.5 Cohesives

Cohesives are gestures which link "thematically related but temporally separated parts of the discourse" (McNeill 1992: 16). They may take the form of iconics, metaphorics, pointing gestures, or beats. They repeat a previous gesture from the speaker's discourse, and in doing so suggest thematic continuity between the two discourse segments (McNeill 1992: 16).

2.2.2.5.1 The gesticulations of interest in the current research

The present study focuses on the expression of locative information in speech and in gesture. Taking into account the sub-categorisation of gesticulations outlined above, it is reasonable to assume that what we have termed *representational spatial gestures* (a type of iconic gesture) and *pointing gestures* will be of primary interest. It is difficult to imagine that speakers will make recurrent use of metaphorical gestures in their descriptions, because our study is not concerned with how speakers localise abstract concepts in gesture space. Instead, it focuses on how speakers describe the locations of visually-represented objects and landmarks. Beats, which fulfil discursive and non-representational functions, will not be examined in what follows; nor will cohesives. The research therefore concentrates on what are known as *representational gestures* in the literature. According to Hostetter and Alibali (2007: 74) these gestures "are movements that convey information that is related to the content of the verbal message", and include the sub-categories of iconic, metaphoric, and pointing gestures. Hence, representational gestures convey information either iconically (iconic and metaphoric gestures) or indexically (pointing gestures) (Debreslioska et al. 2013).

2.2.3 The relationship of speech and gesture

2.2.3.1 An overview of the literature

Representational gestures are tightly related to the speech which they accompany at both temporal and semantic levels (McNeill 1992, 2005; Kendon 2004). Yet what is the purpose of these gestures, and why do they accompany speech? Do they allow us a 'window onto the mind' by representing an imagistic form of utterance content (McNeill 1992, 2005)? Are they part of the final communicative package which a speaker intends for their addressee (Kendon 2004)? Perhaps their role is not so much to communicate information to addressees as it is to assist the speaker in retrieving lexical items (Krauss et al. 1996; Krauss et al. 2000; Hadar and Butterworth 1997). The aim of this section is to understand *why* speakers use representational gestures, and to determine their role in relation to speech. Although this entails discussing several models of speech and gesture production, an intricate presentation of how gestures are generated in relation to speech is not the focus here.

One approach in the literature considers gesture as a modality that helps speakers to access lexical items. Krauss, Chen and Gottesman (2000) propose a model of speech and gesture production which builds upon the model proposed for speech by Levelt. According to the version presented by Krauss and colleagues, gesture arises from spatial and dynamic features of working memory and is generated separately to linguistic propositional content. Gesture develops a relationship with speech at the moment of phonological encoding, by facilitating the retrieval of an appropriate lexical item. De Ruiter (2000, 2007) also uses Levelt's speaking model as a base, but his version takes into account gesture's role as a communicative device. That is, he shows how his 'Sketch Model' allows the speaker's communicative intention to unfold through both the speech and gesture modalities. This brings him to acknowledge a similarity between his model and another account of speech and gesture production: McNeill's 'growth point' theory (McNeill 1992, 2000a, 2000b, 2005; McNeill and Duncan 2000). De Ruiter points out that, in both of these accounts, "gestures and speech are part of the same communicative intention, and are planned by the same process" (de Ruiter 2000: 306). For McNeill this communicative intention, or 'growth point' as he calls it, is "the initial form of thinking out of which speech–gesture organization emerges" (McNeill 2000b: 314). Growth points are units which blend "imagery and linguistic content" (McNeill 2005: 18). Linguistic content is unpacked into the linear structure of spoken language, while imagery receives expression in gesture. Pivotal to growth points are the concerns of context and contrast: the more a growth point stands out in context, the more pronounced the speech and gesture realisation will be. Hence, growth point theory predicts that when this contrast is minimal, the likelihood of gesture is less.

To summarise so far, Krauss and colleagues argue in favour of gesture as a facility for lexical retrieval, while both de Ruiter (2000, 2007) and McNeill (1992) understand gesture as a modality which, together with speech, unpacks the speaker's communicative intention. Also crucial to McNeill's theory is the idea that "gestures are a necessary component of speaking and thinking" (2005: 15). This means that gesture provides us with a 'window onto the mind' (McNeill 1992), allowing us access to a speaker's cognitive state at the time of speaking.

Kendon (1994) also argues in favour of a communicative bond between speech and gesture, stating that "the gestures produced by speakers in association with their speech are produced as an integral part of the same plan of action as the spoken utterance" (p.176). However, while McNeill (1992, 2005) focuses on the role of gesture in relation to thought processes, Kendon (2004) concentrates more on gesture's role as a communicative channel in interaction: "the gestures used by speakers as they speak are partnered with speech as a part of the speaker's *final product* and are as much a part of the utterance's design as the speaker's words." (Kendon 2004: 5; original emphasis). A key phrase here is *final product*. This suggests that gestures are part of the communicative package that a speaker prepares for a listener. These gestures are intended for the utterance recipient because they are *as much a part of the utterance's design as the speaker's words*. In his 2004 book *Gesture: visible action as utterance*, Kendon details the many ways in which gestures communicate different types of information in spoken interaction. His approach pays close attention to hand form and the semiotic properties of gesture. In earlier work (Kendon 1994), he notably takes up a claim by Rimé and Schiaratura that gestures do not communicate information. By assessing evidence from both experimental and observational data, Kendon concludes that gestures do indeed communicate, although there is variability as to when and how they do this.

It is possible that representational gestures occur for many reasons. Undoubtedly, there are times when speakers use these gestures for lexical retrieval purposes (Hadar and Butterworth 1997; Krauss et al. 1996; Krauss et al. 2000). However, it is unlikely that this is their sole function. Yet even if it were, these gestures would nevertheless be assisting speakers to communicate messages: this highlights the essentially communicative function of gesture. It is at this point that the question of gesture visibility comes into play. That is, speakers gesture even when they do not have visual access to their interlocutor: when they are on the phone, for example (see Bavelas et al. 2008 for an in-depth discussion of interlocutor visibility and gesture). In such a context, any information which the speaker expresses solely in gesture will not be accessible to their addressee. This raises the following question: do speakers gesture differently when they share reciprocal visibility with their addressee? Work by Emmorey and Casey (2001) suggests that this is the case. Reporting on an experiment in which a speaker was required to give instructions of a spatial nature to an addressee seated opposite them, the researchers found a higher rate of gesture when the speaker could see their addressees as opposed to when they could not. Furthermore, addressees picked up on information that was only present in their interlocutor's gestures. Additional evidence which shows that addressees attend to information which is only present in gesture has been reported by Tabensky (2001). Tabensky's analysis of conversational interaction found that recipients re-took information which was present in their interlocutor's gestures, and re-expressed this as new units in either speech or gesture. Further empirical support for the view that addressees attend to their interlocutors' gestures is provided by Cassell, McNeill and McCullough (1999). In this paper, the authors describe an experiment in which participants watched a video of a narrator retelling a cartoon story that they had viewed. At certain points in his narration this narrator (one of the article's authors) deliberately expressed information in gesture that was not encoded in speech. The participants who watched this narration were subsequently required to re-tell the story to a naïve listener. The results showed that during this retelling phase, speakers provided information (in speech and in gesture) that had only been available in the narrator's gestures. This therefore provided evidence that addressees do attend to, and take up, information expressed in a speaker's gestures.

2.2.3.2 The view taken in the current study

The present study understands speakers' use of representational gestures in two ways. Firstly, we suggest that the speakers in our study likely used these gestures to impart information to their addressees at different times. This aligns with Kendon (2004), who understands gesture as part of the final product of utterance, as well as with McNeill (1992, 2005), who understands gesture as part of language itself. A degree of support for this interpretation derives from our finding that speakers often used gesture to express salient, unlexicalised directional information. Logically, if speakers did not intend their gestures to communicate, then this information should also have been encoded in speech. Often, however, this was not the case. However, we have not conducted gesture comprehension studies to determine whether addressees actually gleaned information from the gestures made by our speakers: hence, we cannot claim their communicative efficacy with complete confidence. Furthermore, speakers also make small, discrete gestures, which are arguably not intended for their interlocutor's benefit. Therefore, we will lean more heavily on the idea that representational gestures allow us to better understand how speakers conceptualise static locative relationships. This approach is based on the premise that gestures provide us with access into spatial cognition (Alibali, 2005; Hostetter, Alibali and Kita, 2007; Levinson, 2003b) and conceptualisation more generally (McNeill, 1992, 2005). By observing representational gestures, we can understand the types of information that speakers attend to when using different lexical spatial items. For example, our data reveal that some speakers represent the *foreground* of the stimulus pictures by depicting extension along the lateral axis. The concept FOREGROUND designates a spatial area that lies in perceptual proximity to an oriented viewer along a frontal axis. Nevertheless, this area must also possess width along a lateral axis. Gesture reveals how speakers attend to this complementary concern as part of their mental representation of FOREGROUND. Further evidence for understanding gesture as a window onto spatial cognition is the use of different perspectives cross-modally (qv. Chapter 5). Hence, gesture may express location from a particular perspective (i.e. observer perspective), while speech expresses it from another perspective (i.e. character perspective). Given this difference, the information encoded by the lexical spatial item may be inconsistent with the information expressed in gesture. In such a case, it is hard to argue that gesture's role is to facilitate the retrieval of a lexical item: rather, gesture is revealing another way in which the speaker conceptualises the Figure's location.

2.3 Gesture and the expression of spatial information: what we know

The following sub-sections identify the major research which has been carried out into gesture and the spatial domain. These projects have basically targeted three topics of enquiry: gesture's relationship to spatial conceptualisation; the relationship between the spatial information which speakers express in gesture and that which they encode in speech; and gesture's role in expressing information concerning object size and relative position.

2.3.1 Gesture and spatial conceptualisation

When people talk about spatial concepts, they gesture (Alibali, Heath and Myers 2001; Alibali 2005; Emmorey and Casey 2001; Hostetter, Alibali and Kita 2007; Kita and Özyürek 2003; McNeill 2000). In fact, speakers gesture more frequently when they talk about spatial topics than non-spatial ones (Alibali, Heath and Myers 2001; Alibali 2005; Rauscher et al. 1996). Numerous studies have been conducted which examine the relationship between gesture production and spatial cognition. These studies have targeted, for instance, how speakers gesture when completing spatial tasks of varying cognitive difficulty (Hostetter et al. 2007), and whether gesture frequency is linked to speakers' different levels of spatial skill (Hostetter and Alibali 2007). The spatial domain has also been used as a tool for determining the role played by representational gestures in conceptualisation. For example Kita and Davies (2009), using a study based upon the description of geometric shapes, showed that the frequency of representational gestures increases when conceptual demands are higher. In other work, Chu and Kita (2008) used a mental rotation task involving a geometric figure to show that speakers produce gesture in the absence of speech. They concluded that this reveals the pivotal role of gesture in spatial conceptualisation.

2.3.2 The relationship between lexically-encoded and gesturally-expressed spatial information

Other studies have examined whether the spatial information expressed in gesture is mediated by the semantic content of co-occurring lexical spatial items. Hence, Gullberg (2011) looked at the gestures made by speakers of French and Dutch in descriptions of placement events. She hypothesized a difference between the two groups of speakers on the basis of the contrasting semantic granularity of French and Dutch placement verbs. Whereas French placement verbs focus solely on the movement of the Figure in relation to the Ground, Dutch placement verbs are finer-grained and encode information relating to spatial features of the Figure, such as shape and orientation. Gullberg's results showed that the placement gestures of the two groups were indeed different, and that speakers' gestures reflected the lexical semantic contrast between the two sets of verbs. In other research, Kita and Özyürek (2003) examined the gestures of English, Japanese and Turkish speakers when describing a character's trajectory from one building to another in a cartoon stimulus film. The arc-like trajectory of the character is readily encoded by the English verb *swing*, but not by any lexical item in either Japanese or Turkish. This lexical difference led the researchers to hypothesize that English speakers would express the character's arc-like trajectory in gesture more frequently than Japanese or Turkish speakers. This was shown to be the case, thus prompting the researchers to conclude that there was "a linguistic effect on the gestural representation" (p.21). Further evidence for the influence of linguistically-encoded event features on the informational content of gesture has been reported by Özyürek et al. (2005). These researchers showed that speakers gesturally represent features of motion events that are concurrently attended to in speech. In contrast, when a language does not encode a particular event feature (i.e. manner of motion), this is also absent in gesture. Descriptions of motion events have also been used to show how gestures reflect a language's syntactic distribution of information. Hence, Özyürek et al. (2008) report that adult speakers of English and Turkish differ in how they gesturally represent the Path and Manner components of motion events. While English lexically encodes these two strands of semantic information within the one clause, Turkish uses two clauses. Accordingly, adult English speakers execute a single gesture which conflates both strands of information, while adult Turkish speakers express each strand of information in a separate gesture.

The evidence above suggests that the syntactic and semantic-encoding patterns of individual languages influence the type of spatial information which speakers express in gesture, as well as how speakers distribute these gestures alongside lexical utterance structure. In contrast, another study reports that speakers *do* attend to a feature of motion events which is not prioritized by the language spoken. In this study, McNeill (2000b) examined how English and Spanish speakers described motion events which they had viewed in a cartoon-film stimulus. English, a satellite-framed language, and Spanish, a verb-framed language, each accord different importance to the lexical encoding of manner of motion. Hence, this semantic feature is routinely encoded in English but not in Spanish (McNeill 2000b; see also section 2.1.3 above). McNeill found that Spanish speakers seemingly compensated for this by expressing manner in gesture alone. He termed this phenomenon a *manner fog*: "an entire description blanketed with repeated manner gestures in the total absence of manner in speech" (McNeill 2000b: 53). His results therefore suggested that speakers attend to event features other than those prioritized by the language spoken.

2.3.3 The role of gesture in communicating object size and relative position

An important body of research now exists about how speakers express information relating to object size and relative position. This research has been conducted by Geoffrey Beattie, Heather Shovelton and Judith Holler at the University of Manchester. In published work from 1999 onwards, Beattie, Shovelton and Holler have examined the communicative value of spatial information which speakers present in iconic gestures. Beattie and Shovelton (1999) describe an experiment in which observers were played clause-length video clips of speakers narrating different events from a cartoon strip. Some observers were played the audio only, while others also had access to the speakers' iconic gestures. The researchers found that observers were significantly more likely to provide accurate spatial information when they had access to the speakers' iconic gestures as well as to their speech. More precisely, this increase was significant for two particular types of spatial information: size and relative position. Holler and Beattie (2002), using a conversational paradigm, showed that speakers used iconic gestures to express information about relative position which was not present in the co-occurring speech segment. This, they argued, highlights the complementary nature of the speech and gesture systems in the expression of semantic information. In other published work from this same year, Beattie and Shovelton (2002) investigated whether a speaker's use of character or observer viewpoint affected the 'communicative power' of their iconic gestures. Communicative power was determined by having viewers watch iconic gestures without the accompanying speech, and identifying whether these viewers produced more correct information about semantic features (such as size and relative position) depending on whether the speaker used character or observer viewpoint. Their results showed that gestures were significantly more 'powerful' in communicating relative position information when the speaker used a character viewpoint. The same result was also found for size information in one of the two experiments reported. In work to follow, Beattie and Shovelton (2006) focused on how speakers express size information in gesture alone. Their study indicated that this information was of high importance to the narrative, and therefore that speakers were using gesture to communicate important spatial information which was not lexically co-present. Finally, Holler, Beattie and Shovelton (2009) examined whether observers glean information about object size and relative position from their partners' iconic gestures in face-to-face interaction. This diverged from their earlier methodology, which focused on whether observers gleaned information from gestures that were presented to them on video. The face-to-face condition which underpinned this latest study upheld the results found in the earlier work.

2.3.4 Gesture and the expression of static locative information: hypotheses

The sections above show that research into gesture and space has targeted three main areas of interest. One additional study, mentioned in our introduction, is a dissertation by Arik (2009). This work examines which features of motion and locative events are expressed by speakers of seven different languages: Turkish Sign Language, Croatian Sign Language, American Sign Language, Austrian Sign Language, Turkish, Croatian, and English. In addition to this, it investigates how spatial language is used in temporal expressions. As part of this study, Arik looked at the gestures made by speakers of the three spoken languages when they described motion and locative events. However, given the breadth of his investigation, there is little discussion of how English speakers use gesture with speech to express different types of locative information. Nevertheless, the results for English showed that speakers can use different frames of reference in speech and gesture, and that gestures can express unlexicalised spatial information, such as the spatial axis which underpins a locative relationship, in gesture alone. Arik also noted that speakers' hands did not express the idea of contact when describing topological relationships in which two objects were in contact, such as a ruler in a measuring cup or an orange on a mug. His study, however, was not concerned with investigating the relationship between speech and gesture in the expression of location. Hence, there was no particular discussion of how gestures related to different spatial items in speech. A couple of other studies should also be mentioned in this section. Tversky et al. (2009) briefly describe the use of gesture in route descriptions. Certainly, static locative expressions form part of such descriptions, since different landmarks need to be identified in order to navigate from one place to another. However, these expressions are not investigated in the paper, and the only mention of gesture's role in expressing location was that speakers sometimes used deictic gestures to point to locations. Striegnitz et al. (2009) also present a study of route descriptions. Here, the authors' focus is on the different perspectives speakers convey in gesture: hence, their aim is not to establish gesture's role in expressing locative semantic information. There is therefore no true precedent for the experiments that we will present. Note also that the Beattie and Shovelton studies which report on relative position do not look at what types of locative information are expressed in gesture, nor do they target static locative configurations. We have nevertheless formulated three basic hypotheses about what we expect to find in our work. These hypotheses, which were initially presented in our introduction, concern how we believe speakers will use gesture when expressing static locative relationships.

– Speakers will use representational gestures (qv. Chapter 2) when describing locative configurations. This follows on logically from the following findings: speakers use representational gestures when describing dynamic motion events (e.g. Kita and Özyürek 2003; McNeill 2000b); preventing speakers from gesturing reduces speech fluency when speakers express spatial information (Krauss, Chen and Chawla 1996); speakers gesture more often when they talk about spatial topics as opposed to non-spatial ones (Alibali, Heath and Myers, 2001; Alibali, 2005; Rauscher et al., 1996).

– Speakers' gestures will express salient, unlexicalised locative information. This is based on earlier research which shows that not all aspects of a spatial event receive form in speech – some emerge in gesture only (Alibali 2005; Arik 2009; Emmorey and Casey 2001; McNeill 2000b). As such, representational gestures will provide us with an ideal means of access into spatial cognition (Alibali, 2005; Hostetter, Alibali and Kita, 2007; Levinson, 2003b).

– The use of lexical spatial items with similar semantics in English and French will result in the expression of the same locative information in gesture by speakers of the two languages. This highlights the tight interrelationship of speech and gesture in the expression of semantic information (McNeill 1992, 2005; Kita and Özyürek 2003).

3 Methodology

This chapter presents the experiment which underpins our investigation into static locative expressions. We describe the experiment design, the goals behind it, and justify the use of the two stimulus pictures which were created specifically for the study. We also explain how participants were recruited and the conditions under which data were elicited. This is followed by a description of the transcription process and an explanation of the way in which the data were analysed. Finally, we detail how examples from the data will be presented in subsequent chapters, and present a brief transcription code to explain the conventions used in these examples.

3.1 Background to the experiment

The aim of our experiment was to understand how English and French speakers use speech and gesture to express the nature of static locative relationships. Given that no previous study had targeted this question, there were no precedents as to the experimental format which we should follow. There were, however, some obvious conditions which needed to be observed. Firstly, given the interest in gesture, the experiment needed to be filmed. Secondly, given the inter-linguistic nature of the study and the fact that data would be collected in both Australia and France, the experimental conditions had to be controlled and kept constant for all participants (as far as reasonably possible). Thirdly, speakers had to be engaged in the task so that their inhibitions would be lessened. If participants felt ill-at-ease, then this would negatively affect their implication in the experiment and potentially their use of gesture. Finally, research into spatial language and gesture by Emmorey and Casey (2001) has revealed that "subjects gestured much more when they could see their addressee" (p.42). Therefore, we decided that it would be better to have an experimental situation in which speakers were in the physical co-presence of their addressees. With this in mind, we developed a pilot study[13] in order to better understand the methodological issues at play in our research.

---

[13] This study has also been described in Tutton (2007).

3.2 Pilot study

Pivotal to the pilot study was creating an appropriate experimental task. As suggested above, we decided to have speakers describe location to a physically co-present addressee. However, how could we incite speakers to talk about locative relationships, and also control for the types of locative relationships which they described? The solution was to create a stimulus picture and to ask speakers to describe the locations of specific objects in this picture. We devised a basic sketch of a lounge room scene, which was subsequently reproduced by a fourth year student in Visual Arts at the University of New South Wales[14]. This picture is shown as figure 2 below. A comprehensive range of locative relationships is targeted by the stimulus picture: for example, the rug is *in front of* the fireplace, the dvd player is *underneath* the television and *in* the cabinet, the mirror is *above* the fireplace, while the book, the bone and the ball are all *on* the floor.

Fig. 2: Pilot test stimulus picture

Eight native speakers of Australian English and eight native speakers of French were recruited to participate in the study. All were students at the University of New South Wales, Sydney at the time of the experiment. Participants were part-

---

14 This picture, along with the other pictures used in our experimental tasks, was drawn by Peta Dzubiel.

nered with another speaker of the same language, thus enabling the filming of four English and four French dyads. One speaker was the designated 'describer', who had the task of describing the picture to their partner, who was known as the 'receiver'. The two speakers were seated opposite each other and both had a copy of the picture on a stand next to them. On the receiver's copy of the picture however, three items were missing (the cat, the bone and the ball). The describer was instructed to describe the lounge room to the receiver, focusing on the location of 14 items which were listed next to the picture. The describer was also told to describe the location of these items as clearly as possible. Based on the description provided by the describer, the receiver had to work out which three of the 14 items were missing in their copy of the picture. Once the describer had completed their description, the receiver was allowed to ask questions. No time limit was imposed for this task. The researcher then debriefed both participants following their completion of the experiment.

The results of the study highlighted several methodological issues which required attention. One major issue was that the receiver's attention was focused on their copy of the picture during the describer's description. This was unavoidable, because receivers had to determine which three items had been removed from their version of the stimulus image. However, this impeded visual interaction between the two participants, and so potentially impacted on the describers' use of gesture to communicate locative information. Indeed, several describers made little use of gesture at all.

The researcher debriefed participants following their completion of the task, and this provided helpful feedback concerning their experience and opinion of the experiment. For instance, certain participants stated that they thought they were *not allowed* to gesture, because they understood the focus of the study to be on language. Some participants also thought that it would be *too easy* if they could use gesture, and therefore did not do so. Both of these comments indicated that the instructions for the task needed to be modified so that participants would not consciously suppress the use of gesture.

Another flaw in the study was the stimulus picture itself. The picture is not naturalistic enough in its depiction of a lounge room, and there are noticeable anomalies – such as the sofa's orientation to face the table, as opposed to the television. Moreover, the light is hanging above a coffee table as opposed to a large dining table with chairs, which seems somewhat incoherent. With this in mind, we set about creating a revised version of the stimulus picture. Other considerations also influenced the new experimental design, and these are described in the following section.

3.3 The revised study

3.3.1 Theoretical considerations

Following the pilot study, it was decided that speakers should describe two different types of spatial scenes instead of just one. Research has shown that the ways in which we understand space depend on the factors of scale (Montello 1993) and the salience of motion events (Montello 1993; Tutton 2013). For example, the spatial language which we use is likely to differ when we describe a larger-scale space like a city street, as opposed to a smaller-scale internal space like a lounge room: this is because spatial language is sensitive to fluctuations in scale (Lautenshütz et al. 2007). This is demonstrated in the two invented examples below.

(24) *the post-office box is at the end of the street, before the roundabout*
(25) **the table is at the end of the lounge room, before the sofa*

The spatio-temporal preposition *before* encodes location in terms of a sequence. That is, the Figure occupies a point prior to the Ground in the trajectory of a real or virtual agent in motion (Tutton 2013; cf. Vandeloise 1986 for *avant*). Hence, in example (24), the addressee will encounter the post-office box at an earlier point in their trajectory than the roundabout. The concept of a physical trajectory is more salient to a large, external space like a city street than it is to a smaller, enclosed space like a living room: this explains the difficulty of using *before* in example (25). The spatial nominal *end*, such as it is used in both of these examples, refers to the final point in an agent's trajectory. This foregrounding of physical motion and an extended path is compatible with the external expanse of a street (example 24), but not with the restricted interior space of a lounge room (example 25). With this in mind, we decided to create a second picture which would potentially highlight this contrast in the use of spatial language.

3.3.2 The use of two pictures

The idea of a lounge room was retained for the first picture, while a second picture of a street scene was created. A substantial variety of spatial configurations are represented in both pictures in order to trigger descriptions that recruit a wide range of spatial items. Hence, the spatial configurations varied from objects *on*, *on top of* and *in* others, to objects *above*, *to the left of*, *to the right of*, and *in front of* others. Participants' attention could be guided towards these specific configurations by instructing them to focus on the location of certain objects, as was the case in the pilot study. Once basic sketches had been made, the artist who had sketched the stimulus picture for the pilot test created the two desired black and white images. These pictures are shown below[15].

Fig. 3: Lounge room scene

Fig. 4: Street scene

Figure 3 is a re-working of the scene initially used in the pilot study (see Figure 2). Firstly, the artist's use of shading along the back wall in the picture creates a more naturalistic effect. The orientation of the sofa has shifted so that it now

---

15 Larger versions of both pictures can be found in Appendices A and B.

faces the back wall and the television. The table has become a dining-room table with two chairs and a tablecloth. The lamp now hangs down over it, as opposed to being suspended awkwardly in midair. This positioning of the lamp close to the table is intentional, in order to discover whether English speakers favour the use of *above* (which highlights presence along the vertical axis), or *over* (which suggests horizontal coverage). In terms of cross-linguistic comparison, French speakers can encode this vertical relationship using *au-dessus de* ('above'), but there is no ready equivalent for English *over*. The picture was also devised to allow speakers to make ample use of both intrinsic and relative frames of reference. Hence, the rug is in front of the fireplace (intrinsic frame of reference), while the bone is in front of the rug (relative frame of reference). Topological relationships were also targeted, as speakers were required to locate the tablecloth (which is *on* the table), and the curtains (which are *on* the window).

A range of locative relationships was also targeted in the street scene (figure 4). One point of particular interest was to see whether speakers would use spatio-temporal prepositions, such as *before/avant* and *after/après*, to encode location. Hence, the post-office box is located just *before* the pedestrian crossing, while the telephone booth is just *after* it. Various topological relationships were depicted, from the bird *on* the branch *in* the tree, to the satellite dish *on top of* the hotel. We also wanted to see how speakers used gesture when confronted with a Figure which is difficult to localise. Hence, the lady is neither in front of the café nor of the youth hostel, but somewhere in between them. She is also standing near a pathway. Establishing her precise location is therefore a complicated affair. Faced with such a situation, would speakers use gesture to assist spatial conceptualisation?

A major concern when devising these two pictures was to create representations of spaces that could be found in either Australia or in France. This meant that they had to possess a certain degree of cultural neutrality. Hence, in the lounge room scene (figure 3), the language of the open book is not legible, nor is there any writing on the television screen. The room contains objects that are regularly found in spaces of this type in Australia and France: a sofa, a television, a dvd player and a rug, amongst others. The street scene (figure 4) was more complicated as far as cultural neutrality was concerned, because Australians drive on the left-hand side of the road while the French drive on the right: this is a major difference which cannot be overlooked. The easiest way to overcome this problem was to create a one-way street and to focus attention on the objects and landmarks on the left and right footpaths. We also deliberately avoided specifying number plates on vehicles and did not include any traffic signs. Another difficulty as far as the street scene was concerned was deciding how to identify the shops along the street. It is difficult to avoid the use of language here, as labels for individual shops provide the most economical and efficient means of landmark identification. Two versions of the street scene were thus created: one in which the shop labels were provided in English, and another in which they were provided in French. The only difference between these two versions is the language in which the shop names are written.

3.3.3 Experimental setup

In order for these pictures to be exploited to their full potential, a careful experimental framework needed to be developed. We decided to keep the basic format of a describer/receiver interactive situation, as used for the pilot study. There was also the same requirement that the describer explain the location of 14 listed items for each picture. The order in which these 14 items appeared on the lists was different for each describer/receiver couple: this was to cancel out any order effects. Ordering was determined randomly in Excel. The order in which the two pictures were given to describers changed from one pair to the next. Hence, the first describer began by describing the lounge room scene, while the subsequent describer began with the street scene. 12 male-female couplings were devised, with one person assigned the role of describer and the other the role of receiver. There was an equal number of male and female participants assigned to each role. Participants were seated a short distance opposite each other in the studio where the experiment was filmed. The first picture to be described was placed back-to-front on a music stand just to the left of the describer. Describers could not visually access the picture until the researcher turned the picture around. Both pictures were laminated and of A3 size. The music stand was positioned so that receivers had maximum visual access to the describers' gestures. Hence, even gestures made in front of the music stand were accessible to the receiver. The experiment setup is shown in figure 5 below.

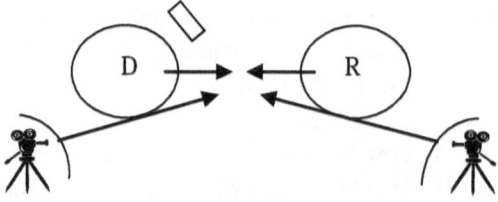

Fig. 5: Experimental setup

The researcher began the experiment by distributing instruction sheets to the describer and the receiver[16]. He read these aloud, beginning with the describer's instructions. These instructions stipulated that descriptions of the picture should focus on the locations of the 14 items listed next to the picture. They also specified that describers had a maximum of five minutes in which to complete their description, after which time they would have to stop. The receiver, who was not allowed to interrupt this description, would then have five minutes to ask the describer any questions about the picture and the locations of the 14 items. Following this, the receiver would be presented with four different versions of the picture. The three incorrect versions would each have just one object in the incorrect location. After the researcher had read these instructions aloud, participants were asked if they had any questions. The researcher then collected the instruction sheets and attached the list of 14 items next to the picture on the music stand. He then turned this picture around so that the describer could see it. The researcher subsequently handed a copy of the list of items to the receiver, and the describer was told to begin their description.

The researcher was present in the room during all recordings and kept track of time, warning describers when their five minutes had expired, and telling both parties when the five minute interactive segment was over. Following this interactive segment, he issued the receiver with the four alternate versions of each stimulus picture: these four versions were presented together on a single, laminated A3 sheet[17]. Once the receiver had made their choice, they passed this sheet to the describer. The describer then told the receiver whether they had selected the correct picture or not by comparing the four versions against their own copy of the picture. This therefore completed the first half of the experiment. The researcher initiated the beginning of the second half of the experiment by placing the next picture on the music stand, and attaching the list of 14 items next to it. He then issued the receiver with their copy of the list, and the describer was once again told to begin their description.

There were two key differences in this set-up which reflected what we had learned from the pilot study. First of all, there was a time limit imposed for each section of the experiment: this was to encourage the participants' full implication in the task. Hence, the describer was given five minutes to describe the first picture. The receiver was not allowed to interrupt the describer or to ask questions during this time: this was so that we could subsequently analyse how

---

16 Copies of these instruction sheets can be found in Appendix C. Both English and French versions are provided.
17 These four alternate versions of each picture are provided in Appendices A and B.

speakers expressed location without the content of their discourse being influenced by their partner. Similarly, there was a time limit of five minutes for the interactive segment. The second major difference was that receivers were not provided with their own version of the stimulus picture. Instead, they were simply given a list of the 14 items which needed to be located. This was to encourage the visual interaction of the two participants, and hence facilitate the describer's use of gesture to communicate locative information. By altering the set-up of the experimental task in this way, describers were steered towards providing clear, detailed descriptions of location.

3.3.4 Further precisions concerning experimental procedure

On the day of the experiment, Australian participants were met by a research assistant prior to entering the studio. They completed information sheets requesting personal details, and signed consent forms. French participants were met directly by the researcher (MT), who oversaw that the necessary administrative duties were completed prior to the experiment commencing. Once both participants were seated, the researcher engaged them in a warm-up exercise. This required the participants to ask each other two questions which the researcher handed them on a piece of paper. Hence, the describer asked the receiver "What is your name?" and "What is your favourite meal?" while the receiver asked the describer "What is your name?" and "What would you do if you won the lottery tomorrow?" These questions were designed to create an element of humour and to diffuse the tension of the experimental situation. Following this, the instruction sheets were issued and the experimental process outlined in section 3.3.3 began.

12 dyads were filmed for English. 16 were filmed for French, because four of the original 12 were unsuitable for analysis. One dyad was eliminated because the receiver interrupted the describer during the free discourse segment; another because the describer had their back to the camera, thus obscuring their gestures; the third because the describer was not a speaker of metropolitan French; and the fourth because the participants did not fully comply with the experimental procedure. Other pairs of participants thus replaced these four. These replacement pairs undertook the experiment in exactly the same conditions as those whom they replaced: this included using the same lists as those distributed to the original participants, and maintaining the same attribution of male and female describers and receivers.

3.4 Recruitment of participants

Prior to data collection, ethics approval was sought and obtained from the relevant authority at the University of New South Wales. Following this, native monolingual speakers of Australian English were recruited as participants for the experiment. We decided to limit the study to speakers of this variety of English on account of potential lexical differences between different varieties of the language. For example, in American English the prepositional phrase *in back of* is used in addition to *behind*, whereas in Australian English only the latter preposition is used. In order to achieve consistency in the data, it was therefore considered more prudent to restrict the study to speakers of Australian English.

Advertisements were placed in various locations around the university and students were approached directly and told about the experiment. 24 participants were recruited: 12 male and 12 female. All participants were students at the university. Their ages ranged from 18 to 31 and the mean age was 23.75 years. Participants received $15 for their time. Recording of all participants took place on Thursday December 7, 2006 at the University of New South Wales, Sydney. This recording was undertaken by a professional technician employed by the university. The expenses incurred by the experiment, including the payment of participants, studio hire and subsequent editing of the raw data, were covered by a research expenses grant awarded to the researcher by the University of New South Wales.

French data were obtained during the researcher's stay in 2007 at the Université Lille 3, France. Native speakers of the metropolitan variety of French spoken in France were sought. Although these speakers had knowledge of English, they were not bilingual. Participants were recruited by directly approaching students on campus as well as via an email sent out to students enrolled in the university's Department of English. We recruited an equal number of male and female participants. These participants were between 18 and 28 years old and had a mean age of 20.72 years. Recording of participants took place across three separate days in October, 2007 and January, 2008. Data were recorded in the university studio by a technician employed by the university. Participants were not paid, in accordance with university regulation, and were instead invited to select a gift at the end of the recording. These gifts included boxes of chocolates and assortments of teas. This expense was covered by the researcher.

3.5 Editing and transcription of data

Editing of the data was undertaken by the technicians who filmed the experiments. A split-screen system was applied so that edited files showed both the describer and the receiver (see figures 6 and 7 later in this chapter). This was to ensure that the speech and gesture of both participants was accessible at all moments of the analysis.

Spoken data were originally transcribed in Word. No punctuation was used. Instead, a small series of devised conventions indicated pauses, interruptions and other phenomena observable in oral discourse[18]. Following this process, transcriptions were checked to ensure accuracy. Transcriptions initially included both the describer's five-minute monological discourse, as well as the subsequent five-minute interactive segment. Given the enormous amount of data, we decided to focus purely on the first part of the description – that is, the discourse produced by the describer alone. There were two reasons for this decision. The first is that this would enable a clearer picture of how the *describer* actually considered the two different spaces and broke them down for analysis: this is because the receiver was not allowed to interrupt the describer during their monologue. Secondly, it would allow us to examine how describers construed the location of individual objects, and which components of this construal achieved expression in speech and gesture. It is harder to know how describers actually construed the location of the 14 objects in the interactive half of the experiment, since the information which describers provided was regulated by the questions asked by receivers. Hence, by proceeding in this way, we were able to examine how describers conceptualised location.

Instead of drawing on the 12 descriptions as originally planned, it was decided to use the discourse of the first ten describers for each language. This was a necessary measure to reduce the vast amount of data for analysis. As far as the French data are concerned, the discourse of describer 11 was used in the place of that of describer 9. This is because the latter's discourse differed markedly to the descriptions of the other participants: the speaker engaged in a minimum of contact with his partner and described the picture more to himself than to his addressee. This was mirrored in his pattern of gesture behaviour, which largely consisted of the speaker executing gestures on the picture in front of him.

Following transcription in Word, each describer's discourse was transferred into individual files in the video annotation software ELAN. This firstly enabled

---

[18] Please see Appendix D for a sample transcription in Word.

the isolation of lexical locative expressions[19] in the speaker's discourse. We began by coding each of these expressions in terms of the following subcategories.

Object(s). This tier indicates which of the 14 listed items was/were referenced in the locative expression.
Figure. The Figure of the locative expression.
Ground. The Ground of the locative expression.
Spatial linguistic item. This identifies any lexical item – excluding verbs – which encodes spatial information. For reasons mentioned in Chapter 2, our study does not focus on the use of lexical verbs in locative expressions.
Perspective. This tier identifies whether the lexical locative expression encodes location from an observer (scene-internal) perspective, or from a character (scene-external) one.
Frame of reference. This codes whether the lexicalised directional information used an absolute, intrinsic, or relative frame of reference. In instances where a topological preposition such as *on* or *sur* was used, the annotation [NIL (topology)] was applied.

We then identified the gestures that occurred during each of these locative expressions. Gestures were coded in terms of the stroke phase: that is, "the meaningful part of the gestural movement where the spatial excursion of the limb reaches its apex" (Gullberg et al. 2008: 213). Coding the stroke phase allowed us to identify individual gestures in a speaker's discourse. It does not, however, mean that we ignored the preparation phase or pre-or post-stroke holds in our discussion of the data. In subsequent chapters, we discuss examples in which the preparation phase and post-stroke holds played a clear role in the communication of locative information.

Each of the gesture strokes identified on the parent tier 'gesture' was coded for the central information that it expressed. This was achieved by devising a large set of labels, which were defined in terms of the core semantic and pragmatic functions of gestures in our data[20]. For example, an iconic gesture for the rug in a description of the lounge room scene would be coded as [ICON-OBJ 'rug']: this means that the gesture is iconic in nature. These labels identify many features of gestures, such as iconicity of physical form (label: [ICON-OBJ]), the

---

19 A presentation of how we define static locative expressions is forthcoming in Chapter 4.
20 For a full list of these labels, please see Appendix E 'Gesture code for transcriptions in Elan.

representation of lexically encoded locative information (label: [REP-SPACE]), and the expression of unlexicalised locative information (label: [UNLEX-LOC]). A single gesture could be attributed any number of these labels, and there was no necessary connection between any of them: that is, the application of one label to a gesture did not automatically trigger the application of another. Furthermore, there was no range of values for the majority of these labels. For example, the label [ICON-OBJ] was applied to all gestures that were judged to be iconic, irrespective of whether we considered the gesture to have a high or a low iconic loading: the establishment of such ranges in most categories was not essential to our analysis of how gestures express locative semantic information. However, the labels [UNLEX-LOC NEW], [UNLEX-LOC ANAPH], [UNLEX-LOC CONTEXT], and [LOC-CONTEXT], all of which code for locative information, required specification of the spatial axis or axes referenced by the gesture. There were three possible values here: frontal (frontal axis), lateral (lateral axis), and vertical (vertical axis).

One specific example of a gesture and the labels which were attributed to it is shown below.

(26) *there's a cinema.. at the end*
      Gesture: ICON-OBJ 'cinema'; REP-SPACE 'end'; UNLEX-LOC NEW (lateral)

In example (26) the speaker expresses the cinema's location in the street scene using both speech and gesture components. The end of the gesture stroke phase is captured in the still above. The speaker adopts a flat form of the right hand which is oriented so that the palm faces forward: this iconically suggests the flat surface of the cinema as well as its height. This iconicity of form is acknowledged by the label [ICON-OBJ 'cinema']. Secondly, the speaker's right arm is extended straight out in front of his body: this suggests the idea of distance encoded by *end*, and is therefore coded using the label [REP-SPACE 'end']. Finally, in the locative expression which precedes our example, the speaker represents the locations of the two rows of shops on the left- and right-hand sides of gesture space. The gesture in the present example sits in between these two locations, and therefore provides information about the cinema's location along the lateral axis. This information is not encoded in speech, nor has it been mentioned previously in discourse. Hence, we use the label [UNLEX-LOC NEW (lateral)]: this means that the gesture contains unlexicalised locative information which is new in the speaker's discourse, and which concerns the lateral axis.

In addition to this, we established a set of dependent gesture tiers. These tiers, which borrow from those outlined in Bressem (2008), code individual aspects of a gesture, such as the hand(s) used and the direction of the gestural movement. Each of these tiers is specified as follows.

Hand. This codes whether the left hand, the right hand, or both hands were used.
Hand configuration. This provides a basic description of the hand's configuration: i.e. a fist, a flat hand, a single finger, a 'finger spread' (i.e. fingers clearly separated and not touching), etc.
Numbering of fingers. Fingers used in the gesture were numbered from 1-5, the thumb being 1 and the pinkie being 5.
Shape of digits. Digits were described as stretched, bent, crooked, flapped down, connected, or touching.
Palm. The palm was described in terms of its orientation. For example, 'PU' means that the palm was facing upward, and 'PF' means that the palm was extended so that the fingers pointed forward along the frontal axis.
Position in gesture space. We use the gesture space proposed in McNeill (1992: 89).
Movement. This provides a description of the hand's trajectory through space. For example, "hand rises up then moves slightly left".
Perspective. This codes whether the gesture presents locative information from an observer or a character perspective.
Co-occurring lexical item(s). This identifies the lexical item(s) which co-occur(s) with the gesture stroke. For a word to be considered as 'co-occurring' at least one syllable and vowel nucleus had to be enunciated.
Grammatical category. This is a dependent tier for 'co-occurring lexical item(s)', and identifies the grammatical category of the co-occurring phrase. For example, *down the page* would be PP (prepositional phrase).

Ultimately, our investigation in the following chapters is largely concerned with how speakers express location along the horizontal spatial axes. This involves the expression of directional information in gesture. Such information is often expressed by a hand in motion, thus highlighting the importance of the 'movement' sub-category above. Another important sub category is 'palm', since the palm's orientation readily expresses directional information. In contrast, 'shape of digits' and 'hand configuration' are less important to our study.

Below are two full examples of how we coded locative expressions in Elan. We present one example from the English data, and another from the French data. In both examples, the speaker executes more than one gesture as part of the locative expression. Our analysis concerns the first of these gestures in both cases.

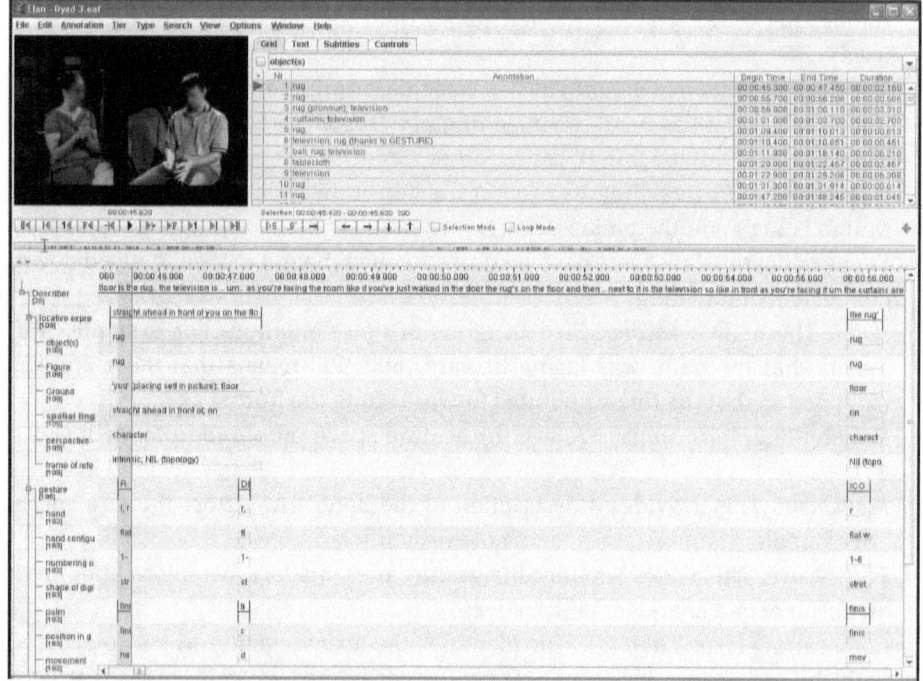

Fig. 6: Fully coded English example in Elan

Lexical locative expression: *straight ahead in front of you on the floor is the rug*
Object(s): *rug*
Figure: *rug*
Ground: *you* (placing self in picture); *floor*

Spatial linguistic item: *straight ahead in front of*; *on*
Perspective: character
Frame of reference: intrinsic; NIL (topology)
Gesture: REP-SPACE 'straight ahead in front'
Hand: l, r (i.e. left and right hands)
Hand configuration: flat hand
Numbering of fingers: 1-5
Shape of digits: stretched
Palm: both hands finish PF (palm frontal: i.e. palms lie forward along frontal axis)
Position in gesture space: finish centre-centre
Movement: hands move down and forward along frontal axis
Perspective: character
Co-occurring lexical item(s): *straight*
Grammatical category: AdvP (adverb phrase)

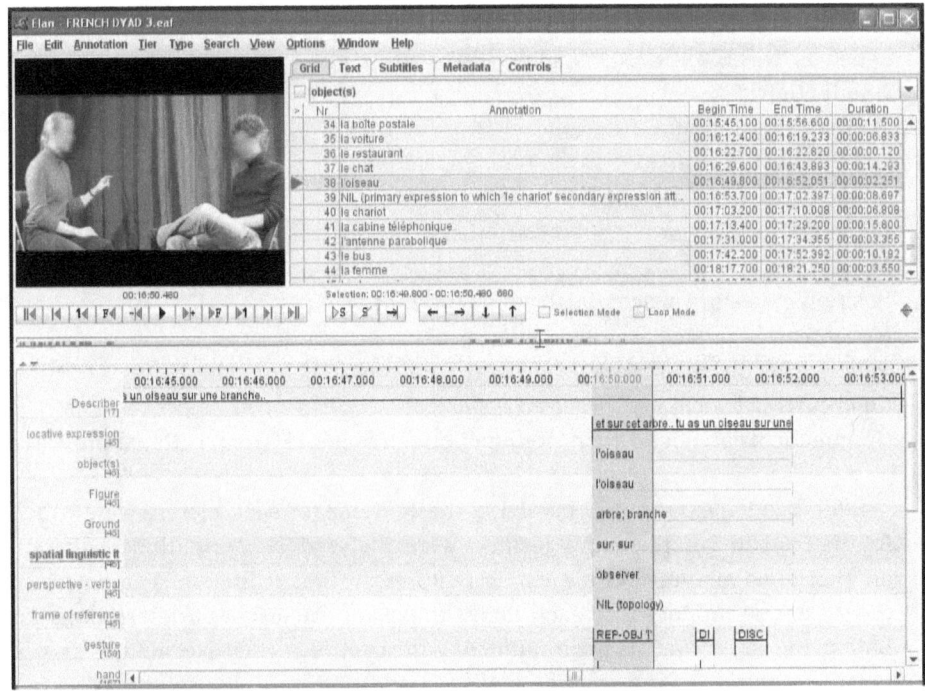

Fig. 7: Fully coded French example in Elan

Lexical locative expression: *et sur cet arbre.. tu as un oiseau sur une branche* and on this tree.. you have a bird on a branch

Object(s): *l'oiseau* ('bird')
Figure: *l'oiseau* ('bird')
Ground: *arbre* ('tree'); *branche* ('branch')
Spatial linguistic item: *sur* ('on'); *sur* ('on')
Perspective: observer
Frame of reference: NIL (topology)
Gesture: REP-OBJ 'l'oiseau'; (possibly also HOLD-OBJ 'l'oiseau'); PLACE-OBJ 'l'oiseau'; UNLEX-LOC CONTEXT & NEW (vertical)
(The code 'REP-OBJ', unlike 'ICON-OBJ', means that the speaker provides a non-iconic representation of a physical referent. It is possible that the speaker is holding the conceptualised object between her fingers, hence the label 'HOLD-OBJ'. She places the conceptualised object into her gesture space: this is coded by 'PLACE-OBJ'. Her hand also rises, suggesting the elevation of the bird in the tree. This information is unlexicalised, but pragmatically inferable from our world knowledge of tree height and the locations of birds in trees. It is therefore coded as 'UNLEX-LOC CONTEXT & NEW (vertical)').
Hand: 1 (left)
Hand configuration: C-fingers
Numbering of fingers: 1-2
Shape of digits: 1: stretched, 2: bent
Palm: PVFaceForwardSlopeForward (i.e. palm vertical, facing forward and sloping forward)
Position in gesture space: finish centre/periphery left
Movement: high arc back in towards speaker
Perspective: observer
Co-occurring lexical item(s): *et sur cet arbre*
Grammatical category: ConjP (conjunction phrase) & PP (prepositional phrase)

All locative expressions involving the 14 items for each picture were coded for the English Describers. All gestures were analysed. However, this resulted in an enormous amount of data which required further reduction. The length of the discourse produced by each English speaker (inclusive of descriptions for both pictures), as well as the number of gesture strokes they executed, is shown in table 1, below.

Tab. 1: Length of discourse and number of gesture strokes produced (per speaker)

Speaker	Length of discourse (minutes)	Number of strokes
EngDesc1	7:06	16
EngDesc2	12:17	162
EngDesc3	10:39	185
EngDesc4	11:49	148
EngDesc5	5:59	36
EngDesc6	3:16	71
EngDesc7	8:01	59
EngDesc8	13:05	172
EngDesc9	11:34	269
EngDesc10	11:21	173
TOTAL	95:07	1291

It was therefore decided that only locative expressions in which each of these 14 objects appeared as a Figure *for the first time* would be used[21]. An object could appear as a Figure in speech, in gesture, or in both modalities[22]. The coding of the French data, which occurred after the English data had been treated, solely targets the first mention of the 14 items as Figure. The data analysis presented in the following chapters draws uniquely on locative expressions from this 'first-mention' pool. There are several benefits to be gained from this approach. The most obvious is that a substantial amount of locative information is likely to be supplied when an object's location is described for the first time in discourse. This should favour a rich use of linguistic spatial items, such as prepositions. In contrast, second and subsequent mentions of an object's location may involve the use of anaphoric strategies, such as pointing to a previously-established location for the object concerned. This provides us with less scope for investi-

---

21 We thank Asli Özyürek for suggesting the 'first mention' of an object in discourse as an analytical strategy. Note, however, that we do not simply target the 'first mention' of an object: we are interested in the first mention of an object *as a Figure*.
22 Please refer to Chapter 4 for details of how Figures may emerge in gesture only.

gating the relationship between lexically-encoded and gesturally-expressed spatial information. Since the present study is interested in the semantic interaction of linguistic spatial items and gesture, the application of the first-mention principle allows for a more pertinent set of data to be cultivated.

3.6 Structure of data analysis

As suggested previously (see Chapter 2), a productive way of structuring our analysis is in terms of the three spatial axes: that is, the frontal (front-back) axis, the lateral (left-right) axis, and the vertical (top-bottom) axis. These axes, or 'orientations' (Fillmore 1975) as they are also known, are a factor in "the semantic organization of lexical items in all languages" (Fillmore 1975: 19). They also provide a ready way to examine how speakers express directional information in speech and gesture. However, prior to our analysis of how speakers express location along the frontal and lateral axes, we need to explain how we defined and separated locative expressions in our data set. This concern is addressed in the following chapter. We then investigate how speakers express location along the frontal axis in both speech and gesture (Chapter 5), before turning our attention to the lateral axis. We subsequently focus on how speakers gesture when encoding topological configurations with the prepositions *on* and *sur*. This allows us to examine what locative information, if any, speakers express in gesture when a Figure shares a common location with a Ground. The final analytical chapter looks at two major ways in which speakers used gesture to express unlexicalised locative information in the experiment. This allows us to come to a fuller understanding of gesture's role in expressing location.

3.7 Presentation of examples in the analysis

The numbering of examples recommences at the beginning of each chapter. The following conventions are adopted when presenting examples from our data.

..	Indicates a pause of less than three seconds.
....	Indicates a pause of more than three seconds.
[...]	Indicates that part of the locative expression has not been included in the example.
<u>stroke</u>	The underlining of a lexical item or group of items shows that they co-occur with the gesture stroke phase.
bold	Bold type indicates the author's emphasis on part of the locative

	expression. It does not concern emphasis by the speaker.
( )	Brackets indicate a segment which is included to provide context for the example. It is not part of the locative expression in the example.
EngDesc4	This is the code for the individual speaker. 'EngDesc' means 'English describer', while 'FrenDesc' means 'French describer'. The number which follows identifies the speaker amongst the ten describers for each language.

Several of these conventions are highlighted in example (27) below.

(27) [...] au <u>premier plan</u>..   sur la gauche (FrenDesc6)
     in the <u>foreground</u>..   on the left

Firstly, [...] indicates that the preceding part of the locative expression is not included in the example. The <u>underlining</u> indicates that the gesture stroke co-occurs with *premier plan* ('foreground'), and .. signals a pause of up to three seconds. The code 'FrenDesc6' identifies the speaker as French describer 6.

As far as French examples are concerned, we provide literal English translations on the line below the transcribed French (as in example 27 above). When this results in non-idiomatic English, we also provide an idiomatic translation between single inverted commas.

For many examples of gestures we provide three still images. These normally represent the gesture stroke phase and should be observed from left to right. In certain instances we provide numbers beneath the stills (i.e. 1, 2, and 3). This is because our written explanation of the example makes reference to one or more of the individual stills, and the numbering helps to facilitate the reader's access to the still(s) concerned.

4 Defining and separating static locative expressions in oral discourse

Having outlined the methodology for the collection and transcription of our data, the current chapter proposes a definition of the term *static locative expression* and presents the reasons behind this definition. It then discusses how static locative expressions are separated within the continuous flow of a describer's discourse. This discussion of the definition and separation of static locative expressions introduces some of the key ways in which speakers use speech and gesture to communicate locative information in oral discourse.

4.1 Defining static locative expressions

In Chapter 2, several ways in which different researchers have understood the concept of locative relationships were presented. The task of the current chapter is to present the interpretation of static locative expressions which will be applied in this study, and to detail the reasons behind this choice. The definition which we propose is as follows:

Static locative expressions: Static locative expressions communicate the fixed location of an object or group of objects (the Figure) in space.

The choice of the verb *communicate* in this definition is deliberate. It suggests that the expression of locative information is not modality specific, and therefore that both speech and gesture may play a part in this expression. The definition is simple and unrestrictive, and aims to cover the complete variety of ways in which speakers communicate location. Although not explicitly stated in the definition, there are other semantic components, apart from the Figure, which are inherent to locative expressions. As discussed in Chapter 2, Talmy identifies these other components as the Ground, Path and Motion. Given that we do not agree that static locative expressions can be categorised as Motion events, we will instead refer to this last semantic role as Location instead of Motion. These components are readily identified in locative expressions from our data.

(28) *the tablecloth is on the table* (EngDesc1)

(29) *l'oiseau* est *sur un arbre* (FrenDesc1)
 the bird is on a tree

In example (28) the Figure is encoded by the noun phrase *the tablecloth*, the Ground by the noun phrase *the table*, Location by the copula *is* and Path by the preposition *on*. The same pattern of lexical encoding is observed in French example (29): the Figure is encoded by *l'oiseau* ('the bird'), the Ground by *un arbre* ('a tree'), Location by *est* ('is') and Path by *sur* ('on'). This type of expression, in which two noun phrases are linked by a spatial preposition, is frequently presented as a way in which locative relationships are encoded in English and in French (see Herskovits 1986; Vandeloise 1986). Hence Costello and Kelleher (2006: 1), working on the preposition *near*, define locative expressions in the following way: "A spatial locative expression consists of a locative prepositional phrase together with whatever the phrase modifies (noun, clause, etc.). In their simplest form, a locative expression consists of a prepositional phrase modifying a noun phrase, for example *the man near the desk*." Locative expressions are therefore no longer just expressions which communicate the location of a Figure in relation to a Ground: they are expressions which use spatial prepositions to do so. This approach to the subject is also advocated by Hörberg (2007: 3–4), who proposes that "In English and Swedish, locative expressions are constructed using a complement or adjunct prepositional phrase". Approaches to locative expressions which target the category of spatial prepositions as the typical encoder of locative information are, however, deficient, since such information is also encoded by other lexical categories (Levinson and Meira 2003; Sinha and Kuteva 1995; Svorou 1986). As far as the identification and division of locative expressions is concerned, the citation from Costello and Kelleher above suggests the centrality of a phrase-based approach, a method also followed by Schober (1998) in his study. Naturally, different studies have different aims, and these approaches may be perfectly suited to the needs of the researchers undertaking them. However, such a grammatically driven approach is not always suitable where oral discourse is concerned. First of all, spoken discourse is, by its very nature, hard to break down into neatly defined grammatical boxes. Secondly, as far as the present study is concerned, the speaker's addressee was co-present and both parties had visual access to each other: this therefore made it possible to use gesture to express information. In fact, gesture alone may carry the entire locative charge, as shown in the example below.

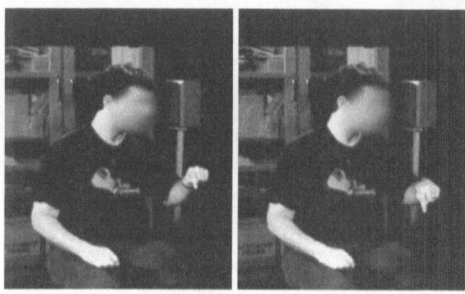

(30)   *cat* (EngDesc10)

In example (30) above, the speaker simply uses a noun with a pointing gesture to indicate the location of the Figure. The gesture stroke is executed close to the speaker on the left-hand side of gesture space: this reflects the location of the cat in the foreground of the picture, on the left-hand side of the street. No spatial linguistic item is employed, and gesture carries the entire locative semantic load[23]. This suggests that any definition which seeks to account for all of the ways in which speakers express static location cannot be developed around a particular grammatical category, such as prepositions. Rather, it is preferable to adopt a more simplistic definition along the lines of Fillmore (1975: 18): "The typical kind of locating expression in a language is one which indicates the location of one object with respect to some other object." A certain amount of fine-tuning of this definition is nevertheless required. Fillmore defines locative expressions as locating 'one object' in relation to 'some other object'. However, locative expressions can indicate the location of *multiple* objects – as opposed to just one object – in relation to a Ground.

(31)   *and on the right is a café youth hostel restaurant bank and a bar* (EngDesc1)

In example (31) the speaker locates a series of objects, all of which share the common spatial property of being located on the right-hand side of the street. Each of these objects relates back to the same Path and Ground (encoded by *on*

---

23 This type of locative expression is typically used by speakers once the location of an individual object has already been presented in their discourse: it therefore serves an anaphoric function. Given that the present study focuses on the first mention of an object as Figure in a speaker's discourse, this type of gesture will not be very frequent. It is nevertheless important to acknowledge that location is communicated in this way when devising a competent definition of static locative expressions.

and *the right* respectively), and they are presented as a single package: they are lexicalised in succession and are coordinated by a final *and*. This common dependency on the one Path and Ground unit, along with their successive syntactic distribution, encourages their construal as a collective Figure. Locative expressions may therefore locate a *group* of objects in relation to another object (see Lemmens 2005) as opposed to just *one* object in relation to another object. Just as it is feasible to have a Figure which is comprised of multiple objects, so too is it possible to have a multiple-object Ground. In an expression like "Joe stood opposite Jane and Mark" the Figure (*Joe*) is located in relation to a Ground which is comprised of two objects (*Jane* and *Mark*). These objects are presented as entities which share a common spatial area, thereby triggering their construal as a single Ground.

4.1.1 Functional versus grammatical concerns in defining static locative expressions[24]

Matters become more complicated when speakers encode multiple Ground entities which do *not* share a common spatial area. In such cases, sequential phrases may encode the location of the Figure with respect to each of these Ground entities. These sequential phrases may either be taken as separate locative expressions or as one single expression. In the latter instance, the common function of the successive phrases in localising the same Figure is accentuated.

(32)   *there's a cat to the left of the bus.. on the path* (EngDesc1)

In example (32) the speaker encodes the location of the Figure, *a cat*, in relation to a Ground, *the bus*, before bringing into play a second Ground object, *the path*. These two Ground objects do not share a common spatial area: *the path* is understood to be to the left of the first Ground object, *the bus*. The question therefore arises as to whether this example should be seen as one or as two locative expressions: that is, should the common locative function of the two phrases override their grammatical separability into different prepositional phrases?

---

24 In what follows, we use the terms function and functional in our discussion of static locative expressions. These terms, such as they are used here, have nothing to do with systemic functional grammar. Rather, they relate to the idea of 'purpose'. Therefore, the function of a locative expression means the purpose of the locative expression, just as functional concerns have to do with the purpose of the locative expression.

The identification of locative expressions on the basis of separability into phrases is follow ed by Schober (1998). However, this phrase-based approach is inadequate when it comes to accounting for how gesture expresses locative information, as revealed in the following example.

(33)   *and a ball.. a bit further in front* (EngDesc2)

In example (33) the speaker moves her hand forward and to the right in one continuous motion. In doing so she not only communicates the lexically encoded information that the ball is in front of the bone, but also that it is *to the right* of it. The two pieces of locative information are laminated together in speech and in gesture: speech encodes location along the frontal axis, while gesture expresses this information as well as the Figure's location along the lateral axis. The upshot of this is that the speaker uses gesture to communicate a piece of unlexicalised locative information which has not been previously presented in discourse. Had the speaker lexicalised the lateral information instead – perhaps through the use of a prepositional phrase such as *to the right* – the example would have contained two locative phrases. Following the phrase-parsing method outlined above, two locative expressions would be counted. However, because this information was just expressed in gesture, the phrase-parsing approach would count just one expression. The problem here is that any comparison concerning the number of locative expressions made by different speakers can easily be skewed if one speaker routinely encodes location in speech, while another does so in both speech and gesture. This means that a speaker who routinely encodes locative semantic information in speech but not in gesture would be seen as producing more locative expressions than a speaker who also uses gesture to express unlexicalised locative information. This leads to an unfair bias in speech's favour, and ultimately shows that understanding locative expressions in terms of locative phrases is not reliable when gesture is taken into account.

It therefore follows that locative expressions are better determined by identifying the function of sequential locative phrases: when such phrases share the common function of localising the same Figure, they should be considered parts of a single locative expression. This approach to the matter, although simplistic, nevertheless allows for the variety of ways in which speakers express location in both speech and gesture to emerge. Static locative expressions are therefore *the continuous stream of information which a speaker provides about a Figure's fixed location in space.* Numerous phrases or clauses may make up this stream, all of which are linked by their specification of the same Figure's location. Further justification for this approach comes from the gestures that speakers make when expressing a Figure's location. Seeming discrepancies in the information expressed in speech and gesture can be explained when locative expressions are considered as the complete package of sequential phrases concerning a Figure's location.

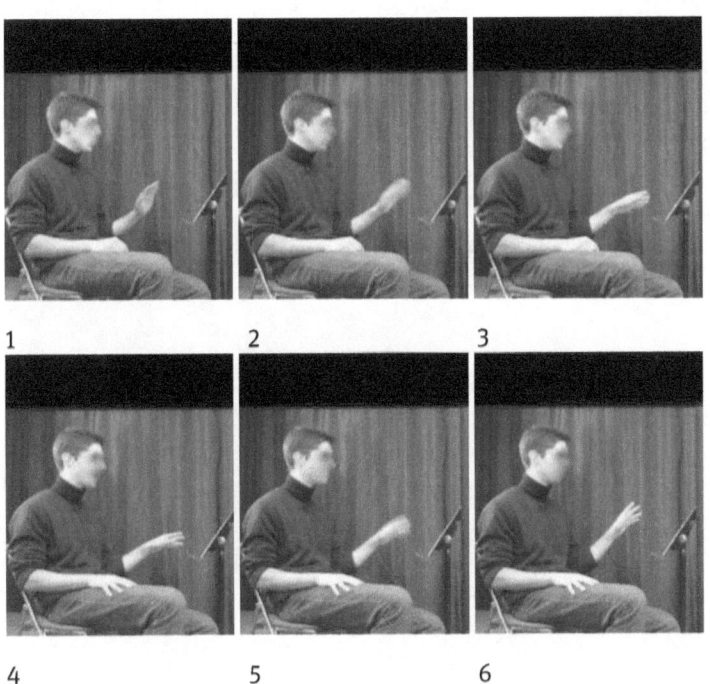

(34) <u>au-dessus</u> du chat   donc on retourne à gauche [laughs]   il y a
       <u>above</u> the cat   so we're going back to the left   there is
                        [laughs]
       <u>un portrait</u>   (FrenDesc7)

a portrait

In example (34) the speaker gestures across to the left (stills 1–3) while uttering *au-dessus de* ('above'). There is a contradiction between the directional information expressed in speech and gesture: the speaker expresses direction along the lateral axis in gesture, while encoding location along the vertical axis in speech. However, when the speaker presents the Figure, *un portrait* ('a portrait'), in speech, he gestures upwards (stills 4–6): this is the gestural partner of the earlier use of *au-dessus de*. The lexical spatial items and their representational gestures are therefore not aligned, but this temporal incongruity is not an issue if this whole example is understood as a single expression. Following such an approach, the locative expression is a package of information that needs to be considered in its entirety: corresponding speech and gesture units may occur at non-synchronous points throughout the expression. Indeed, not only is there temporal non-alignment between *au-dessus de* and its representational gesture, such non-alignment is also noted for *à gauche* ('to the left') and its gestural affiliate. Here, the gesture to the left is executed at the very beginning of the expression, with the corresponding prepositional phrase occurring several words later. This suggests that example (34) should not be broken down into two separate expressions on the basis of the spatial phrases *au-dessus du chat* and *à gauche*, as would be the case if the phrase-parsing method of Schober (1998) were followed. Rather, it should remain as a single expression, whose component parts are linked by a common locative function.

4.1.2 Static locative expressions and the clarification of directional information

A further reason for taking a function-based approach to locative expressions concerns the semantic interconnectivity of consecutive locative phrases or clauses which localise a common Figure. Often, a locative phrase or clause serves to clarify the directional information encoded by the previous one.

(35) *just behind the dog there's a ball on the floor.. so this is between the dog and the television* (EngDesc5)

This speaker begins by locating the Figure at a point along the frontal axis *just behind the dog*. Two possible interpretations exist for this phrase. The first interpretation uses an intrinsic frame of reference. The second interpretation uses a relative frame of reference, since the ball is not located at the dog's intrinsic behind. The provision of the locative information in the *between* phrase shows that the non-intrinsic interpretation is the correct one. Hence, the directional information encoded by *behind* cannot be correctly understood without considering the *between* phrase. It therefore makes little sense to segment this example on the basis of there being two clauses: the example is clearly meant to be taken as a coherent whole.

A second reason against this type of division is that only the first mention of an object as Figure is considered in this study. The segmentation of examples such as the one above into two separate expressions would mean that the second clause would not be taken into account. This would be methodologically erroneous, since this second clause bears upon the first in providing clarification of how the speaker intends the location of the ball to be understood. Such a problem is avoided if both clauses are understood in terms of their common locative function of localising the same Figure, and therefore considered as a single expression.

4.2 Segmenting static locative relations in oral discourse

It is helpful at this point to recall the definition of static locative expressions that we proposed at the beginning of the chapter.

Static locative expression: Static locative expressions communicate the fixed location of an object or group of objects (the Figure) in space.

This definition aims to cover all of the different ways in which speakers use speech and gesture to express location. Taking into account the arguments laid out in the previous section, it should also be stated that these expressions are comprised of the continuous stream of information that a speaker provides about a Figure's fixed location in space.

Now that we have justified our definition, we need to specify how we separate consecutive locative expressions in discourse. This is not as easy at it may seem. We identify boundaries for our expressions by looking at speech. This is because describers must use speech in their descriptions of the pictures: it is impossible not to do so. The same is not true of gesture, however: speakers may feasibly describe the locations of all of the objects in both scenes without gesturing at all. Identifying the boundaries of locative expressions in speech also enables a framework for the interpretation of co-speech gestures to be established. In this way, the semantic interaction between the information encoded in speech and the information expressed in gesture can be explored. Speech, therefore, provides a logical starting point for retrieving locative expressions from the data pool.

However, it is not always enough to identify locative expressions on the basis of speech alone. As shown in example (30), speakers can communicate locative information in gesture even when a locative expression is not present in speech. Therefore, those parts of a speaker's discourse which did not contain lexical locative expressions were also examined for any location-expressing gestures. These gestures, along with their accompanying lexical segment (i.e. *cat* in example 30), were also coded as locative expressions.

As far as the speech stream is concerned, in many instances the separation of locative expressions was transparent. This was due to the clear change in the Figure being located, as shown in the following example.

(36)   *le canapé..*   *en bas de l'image aussi*   *dans le coin gauche*
         the sofa..   at the bottom of the picture as well   in the corner left
         les rideaux..   *euh dans le coin droit en haut*   (FrenDesc1)
         the curtains..   uh in the corner right up the top
         'the sofa.. at the bottom of the picture as well in the left corner
         the curtains.. uh in the right corner up the top'

In example (36) the locations of two different Figures are encoded. The second of the two Figures, *les rideaux* ('the curtains'), is located *dans le coin droit en haut* ('in the right corner up the top') while the preceding Figure, *le canapé* ('the sofa'), is located *en bas de l'image aussi dans le coin gauche* ('at the bottom of the picture as well in the left corner'). The change in Path and Ground components from the first expression to the second signals the establishment of a new Figure in a new location, and hence a new locative expression is noted.

However, understanding when a new Figure comes into play is not always a transparent exercise. This is particularly the case when it is not clear whether a speaker intends multiple objects to be taken as a group Figure, or whether they are intended as individual Figures instead.

(37) *then for the buildings that are on the right hand side of the street.. there's a café.. there's a restaurant.. and a bar* (EngDesc10)

In example (37) above, the existential phrases *there is* and *there are* separate the Figure objects *a café* and *a restaurant*. These linguistic expressions encode existence but not location: it is therefore feasible that *a café* and *a restaurant* should be taken as a single, group Figure. However, the fact that each object is prefaced by the existential *there's* suggests a division between them. Therefore, when the passage from one Figure to the next was not transparent, lexical markers were taken as cues. Existential phrases such as *there is* and *there are* were taken as markers of new locative expressions, as well as sequential items like *then*. Example (37) would therefore be divided into the following two expressions:

(38) *then for the buildings that are on the right hand side of the street.. there's a café..*
(39) *there's a restaurant.. and a bar*
      (EngDesc10)

In example (39) the Path (*on*) and Ground (*the right hand side of the street*) components are inferable from the preceding expression.

In many situations the separation of locative expressions is a transparent exercise: for example, when a speaker explicitly encodes a new Figure at a different point in space (e.g. example 36). However, in other instances there is room for doubt. In such cases, as mentioned above, we divide on the basis of lexical cues. These cues are the existential phrases *there is*, *there are* and *il y a*, along with sequential markers such as *then* and *puis*. Such lexical phrases signal individuation between consecutive Figures. Note that Path and Ground components may not always be explicitly encoded for each new locative expression (e.g. example 39). However, these components are immediately retrievable from the preceding context. It is simply a feature of oral discourse that elements which may be accessible contextually do not need repeating.

Another possibility was to use pauses as signals for the end of a locative expression. However, this is not a reliable method because pauses do not necessarily suggest the passage from one piece of locative information to the next. Rather, pauses may reflect other phenomena, such as hesitation. Furthermore, if pauses were to be used, how long should a segmenting pause be? It therefore seems more solid to understand locative expressions in terms of the Figure and, where necessary, to use lexical markers as a segmenting device.

The key to separating static locative expressions is therefore the identification of the Figure. The Figure must always be lexicalised by the speaker. In contrast, Path and Ground components may be contextually inferable. Understanding what constitutes a new Figure depends on the guidelines laid down for the separation of locative expressions. In this study, speech is taken as the starting point. A locative expression is the stretch of speech which expresses the location of a Figure, irrespective of how many phrases or clauses this involves. A new locative expression begins when a new Figure is targeted. New Figures can be identified in one of two ways. Firstly, they may be entities which are located at a different location in space to the preceding Figure (e.g. example 36): this necessarily means a new locative expression. Secondly, they may be located at the same location in space as the Figure which precedes them, but the speaker signals a division between them: this involves the recruitment of a lexical divider, such as *there is/there are* or a sequential term like *then*.

4.2.1 Differences in lexical and gestural Figures and Grounds

While attending to the gestures which co-occur with locative expressions in the speech stream, an important tendency across both English and French speakers was noted. This was the fact that speakers recurrently expressed a different Figure in gesture to that which was encoded in speech. This type of gesture-only Figure will be termed a *gestural Figure*. The following example shows how such Figures occur.

Defining static locative expressions — 79

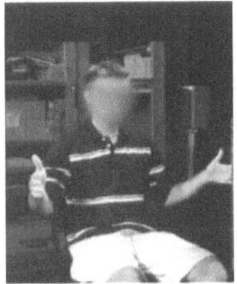

(40) *in between.. um <u>the</u> couch <u>and the</u> table.. um there's a book and a a small dog* (EngDesc9)

The Figures of the lexical locative expression in (40) are *book* and *small dog*, which are located in relation to a lexical Ground (*the couch and the table*). The still image shows how the speaker uses his hands to mark the respective locations of these two Ground entities in gesture space. The speaker initially moves his left hand down to indicate that the couch is located on the left-hand side of the lounge room; this is followed by movement of the right hand down to mark the location of the table on the right-hand side. The space between the speaker's hands suggests the distance between the two objects. Two semantic roles are attributed to the couch and the table here: they are the Ground objects of the lexical expression, whilst also being the Figures of their own gestural locative expressions. They are Figures because the speaker establishes their location in space: this is precisely what constitutes a Figure in a locative expression. The Path and Ground components that round out these gestural locative expressions can be identified as follows: Path is expressed by the placement of the speaker's hands at the objects' isomorphic locations in gesture space, while the Ground is understood contextually, with the speaker's gesture space representing the space of the lounge room. Therefore, the placement of the speaker's left hand establishes the location of the couch on the left-hand side of the lounge room, while the placement of his right hand communicates the location of the table on the right-hand side of the room. Importantly, gesture alone carries the locative charge in these two examples. These gestural expressions are secondary in nature, and attach to the lexically encoded Ground objects. They function in a similar way to a relative clause: they modify the noun to which they are associated and cannot survive as 'stand-alone' expressions. The conclusion to be drawn from the existence of gestural Figures is that there are multiple levels to locative expressions. In addition to the lexical Figure, there may be other Figures that emerge at the gestural level. This shows that the semantic roles that speakers assign to objects can only be revealed when both speech and gesture are attended to.

The second way in which gestural Figures occur is when multiple objects are lexically encoded as a group Figure. Gesture may signal division between these objects by showing differences in their respective locations. This is reflected in the following example.

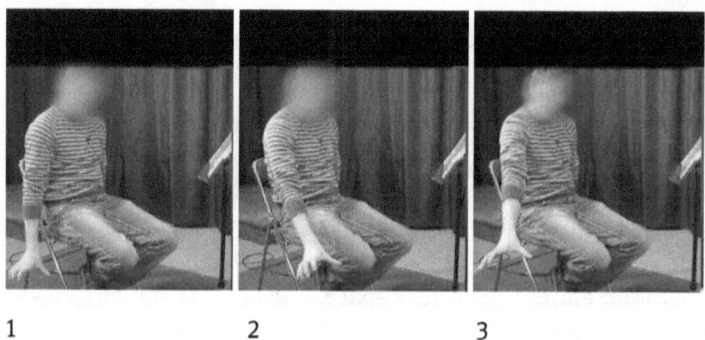

1   2   3

(41) [...] *le livre*   *l'os*   *la balle*..   *qui sont les trois objets par terre* [...]
      [...] the book   the bone the ball..   which are the three objects on the floor [...]

(FrenDesc10)

The three stills show the end of three successive gesture stroke phases. The speaker lexically encodes a group Figure comprised of three objects: all three of these objects are bundled by the one verb form *sont* ('are') and are collectively located at the one point in space *par terre* ('on the floor'). However, the information which the speaker's successive gestures provide captures individual differences in the location of each object. The bone is gesturally depicted as being in front of the book (still 2, compared to still 1), while the ball is shown to be to the right of the bone (still 3, compared to still 2). This information can only be understood if the book is conceptualised as a gestural Ground for the bone, and the bone a gestural Ground for the ball. The upshot of this is that the lexical group Figure is *not* a group Figure in gesture: gesture is expressing different, yet complementary, information to that encoded in speech. These gestures present the three objects as individual Figures whose spatial distribution relative to each other is at issue. As such, three gestural expressions of location emerge. These expressions attach to the nouns that encode each object. Path and Ground information for each expression are retrievable from gesture. Therefore, the combined consideration of the two modalities in this example reveals that the speaker is expressing far more than a lexically encoded topological relationship. In fact, he is also expressing the directional distribution of the objects that comprise the lexically encoded group Figure.

Examples (40) and (41) show how gesture can play a pivotal role in expressing locative information in both English and French. This role will be examined in greater detail in the following chapters. For the moment however, the key point to retain is that gesture adds *layers of meaning* to lexical expressions of location. It is not enough to consider speech alone: gesture provides information about Figure/Ground configurations which is not encoded in speech at all.

4.2.2 Primary locative expressions and secondary locative expressions

Having established how to define and separate static locative expressions in oral discourse, it is necessary to introduce a final idea which is central to understanding how these expressions work. This is the idea that locative expressions are comprised of two sub-types of expression: *primary locative expressions* and *secondary locative expressions*. Primary locative expressions introduce a new Figure and can 'stand alone': they do not depend on another locative expression for existence. Secondary locative expressions on the other hand, create a new Figure from an object(s) which is/are already engaged in a locative expression. The difference between these two types of locative expression is highlighted in the example below.

(42) and in the in just in the foreground of the supermarket **which is actually the first shop that you'll see on the left**.. there's a tree
(EngDesc4)

This expression can be broken down into primary and secondary locatives as follows:
Primary locative: [and in the in just in the foreground of the supermarket.. there's a tree]
Secondary locative: [which is actually the first shop that you'll see on the left]

The Figure, *the tree* is located in relation to the Ground *the foreground of the supermarket*. This Ground, or rather part of it (*the supermarket*) is then described as 'the first shop that you'll see on the left'. The speaker therefore creates a new Figure from the existing Ground (*supermarket*), which means that this one object plays both Ground and Figure roles. The overall locative expression is comprised of the primary and secondary sub-parts. Definitions of these two types of locative expressions may be proposed as follows:

Primary locative expression (or primary locative): A primary locative communicates the location of a new Figure.

Secondary locative expression (or secondary locative): A secondary locative communicates the location of a new Figure. This is achieved by making use of a Figure or Ground entity that is already engaged in a locative expression.

Three of the main ways in which secondary locatives manifest themselves are as follows.

– Relative clauses

The speaker uses a relative clause to assign a second role to an existing Figure or Ground entity.

(43)   *in front of her to the right like in front of the book* **which is next to the sofa** *there's a bone* (EngDesc2)

In this example, the relative pronoun *which* allows the secondary role of Figure to be assigned to the existing Ground 'book'. A relative pronoun may or may not be used, as the speaker may choose to use an *–ing* participial clause, as in the following example.

(44)   [...] *there's a cat.. which is directly under the bird* **sitting in the tree** (EngDesc5)

The phrase *sitting in the tree* encodes the location of the lexical Ground *the bird*.

– Embedding

A clause or phrase, detailing the location of an object, is inserted within the primary locative.

(45)   *um on top of the hotel* **so that was the second shop** *there's a satellite dish* (EngDesc3)

The phrase *so that was the second shop* is inserted into the primary locative expression immediately after the Ground object *hotel*. This allows for the location of the Ground to be revealed: *hotel* is now also a secondary Figure. The Path in this expression is encoded by the sequential term *second*: this indicates that the hotel is the shop *after* the one closest to the observer's perspective. The Ground is therefore contextually inferable as the *first shop*. This example shows how juxtaposition can be used to create a secondary locative expression within the structure of a primary, matrix expression.

– Gesture
A speaker may provide the location of a lexicalised Ground object in gesture alone: this creates a gestural Figure. This object is therefore a lexical Ground and a gestural Figure simultaneously (see example 40). The respective locations of individual entities which collectively comprise a lexical Group Figure may also be given in gesture (see example 41): this then establishes these entities as individual gestural Figures.

Finally, speakers sometimes use phrases that function as pre-head modifiers in larger phrases. This strategy allows them to provide information about a Ground's location.

(46) on the **left hand** side of the road past the trolley.. is a phone box
      (EngDesc8)

In example (46) the modifying noun phrase *left hand* identifies the location of the Ground *side of the road*. However, it also serves the purpose of disambiguating this particular side of the road from the other one (i.e. the right-hand side). The use of these pre-head modifying phrases occurs in our data when there is more than one of the same Ground (for example, sides of a road). We do not consider that they serve the same purpose as the linguistic and gestural phenomena above, which express the locations of unique Grounds in our stimulus pictures. Rather, these modifying phrases serve the purpose of disambiguating between multiple Grounds of the same nature. Therefore, we do not consider them as secondary locative expressions.

4.2.3 Overall locative expressions

The crucial difference between primary and secondary locatives relates to the notion of dependency. A secondary locative attaches to, or is embedded within, a primary locative (or even another secondary locative). Crucially, it creates a Figure from an object which is already engaged in a Figure or Ground role. In contrast, a primary locative does not have this same relationship of dependency, and does not assign another semantic role to an object which is already engaged in a locative expression.

One of the advantages of secondary locative expressions is the ease and economy with which they allow speakers to describe new locative configurations. In our study, locative expressions are understood as the combination of primary and secondary locatives. It is necessary to understand locative expressions in this way because secondary locative expressions are designed to be considered alongside primary ones. When the overall expression needs to be distinguished from its primary and secondary sub-parts, it will be referred to as an *overall locative expression*.

As mentioned in the previous chapter (Chapter 3), our analysis focuses on the first mention of an object as Figure in discourse. We look at the *overall locative expression* in which this occurs. Hence, even if an object's location is described in a primary locative, we also consider any secondary locatives that accompany it. Similarly, if a Figure's location is expressed in a secondary locative, we also consider the primary locative to which it is attached. One of the objects which speakers were required to localise in their descriptions of the street scene was the shopping trolley. In the following example, the speaker describes its location in a primary locative, but also embeds a secondary locative that describes the location of the Ground *le supermarché* ('the supermarket').

(47) *devant le supermarché..*   *donc euh le premier bâtiment..*
      in front of the supermarket..   so uh the first building..
      un chariot   (FrenDesc7)
      a trolley

In the following chapters we examine how speakers use lexical spatial items and gesture. As far as the example above is concerned, we would therefore not only consider the use of *devant* ('in front of') in the primary locative, but also the occurrence of *premier* ('first') in the secondary locative. Now, this is the *second* time that the speaker has described the location of the supermarket in his discourse. Hence, our approach means that we sometimes include incidences of items which do not describe an object's location for the first time: this is the case for *premier* in the example above. We believe that it is important to include such occurrences of items in our analysis because they comprise part of an overall locative expression which localises a target object (i.e. 'the trolley') for the first time. To omit such occurrences from our analysis would be to suggest that we can selectively consider parts of a locative expression while simultaneously rejecting others. As we have argued throughout this chapter, locative expressions are comprised of the continuous stream of discourse that describes a Figure's location; this stream of discourse may be comprised of primary and secondary sub-parts. Hence, the two parts are necessarily related and they must not be separated.

It is important to point out that the inclusion of such items, which describe an object's location for a second or subsequent time in discourse, are rare in our set of overall locative expressions. Crucially, their inclusion in our analysis does not change the conclusions that we reach in subsequent chapters. To ensure the transparency of our results we have included a list of all these items, along with their frequencies, in Appendix F.

4.3 Summary

The expression of location is, above all, a semantic concern. Certain researchers separate locative expressions on the basis of phrases (i.e. Schober 1998; Costello and Kelleher 2006). However, this is insufficient for two reasons. Firstly, such a grammatically-based approach fails to capture the fact that the location of a Figure is often expressed across successive phrases or clauses. The individual phrases and clauses within this overall stretch of information do not operate independently: they are linked functionally and semantically, and cannot be considered in isolation from each other. Secondly, speakers use gesture to communicate locative information. This information may pertain to the lexically encoded Figure (example 33), or alternatively it may create a gestural Figure out of a lexical Ground (example 40) or a group lexical Figure (example 41). The observation that a lexical Ground can simultaneously be a gestural Figure is crucial: it reveals that speakers localise objects other than those that are specifically marked as Figures in speech. It also shows that speakers can present multiple locative relationships simultaneously, and that productive use is made of both speech and gesture to express such relationships.

As far as the segmentation of locative expressions in oral discourse is concerned, locative expressions are firstly identified in the speech stream. The complete, uninterrupted stretch of information provided about a Figure's location is counted as an expression. This expression may include dependent parts which we have termed *secondary locatives*. When the separation of Figures is not transparent, lexical cues such as *there is* and *then* are taken as signs of Figure individuation. Co-speech gestures are then identified and analysed. This allows for the identification of gestural Figures, and hence the coding of another type of secondary locative. The parts of a speaker's discourse which do not contain lexical locative expressions are also analysed for any gestural expressions of location. Overall, this definition and approach to the separation of locative expressions seeks to account for the maximum amount of ways in which speakers communicate location across the two modalities. The results which this method achieves are presented in what follows.

5 Describing location along the frontal axis

This chapter examines how speakers express location along the frontal (front/back) axis. We show that gestures express unlexicalised directional information which relates to the use of directionally non-specific items (for example, *between* and *entre*): this reveals the integrated, complementary nature of speech and gesture in the expression of location. As far as front-encoding items are concerned, gesture helps to clarify the direction encoded by *in front of* when speakers use a relative frame of reference. Our examples also reveal that English speakers assign 'fronts' to Ground objects using the process of translation, as opposed to 180-degree rotation: this runs contrary to the established view in the literature (see Levinson 1996: 369–371; 2003). Furthermore, we show that French speakers use the spatial item *en face de* ('in front of'/'opposite') to encode relationships of both proximity and distance. When *en face de* is recruited to encode the latter type of relationship, speakers supply additional distance information in the locative expression. This information may be expressed in speech, in gesture, or in both modalities.

5.1 The frontal axis

The frontal axis corresponds to the imaginary lines which extend forward and backward from the region understood as a reference object's 'front' and 'back'. As described in Chapter 2, it subsumes the componential 'front' and 'back' half-line axes described by Herskovits (1986): it therefore incorporates location which is both *in front of* and *behind* an object. An object may possess intrinsic front and back spatial properties. This is the case, for example, of animate entities such as human beings and animals. Both French and English have prepositions which allow speakers to reference an object's intrinsic front and back when encoding location: these are *in front of* and *behind* in English, and *devant* ('in front of'), *en face de* ('opposite'/'in front of') and *derrière* ('behind') in French. *En face de* is spatially polysemous: while recurrently used to convey a meaning similar to the English *opposite*, it can also be used in the sense of *devant* ('in front of'). The potential implications of such polysemy on the use of co-speech gestures are investigated in the data analysis which follows.

When an object does not possess an intrinsic front/back distinction, viewers may attribute these properties in one of several ways. Firstly, our habitual interaction with an object may lead to the attribution of a front and a back. Hence, the 'front' of a classroom is associated with the side of the room from which the teacher conducts class: this suggests that cultural convention can play a role in how the frontal axis is considered (Levinson 1996). Fronts and backs may also be assigned according to the direction of an object's movement (Fillmore 1975). Therefore, the *front* of a train is the part that determines the train's direction; it is also the part that is most proximate to the train's final destination. Finally, objects may acquire a front and back distinction when such properties are projected onto them through a relative frame of reference (see Chapter 2). According to Levinson (1996: 369–371), this involves the 180-degree rotation of the human subject's front onto the object concerned. Hence, the *front* of an object which does not have an intrinsic frontal orientation, such as a pole, is the part opposite an intrinsically-oriented viewer. Borillo (1998), in her discussion of French, also suggests that speakers attribute a front to the part of an object which is opposite them. She terms this *orientation en miroir* ('mirror orientation'). However, the evidence presented in this chapter shows that speakers do not always assign a 'front' to the side of the object which is opposite the intrinsically-oriented viewer. This indicates that there is a certain degree of flexibility in how speakers attribute frontal properties when using relative frames of reference. A similar type of flexibility has been noted for the language Hausa (Hill 1982). In contrast to English and French however, Hausa normally uses the process of 'translation' (Levinson 2003b) to assign spatial properties under a relative frame of reference (see Chapter 2). Hence, the 'front' of an object is not the side opposite a viewer, but the one *behind* it. Nevertheless, speakers of Hausa do sometimes assign frontal properties in the same way as English and French speakers (see Hill 1982). This provides a precedent of sorts for our own finding of flexibility in the linguistic attribution of frontal properties.

One concept introduced earlier (Chapter 2) which is pivotal to the analysis which follows is that of origo (Bühler 1982). An origo "is conceptually understood as the origin of a coordinate system" (Fricke 2003: 71). Hence, if I were to describe a bag's location as being *in front of me*, the origo would be *me*: this is because my intrinsic front/back distinction provides the point of origin for the directional information encoded by *in front of*. Similarly, if I were looking at a pole and described a piece of paper *in front of* it, I would also constitute the origo: this is because the pole is attributed a frontal value thanks to presence of my own intrinsic front opposite it. An origo is therefore an oriented base in relation to which direction is established.

As outlined in Chapter 3, spatial language may differ according to the type of space described. We will therefore analyse the data for each picture separately. This approach should reveal any differences in the use of language and gesture which are triggered by the change in the visual stimulus. Furthermore, it will also enable a contrastive analysis of the English and French data for each picture to be undertaken. Our intra- and inter-linguistic comparisons of the data appear at the end of the chapter (section 5.6 'Comparison and discussion').

5.2 Lounge room scene – English descriptions

An ideal starting point is to identify the lexical spatial items which English describers used to encode location along the frontal axis. An 'item' is understood as a lexeme or lexical unit which encodes a piece of spatial information: for example, *behind*, *in front of* or *closer to*. Table 2 below presents all such items for descriptions of the lounge room scene. Three categories have been devised around the semantic criterion of direction. In this chapter, we understand direction as the two endpoints which make up the frontal axis: i.e. front and back. Items which encode reference to either of these endpoints are 'directionally specific' and divided into two categories: those which reference the Ground's front ('front-encoding items'), and those which reference its back ('back-encoding items'). In contrast, items which reference neither of these points are termed 'directionally non-specific' items. An example of such an item is the preposition *between*, which does not encode a front or back for either of the Ground objects in the locative relation. This contrasts, quite obviously, to a directionally-specific, front-encoding item like *in front of*. We include directionally non-specific items in our analysis because they combine with lexical or gestural units which do reference location along the frontal axis. For example:

(48)   *the bone is in front of the rug.. um **closer to** the foreground* (EngDesc3)

Taken alone, the phrase *closer to* encodes proximity without specifying direction along a particular spatial axis. However, its use here introduces the noun phrase *the foreground*, making it part of an expression which establishes location towards the front point of the picture's conceptualised frontal axis. This occurrence of *closer to* is therefore included in the analysis.

Directionally non-specific items are also counted when location is established in relation to the speaker's front, even though this frontal axis is not lexically specified.

(49)   *ok there's a portrait.. on the the far wall* [...] (EngDesc7)

In example (49), the distance encoded by *far* concerns the frontal axis which extends out from the intrinsically-oriented speaker as they view the picture.

Although this frontal axis is not lexically specified, it nevertheless licenses this occurrence of *far* and is therefore included in the analysis.

Any spatial item may therefore be included in our 'directionally-non specific' category as long as it fulfils one of the two criteria listed above: that is, it combines with a lexical phrase or gesture to express location along the frontal axis; or it establishes location in relation to the speaker's understood front. We do, however, exclude from this category the basic, topological prepositions *at*, *on* and *in* (as well as *à*, *sur* and *dans* in the French analysis). Topological relationships are dealt with separately in Chapter 7.

In table 2 below, distinctions between similar lexical items are made when individuation is justified. For example, there is no single category which collates all items which include the lexeme *front*. Doing so would fail to acknowledge important distinctions between different lexical units. For example, *in front of* encodes a completely different relationship to a unit such as *at the front of*. These two items are therefore in different sub-categories.

If an item was used more than once in an expression to refer to the same Figure/Ground relationship, each individual use was counted: this is because individual uses of an item may be distinguished by the presence of lexical modifiers or co-occurring gestures. The exception to this rule was when repetition was triggered by a lexical correction. In such cases, just one use of the item was noted. This is shown in the example below.

(50) *in front of the couch is a rug.. or a sofa.. in front of the sofa there's a rug* (EngDesc2)

The second occurrence of *in front of* in example (50) is triggered by the lexical switch from *couch* to *sofa*. Hence, we only count one use here.

Tab. 2: Lexical items used to encode location along the frontal axis in English descriptions of the lounge room scene

	Front-encoding items	N	Back-encoding items	N	Directionally non-specific items	N
A	in front of	18	behind	3	(in) between	7
B	the front[25]	5	OTHER *back* (modifier) *at the back* (1)	3	far	6
C	the foreground[26]	4			closer/closest to	3
D	OTHER *in front* (2) *ahead* (1)	3			next to	1
	TOTAL	30		6		17

Table 2 shows that speakers used front-encoding items far more frequently than back-encoding ones: 30 examples of the former were noted, as opposed to just six of the latter. There were also 17 occurrences of directionally non-specific items. In order to understand why this distributive pattern emerged, a closer look at how speakers used the members of each category is required.

5.2.1 The use of front-encoding items

In front of was the lexical phrase which speakers most commonly recruited to encode a Figure's location in relation to a Ground's front. The 18 examples of *in front of* far outweigh the five examples of *the front*, or the four of *the foreground*. Nevertheless, the two latter sub-categories collectively account for nine references to the picture's foreground: this shows that speakers conceptualised the picture as a three-dimensional space. However, speakers did not make specific lexical reference to an area defined as the *background*. Instead, they made indirect reference to this area through the use of the modifiers *far* (six uses: category 'directionally non-specific items', row B) and *back* (2 uses: category 'back-encoding items', row B). Note that the modifiers *far* and *back* localise objects in

---
[25] Includes two examples of *at the front of*, and one example each of *to the front of*, *at the forefront of* and *to the front*.
[26] Includes three examples of *in the foreground of*, and one example of *the foreground*.

relation to the back point of the picture, as opposed to a larger, more extensive background region.

The high frequency of *in front of* in the data may be explained, to some extent at least, by the locative distribution of objects in the picture. For example, seven of the ten speakers described the location of the rug *in front of* the fireplace. Fireplaces, with their stable, fixed anchorage in space, are characteristically typical of Ground objects. The proximity of the rug to the fireplace, coupled with the latter object's readily distinguishable front, is a clear trigger for the use of *in front of*. As far as other uses of this spatial item are concerned, several are particularly worthy of attention. These are presented in the following section.

5.2.1.1 The role of gesture in clarifying frontal direction

Certain uses of *in front of* reveal unexpected ways in which speakers attribute frontal properties to Ground objects.

(51)   just <u>a bit in</u> front of those items there is a bone (EngDesc10)

In example (51), *those items* are the previously lexicalised *sofa*, *book* and *dog*. The Figure, *a bone*, is described as being *in front of* this group of objects. Yet the three objects which comprise this group do not possess a collective front, nor are their individual intrinsic fronts facing in the same direction (see picture extract above). In example (51), *those items* are the previously lexicalised *sofa*, *book* and *dog*. The Figure, *a bone*, is described as being *in front of* this group of objects. Yet the three objects which comprise this group do not possess a collective front, nor are their individual intrinsic fronts facing in the same direction (see picture extract above). Specifically, the dog is facing the viewer, the sofa is facing the back of the room (from the speaker's viewpoint as an external observer), and the book is lying open and does not appear to have an intrinsic 'front' in this context. Only the front of the sofa is correctly oriented to establish a frontal 'search domain' (Levinson 2003b) within which the bone may be located. Yet how is this front attributed to the book and the dog, such that the bone is *in front* of these items? Not only are the three Ground objects close to each other, but they are also located along a common lateral axis: this means that they are readily conceptualised as a linear group. The use of *in front of* appears to be licensed by this linear arrangement, relying on a conceptualised extension of the sofa's frontal surface to include its two laterally-aligned neighbours. The speaker therefore maps the sofa's front onto the neighbouring objects, using the process of translation normally associated with languages like Hausa (see Hill 1982). That is, there is no 180-degree rotation of the sofa's frontal surface, such that the 'front' attributed to the group of objects now faces in the opposite direction (i.e. towards the speaker). This example clearly shows that the speaker has attributed a 'front' in a manner which is not conventionally associated with English (cf. Levinson 1996: 369–371; 2003b). While we can deduce this explanation from having visual access to the picture, the receiver in the experiment has no such visual privilege. Hence, they cannot know that the *front* of this group of objects results from an extension of the sofa's frontal surface to incorporate its laterally-aligned neighbours. Furthermore, they cannot know whether this encoded *front* faces the back of the room, or the viewer instead. The describer needs to resolve this directional ambiguity so that the addressee can correctly understand the Figure's location in the picture. This directional explication occurs in the gesture shown in the stills above. The speaker's left hand, fingers bunched together as though holding the conceptualised bone, moves forward and down: this reveals that the bone is located further back into the picture, away from the viewer. The gesture shows that the *front* which the speaker has assigned to the group of Ground objects faces the back of the room from the speaker's viewpoint. It therefore resolves directional ambiguity and works alongside the lexical expression to create an expression of location.

The process of attributing a front to a neighbouring, laterally-aligned object is also noted in another speaker's discourse.

(52)   *in front of her to the right like <u>in front of the</u> book which is next to the sofa there's a bone* (EngDesc2)

Books which are lying open, such as the one in the picture, do not have intrinsic 'frontal' surfaces in relation to which location may be established. In example (52), the region referenced by *in front of* lies away from the book, back into the picture (see picture extract above). As in the preceding example, the *front* of the book borrows from the intrinsic front of another, laterally-aligned object: this is the preceding Ground *her*. In the previous expression in her discourse, the speaker establishes the lady's location on the sofa. It is therefore possible that the speaker's attention is also drawn to the frontal orientation of the sofa, which may help to trigger the use of *in front of* in example (52). The lady, the sofa on which she is sitting, and the book, are all aligned along a common lateral axis. The speaker acknowledges this when she states that the book is *next to the sofa*: as she does so, she gestures to the right (this gesture is not shown here). Just as in example (51), this alignment along the lateral axis triggers the mapping of the lady's front onto the book. Once again, gesture expresses directional information which establishes the location of the Figure further back into the picture: this gesture is shown in the stills above. As in example (51), speech and gesture collaborate to express location and direction along the frontal axis. In both instances, this involves a spatial context in which the frontal surface of one object is mapped onto a neighbouring, laterally-aligned object. This does not involve the 180-degree rotation of front/back spatial properties in either example. Gesture clarifies the direction which the attributed 'front' faces by expressing movement forward and away from the speaker: this shows that it faces the back of the room from the speaker's viewpoint.

The mapping of a frontal property onto laterally-aligned Ground objects highlights the interconnectivity of the frontal and lateral axes. A certain amount is already known about how this axial interconnectivity affects the attribution of spatial properties. We know, for example, that lateral properties are dependent on frontal ones. As pointed out by Lyons (1977: 694): "Recognition of the difference between right and left is dependent upon the prior establishment of directionality in the front-back dimension". However, examples (51) and (52) above show that frontal properties can also be determined by the alignment of objects along the lateral axis: this means that the lateral axis can play a role in the attribution of frontal properties. Nevertheless, examples (51) and (52) both attribute fronts using intrinsically-oriented objects (i.e. the 'sofa' and the 'lady'): this means that a 'front' has to exist in the first place. The way in which the speakers assign these fronts in the two examples above is important. That is, they do not use the 180-degree rotation of the intrinsic front of either the sofa or the lady. Rather, the mapping is achieved by a process of translation onto the laterally-aligned objects. As far as we are aware, this finding has not previously been reported for static locative expressions in the literature. However, Hill (1982: 23) has reported that speakers can attribute frontal properties which 'align' with their own when motion is involved:

> When people are, say, riding in a vehicle, they are more likely to describe a further object as *in front of* a nearer one (e.g., *Oh, look at that cemetery up there in front of those trees*). When *in front of* is used with an aligned field in their way, we often find such elements as *out, out there*, or *up there* in the utterance. It is as though a need is felt to signal that the constructed field is not, as it usually is, a facing one.

Hence there is a precedent of sorts for our discovery, although Hill's observation works within the context of a motion event. Miller and Johnson-Laird (1976: 396) also discuss an example which has a certain degree of similarity to what we have noted in our data.

(53) *Put it in front of the rock*

One interpretation of this phrase is that the object 'it' should be placed in front of the rock's surface which 'ego' is facing (Miller and Johnson-Laird 1976: 396). However, Miller and Johnson-Laird (1976: 396) also suggest that "if ego is thinking of himself as in a row of objects behind the rock, "in front of the rock" can mean on the far side of ego". This means that the front of the rock would be facing in the same direction as ego. On one level, this is similar to our finding because it suggests that English speakers can use the process of translation to apply front and back properties to reference objects. On another level, there are important differences to what we have discovered. Firstly, in Miller and Johnson-Laird's example, it is ego which is in a row of objects. However, in our data it is the Ground objects, not the speaker, which are part of a row (see examples 51 and 52). Secondly, the 'front' attributed to the Ground in our examples borrows from the intrinsic frontal property of a neighbouring object in this row. In contrast, Miller and Johnson-Laird do not state any such condition in their explanation of example (53). We have therefore brought to light a new way in which speakers attribute frontal properties when using a relative frame of reference in static locative expressions.

5.2.1.2 A different origo and Ground in speech and gesture

Speakers' use of gesture also reveals that different Grounds and origos can exist multimodally (Fricke 2003). In the following example, the speaker describes the location of the rug in front of the fireplace.

1   2

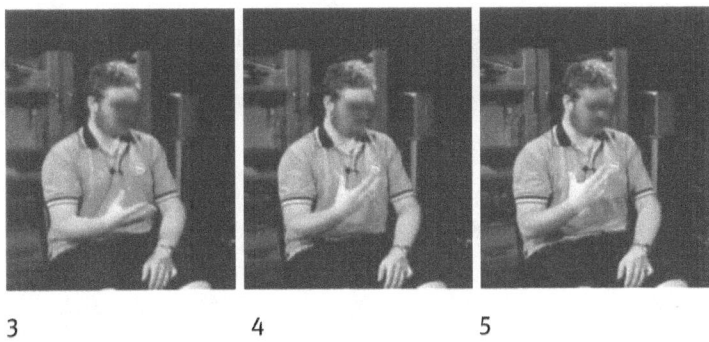

3   4   5

(54)   the *fireplace* has.. *a rug*.. in *front of it* (EngDesc8)

To begin with, the speaker establishes the location of the fireplace in his gesture space. The end of this gesture stroke, which synchronises with *fireplace*, is shown in still 1. He subsequently indicates the location of the rug which is in front of it, by moving his hand down and slightly in towards himself; the end of this gesture stroke is shown in still 2. Then, while verbally stressing the phrase *in front of it*, the speaker makes a clear, and clearly pronounced, movement of the right hand in towards himself: this gesture is depicted in stills 3-5 above. The timing of the gesture to coincide with *front*, along with its trajectory in space, clearly emphasises direction towards the speaker's front. This gestural expression of direction warrants investigation. Firstly, the Ground in the lexical expression is *fireplace*. The fireplace has an intrinsic frontal orientation and is also understood as the origo for the direction-encoding phrase *in front of*. As shown in stills 1 and 2 above, the speaker executes two gestures which depict the rug's location in front of the fireplace. However, the gesture shown in stills 3-5 does not express this same information. Rather, the hand moves up and in towards the speaker: this suggests that the speaker is now locating the rug in relation to his own front. Under such an interpretation, the speaker would be the Ground of the gestural expression. He would also constitute the origo, since the gesture is suggesting the rug's location in relation to the speaker's intrinsic front: that is, the rug is in front of the speaker (as he views the picture).

This interpretation is given further weight by the following example, in which the same speaker again uses gesture to reference his own location in space. This time however, he also lexically encodes himself as the Ground and origo of the directional relationship.

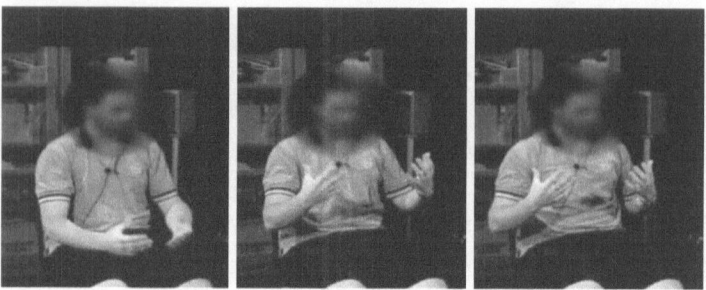

(55)   there's um <u>in front of us</u>.. so where you're viewing it from ah on the far left there's a couch (EngDesc8)

Although bi-manual in nature, the gesture above retains a similar form and trajectory to that represented in stills 3–5 of example (54). It shows that the speaker uses gesture to reference himself when he fulfils the roles of Ground and origo, and thus that our interpretation of example (54) is possible. This interpretation holds that the Ground and origo may vary across speech and gesture.

5.2.1.3 Different perspectives in speech and gesture

An origo is a conceptually mobile entity which may be instantiated by a scene-external observer or a scene-internal character (Fricke 2003). Hence, a speaker may express location in relation to their own position in front of the picture (as a scene-external observer), or in relation to an imagined location within the picture itself (as a scene-internal character). In both cases the speaker constitutes the origo, but there is divergence as far as the speaker's (real or imagined) location is concerned. The following example suggests that different perspectives may occur in speech and gesture[27], and that both perspectives may potentially be present within a single gesture. The speaker imagines herself near the door in picture ('you've just walked in the door'). This reveals the use of a character perspective in speech.

---

[27] I would like to thank Asli Özyürek for suggesting the idea of a dual perspective in this example.

Lounge room scene – English descriptions — **99**

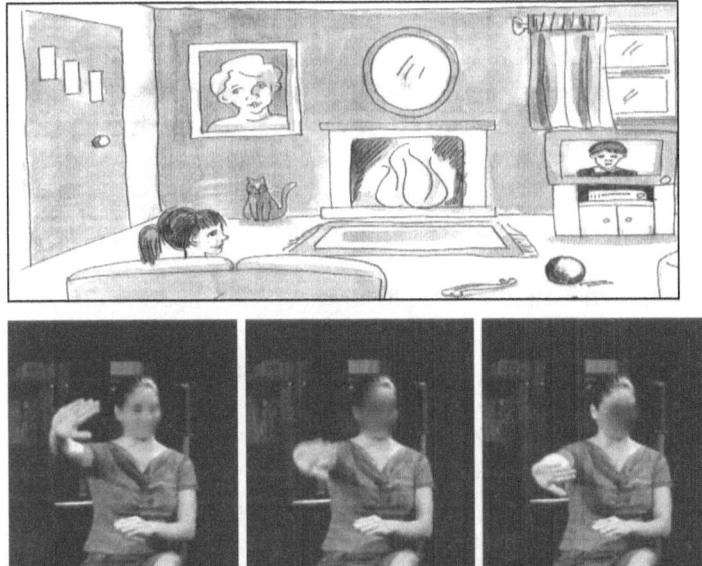

(56) *(if you've just walked in the door the rug's on the floor) and then.. next to it is the television so like in front as you're facing it*

Just before uttering *next to* the speaker moves her hand forward and down, in keeping with the idea of frontal direction encoded by *in front as you're facing it*. This gesture, which concerns the location of the television, is shown in the stills above. The speaker's body is turned slightly to the right, such that we understand her hand placement to indicate forward direction. While the gesture's trajectory is consistent with the use of character perspective, its hand shape and orientation are not. The rectangular form of the hand iconically suggests the flat screen of the television, and its orientation in relation to the speaker suggests that she is viewing this screen. However, the speaker would see the side of the television from her imagined location near the door in the picture – not its front. Instead, her hand's depiction of shape, as well as its orientation, is consistent with the television as seen by an *external observer*. Furthermore, the speaker executes this gesture with her right hand, although the television would be on her left-hand side when viewed from her imagined location in the picture. However, the television is on the right-hand side when viewed by an external viewer: this provides further evidence for the use of an observer perspective in gesture. Hence, it would seem that the speaker is using a character perspective in speech, and a dual observer/character perspective in gesture. Let us recapitulate why a dual perspective potentially exists in gesture here. The speaker's hand moves forward along the frontal axis: this is consistent with the location of the television when the scene-internal character perspective is used. In contrast, the shape and orientation of the hand suggest that the speaker is facing the television screen: this indicates the use of a scene-external observer perspective. This is bolstered by the speaker's use of her right hand, which seemingly reflects the television's location on the right-hand side of the picture. If our interpretation of this example is correct, then this dual perspective in gesture clearly brings to light the multi-layered nature of spatial conceptualisation: that is, speakers can simultaneously conceptualise location using both observer and character perspectives. It is also important to realise that the observer perspective occurs in gesture alone, while speech focuses solely on character perspective. This indicates that a choice of perspective is not binding for both modalities, and that variation across speech and gesture can exist.

A slightly different interpretation of (56) is that the gesture uses an observer perspective only, as opposed to a conflated character/observer one. In our explanation above, we suggested that the hand's forward trajectory suggests the distance of the television in relation to the speaker's imagined location within the picture. However, it may also represent the television's location in the background of the picture as viewed by the scene-external observer: hence the gesture may represent location exclusively from an observer perspective. Ultimately, whether the speaker conflates both perspectives in gesture or simply uses observer perspective alone is not a critical distinction. The fact remains that speech encodes location from a character perspective only, and this is clearly different to what occurs in gesture.

5.2.1.4 Gestural representations of foregrounds

There are four examples in which the lexical encoding of a foreground is accompanied by a representational gesture. Three of these gestures establish proximity to the speaker along the frontal axis. The fourth gesture, however, is a bi-manual depiction of extension along the lateral axis. The speaker's hands are slightly bent at the knuckles, as though ready to cut up a portion of space. The left and right hands then move out towards the left- and right-hand sides respectively, before moving up and down repeatedly. The first part of this gesture, in which the speaker's hands move out along the lateral axis, is captured in the stills below.

 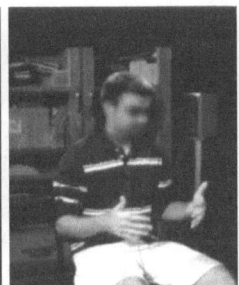 

(57)   *in the the foreground of the picture* [...] (EngDesc9)

This example suggests the implication of the lateral axis in how the speaker understands the concept FOREGROUND. A foreground is the region which is most proximate to a speaker's front as they view a picture. Foregrounds, however, must also possess width along a lateral axis, and the gesture above shows how the speaker takes this into consideration. The speaker subsequently executes a second gesture (this is not shown here) which references the frontal axis: this takes the form of a large, arc-like movement in towards the body. The two consecutive gestures therefore target different spatial axes, and together show how each axis informs the speaker's conceptualisation of the picture's foreground.

5.2.2   The use of back-encoding items

Speakers made very little use of back-encoding items in their descriptions of the lounge room scene. Just six occurrences of such items were noted, and three of these were due to one speaker. There were no representational gestures for these six occurrences; indeed, in five of the six expressions in which these items were found, speakers did not produce any representational gestures at all. The paucity of back-encoding items possibly shows that speakers did not generally distinguish a *background* in the picture. It also reflects the fact that objects could not readily be located *behind* others. For instance, the stimulus picture presents objects *in front of* the fireplace, the sofa and the television, but not *behind* them. Hence, the lack of back-encoding items – and therefore of gestures expressing back-directional information – is potentially a result of the stimulus picture itself. These observations will be revisited when we analyse how French speakers use back-encoding items (qv. section 5.3.2).

5.2.3 The use of directionally non-specific items

Table 2 shows that *far* was the second most frequently used directionally non-specific item. *Far* encodes the idea of distance, with the understood value of this distance contingent on the types of Figure and Ground objects in the locative configuration (Carlson and Covey 2005). Therefore, within the framework of a small-scale space like a living room, a pen is *far* from me if it is located in a drawer at the opposite end of the room. Within the context of large-scale space, New Zealand is *far* from America on account of its location in a different hemisphere. Hence, the distance understood by *far* depends crucially on the objects which fulfil the Figure and Ground roles[28].

In five of the six locative expressions containing *far*, speakers express direction along the frontal axis in either speech or gesture[29].

(58) the cat um.. is um near the door.. against the **far** wall.. um which is yeah like **at the back** (EngDesc7)

The speaker clarifies the spatial axis underpinning the use of directionally non-specific *far* with the prepositional phrase *at the back*. This phrase encodes a back property which results from the location of the intrinsically-oriented speaker in front of the picture: the speaker is therefore the origo of the directional relationship. This same front/back distinction can also be expressed in gesture alone.

---

28 Our understanding of *far* is not strictly spatial in nature: it may also be shaped by temporal concerns. For instance, London may be described as *far* from Paris if a traveller is about to embark on a ten-hour bus journey from one city to the other. In contrast, the same journey between the two cities would no longer be *far* if the traveller were going by plane instead. Therefore, like other spatial items such as *before* and *after* (which will be discussed later), there is often a tight interrelationship between spatial and temporal concerns. For the moment however, temporal concerns will not be of foremost interest.

29 Although this information was not expressed in the 6th example, it was nevertheless pragmatically inferable.

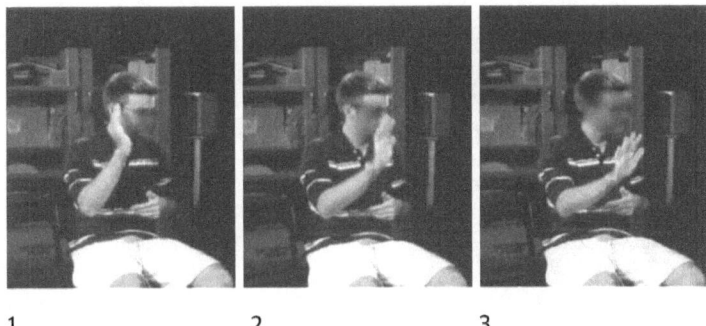

1   2   3

(59)   <u>on the far</u> wall.. um just next to the.. ah the door.. ah hanging on the wall is a a picture of a boy.. [...] (EngDesc9)

This gesture begins at a location next to the speaker's head, with the hand straightening out as it moves out along the frontal axis. The flat, extended form which the hand acquires at the end of the stroke phase (still 3) iconically represents the flat shape of the portrait. Notice how the speaker singles out the frontal axis as salient: instead of executing his gesture on the left of gesture space – thereby representing the portrait's location on the left-hand side of the room – he executes it in the centre. This possibly suggests that the speaker conceptualises the Figure's location in terms of the frontal, but not the lateral, axis. Moreover, while the speaker in example (58) clarifies the use of *far* with the prepositional phrase *at the back*, the speaker in example (59) specifies direction in gesture alone. This involves the use of the speaker as origo, with the directional information understood in relation to the speaker's intrinsic frontal property.

Speakers also used speech and gesture to express direction relating to uses of *closer to* and *closest to*.

(60)   in the the **foreground** of the picture so **closest to** to you.. um there's a couch over on the left hand side [...] (EngDesc9)

In example (60) *closest to you* encodes proximity and qualifies the use of *foreground of the picture*, which expresses a directional region along the frontal axis. In another example with *closer/closest to*, the speaker expresses direction along the frontal axis in gesture alone. Interestingly, this references a diagonal spatial axis which conflates both the frontal and lateral axes.

(61) *between.. the ball.. and the sofa.. ah <u>closer to</u> the ball.. and in fact it's almost aligned with the book is a bone* (EngDesc8)

The speaker does not lexically encode direction along any spatial axis in example (61). *Between* establishes the intermediate location of a Figure with respect to two Ground objects; *closer to* encodes general proximity; and *aligned* establishes the linear arrangement of a Figure and a Ground along a non-specific spatial axis. The speaker complements these lexical encoders of location with directional information in gesture. The stills above show how the speaker moves his hand forward and to the right: this indicates that the ball is in front and to the right of the sofa. Crucially, neither piece of directional information is present in the co-occurring speech.

Example (61) also features one use of *between*, which was the most frequently recruited directionally non-specific item. *Between* occurs six times in the lounge room scene data and *in between* once, resulting in a combined total of seven occurrences (see table 2). This is particularly noteworthy because *between* does not make reference to either front or back direction along the frontal axis. Rather, it can encode location along any horizontal axis which projects out from a Ground (see Kemmerer and Tranel 2000), thus enabling its recruitment in expressions of location which concern the lateral axis (qv. Chapter 6). As far as locative semantics are concerned, *between* encodes "the minimal space bounded by the pair of reference objects" (Landau and Jackendoff 1993: 230). The respective locations of the two Ground objects are salient because they define spatial boundaries for the Figure's location. Importantly, speakers express the locations of the Ground objects in gesture, yet do not concurrently encode this information in speech.

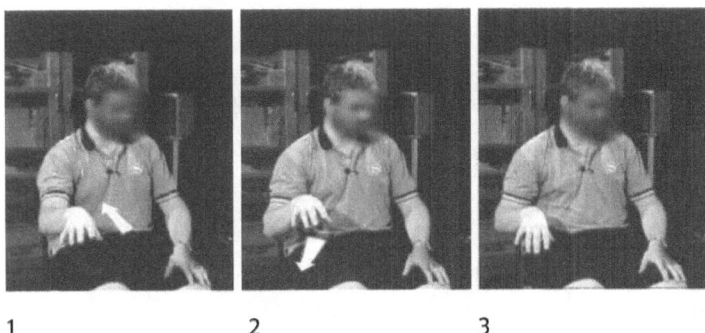

1   2   3

(62)   in between the <u>television and the dog</u>.. um almost aligned with the right hand edge.. of the television as well.. you have a ball (EngDesc8)

The stills above show how the speaker uses gesture to mark the isomorphic locations of the two Ground objects in gesture space. Still 1 captures the end of the movement which marks the television's location; the arrow indicates that the hand subsequently retracts along the frontal axis, resulting in the location shown in still 2. The arrow here indicates that the speaker's hand then moves down and back in towards the speaker, thus marking the dog's location in gesture space (still 3). The gesture ends with the speaker moving his hand slightly forward along the frontal axis (this is not shown here): this establishes the ball's location in the middle of these two locations. Example (62) highlights two important ways in which gesture expresses unlexicalised locative information. Firstly, gesture establishes the unlexicalised locations of the two Ground objects along the lateral axis: both are on the right-hand side of the picture[30]. Secondly, and more importantly for the current discussion, gesture expresses the respective locations of these two objects along the frontal axis. Hence, the speaker shows that the television is located further back into the picture than the dog is. This marking of the Grounds' respective locations along the frontal axis is an important feature of the use of *(in) between*: such gestures were produced for five of the seven occurrences of the preposition in the lounge room scene data, and these gestures were made by three different speakers. Furthermore, this information concerning the location of the Ground objects was not encoded in speech. This highlights the complementary nature of speech and gesture in the expression of locative information: while speech focuses on establishing the

---

[30] The use of gesture to communicate unlexicalised directional information will be explored in more detail in Chapter 8.

location of the Figure, gesture attends to the respective locations of the two Ground objects.

Somewhat paradoxically perhaps, speakers also use directionally non-specific *between* to provide directional clarification for *in front of* and *behind*. The following example shows how this occurs.

(63) and in front of the doo dog.. between the dog and the tv.. is the ball
(EngDesc6)

The use of *in front of* in (63) does not encode the intrinsic front of the dog, as the picture extract reveals. Rather, the speaker has mapped a *front* onto the dog using a process other than 180-degree rotation, which we normally associate with relative frames of reference (Levinson 1996: 369–371). Once again, this shows that English speakers use the process of translation to assign frontal properties. The speaker clarifies her use of *in front of* with the phrase *between the dog and the tv*. While doing so, she marks the dog's location in gesture space before moving her hands forward along the frontal axis to mark the television's location. The use of *between* is therefore complemented by these two gestural expressions of location. Together, the strands of information in speech and gesture provide the necessary clarification for the preceding use of *in front of*.

The expression of the Ground objects' locations alongside the use of *(in) between* reveals an important way in which gestures express unlexicalised directional information. This information concerns the locations of the Ground objects in relation to the front and back points of the picture. Such a use of gesture shows that the lexical Ground objects are simultaneously gestural Figures: a Figure is an object whose location is at issue (Talmy 2000). The semantic roles of Figure and Ground are therefore fluid cross-modally, and a lexical Ground may simultaneously function as a Figure in gesture. The presence of different

Figures in speech and in gesture builds on to Fricke's (2003) finding that different Grounds may be present in the two modalities. A closer examination of gestural Figures is undertaken in Chapter 8.

5.2.3.1 The use of gesture with directionally non-specific items

As represented in table 2, there were 17 occurrences of directionally non-specific items. For these items we ask the following question: does the speaker provide directional information which relates their use to the frontal axis? For instance, in example (62), the speaker's gestures identify the respective locations of the two Ground objects. These gestures reveal that one object is located further back into the picture, while the other is found more towards the front. In example (60), *closest to you* occurs as an explanation for *the foreground*, which encodes a sub-part of the picture defined by the frontal axis. Speakers may use speech, gesture, or indeed both modalities, to provide this sort of directional information concerning the frontal axis. One example in which gesture alone does this is example (62) above. Speakers specified information concerning the frontal axis for 14 of the 17 (82%) examples of directionally non-specific items in our data.

Graph 1: How speakers specify directional information concerning the frontal axis for occurrences of directionally non-specific items

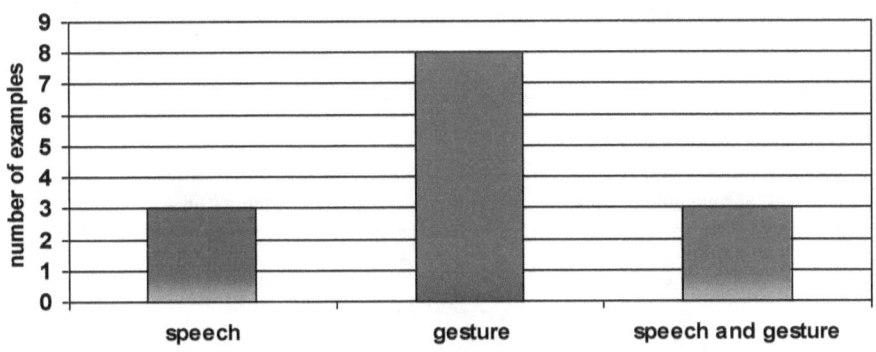

There were eight instances (57%) in which gesture alone expressed directional information concerning the frontal axis, three (21%) in which speech did, and a further three (21%) in which both modalities fulfilled this role. Although drawing on a small pool of examples, these results therefore show that speakers most commonly used gesture alone to provide this information. However, it should be pointed out that two of the examples in which gesture alone was used concerned a diagonal horizontal axis (see example 0): this implicates the lateral, as well as the frontal, axis.

5.3 Lounge room scene – French descriptions

This section examines how French speakers express location along the frontal axis in descriptions of the lounge room scene. The protocol for identifying pertinent lexical items was the same as that established for the English data. However, an additional issue concerning the nouns *milieu* ('middle') and *centre* ('centre') arose: certain uses of these items were ambiguous as to whether they referenced location along the frontal or lateral axis. An example of this is as follows.

(64) *au milieu de la pièce.. il y a un tapis.. posté devant la*
in the middle of the there is a rug.. placed in front of the
room..
cheminée (FrenDesc4)
chimney

In example (64) it is unclear whether *au milieu de* refers to location along the frontal axis, along the lateral axis, or along both axes. In such cases, the use of *milieu* or *centre* was excluded from the analysis as a precautionary measure.

Tab. 3: Lexical items used to encode location along the frontal axis in French descriptions of the lounge room scene

	Front-encoding items	N	Back-encoding items	N
A	au premier plan 'in the foreground'	13	au fond de 'at the back of'	7
B	devant 'in front of'	11	du fond 'of the back'	3
C	en face de 'in front of'/ 'opposite'	10	dans le fond (de) 'in the back (of)'	2

Tab. 3 (cont'd): Lexical items used to encode location along the frontal axis in French descriptions of the lounge room scene

	Front-encoding items (cont'd)	N	Back-encoding items (cont'd)	N
D	en face 'in front'/ 'opposite'	1	OTHER à l'arrière-plan 'in the background' (1) derrière 'behind' (1)	2
E	TOTAL	35		14
	Centre-encoding items	N	**Directionally non-specific items**	N
F	au milieu de 'in the middle of'	1	DEICTIC ITEMS là-bas 'over there' (2) là 'there' (1) ici 'here' (1)	4
G	au second plan 'in the second foreground'	1	entre 'between'	2
H			près de 'near'	2
I			vers 'towards'	2
J	TOTAL	2		10

5.3.1 The use of front-encoding items

French speakers made greatest use of front-encoding items in their descriptions, with the two most common items in table 3 being *au premier plan* ('in the foreground') and *devant* ('in front of'). The third most frequently recruited item was *en face de*. Commonly translated as 'in front of' or 'opposite' in English, *en face de* encodes location with respect to the positive side of the Ground's frontal axis (Vandeloise 1986). Despite differences in the semantics of *devant* and *en face de*, speakers sometimes use both prepositions to describe the same Figure/Ground configurations. This is explored in the analysis which follows, after an initial examination of how French speakers use *au premier plan* to encode location.

5.3.1.1 Gestural representations of foregrounds

French speakers most commonly encoded location along the frontal axis by localising the Figure *au premier plan* ('in the foreground') of the picture. The 13 uses of this prepositional phrase occurred across 12 locative expressions, with one expression containing two uses. Speakers produced seven representational gestures for the concept PREMIER PLAN ('FOREGROUND'). Interestingly, the example which featured two occurrences of *au premier plan* featured two of these gestures – one for each use. Of these seven representational gestures, two basic types were noted. The first type focused on the frontal axis with the speaker's hand(s) moving in towards the body. These gestures highlight a conceptualisation of the foreground as the part of three dimensional space closest to the speaker's intrinsic front.

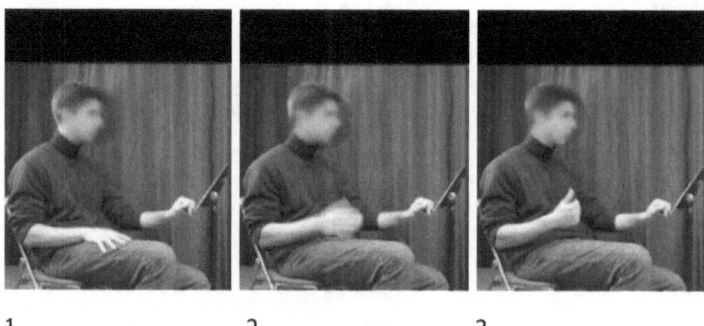

1   2   3

(65)   *donc*   *la lampe sera..*   *est située*   *au-dessus de*   *la table*
       so   the lamp will be..   is situated   above   the table
      donc   *au premier plan*   (FrenDesc7)
       so   in the foreground

In example (65) the speaker elevates his hand from an initial rest position (still 1) and moves it in towards his torso (stills 2 and 3). This contrasts to the second type of representational gesture, which suggests the primacy of the lateral, as opposed to the frontal, axis.

(66) [...] *au premier plan..*   *sur la gauche* (FrenDesc6)
           in the foreground..   on the left

In example (66) the speaker establishes distance between her hands along the lateral axis. This is achieved through the downward movement of the right and left index fingers, which move across to the right and left respectively. The information which the speaker presents in gesture focuses on a different strand of directional information to that provided in speech: whereas *premier plan* highlights the salience of the frontal axis, the speaker's gesture draws attention to extension along the lateral axis. This suggests the conceptualisation of PREMIER PLAN in terms of direction along both horizontal axes. Gestural reference to the lateral axis also accompanies speakers' use of the English *foreground* (see section 5.2.1.4). This cross-linguistic parallel in gestural behaviour suggests the similar conceptual material encoded by the lexical items *foreground* and *premier plan*.

5.3.1.2 How speakers use 'devant' and 'en face de'

Table 3 shows that French speakers use both *devant* ('in front of') and *en face de* ('opposite'/'in front of') to encode location relative to a Ground's front. There is overlap in the semantic networks of these two prepositions. *Devant*, when used to encode a locative configuration, has a sense similar to that of English *in front of*. *En face de* is also often used in this sense. Yet neither *devant* nor *en face de* is substitutable for the other in all contexts of use. The difference between the two prepositions has to do with how the Ground's front is established (Vandeloise 1986). To re-take an example from Vandeloise (1986), if I were standing with my head turned to the left I could describe the location of an object in my field of vision using *devant* – despite the fact that the rest of my body is not facing the object concerned. Such a use of *devant* is motivated by the salience of my line of sight in establishing a frontal direction. In contrast, the use of *en face de* would be less apt (Vandeloise 1986: 125): this is because *en face de* encodes location relative to the front side of a Ground (Vandeloise 1986: 126). Hence, the salience of vision is not sufficient to override the role of the intrinsic front in uses of *en face de*. Rather, *en face de* requires the Figure and Ground to be opposite each other – thus explaining the frequent use of *opposite* to translate the preposition in English. In contrast, English *opposite* does not necessarily encode location in relation to a Ground's front.

Data from our study suggest that additional spatial considerations determine the use of *en face de*. As far as the small-scale space of a lounge room is concerned, *en face de* encodes relationships of distance which are not encoded by *devant*. Strikingly, seven of the ten uses of *en face de* encode locative relationships between the sofa (or the woman on it), and an object at the opposite end of the lounge room. One of these examples is provided below.

(67) **en face de** la cheminée donc du portrait et du chat.. i'y a
opposite the fireplace so the portrait and the cat.. there's
un canapé avec une jeune fille (FrenDesc11)
a sofa with a young lady

In contrast to this, only two of the ten uses of *en face de* encode relationships of Figure/Ground proximity. The first of these, example (68) below, locates the rug in relation to the fire. The second, example (69), establishes the rug's location vis-à-vis the mirror.

(68) euh le tapis il est **en face du** *feu* (FrenDesc10)
uh the rug it is **in front of the** fire

(69) sur le sol **en face du** miroir il y a le tapis (FrenDesc2)
on the floor **opposite** the mirror there is the rug

The final example with *en face de*, shown in example (70) below, locates the sofa *en face de* ('in front of'/'opposite') the rug: this is neither a clear relationship of distance nor of proximity.

(70) et euh au premier plan donc à côté du canapé.. qui est
and uh in the foreground so next to the sofa.. which is
en face du tapis.. i'y a un livre ouvert
opposite the rug.. there's a book open
'and uh in the foreground so next to the sofa.. which is opposite the

rug.. there's an open book'

Leaving this example aside, there are seven uses of *en face de* that encode relationships of distance, and two which encode relationships of proximity. The recruitment of *en face de* to encode both types of relationship may potentially create ambiguity as to how the locative expression should be interpreted. While pragmatic inferencing may help to neutralize this, our results show that speakers supply additional information when the desired interpretation is one of distance. This information is supplied in speech in example (71) below.

(71) **au fond**   *de la pièce..*   *il y a*   *à gauche*   **en face de**
     at the back   of the room..   there is   on the left   **opposite**
     la jeune fille   [...] (FrenDesc4)
     the young girl   [...]

In this example the speaker encodes the portrait of the young boy *au fond de la pièce* ('at the back of the room') and *en face de la jeune fille* ('opposite the young girl'). Half-a-minute earlier in discourse the speaker establishes the girl's location in the foreground of the picture. Hence, the use of *au fond de* ('at the back of') in the current example establishes a contrast between a location in the background and another in the foreground: this leads to a reading of distance for *en face de*. Making reference to the foreground or the background of the picture is a common feature in the ten locative expressions which use *en face de*, and this triggers an interpretation of distance. This is revealed in example (72).

(72) [...] **en face du** *canapé*   *il y a le chat..*   *euh* **vers le mur**
     [...] **opposite the** sofa   there is the cat..   uh **towards the wall**
     du fond *en fait*   (FrenDesc10)
     of the back in fact
     'opposite the sofa there is the cat.. uh towards the back wall in fact'

Previously in this speaker's discourse the Ground object *sofa* was localised in the foreground of the picture. In (72) the speaker suggests the distance which separates the sofa and the new Figure *le chat* ('the cat') by localising the latter as *vers le mur du fond en fait* ('towards the back wall in fact'). In doing so, the speaker directs the listener towards the desired interpretation of *en face de* as an expression of distance. Information relating to distance may also be present in gesture. In example (73) which follows, the speaker describes *le mur en face de nous* ('the wall opposite us'). She executes two gestures which conflate the concerns of distance and direction. The first of these gestures accompanies *sur le mur* ('on the wall'), while the second accompanies *en face de*. Both gestures execute the same movement forward and out from the speaker's front. In contrast, the second gesture has a slighter shorter trajectory than the first one, possibly because it begins from a location further out from the speaker. This second gesture is shown below.

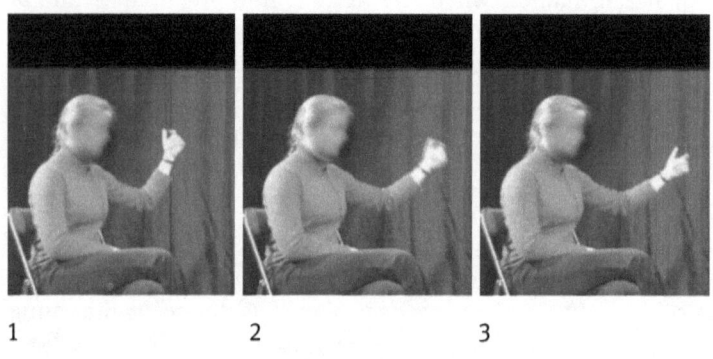

1   2   3

(73)   sur le mur..   euh <u>en face de</u> nous [...] (FrenDesc3)
       on the wall..   uh <u>opposite</u> us [...]

The movement of the left hand begins from a position already some way along the frontal axis (still 1). The speaker then lowers this hand, moving it forward along the frontal axis as she does so (stills 2 and 3). She therefore establishes the idea that the wall is located towards the back of the picture, thus expressing both distance and directional information.

The discussion above shows that *en face de* encodes relationships of distance, and that speakers signal this distance in speech and/or in gesture. In contrast to this, *devant* is used preferentially to encode relationships of proximity. This is neatly revealed by expressions which localise the rug in relation to the fireplace, shown below.

Of the seven examples which localise the rug in relation to the fireplace, six use *devant* while just one uses *en face de*. Although drawing on a small pool of data, this result, combined with the analysis of *en face de* above, suggests that distance plays a factor in the choice between the two prepositions to encode location.

5.3.2 The use of back-encoding items

13 of the 14 back-encoding items establish reference to the background of the picture. The remaining example is a single occurrence of *derrière* ('behind'), which was recruited to encode the bone's location in relation to the book. As far as the other 13 items are concerned, ten occur in examples which include representational gestures for the lexically-encoded concept. In all instances these gestures establish the background as an area defined in relation to the frontal axis which extends out from the speaker's front. This is highlighted in the following example.

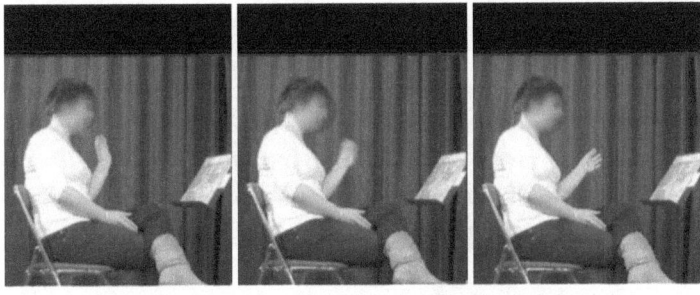

(74)   [...]   <u>près du</u> *mur*   *dans le fond* (FrenDesc5)
           [...]   <u>near the</u> wall   in the back(ground)

The gesture shown above synchronises with the prepositional phrase *près du* ('near the'), yet expresses directional information which semantically partners with the subsequent spatial item *fond* ('back'/'background'). The crucial elements in the gestural representation of a background are direction and distance. These are expressed by the forward-directional movement of the speaker's hand in relation to her front, as shown in (74). However, as far as hand shape is concerned, there is variability across speakers. Such differences reflect the salience of other spatial considerations at the time of utterance encoding. Hence, in the following example the speaker orients his hand so that the palm stands upright and faces outward. This is an iconic representation of the lexical Figure *miroir* ('mirror').

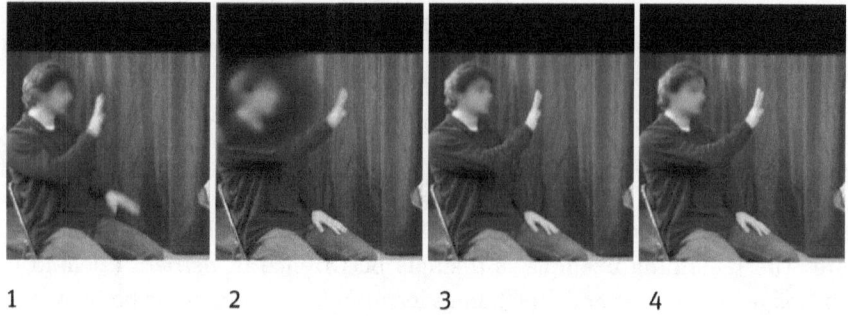

(75) [...] un <u>miroir collé au fond de la</u> pièce [...] (FrenDesc11)
      [...] a <u>mirror stuck at the back of the</u> room [...]

The speaker blends three key elements of his lexical locative expression in gesture. Firstly, the upward, forward-facing palm is an iconic depiction of the Figure *miroir* ('mirror'). Secondly, the speaker moves his hand forward along the frontal axis (stills 1-2), retracts it (still 3), and then moves it forward again (still 4): this possibly represents the physical action leading to the manner of location encoded by *collé* ('stuck'). Thirdly, the movement away from the speaker also suggests the location associated with the lexical Ground *fond de la pièce* ('back of the room'). The combination of hand-form, trajectory and location therefore enables the blend of three informational elements in a single gesture.

In our analysis of back-encoding items for the English data (section 5.2.2) we suggested that speakers could not readily encode the locations of objects *behind* others in the picture. This is confirmed by the French data, which reveal just one occurrence of the preposition *derrière* ('behind'). The more frequent use of back-encoding items in French descriptions (14 occurrences), as opposed to English ones (six occurrences), is discussed in section 5.6.3.

5.3.3 The use of directionally non-specific items

There were ten occurrences of directionally non-specific items in the French data. Of these, four were deictic items employed by the one speaker. Each occurrence of these deictic items was accompanied by a directional gesture. In the example below, the speaker encodes location with deictic *là* ('there') while executing a gesture to the front right of his location in space.

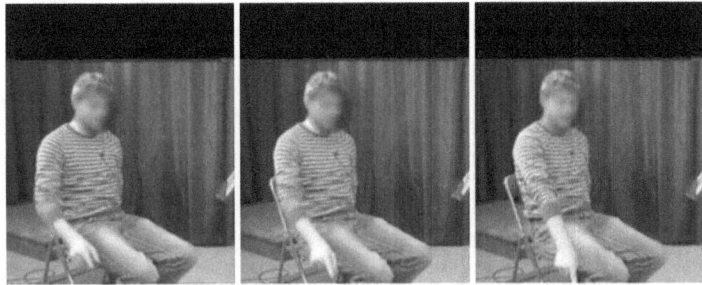

(76) *il y a un os..*   *qui se trouve <u>là</u>..*   *presqu'à mes pieds..*
      there is a bone..   which is found <u>there</u>..   almost at my feet..
      mais un peu   *à droite du canapé*   (FrenDesc10)
      but a little   to the right of the sofa

Example (76) shows how the speaker uses his own location at the time of utterance encoding to command attention to locative information. Using the deictic adverb *là* ('there'), he points to the isomorphic location of the Figure in gesture space. The localisation of the Figure within the speaker's spatial surrounding is continued in the topological phrase *presqu'à mes pieds* ('almost at my feet'). The speaker therefore adopts a character perspective within the picture and plays this out within the context of his own physical reality. More specifically, he imagines himself on the sofa, possibly in the location occupied by the lady. He verbally re-encodes the lateral directional information expressed in his deictic gesture with the phrase *un peu à droite* ('a little to the right'). The speaker does not, however, lexically encode the Figure's location along the frontal axis. The gleaning of this information requires the addressee to attend to two aspects of the speaker's spatial situation. The first of these is the location of the speaker's feet in gesture space: it is in relation to this point that the speaker localises the Figure, as indicated by the phrase *presqu'à mes pieds* ('almost at my feet'). The addressee then needs to attend to the direction of the gesture in relation to this location. By identifying the speaker as origo and by attending to the direction of the gesture in relation to the speaker's feet, the addressee can ascertain the Figure's location along the frontal axis. This information is not encoded in speech; at best, it is a vague pragmatic inference which results from our knowledge of where feet are normally placed in relation to sofas. It is gesture, however, which renders this information specific and which eliminates directional ambiguity: the bone is in front of the speaker's feet.

The role of gesture in expressing locative information is also highlighted by the two occurrences of *entre* ('between') in the data. In both instances, speakers execute gestures which express the locations of the Ground objects along the frontal axis. One of these examples is provided below.

1   2

(77)   <u>*entre le livre et le tapis qui se trouve devant* la cheminée</u>
<u>between the book and the rug which is found in front of</u> the fireplace
il y a un os (FrenDesc 6)
there is a bone

The speaker firstly uses her left hand to mark the location of the book (still 1), before establishing the location of the rug along the same frontal axis (still 2). Each of these locations is understood in relation to the conceptualised frontal axis of the picture: that is, the book is located near the front of the picture (still 1), while the rug is located towards the back (still 2). Notice also that the speaker uses her right index finger to point to the locations targeted by the left hand: the right index points down in the first still, but it points forward in the second. This draws attention to the respective locations of the two Ground objects. Finally, the directional information which the speaker expresses in gesture is not concurrently encoded in the lexical expression.

Table 3 shows that there were ten occurrences of directionally non-specific items in the French data. The two occurrences of *vers* and one of the uses of *près de* are all attributable to the one speaker. This same speaker also accounts for the four uses of deictic items. Hence, seven of the ten uses of directionally non-specific items are due to one describer alone. This shows that, as a group, French speakers made very little use of such items in descriptions of the lounge room scene. With this in mind, we shall not present a graph of these results, nor attempt to draw further conclusions here. Notably however, the results for the French speakers contrast with those obtained for the English speakers. This difference is explored in our comparison and discussion section at the end of the chapter.

5.4 Street scene – English descriptions

Speakers recruited a wide range of lexical items to encode location along the frontal axis in descriptions of the street scene. This range included what we will term *sequence-encoding items*: a particular sub-type of directionally non-specific item. Members of this category encode location in terms of a sequential progression, and do not provide any other spatial information concerning the nature of the Figure/Ground relationship. Examples include numerical values (i.e. *first* and *second*) as well as spatiotemporal prepositions (i.e. *before* and *after*). Note that *next to* does not satisfy this definition, because it also encodes the adjacency of the Figure to the Ground. In contrast, the adjective *next* in a phrase such as 'the *next* item on the street' does not encode adjacency, and is therefore counted as a sequence-encoding item. The accuracy of this decision is reinforced by the following example.

(78)   *the next gas station is not for 100 miles*

Clearly, the *next gas station* is not adjacent to any landmark in the speaker's surrounding environment. Rather, it is 100 miles away from the location at which the expression is uttered. Hence, while *next* encodes a sequence, it does not encode adjacency (although this may be pragmatically inferable).

Expressions which encode purely frontal *orientation*, as opposed to *location* along the frontal axis, have not been included in the analysis. This therefore excludes expressions such as 'she's facing the bus'.

All occurrences of relevant lexical items were counted, even when the one item was used more than once to describe the same Figure/Ground configuration. An exception to this was when the repetition of an item was triggered by a lexical correction: for example, *the third um hotel ah the the third shop*. Here, the repetition of the numerical value *third* is triggered by the lexical switch from *hotel* to *shop*, and so *third* is counted just once.

Items are only counted in one sub-category. Therefore, uses of *from* in examples of *in order from* (table 4, row M) are not also counted under the sub-category *from* (table 4, row K).

Speakers often appealed to the idea of motion to encode static locative relationships in this scene. Spatial items (excluding verbs) which were used to express location were therefore included in the analysis.

(79)   as you go **down** the street on the street on the left there's a trolley (EngDesc10)

In example (79) the adverb *down* encodes the trajectory of the agent *you* along the frontal axis. *Down* does not encode reference to either a front or a back: we therefore consider it to be directionally non-specific as far as the frontal axis is concerned. Hence, examples of *down* are counted in the category 'directionally non-specific items'.

Distance-encoding modifiers of spatial items have not been counted separately in our table. For example, there were four uses of *halfway* in the data, each of which occurred as a modifier to *up* or *down*. There is no need to account for these modifiers separately, since any specification of frontal direction relating to the use of *up* or *down* will also relate to *halfway*: the two items should therefore be considered as one unit. The same holds for the two uses of *further* and *furthest* in our data, as well as sequence-encoding items which act as distance modifiers. One example of the latter is presented below.

(80)   ah the bar is **two doors** down from the restaurant [...] (EngDesc8)

The pivotal phrase here is *down from*, in relation to which *two doors* functions as an expression of distance. In contrast, such items are included in our data analysis when they are **not** modifiers of other spatial items. This is because they are the sole item in relation to which we may attribute a complementary (lexical or gestural) expression of direction along the frontal axis.

(81)   in the **fifth** square.. there's the telephone booth (EngDesc3)

Tab. 4: Lexical items used to encode location along the frontal axis, English, street scene

	Front-encoding items (cont'd)	N	Back-encoding items (cont'd)	N
A	in front of	16	the back	6
B	(the) front	9	behind	3
C	foreground[31]	7	back (adverb)	2
D	in front	3	the background	1
E	out (the) front of	3		
F	the horizon	1[32]		
	TOTAL	39		12
	Directionally non-specific items	N	Sequence-encoding items	N
H	down	13	the end	13
I	close/closest to	8	NUMERICAL VALUE (first, second, etc)	9
J	down from	5	then	5
K	between	4	from	2
L	toward(s)	3	after	2
M	up	4	in order (from/to)	2
N	away from	2	last	2
O	OTHER past (1) just about where (1) about the same spot (1) into (1) far (1) back to (1)	6	next	2
P			OTHER before (1) the beginning (1)	2
J	TOTAL	45		39

Front-encoding items were markedly more frequent than back-encoding ones in the street scene data: 39 examples of the former were noted, as opposed to 12 of

---

31 Includes one use of *forefront*, instead of *foreground*.
32 A *horizon* is the most distal part of a spatial scene in relation to a viewer's front. Hence, the concept HORIZON necessarily implicates the Ground's front.

the latter. This result is potentially triggered by the stimulus picture itself. Many of the items which speakers were asked to localise – such as the trolley, the telephone booth, and the post-office box – were located *in front* of buildings along the street. In contrast, few, if any, of the listed items are readily described as *behind* an object. The analysis therefore begins by looking at how, and why, speakers used the different types of front-encoding items listed in table 4.

5.4.1 The use of front-encoding items

As mentioned in the section above, speakers located objects in relation to the frontal surfaces of buildings along the street. This entailed the description of location along a frontal axis which was perpendicular to their own as they viewed the picture. At other times, speakers encoded location in relation to their own intrinsic front. An example of each of these conditions is provided below.

(82)   *directly in front of of your.. your view.. is a bus* (EngDesc9)
(83)   *there's a post-office box.. in front of the youth hostel* (EngDesc1)

The first of the two visual extracts above shows that the bus aligns with the speaker's intrinsic frontal axis as they view the picture. In contrast, the post-office box is located in relation to the intrinsic frontal surface of the youth hostel (see the second visual extract above). This is perpendicular to the speaker's frontal axis as they view the picture, meaning that the post-office box is to the left of the youth hostel from the speaker's viewpoint.

Now, of the 16 uses of *in front of*, the speaker occurred as Ground on three occasions. The speaker was also the implicit Ground for two of the three uses of *in front*. We observed a particular pattern when speakers filled the role of Ground in these locative expressions: they made gestural reference to their own front. Table 5 below highlights this phenomenon by grouping together all uses of *in front*, *in front of* and *out (the) front of*. For simplicity, these three different lexical items are subsumed under the heading *in front (of)*. Two categories of these items are then proposed: the first collates uses of these items which introduce the speaker as Ground, while the second collates uses which introduce a non-speaker Ground. The occurrence of representational gestures for *in front (of)* is then noted.

Tab. 5: *in front (of)* – street scene

Spatial item and Ground	N
in front (of) and speaker as Ground	
a. + representational gesture	5
b. – representational gesture	0
in front (of) and non-speaker Ground	
c. + representational gesture	2
d. – representational gesture	15
TOTAL	22

Table 5 shows that English speakers executed representational gestures for *in front (of)* on all five occasions on which they featured as Ground. These representational gestures involved the speaker referencing their own front. One of these examples is presented below.

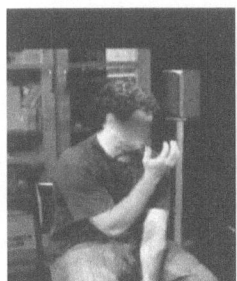

(84)   there's a bird.. and it's.. like right in front of you (EngDesc7)

The speaker draws his hand in towards his face, creating a prominent reference to his intrinsic frontal axis. Notice that he does not represent the bird's isomorphic location on the left-hand side of gesture space: rather, his gesture focuses solely on the frontal axis, and depicts the perceived proximity of the bird to the speaker's location.

In contrast, representational gestures were only noted for two of the 17 occurrences of *in front (of)* which used a non-speaker Ground (see table 5). These two uses of *in front (of)* appeared in the same locative expression, described the same Figure/Ground configuration, and each was accompanied by a gesture which tilted forward and away from the speaker. The first of these gestures is shown below. Note how the superimposed image depicts the forward movement of the speaker's hand. The underlined sections in the example identify the lexical items that accompanied the two strokes.

(85) *directly across.. almost directly across from the car is a telephone booth.. but just <u>slightly in front</u> of it.. so on the on the left hand side there's a telephone booth just <u>slightly</u>.. in front of the car so.. in front towards me*
(EngDesc5)

Hence, in all seven examples that contained a representational gesture for *in front (of)*, the frontal axis was either the speaker's own or one parallel to it. However, there were examples in which speakers did *not* produce such gestures when referencing a frontal axis which was parallel to their own. Hence, it cannot be claimed that speakers routinely gesture when encoding location along a frontal axis which is parallel to their own as they view the picture. One compelling explanation is that representational gestures are more likely to occur when speakers encode themselves as Ground. Such a conclusion, however, is premature. Firstly, in 14 of the 17 examples in which the speaker was *not* the Ground, the directional information encoded by *in front of* was not necessarily salient. This is because *in front of* could be replaced by the directionally non-specific preposition *outside* without the loss of any pivotal locative information: the information that the shops face the street is pragmatically inferable in speakers' discourse. Hence, an object which is located *in front* of a shop may simply be said to be *outside* it, as in the example below.

(86)   *the car is outside the bank on the right* (EngDesc6)

A second reason which may explain the difference in gesture production is the use of modifiers for *in front (of)*. Intensifiers, such as the adverb *right* in example (84), modify the lexical expression of frontal direction in four of the five examples in which the speaker occurs as Ground. These intensifiers highlight the salience of the encoded directional information and potentially explain the expression of this information in gesture. One way of determining the validity of this hypothesis is to examine whether, and how, speakers gesture when encoding themselves as the Ground complement for other spatial items. The eight occurrences of *close (to)* and *closest (to)* (see table 4, row I) each introduce the speaker as Ground and so provide an ideal point of comparison. These eight examples are produced by four speakers. Tellingly, on all eight occasions, speakers execute gestures which reference their intrinsic front.

(87)   closest to your perspective.. there is a bus (EngDesc8)

In example (87), reference to the frontal axis is inferable through the combination of the proximity-encoding *closest to* and the Ground *your perspective*. Gesture confirms this interpretation through the trajectory of the right hand in towards the speaker's front.

An alternative explanation is that the gestures accompanying *close/closest (to)* are triggered by the concern of proximity. However, such directional gestures are also noted when proximity is *not* a concern, as the following example reveals.

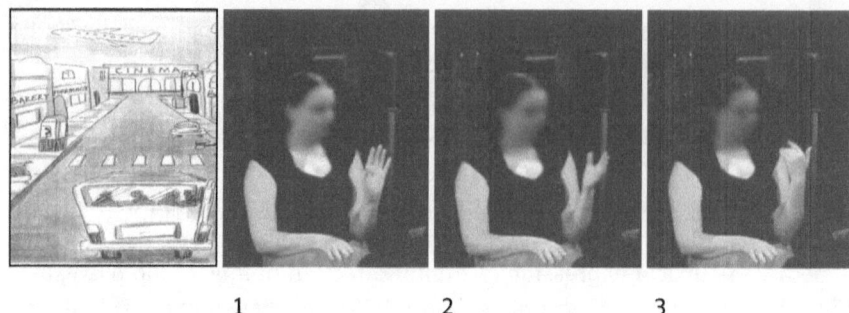

1   2   3

(88) [...] *so on the on the left hand side there's a telephone booth just slightly.. in front of the car so.. <u>in front towards</u> me* (EngDesc5)

In example (88), which is the second half of example (85), *towards* does not encode a relationship of proximity. Rather, it introduces a Ground-encoding complement (*me*) which allows for the Figure's location to be established along the frontal axis. Notice that the prepositional phrase *in front towards me* modifies the preceding use of *in front of*. This modification occurs because the speaker is not referring to the intrinsic *front* of the car. Rather, she is encoding direction relative to her own intrinsic front: the speaker is the origo of the directional information. She confirms this information by rotating her hand (still 2) from an initial forward-facing orientation (still 1) and by beckoning in towards herself (still 3). Another gesture which highlights the role of the speaker as origo of the frontal axis occurs in the following example.

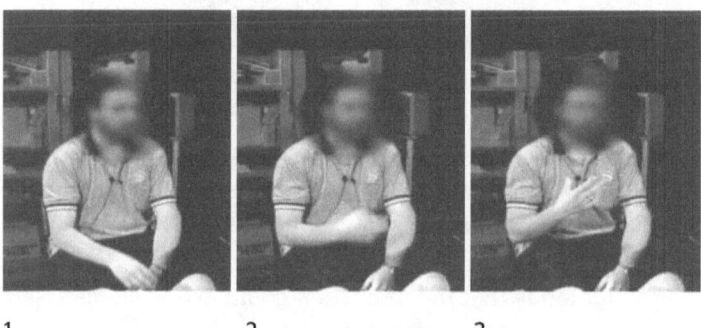

1   2   3

(89) *on the right hand side of the street.. three doors down from.. the um.. viewer.. is a restaurant* (EngDesc8)

The phrase *three doors down from the viewer* encodes distance away from the speaker's perspective. However, the speaker's gesture does not express this information. Rather, his right hand rises from a rest position (stills 1-2) and moves in towards his front (still 3). Once again, this shows that when a speaker encodes themselves as Ground, they make gestural reference to their frontal axis.

To summarise then, all eight occurrences of *close (to)* and *closest (to)* introduce the speaker as Ground, and all are accompanied by gestures which reference the speaker's front. Furthermore, the five uses of *in front (of)* which introduce the speaker as Ground are all accompanied by these same, speaker-indicating gestures. These 13 gestures all draw attention to the speaker's orientation and location in space. Why do these gestures occur? An answer to this question is sought later in this chapter, in section 5.6.1.

5.4.2 The use of back-encoding items

There were just 12 occurrences of back-encoding items in descriptions of the street scene, as opposed to 39 occurrences of front-encoding ones. This striking difference is seemingly due to the visual stimulus itself. Describers were required to localise objects which were out the front of landmarks along the street: for example, the telephone booth is *in front of* the hotel, just as the post-office box is *in front of* the youth hostel. In contrast, very few objects could be localised *behind* others. Hence, seven of the occurrences of back-encoding items concerned the back or the background of the picture, as opposed to relationships in which a Figure was located *behind* a Ground. For five of these seven occurrences, speakers produced representational gestures. These gestures represented the background as a distal region lying forward and away from the speaker's front. All gestures expressed this information using speaker viewpoint and observer perspective, an example of which is shown below.

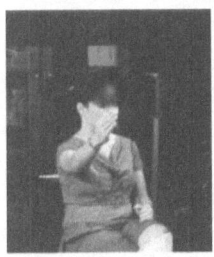

(90)   and then coming down the right hand side we've got the bar so going *from the* back.. the bar (EngDesc3)

The still for example (90) captures the end of a gesture stroke phase in which the speaker establishes the bar's location at 'the back' of the picture. The gesturing arm is positioned in front of the speaker's body and is bent at the elbow so that the forearm leans diagonally forward. This shows two things: firstly, that the back of the picture is considered in relation to the speaker's intrinsic frontal axis; and secondly, that the area designated as 'back' is distal in relation to the speaker's front. Hence, the concerns of distance and direction both underpin the gestural representation.

Overall, speakers produced representational gestures for eight of the 12 occurrences of back-encoding items. As in (90) above, these gestures all represented direction by establishing distance forward and away from the speaker's front.

5.4.3 The use of directionally non-specific items

Down and *up* encode the two polar directions associated with the vertical axis. In addition to this, speakers also use these items to establish location along the frontal axis. This involves conceptualising the Figure's location within a motion-event framework. However, a difference exists between the two items: *up* profiles the destination of this motion event, while *down* does not. The following example of a motion event highlights this contrast.

(91)   *Mary came up to me*
(92)   *??Mary came down to me*

The deictic verb *come* encodes motion in the direction of the speaker's location. This location constitutes the Figure's destination, and so explains the use of destination-profiling *up* in (91). In comparison, the use of *down* in (92) is less felicitous. This understanding of *up* as an item which profiles the end point of a trajectory is consistent with an analysis of the satellite *up* by Talmy (2000). Talmy claims that *up* is used to encode the end of a process: this is revealed by verb phrases such as *cook up*, *turn up*, *show up*, etc. It therefore follows that *up*, when used to encode location along a frontal axis, highlights the completion of a conceptualised trajectory.

When speakers use *down* and *up* to encode location, the direction of the trajectory along the frontal axis needs to be established in relation to an origo. Consider the following example.

(93) *then like not the shop next to the letter-box <u>but the one just</u> down from the letter-box is a restaurant* (EngDesc2)

In order to know the location of the lexically-encoded Figure *restaurant*, we need to understand the direction of the locative progression encoded by *down*. This direction needs to be established in relation to an origo that is located at a specific point in space. The speaker in example (93) provides this information in gesture alone. The stills above show how the speaker's right hand moves forward in relation to her intrinsic frontal axis. This establishes direction in relation to a speaker-based origo, located in front of the picture. Notice that *down* does not necessarily encode direction away from the speaker-based origo. In the following example, the speaker uses this spatial item to signal a trajectory back along the frontal axis and in towards her own location.

(94) *and then coming **down** the right hand side we've got the bar so going from the back.. the bar* (EngDesc3)

In example (94), the use of *down* combines with the deictic verb *come* to reference a movement back in towards the speaker. In contrast, example (93) presents a use of *down* which combines with a gesture to express movement away from the speaker. These two examples show how *down* can reference different directional movements along the frontal axis, in relation to the same origo. The information that gesture expresses in (93) is therefore salient, because it provides directional colour for the trajectory encoded by *down*. In doing so, it highlights the complementary interaction of speech and gesture in the expression of location.

The use of *up* and *down* to describe location along the frontal axis is tightly related to the ideas of motion and a clearly demarcated path. Hence, I may describe the location of a kitchen *down the hallway*, but it would be more difficult to describe the location of a wardrobe **down the bedroom*. Furthermore, a supermarket may be *down the street* but not **down the square*, since town squares are not readily conceptualised as paths. The ideas of trajectory and path are reenforced by the four uses of the distance-encoding adjective *halfway*, each of which occurs as a modifier for *up* or *down*.

(95)   telephone booth.. um it's on the left hand side of the road.. and it's about **halfway down** (EngDesc7)

Speakers also use other distance-encoding phrases as modifiers of *up* and *down*. One such phrase is *a third of the way* in the following example.

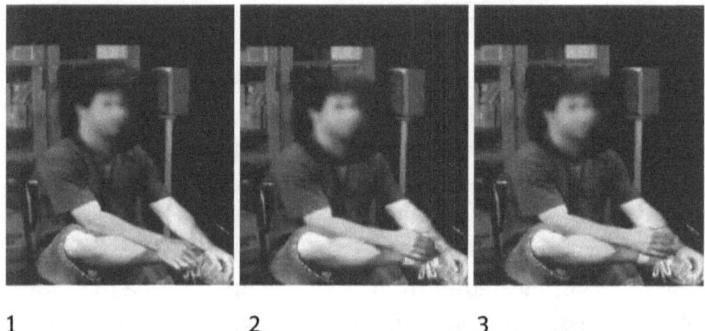

1   2   3

(96)   trolley's on the footpath left hand side.. about a third of the way <u>down the page</u> (EngDesc7)

The use of *down* in this example is ambiguous. Taking the lexical expression without the gesture shown above, it is unclear whether the speaker is encoding the Figure's location *down* the vertical axis from the top of the visual stimulus, or *down* the frontal axis which extends out from the viewer. Gesture provides the necessary directional clarification here. The stills show how the speaker's right hand rises off his shoe and moves slightly inwards (stills 1–2) in order to execute a movement out along the frontal axis (still 3). This gesture communicates what speech has left unexpressed: it shows that this use of *down* concerns the frontal axis, that this frontal axis has the speaker as its origo, and that the encoded trajectory moves forward from the speaker's location. The different strands of information that speech and gesture present are crucial and non-redundant, and must be considered together in order for the Figure's location to be understood.

At other times in the data, *down* and *up* introduce the directionally-specific noun phrases *the front* and *the back*. There are three examples in which *down* introduces *the front*, and two examples in which *up* introduces *the back*. Such collocation highlights one way in which directionally non-specific items combine with directionally-specific ones to express location.

(97) on the road right in the middle of the picture **right down the front** there's a bus (EngDesc5)

Other directionally non-specific items, such as *closest to*, occur in phrases which provide directional qualification for a preceding, direction-encoding item.

(98) um in the very in the middle of the foreground.. so **closest to** us there's um a bus (EngDesc3)

In (98) *closest to us* functions as a directional qualification for *foreground*: this highlights how directionally non-specific items (i.e. *closest to*) can team with certain Grounds (i.e. *us*) to provide directional clarity. At other times speakers provide such clarity in gesture alone, as in example (99) below.

(99) on the left hand side of the road <u>past</u> the trolley.. is a phone box (EngDesc8)

Past, like *up* and *down*, encodes location within the framework of a motion event. It specifies the location of the Figure at a point which is subsequent to the Ground in the trajectory of a real or virtual agent in motion (cf. Tutton 2013). However, the direction of this trajectory in relation to an origo must be known if the Figure's location is to be understood. This directional information is not lexically encoded in (99), yet may be inferred from the speaker's gesture. The stills show how the speaker's hand slices forward and down, expressing direction in relation to the speaker's intrinsic front. This suggests that the speaker conceptualises the relationship encoded by *past* in terms of a forward progression along the frontal axis which extends out from his location in front of the picture. The example therefore indicates that direction expressed in gesture may combine with the semantic of *past* to convey a Figure's location in space.

5.4.4 The use of sequence-encoding items

Speakers frequently employed sequence-encoding items to establish a Figure's location along the frontal axis. Numerical values such as *first* and *second* were the most common examples of such items (see table 4). In certain instances, the starting point of the numerical sequence was pragmatically inferable and speakers did not specify direction along the frontal axis in either speech or gesture. This was the case in the following example.

(100) so in the first square.. we have a cat.. a black cat (EngDesc3)

Prior to the expression in (100), the speaker signals her imagined trajectory along the left-hand side of the street in the following way: "ok we'll go on the left hand side of the road onto the shops onto the sidewalk". This implies a progression from the frontal space closest to the viewer (the foreground), to the frontal space furthest away (the background). In other instances, directional information was inferable from the Path- and Ground-encoding items in the lexical expression. One such example is as follows.

(101) on the right hand side of the street.. three doors **down from.. the** um.. **viewer**.. is a restaurant (EngDesc8)

In (101) the numerical encoder *three* serves as an indicator of distance. *Down from* introduces the Ground *the viewer*, and so encodes a trajectory which departs from the speaker's location. While none of the items *three*, *down from* or *viewer* individually encodes direction along the frontal axis, their collective interpretation allows for this information to be understood. At other times, this directional information cannot be inferred and is left unspecified. In such instances, the listener may potentially understand the speaker as the default origo of the directional trajectory.

(102) *in the fifth square.. there's the telephone booth* (EngDesc3)

As far as the nine occurrences of numerical values are concerned, there were no examples in which gesture alone expressed the direction of the sequential progression. Nevertheless, speakers did use gesture to express directional information relating to other sequence-encoding items.

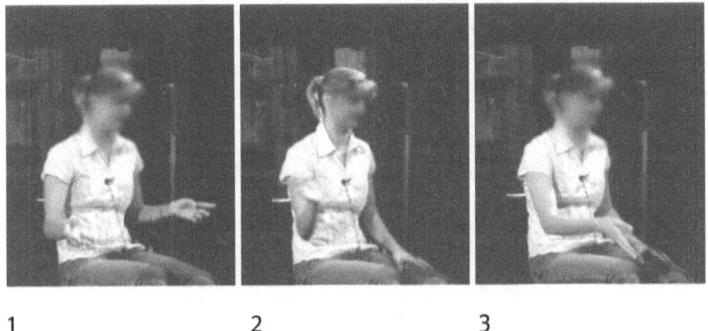

1   2   3

(103) *(right is the.. bank..) and then there's <u>the bar on</u> your right* (EngDesc6)

The use of sequence-encoding *then* establishes the location of the *bar* at a point which is subsequent to that of the *bank*. However, in order to clearly communicate the bar's location, the speaker needs to establish the direction of this sequential progression along a particular spatial axis. In example (103), this occurs in gesture alone. At the end of the preparation phase (still 1), the speaker raises her right hand (still 2), which she subsequently launches forward and away from her intrinsic front (still 3). This shows that the bar is located further back into the picture than the bank is, when the picture is viewed from the speaker's location. Hence, the gesture provides the necessary directional colour for the sequence-encoding lexical item. Notice, however, that the gesture does not synchronise with *then*: instead, it accompanies *the bar* and *on*. Far from denying its semantic partnership with *then*, this alignment simply shows that the gesture also relates to *the bar*, which is the Figure of the locative expression, as well as to the prepositional phrase *on your right*, which encodes additional directional information. As we showed earlier, directional gestures and their lexical partners do not necessarily synchronise (see Chapter 4, example 34).

The second most frequently occurring sequence-encoding item was the noun phrase *the end*. Used in the sense of a spatial sequence, *the end* encodes the ultimate point in the trajectory of a real or virtual agent in motion. The association of beginning and end points with the visually-represented street may lead to the speaker localising these points relative to their own location in space, as in the following example.

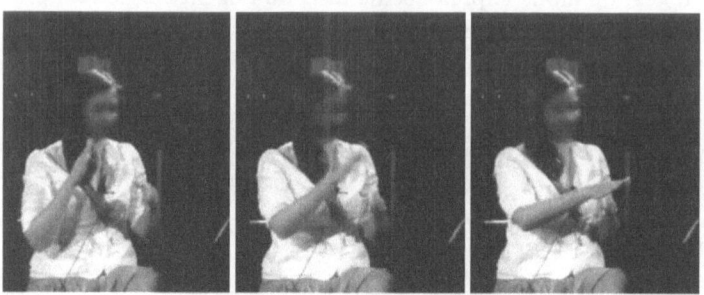

(104)   um at the <u>very end</u> at the of the street is a cinema (EngDesc4)

In (104) the speaker's right hand establishes a path which extends out from her intrinsic front: this highlights the salience of the frontal axis to her conceptualisation of the street's *end*. The speaker serves as origo of this frontal axis, and the movement of her hand forward establishes the *end* as the most distal point in relation to her front. Notably, the directional information which is expressed in gesture is not concurrently encoded in speech, although it is quite possibly pragmatically inferable.

Examples (103) and (104) show how speakers use gesture to express distance and directional information relating to the use of sequence-encoding items. Underpinning the interpretation of many such items is the conceptualisation of location within a motion-event framework (see Tutton 2013). Hence, a location encoded as a *beginning* or *end* requires the conceptual presence of an agent in motion to validate the locative sequence. The same is true for spatio-temporal prepositions like *before* and *after*. In the following example, the speaker encodes the location of the post-office, pronominalised as *it*, in terms of the progression encoded by *after*.

1   2   3

(105)   *it's in front of the youth hostel.. so it's on the right hand side um.. just <u>after the old lady</u>* (EngDesc7)

As shown in the stills above, the speaker's hand rises (still 2) and moves away from his front (still 3): this communicates progression along a frontal axis which has the intrinsically-oriented speaker as origo. While speech encodes location within the framework of a motion event, gesture expresses the unlexicalised direction of this trajectory. This direction is established relative to a speaker-based origo who is located in front of the picture. Notice also that the speaker uses his left hand to express this directional information, even though in speech he states that the Figure is located on the right-hand side of the street: the speaker's gesture is clearly focusing attention on the Figure's location along the frontal, as opposed to the lateral, axis.

5.4.5 The overall use of gesture with directionally non-specific and sequence-encoding items

Overall then, did gestures play a major role in expressing directional information relating to directionally non-specific and sequence-encoding items? To begin with, we will look at the 39 occurrences of sequence-encoding items. Our analysis seeks to determine whether speakers specified the direction of a lexically-encoded sequence in relation to an origo. This information may be provided in speech, in gesture, or in both modalities. Three instances in which gesture alone expressed this information are provided in examples (103)–(105). We understood this information to be provided in speech even if a specific direction was not overtly encoded, but was nevertheless strongly inferable, as in the following example.

(106)   ok the restaurant is closest like it's.. close towards you that from the bank there's a bank.. then there's a restaurant (EngDesc7)

In (106), we consider that speech provides directional clarification for the use of sequence-encoding *then*. Why do we think this? The speaker encodes the restaurant's location as *close towards you*. He subsequently establishes the existence of the bank (*there's a bank*), before referring to the location of the restaurant once again (*then there's a restaurant*). Hence, we can clearly infer that the speaker is moving away from the bank's location and into the foreground of the picture (and hence *close towards you*). We therefore consider that directional information is provided in speech.

In certain instances, salient directional information may accompany the use of another spatial item in the locative expression. Consider the following example:

(107)   then if you were to walk **down** on the right side of the road towards the cinema just **before** you got to the cinema is a bar (EngDesc2)

The speaker accompanies the use of *down* at the beginning of this expression with a motion of the hand forward along the frontal axis. Although this gesture does not occur with *before*, it nevertheless allows us to understand the direction in which the sequence advances: it moves forward from a speaker-based origo at the front of the picture. Hence, as far as the use of *before* is concerned, we consider that directional precision has been provided in the locative expression, and that this occurs in gesture only.

In the rare examples where a spatial item occurs on multiple occasions and refers to the same Figure/Ground combination (i.e. imagine that the speaker had repeated the *before* phrase in the above expression), we only count the item once.

Graph 2: How speakers express directional information concerning the frontal axis for occurrences of sequence-encoding items

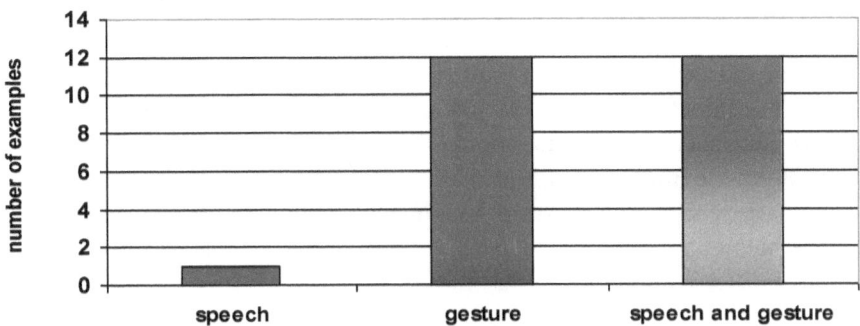

Speakers provided directional specification for 25 of the 36 (69%) occurrences of sequence-encoding items in our analysis. Of these 25 examples, speech and gesture carried the directional charge on 12 (48%) occasions, while gesture alone did so on 12 (48%) occasions as well. In contrast, the use of speech alone to specify direction along the frontal axis was far less frequent: just one (4%) example was noted. Overall, speech expressed directional information in 13 of the 25 examples (52%; taking into account the columns 'speech' and 'speech and gesture'). In contrast, gesture did so in 24 of the 25 examples (96%; adding the columns 'gesture' and 'speech and gesture'). One interpretation of these results is the following. Speakers generally use gesture to provide directional complementation for lexically-encoded locative sequences. When they wish to draw attention to this information, they express it in both speech and gesture. Crucially however, speech alone is very rarely used. This suggests the propensity of gesture for expressing directional information.

We also sought to determine whether speakers provided directional information concerning the frontal axis for uses of directionally non-specific items. For example, the forward-directional gesture in example (93) shows that the Figure is further towards the back of the picture than the Ground is (when viewed from the speaker's viewpoint). This would therefore count as an example in which gesture alone expresses directional information relating to the use of *down from*.

We assessed our examples using the same process as that outlined above for sequence-encoding items. Overall, of the 45 examples, we excluded six from the analysis which follows. Four of these were omitted on the basis that directional information was irrelevant. These were uses of *up* or *down* which were modified by the distance-encoding item *halfway*. If an object is *halfway up* or *halfway down* a street, the specific direction along the frontal axis in which the object is approached is irrelevant: this is because the object's location can simply be determined by scanning for the mid-point of the frontal axis. In addition to these four examples, another two items were excluded because it was ambiguous as to whether both speech and gesture carried the directional charge or not. This therefore left us with 39 occurrences of directionally non-specific items. Speakers provided directional information concerning the Figure's location along the frontal axis for 33 of these 39 occurrences. The expression of this information in speech, gesture and in both modalities is represented in the graph below.

Graph 3: How speakers specify directional information concerning the frontal axis for occurrences of directionally non-specific items

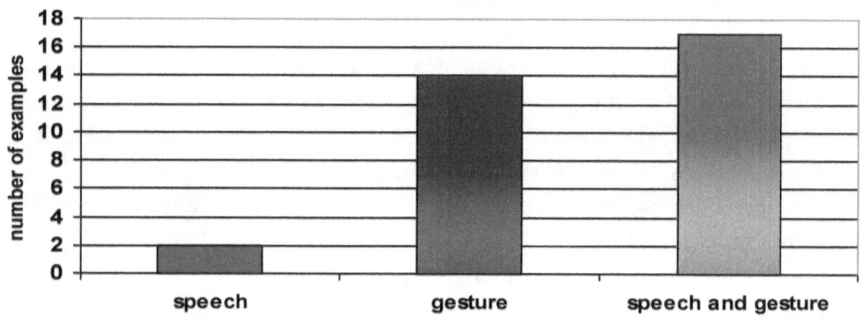

Speakers most frequently expressed directional information relating to directionally non-specific items in both speech and gesture (17 examples; 52%). They also made productive use of gesture alone to express this information (14 examples; 42%), but the same was not true of speech (two examples; 6%). These results are similar to those achieved for sequence-encoding items (cf. graph 2). To highlight this, table 6 below compares the results for sequence-encoding and directionally non-specific items.

Tab. 6: The expression of directional information relating to sequence-encoding and directionally non-specific items

Modality	Sequence-encoding items	Directionally non-specific items	TOTAL
Speech only	1	2	3
Gesture only	12	14	26
Both speech and gesture	12	17	29
TOTAL	25	33	58

As far as directionally non-specific items are concerned, gesture expressed directional information in 31 of these 33 examples (94%; rows 'gesture only' and 'both speech and gesture'), while speech did so in 19 (58%; rows 'speech only' and 'both speech and gesture'). Once again, this shows that speakers used gesture more often than speech to provide directional information relating to directionally non-specific items. It also suggests the particular suitability of gesture for expressing this type of information (qv. Chapter 8).

5.5 Street scene – French descriptions

Just like English describers, French describers recruited a wide range of items to encode location along the frontal axis in descriptions of the street scene. This also involved the use of what we have labelled *sequence-encoding* items. We observed the same protocol for identifying relevant lexical items in the French descriptions as we did in the English descriptions. Hence, we account for all lexical items which speakers used to encode locative information, except for verbs. All occurrences of such items are counted, except when an item was repeated on account of a lexical correction. An example of this is provided below.

(108) *la boîte postale elle est.. encore avant le.. avant la voiture* (FrenDesc2)
    the post-office box it is.. still before the.. before the car
    'the post-office box it is.. further before the.. before the car'

In (108) the speaker follows the first use of *avant* ('before') with the masculine article *le* ('the'). She then pauses, before beginning the prepositional phrase again. This is triggered by the change of article from *le* to *la*, in order to introduce the feminine noun *voiture* ('car'). Hence, we count just one occurrence of *avant* here.

Tab. 7: Lexical items used to encode location along the frontal axis in French descriptions of the street scene

	Front-encoding items	N	Back-encoding items	N
A	*en face de* 'in front of'/'opposite'	22	*au fond*	4
B	*au premier plan* 'in the foreground'	21	OTHER *au dernier plan* ('in the background') (1) *en arrière-plan* ('in the background') (1) *au fond de* ('at the back of') (1) *derrière* ('behind') (1)	4
C	*devant* 'in front of'	20		
D	*en face* 'in front'/'opposite'	3		
E	*le point de fuite* 'the vanishing point' (i.e. horizon)	2		
F	OTHER *plein axe* ('straight ahead') (1) *à l'horizon* ('on the horizon') (1) *un plan en perspective* ('a part in perspective') (1) *en premier plan* ('in the foreground') (1)	4	N/A	
G	TOTAL	72		8
	Directionally non-specific items	**N**	**Sequence-encoding items**	**N**
H	*entre* 'between'	9	NUMERICAL ENCODER	12
I	*vers* 'towards'	5	*après* 'after'	10
J	*à côté de* 'next to'	6	*au bout (de)* 'at the end (of)'	8
K	*près de* 'near' (preposition)	2	*ensuite* 'then'	4

Tab. 7 (cont'd): Lexical items used to encode location along the frontal axis in French descriptions of the street scene

	Directionally non-specific items (ct'd)	N	Sequence-encoding items (ct'd)	N
L			*puis* 'then'	4
M			*avant* 'before'	2
N			*au début de* 'at the beginning of'	2
O			OTHER *à l'autre bout* ('at the other end') (1) *tout d'abord* ('first of all') (1)	2
P	TOTAL	22		44

Table 7 above reveals a similar pattern to that noted in the English data: that is, speakers used spatial language differently when describing the street scene, as opposed to the lounge room scene. This is immediately evident through the productive use that speakers made of sequence-encoding items. The analysis which follows begins by targeting front-encoding lexical items, before moving on to address the constituents of the other three categories.

5.5.1 The use of front-encoding items

A point of similarity with French descriptions of the lounge room scene is the use of both *devant* and *en face de* to encode location along the frontal axis. Our analysis of the lounge room scene data suggested that speakers use *devant* to encode relationships of proximity. This hypothesis is confirmed by the street-scene data: 19 of the 20 uses of *devant* describe relationships in which the Figure is in front of the Ground, and both are located on the same side of the street[33]. The following expression provides an example of this.

---

[33] The one example in which the Figure and Ground were not located on the same side of the street described the location of the car *devant* ('in front of') the bus: this concerns location down the middle portion of the street.

(109) juste **devant** l'hôtel   il y a   *un chariot* (FrenDesc8)
       just   **in front of** the hotel there is a trolley

Speakers recruited *en face de* to encode location in similar measure (22 occurrences; see table 7). Our analysis of the lounge room scene data indicated that speakers made preferential use of this spatial item to encode relationships of distance. This finding, however, is not corroborated by the street-scene data: just four of the 22 occurrences of *en face de* encode relationships of distance. By 'relationship of distance', we mean a relationship in which the Figure is located on the opposite side of the street to the Ground. These four occurrences occur in three locative expressions. In each of these three expressions the speaker signals the distance between the two objects, thereby eliminating the reading of Figure/Ground proximity. This is shown in the example below, which features two occurrences of *en face de* to encode a relationship of distance. Note that both occurrences refer to the same Figure/Ground relationship.

(110) *ensuite la femme..*   *se trouve sur le trottoir en face du chariot..*
       then the woman..   is found on the footpath opposite the trolley..
       sur le trottoir de droite   *donc elle est <u>en face du chariot</u>..*
       on the footpath of right   so she is <u>opposite the trolley</u>..
       elle est devant le café   (FrenDesc10)
       she is in front of the café
       'then the woman.. is on the footpath opposite the trolley.. on the right footpath so she is <u>opposite the trolley</u>.. she is in front of the café'

The gesture shown above synchronises with the second occurrence of *en face de* in the locative expression; no such directional gesture accompanies the first use of the item. Notice how the gesture not only indicates the distance between the Figure and the Ground, but also the fact that the two objects are on the left- and right-hand sides of the street respectively. A very similar use of gesture is noted in the two other examples which recruit *en face de* to encode relationships of distance. Both these locative expressions are uttered by the one speaker, and the first is shown below.

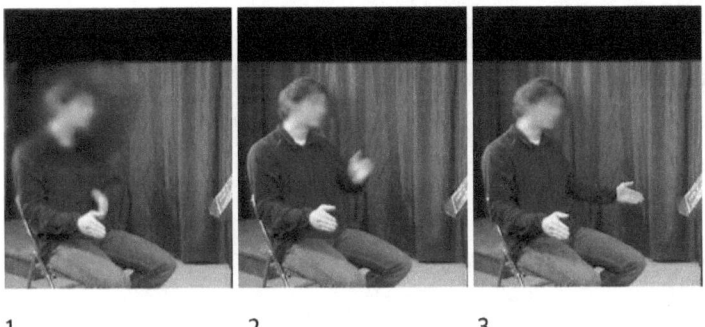

1　　　　　　　　2　　　　　　　　3

(111)　*et* **en face de**　　*cette boîte à lettres..*　　*donc* **de l'autre côte**
　　　　and **opposite**　　this post-office box..　　so **on the other side**
　　　　de la rue..　　　　*i' y a le chariot*　　　　*pour faire les courses*
　　　　of the street..　　　there's the trolley　　　　to do the shopping
　　　　(FrenDesc11)

The speaker in example (111) clarifies the use of *en face de* with *de l'autre côté de la rue* ('on the other side of the street'): this suggests the distance between the Figure and the Ground. In addition to this he makes a pronounced, arc-like trajectory with his left hand, which rises from the right-hand side of gesture space and moves to the left (see stills 1-3 above). This gesture trajectory suggests the distance between the post-office box and the shopping trolley, and also provides the directional specification that the *autre côté* ('other side') is on the left-hand side of picture (as viewed by the speaker). The final use of *en face de* to encode a relationship of distance occurs in the example below.

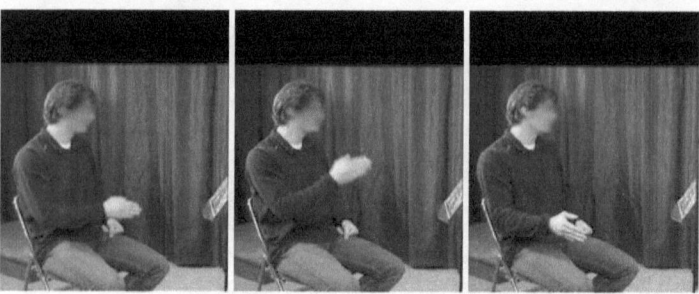

(112) −onc en face de   cette cabine téléphonique   i' y a une voiture
       so   opposite   this telephone booth   there's a car
       (FrenDesc11)

The stills above show how the speaker arcs his hand over to the right from an initial position on the left-hand side of gesture space. In doing so, he indicates that the Figure and Ground are located on separate sides of the street. Moreover, he also identifies the particular side of the street upon which each object is located: hence, the telephone booth is on the left-hand side of the street, while the car is on the right-hand side.

Examples (110)–(112) are the three locative expressions in which *en face de* encodes a relationship in which the Figure is on the opposite side of the street to the Ground. In these three expressions, the two speakers who utter them use gesture to express the distance separating the Figure and Ground. The gestural expression of this information highlights its status as newsworthy in context (McNeill 1992). Its salience is explained by the fact that speakers more commonly use *en face de* to encode relationships of proximity in the street-scene data: this type of use accounts for 17 of the 18 remaining occurrences of *en face de*[34].

---

[34] The final occurrence of *en face de* locates the bar in relation to the cinema. This is unlike our other examples, because it is ambiguous between a reading of proximity and distance. We have therefore left it aside in our analysis of *en face de* here.

(113) la cabine téléphonique.. **en face de** la boulangerie (FrenDesc2)
the telephone booth.. **in front of** the bakery
(114) la cabine téléphonique est euh.. **devant** la boulangerie (FrenDesc6)
the telephone booth is uh.. **in front of** the bakery

In (113) *en face de* encodes the Figure's location in relation to the intrinsic front of a proximate Ground (see picture extract above). The use of *en face de* to encode such relationships of proximity means that there is semantic overlap with *devant* ('in front of'), as highlighted by example (114). These two locative expressions suggest that both *devant* and *en face de* can encode the same relationships of proximity along a frontal axis.

In examples (110)–(112) we showed that speakers used gesture to express distance information relating to uses of *en face de*. However, speakers do not routinely gesture when *en face de* encodes relationships of proximity, which appears to be the default case in descriptions of the street scene. The use of gesture thus serves to eliminate this default interpretation of the spatial item.

Strikingly, speakers frequently used *en face de* to encode relationships of proximity in descriptions of the street scene (17 occurrences), but not in descriptions of the lounge room scene (two occurrences). One potential reason for this is that the default interpretation of the spatial item fluctuates as a function of the space described. Hence, within the context of a larger-scale external space such as a street, *en face de* generally encodes relationships of proximity. In contrast, within the context of smaller-scale internal spaces such as lounge rooms, it encodes relationships of distance. Another explanation is that speakers used *en face de* to encode location relative to a building's *face* ('front') in descriptions of the street scene. This is confirmed by the data: 15 of the 17 occurrences of *en face de* which encode relationships of proximity localise the Figure in relation to the front of a building. This therefore helps to explain the discrepancy in our results for the lounge room and street scene descriptions.

As in descriptions of the lounge room scene, we noted that French speakers made frequent reference to the foreground of the picture in their descriptions of the street scene. All ten French describers referred to this sub-section of the visual stimulus, resulting in a total of 22 lexical references: this includes twenty-one uses of **au** *premier plan* ('in the foreground') and one of **en** *premier plan* ('in the foreground'). Seven of the ten speakers executed representational gestures for *premier plan* ('foreground') when encoding the location of the bus in the picture. These gestures can be divided into three subtypes: those which reference the frontal axis, those which reference the lateral axis, and those which reference both axes.

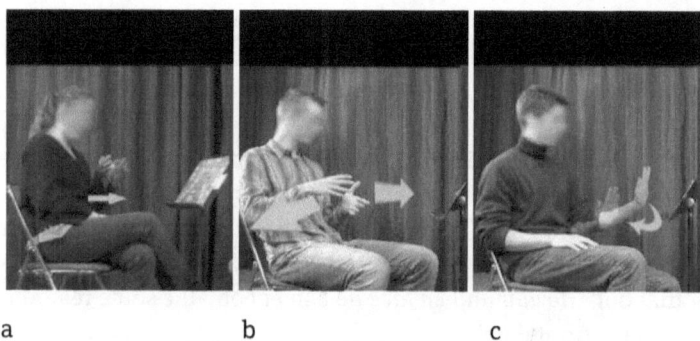

a　　　　　　　　　b　　　　　　　　　c

The gestures above reveal that speakers attend to both the frontal and lateral axes when conceptualising foregrounds, with different levels of attention paid to each axis. The gesture in still 'a' moves forward and away from the speaker, thus targeting the frontal axis exclusively. In still 'b' the speaker's left hand moves across to the left and his right hand across to the right: these directed movements are indicated by the arrows on the still. This particular speaker therefore targets the lateral axis in his gestural representation of the foreground. Finally, still 'c' shows how the speaker attends to both the frontal and lateral axes in gesture: his left hand moves across to the right and in towards himself in one continuous motion. Therefore, while the lexical item *premier plan* foregrounds the centrality of the frontal axis, the gestures in 'b' and 'c' reveal the importance of the lateral axis to the lexically-encoded concept. These gestures cast further light on the complementary interaction of the frontal and lateral axes in spatial conceptualisation.

5.5.2 The use of back-encoding items

Speakers made far less use of back-encoding items than they did of front-encoding ones (see table 7). This is explained, in large part, by the stimulus picture itself: the majority of the objects which speakers were required to locate were positioned in front of intrinsically-oriented landmarks. Thus, the car is in front of the bank, the trolley is in front of the hotel, and the post office box is in front of the youth hostel. In contrast, no objects were positioned behind intrinsically-oriented landmarks.

Speakers made reference to the background of the picture, but such references occurred less frequently than references to the picture's foreground. Once again, this is explained to some extent by the particular objects which speakers were required to locate. While at least six of these 14 objects are in the foreground of the picture (the bird, the trolley, the lady, the café, the bus and the post-office box), just three are in the background (the cinema, the pharmacy and the bar). Moreover, the way in which speakers lexically referenced the background differed from how they referenced the foreground. For example, three of the four uses of *au fond* ('at the back') were unclear as to whether the speaker was referring to the background of the picture or to the back end of the street (i.e. the more distal end in relation to the speaker's location). Ultimately, the distinction is unimportant because both of these Grounds occupy the same, distal space along the frontal axis that extends out from the observer. Speakers also used the sequential item *bout* ('end') to reference the background. *Bout*, like *end*, can be interpreted in two ways. Firstly, it can be understood as one of two points that marks the length of a street: hence, a street has two *bouts* ('ends'). However, when used in the singular, *le bout* is generally understood as the more distal of these points in relation to an oriented observer: this equates to the background of the picture as far as the present visual stimulus is concerned. Therefore, while speakers encoded specific reference to the foreground of the picture, they referred to its background in a less direct manner.

5.5.3 The use of directionally non-specific items

There were 22 occurrences of directionally non-specific items in the data, with *entre* ('between') accounting for nine of these. For three of these nine uses of *entre*, speakers executed gestures which marked the locations of the two Ground objects along the frontal axis. This shows that speakers do not merely attend to establishing the location of the lexical Figure in locative expressions:

they also attend to establishing the locations of the lexical Grounds. This is revealed in the following example.

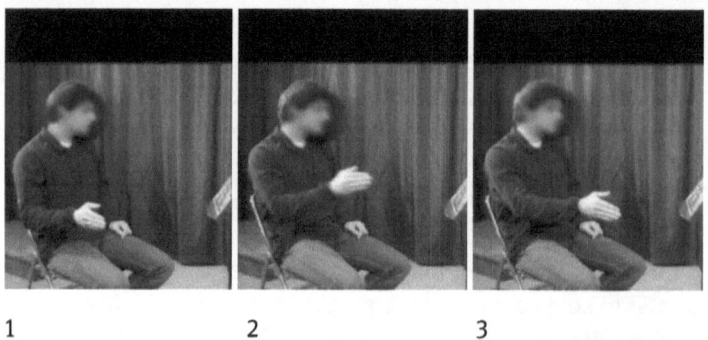

1　　　　　　　　2　　　　　　　　3

(115)　　de l'autre côté du trottoir　　　　donc　　entre le café
　　　　on the other side of the footpath　so　　between the café
　　　　et l'auberge de jeunesse [...]　　　　　　　(FrenDesc11)
　　　　and the youth hostel [...]

The stills for example (115) show the speaker's right hand just after he has marked the location of the café (still 1), its subsequent progression up and forward (still 2), and its marking of the youth hostel's location (still 3). This indication of the Ground objects' locations in gesture with the use of *entre* was also noted in descriptions of the lounge room scene (cf. section 5.3.3). These gestures reveal two things. Firstly, they show that speakers establish the locations of lexical Ground objects in gesture. These locations are not encoded in the co-occurring speech. Secondly, they reveal that although these objects are lexically encoded as Grounds, they are simultaneously conceptualised as Figures: this is because speakers establish their locations in gesture space. Therefore, as stated previously (in section 5.2.3), one object can simultaneously fulfil different semantic roles in speech and in gesture.

There were six uses of *à côté de* ('next to') to express location along the frontal axis. However, five of these were due to one speaker: uses of the preposition were therefore not widespread. Nevertheless, this provides another example of how speakers use gesture to express salient, unlexicalised directional information.

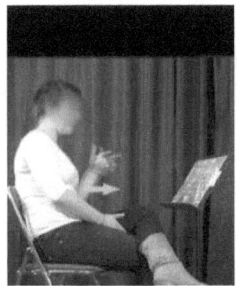

(116) *donc à droite*   *au premier plan*   *il y a un café*
       so on the right   in the foreground   there is a café
       à côté de ce café *il y a <u>une dame</u>* [...]   (FrenDesc5)
       next to this cafe   there is <u>a lady</u>

The still above shows the location of the speaker's index as she points to the location associated with the café. The superimposed image shows how the speaker's hand moves forward to designate the lady's location, thus clarifying the role of the frontal axis in the use of *à côté de* ('next to'). The lexical phrase which accompanies this forward movement is underlined in the example. Note that the directional information is not concurrently encoded in speech.

A small variety of other spatial items completes the range of directionally non-specific items in table 7. These include *vers* ('towards'; five examples) and *près de* ('near'; two examples). This restricted range owes to the speakers' preferential use of sequence-encoding items to encode location along the frontal axis (see section 5.5.4 below).

5.5.4 The use of sequence-encoding items

The semantic category of sequence-encoding items was second only to front-encoding items in terms of frequency of use. Sequence-encoding items are neutral as far as directional information is concerned. Some, such as the prepositional pair *avant* ('before') and *après* ('after'), conflate temporal and spatial concerns (Berthonneau 1993: 41). Vandeloise (1986) explains that *avant* and *après* encode static location by appealing to the idea of motion. Hence, a Figure can be *avant* ('before') or *après* ('after') a Ground when location is conceptualised in terms of a trajectory. Moreover, this sequential distribution of Figure and Ground needs to be established in relation to a third point in space (Vandeloise 1986), which may or may not be the speaker's location (Berthonneau 1993). That is, a Figure can only be *avant* ('before') or *après* ('after') a Ground if its location is considered in relation to another point of reference. Consider the following excerpt from the street scene.

The picture depicts the bus as an entity in motion which is heading towards the end of the street (from our perspective). Taking the bus as our point of reference, we may say that the bakery is *avant* ('before') the pharmacy: this is because the bakery will be encountered prior to the pharmacy in the forward trajectory of the bus. In contrast, if the bus were instead heading towards the front of the picture from the back of the street, the pharmacy would now be *avant* ('before') the bakery: this is because it would be sequentially prior to the bakery when considered in relation to the moving bus. Hence, understanding locative relationships encoded by *avant* and *après* requires establishing direction in relation to an oriented point of origin (i.e. an origo). In the following example the speaker constitutes this point of reference, and directional information emerges in gesture alone.

(117) *après la boulangerie*   *une pharmacie* (FrenDesc7)
       after the bakery   a pharmacy

By moving his left hand forward (stills 1–3) the speaker indicates that he is conceptualising location along a frontal axis which has its origo at the speaker. Secondly, he reveals the direction in which this trajectory is conceptualised: it progresses forward and away from his location in front of the picture. This information is crucial to determining the location of the pharmacy, and it appears in gesture only. Moreover, the speaker does not lexicalise this directional progression in the preceding locative expressions: gesture alone carries the directional charge.

Of the ten occurrences of *après*, five are accompanied by gestures which express this type of directional information. In four of these, this information was not concurrently encoded in speech. Hence, gestures can carry an unlexicalised directional charge which semantically complements lexicalised sequences.

In contrast to the ten occurrences of *après* ('after'), there were only two incidences of *avant* ('before'). This reflects a tendency to establish location out towards the back of the picture, as opposed to back in towards the foreground. Nevertheless, the following example shows how gesture expresses directional information relating to a use of *avant*.

(118) *la boîte postale*   *elle est..*   <u>*encore* avant le..</u>   *avant la voiture*
       the letter box   it is...   <u>further</u> before the..   before the car
       (FrenDesc2)

In (118) the movement of the right hand in towards the speaker establishes the frontal axis as salient. More precisely, it indicates direction along a frontal axis which has its origo at the speaker. The speaker is oriented so that she faces the spatial scene: hence, a Figure which is *avant* ('before') a Ground is necessarily closer to the front of the picture. This directional information is not concurrently encoded in speech.

Speakers also use other sequence encoders, such as *au début de* ('at the beginning of'), to specify location along the frontal axis. The use of such items is potentially triggered by the stimulus picture itself, which depicts the shops as part of two linear extensions (i.e. the sides of the street) which head into the background. The left side of the picture is shown below.

In addition to positing beginning and end points to these row-like extensions, speakers also recruited numerical encoders, such as *premier* ('first') and *deuxième* ('second'), to express location. An example of this occurs in the following locative expression.

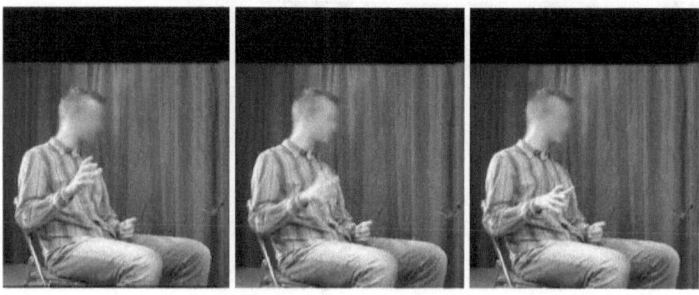

(119)　　*à droite tout à droite*　　　　　　　*t'as*
　　　　　on the right right over on the right　you've got
　　　　　un premier bâtiment [...]　　　　　(FrenDesc8)
　　　　　a　first　building

Here, the speaker uses gesture to establish the starting point of the sequence encoded by *premier*. The execution of the gesture at a point close to the speaker's torso suggests the Figure's location in the foreground of the picture. This sets the scene for a locative sequence which extends forward along a frontal axis defined by the intrinsically-oriented speaker. The subsequent locative expression confirms this interpretation.

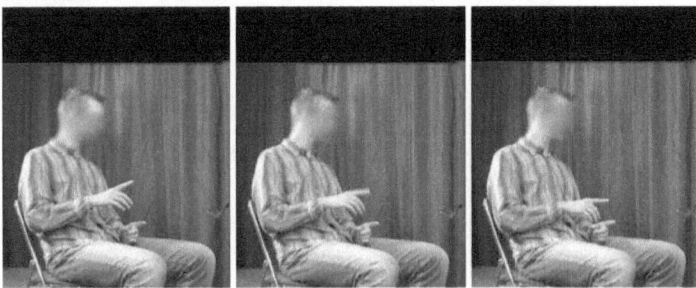

(120)   *ensuite un restaurant* (FrenDesc8)
        then a restaurant

The speaker recruits the sequential encoder *ensuite* ('then') and simultaneously executes a pointing gesture (see stills above). This gesture expresses unlexicalised directional information by showing that the locative sequence extends forward in relation to the speaker's front. Hence, while the speaker encodes a sequential progression in speech, he expresses the directional nature of this progression in gesture. The information which appears in the two modalities is motivated by the common goal of establishing the Figure's location in space, and each modality contributes a different strand of information to achieve this goal. Overall, speakers used gesture alone to express direction relating to five (42%) of the 12 occurrences of numerical values in the data.

5.5.5   The overall use of gesture with directionally non-specific and sequence-encoding items

We examined all uses of sequence-encoding items within the context of the overall locative expressions in which they occurred. In doing so, we aimed to determine whether speakers provided directional information relating to lexically-encoded locative sequences. Four instances of how this occurs in gesture alone are provided in examples (117)–(120) above. We observed the same analytical conditions as outlined for the English data in section 5.4.5. Hence, we understood that salient directional gestures do not always temporally align with sequence-encoding items, and may instead occur at other moments in the overall locative expression. We also discarded four examples which were ambiguous expressions of directional information. This left us with 38 occurrences of sequence-encoding items for analysis. Speakers expressed directional information relating to 23 (61%) of these 38 lexicalised sequences. Again, we observed whether this information was expressed in speech, in gesture, or in both modalities. Graph 4 below presents our findings.

Graph 4: How speakers specify directional information concerning the frontal axis for occurrences of sequence-encoding items

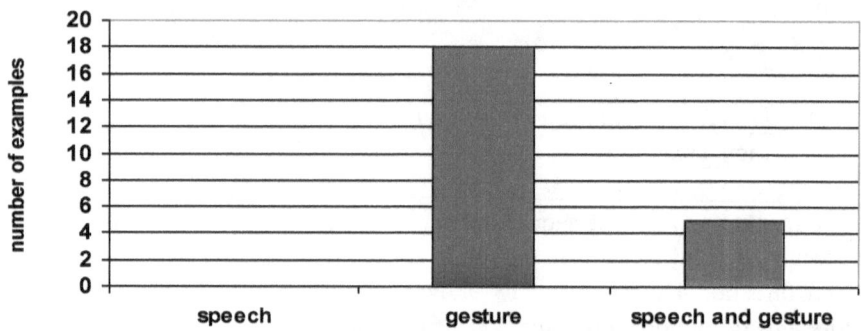

Our results indicate that speakers used gesture alone to express directional information in 18 (78%) of the 23 examples studied. In contrast, speech alone never carried the directional charge, and both speech and gesture expressed direction in just five examples. This keenly suggests that gestures play a clear role in expressing unlexicalised directional information. Nevertheless, it is worthwhile noting that speakers did not express directional information at all for 15 (39%) of the 38 occurrences of sequence-encoding items. This potentially suggests that speaker may have believed such information to be contextually inferable and not requiring expression. A similar total was noted in the English data: speakers provided directional specification for 25 (69%) of the 36 occurrences of sequence-encoding items. In contrast however, English speakers most frequently used *both* speech and gesture to express this information. A fuller comparison of these results will be presented in section 5.8 below.

A slightly different picture emerges when we consider directionally non-specific items. As shown in table 7, there were 22 occurrences of such items in the data. Speakers provided directional information concerning the frontal axis for 11 (50%) of these. An additional four (which would therefore have brought the total to 15) were considered ambiguous and not included in the following analysis. It is worthwhile noting that three of these four examples were due to one speaker: this means that ambiguity of interpretation was not associated with many describers. Of the 11 pertinent examples, gesture expressed directional information on four occasions (36%), speech on one occasion (9%), and both speech and gesture on six occasions (55%).

Graph 5: How speakers specify directional information concerning the frontal axis for occurrences of directionally non-specific items

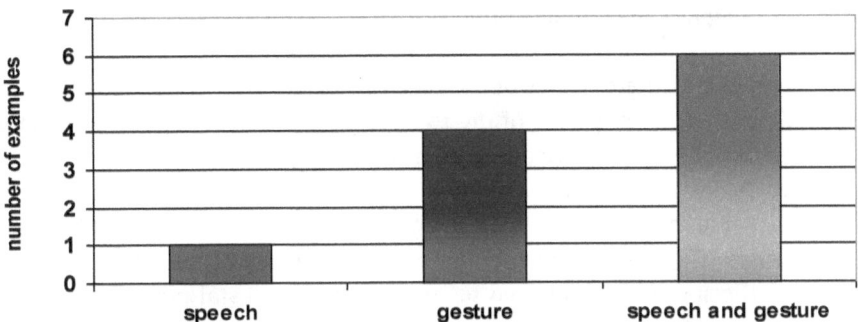

Due to the small number of examples under analysis we cannot draw solid conclusions here. Nevertheless, these results are in line with those found for the English data: that is, speakers most frequently express this type of directional information in both speech and gesture. Furthermore, when just one modality is used, speakers favour gesture over speech. Interestingly, these results diverge from the pattern noted for sequence-encoding items in French (cf. graph 4): this pattern indicated a large preference for the use of gesture alone as opposed to both speech and gesture. Further investigation into directionally non-specific items in French is required before proper comparisons can be made, however. For instance, four of the six examples in which both speech and gesture were used were occurrences of *vers* ('towards'). This means that there was a not a large variety of directionally non-specific items which triggered the use of both speech and gesture to express directional information. Nevertheless, it is important to note that in all of our analyses the use of speech alone is consistently poorly represented, and it is always the least frequent way in which directional information pertaining to directionally non-specific and sequence-encoding items is expressed. This indicates that speakers favour gesture to express this type of complementary information.

5.6 Comparison and discussion

In this section we compare and discuss our findings concerning descriptions of the two pictures. We begin by comparing the English descriptions of the lounge room and the street scene. This same process is then observed for the French data. Following this, we provide a comparative discussion of the English and French results for both stimulus pictures.

5.6.1 Comparison of lounge room and street scene descriptions in English

Speakers made different uses of lexical items to encode location along the frontal axis in their descriptions of the two scenes. The most noticeable difference was the use of sequence-encoding items in descriptions of the street scene. This reflects the visual style of the picture: drawn so that the street runs away from the speaker along the frontal axis, location is readily conceptualised in terms of a sequence. This sequence generally has its *beginning* at the point most proximate to the speaker's front, and its *end* at the most distal point forward along this frontal axis. The ordering of entities in terms of numerical values (*first, second*, etc) or temporal encoders (*before, after, then*, etc) requires the conceptualisation of location within the framework of a motion event: for example, an object can only sequentially precede or be *before* another if there is a conceptualised trajectory along a path. Speakers used gesture to express the direction of sequential progressions in relation to an origo. Individual examples highlighted how this occurred for uses of *then* (example 103), *end* (example 104) and *after* (example 105). These gestures also accompanied directionally non-specific items, such as *down* (examples 93 and 96) and *past* (example 99). The directional information which gesture expresses in these examples is pivotal to localising the Figure, and it is not concurrently encoded in the lexical expression. Gesture's contribution in such a context is to specify direction along the frontal axis in relation to an origo.

While the preposition *(in) between* was the second most frequently occurring item in descriptions of the lounge room scene (seven of 53 items; 13%), its recruitment in descriptions of the street scene was comparatively less (four of 157 items; 3%). This reflects the wider range of lexical items which speakers recruited to encode location in descriptions of the latter scene. For example, speakers made use of a semantic sub-category, 'sequence-encoding items', which was not noted in descriptions of the lounge room, and they also recruited items which appealed to the idea of motion (i.e. *up, down, past*). These differences are likely due to the different types of space described, as well as to the different levels of attention which the pictures draw to the frontal axis. Hence, the prominent frontal axis of the street scene is a trigger for Path-focused items such as *down* and *up*, whereas the box-like enclosure of the lounge room is less easily conceptualised as an extended path. Furthermore, motion events are more salient to external spaces such as streets than they are to smaller, internal spaces like lounge rooms (Tutton 2013). This accounts for the presence of motion-encoding items in descriptions of the street scene, but not in descriptions of the lounge room scene.

Analysis of the street scene discourse also revealed that speakers executed representational gestures for *in front (of)* when they featured as Ground in the locative expression. These gestures involved the speaker manually indicating their own intrinsic front. If we now look at data from the lounge room scene, there are four instances in which the speaker occurs as Ground when expressing location along the frontal axis. On all four occasions, speakers also make gestural reference to their intrinsic front. However, the three speakers responsible for these examples also use gesture to express location along the frontal axis when they are *not* encoded as the lexical Ground: hence, no conclusion can be drawn as far as the lounge room scene is concerned. Nevertheless, the data from the street scene descriptions suggest that the speaker's role as lexical Ground and origo may trigger the use of self-indicating gestures. There are several arguments which support this thesis. Firstly, the human body is paramount to the way in which English speakers describe and understand location. Hence, when providing directions to someone on the street, we orient ourselves in the direction of the location targeted and gesture accordingly. In doing so, we show that our instructions are based upon the current location and orientation of our body, which serves as the origo for the trajectory described. When the speaker fills the semantic role of Ground in addition to that of origo, the salience of the body as a directional instrument is augmented. It is this heightened salience of the body's axes which potentially triggers a speaker's use of gesture to indicate their own oriented frontal axis.

5.6.2 Comparison of lounge room and street scene descriptions in French

In contrast to descriptions of the lounge room scene, French speakers recruited 'sequence-encoding items' to encode location in descriptions of the street scene. This same phenomenon was observed in the English-language data, and very likely results from the linear arrangement of landmarks along both sides of the street. Sequence-encoding items do not encode reference to any particular spatial axis, and speakers recurrently expressed salient directional information in gesture. Examples from the data revealed how such gestures accompanied the use of *avant* ('before'), *après* ('after') and *premier* ('first').

French speakers most frequently recruited front-encoding items in descriptions of both scenes. Recurrent use was made of both *devant* ('in front of') and *en face de* ('in front of'/'opposite'), and there were examples in which speakers used both of these prepositions to encode the same Figure/Ground relationships along the frontal axis. However, the results for the lounge room scene indicated a preference for *devant* when encoding relationships of proximity, and *en face de* when encoding relationships of distance. Nevertheless, readings of proximity and distance were both feasible for *en face de*. Speakers signalled a desired reading of distance by using different strategies. Firstly, they suggested the different locations of the Figure and the Ground in the foreground and background of the lounge room scene. As far as descriptions of the street scene are concerned, speakers expressed the distance between the Figure and the Ground in gesture.

An important contrast was noted in how speakers used *en face de* in descriptions of the two scenes. While this spatial item recurrently encoded relationships of distance in lounge room scene discourse, it most frequently encoded relationships of proximity in descriptions of the street scene. This is an unexpected result for which three possible explanations exist. Firstly, as far as the lounge room scene is concerned, speakers recruited *en face de* to describe location along a frontal axis which was parallel to their own as they viewed the picture. In contrast, speakers used *en face de* to encode location along a frontal axis which was perpendicular to their own in descriptions of the street scene. The contrasting use of *en face de* is therefore potentially linked to the orientation of the frontal axis described. A second explanation is that the size of the surrounding space determines the way in which speakers use the preposition. Hence, speakers may be more likely to use *en face de* in the sense of *devant* ('in front of') when encoding location in larger, open spaces like streets. In contrast, a reading which approaches that of the English *opposite* may be more likely when speakers use *en face de* to describe location in smaller, container-like spaces like lounge rooms. Finally, we showed that 15 uses of *en face de* in descriptions of the street scene encoded the Figure's location in relation to a building's façade. One meaning of the French noun *face* is the 'front' of a building. Hence, speakers may have used *en face de* to establish reference to this side of a building, thus encoding a relationship of proximity as opposed to one of distance.

5.6.3 Comparison of English and French descriptions of the lounge room scene

Both French and English speakers recruited front-encoding items in very similar measure. These items accounted for 30 (57%) of the 53 used by English speakers, and 35 (57%) of the 61 used by French speakers. While English speakers frequently recruited *in front of* to encode location, French speakers used *devant* and *en face de* with almost equal frequency. Speakers signalled the desired interpretation of *en face de* as a relationship of distance through the lexical and/or gestural expression of distance information. Such uses of *en face de* would be encoded by *opposite* in English – yet no uses of *opposite* were noted in the English data. Instead, English speakers encoded relationships of distance with directionally non-specific items, such as *far* and *(in) between*. For five of the seven uses of *(in) between*, speakers deployed gestures which expressed the respective locations of the two Ground objects along the frontal axis. This brought to light a particularly important way in which speakers use gesture to express unlexicalised directional information. French speakers only made two uses of *entre* ('between'), but both were accompanied by the same Ground-marking gestures noted for English *between*. This parity in gestural behaviour suggests the similar semantics of the two prepositions.

Overall, directionally non-specific items accounted for 17 (32%) of the 53 items in the English data, as opposed to ten (16%) of the 61 in the French data. These items were also recruited by a wider range of speakers in the English descriptions: six English describers made use of them, as opposed to three French speakers who did so. This discrepancy can be explained by the different ways in which speakers referenced the back of the visually-represented space. Whereas English speakers recruited the directionally non-specific item *far* to refer to location at the back of the lounge room, French speakers used back-encoding phrases such as *au fond de* ('at the back of'). The numbers re-enforce this observation: back-encoding items account for 14 (23%) of the 61 items in the French data, as opposed to six (11%) of the 53 in the English data.

The analysis also revealed that representational gestures for *foreground* and *premier plan* included examples in which both groups of speakers indicated proximity to their front, as well as extension along the lateral axis. These results show how the locative information expressed in both modalities is interconnected, and that similar lexical semantics yields similar uses of representational gestures.

Finally, analysis of the English data established a connection between the frontal and lateral axes. Speakers assigned fronts to objects using the intrinsic frontal properties of other laterally-aligned objects. A potential example of this in French is provided below.

(121) devant la télévision et le tapis   tu as une balle (FrenDesc3)
       in front of the television and the rug you have a ball

The speaker in (121) encodes the ball's location *devant* ('in front of') the television and the rug. Whereas the television has an intrinsic frontal surface, the rug does not. How then can the speaker posit a collective frontal property for these two objects? There are two feasible explanations. The first is that the speaker is not making reference to the television's intrinsic front. Rather, she has attributed a common frontal surface to the two objects through the mirror-like rotation of her own front as she views the picture. The second explanation is that the television's intrinsic front has been mapped onto the rug, which is the neighbouring item along the lateral axis. One factor which favours this interpretation is that *la télévision* ('the television') precedes *le tapis* ('the rug') in the lexical expression. This invites the possibility that the speaker initially references the television's front before conceptually extending it to include the neighbouring, non-oriented item. Although this particular example leaves room for discussion, the two English examples which we presented in section 5.2.1.1 are straightforward: speakers clearly attribute frontal properties via a process other than 180-degree rotation. This results from the alignment of the Ground objects along a lateral axis, thus highlighting the interaction of the frontal and lateral axes in the determination of spatial properties (cf. Lyons 1977: 694).

5.6.4 Comparison of English and French descriptions of the street scene

Both English and French speakers used back-encoding items in small measure. These accounted for 12 (9%) of the 135 items in the English-language data, and for eight (5%) of the 146 items in the French-language data. In contrast, there was a substantial difference in the frequency with which English and French speakers recruited front-encoding items. This category accounted for 72 (49%) of the 146 items in French, as opposed to 39 (29%) of the 135 in English. This comparative result is presented in the table below.

Tab. 8: Frequency of front-encoding items in street-scene descriptions

	English	French
Front-encoding items	39 (29%)	72 (49%)
Non-front-encoding items	96 (71%)	74 (51%)
Total	135	146

This difference between English and French speakers is partly explained by the recurrent use of *devant* and *en face de* to encode location in French. For example, nine out of ten French speakers used either *devant* or *en face de* to encode the location of the telephone booth, while just four out of ten English speakers used a front-encoding item in the same locative context. Moreover, while eight of the ten French speakers used *devant* or *en face de* to encode the trolley's location, no English speaker used a front-encoding item to do so. Instead, English speakers favored directionally non-specific items.

(122) *on the left hand side of the street.. um.. sort of about* **halfway up** *it.. um there's a trolley* (EngDesc5)

There are no French equivalents of *down* or *up* to encode location along the frontal axis. With this is mind, French speakers are perhaps drawn to encoding location in relation to the intrinsic frontal surface of reference objects: this would explain the productive recruitment of *devant* and *en face de* in the data. Overall, English describers employed directionally non-specific items more frequently than their French-speaking counterparts, as shown in the following table.

Tab. 9: Frequency of directionally non-specific items in street-scene descriptions

	English	French
Directionally non-specific items	45 (33%)	22 (15%)
Other items	90 (67%)	124 (85%)
Total	135	146

Therefore, whereas French speakers used front-encoding items more frequently than English speakers, the inverse was true as far as directionally non-specific items were concerned. These differences ultimately balance each other out.

The two groups of speakers made very similar use of sequence-encoding items, with members of this category accounting for 39 (29%) of the 135 items in English, and 44 (30%) of the 146 in French. Both English and French describers used gesture to express the direction of lexically-encoded sequences in relation to an origo. Such information is pivotal to the clear expression of the Figure's location, and numerous examples revealed how speakers expressed this information in gesture alone. However, we noted a difference in the way in which the two groups of speakers expressed this information overall. Whereas English speakers used both speech and gesture in 12 (48%) of the 25 examples analysed, French speakers did so in just five (22%) of 23 examples. This is represented in table 10 below.

Tab. 10: Uses of both speech and gesture to express direction pertaining to sequence-encoding items

	English	French
Both speech and gesture	12 (48%)	5 (22%)
Speech only or gesture only	13 (52%)	18 (78%)
Total	25	23

The difference between the English and French speakers here is partly accounted for by the following explanation. In the English data, there were four examples in which speakers encoded a sequential progression which ran along the entire side of a street, and which therefore concerned multiple successive Figures.

(123)   *like going from front to back.. café* (EngDesc7)

In (123), the sequence encoding phrase *from.. to* encodes location along the entire frontal axis which the speaker attributes to the left-hand side of the street. He encodes the directional progression of this sequence with the nouns *front* and *back*, whilst also indicating these respective areas in gesture space. We suggest that the speaker expresses this directional information in both speech and gesture here because it affects not merely the Figure of this locative expression ('café'), but also those of subsequent expressions. Hence, the directional nature of the sequence is particularly salient. The same use of both speech and gesture to express direction also occurs in the other three examples in which the speaker encodes this type of sequence. In contrast, there are no examples of such sequences in the French data. Therefore, part of the reason for the increased use of the two modalities in the English data appears to be due to this phenomenon.

Our results also showed that gesture allows us a point of access into spatial conceptualisation. One example of this is the gestural reference which speakers made to the lateral axis when encoding foregrounds. While the lexical items *foreground* and *premier plan* place emphasis on the frontal axis, gesture reveals the salience of the lateral axis to the encoded concept. Another example is English speakers' use of gesture to reference their front when they function as Ground in a locative expression. This suggests the crucial role of the speaker in the conceptualisation of directional information, and underscores the speaker's status as both Ground and origo. Whereas the analysis identified 13 examples in which English speakers featured as Ground in a lexical expression, just one such occurrence was noted in the French data. This indicates that French speakers tended to recruit Ground entities which were scene-internal, as opposed to scene-external. As such, future research is required to determine whether French speakers make gestural reference to their fronts in the same manner that our English describers did.

6 Describing location along the lateral axis

This chapter examines how speakers use speech and gesture to express location along the lateral axis. More precisely, it reveals that speakers encode location with lexical items that encode neither left nor right directional information (i.e. *next to* and *à côté de*). In such cases, we show that speakers frequently express this information in gesture alone: this highlights the complementary nature of the two communicative modalities. Additional support for this thesis is provided by an analysis of the prepositions *between* and *entre*. As noted previously (see Chapter 5), these two prepositions can be used to encode location along any horizontal axis (Kemmerer and Tranel 2000). We show that speakers reveal the salience of the lateral axis to individual uses of these prepositions by marking the locations of the Ground objects in gesture space. In addition to providing directional clarification, these gestures also express the unlexicalised locations of the Ground entities. Our analysis therefore argues that gesture plays a pivotal role in the expression of directional information, and that this information is tied to the semantics of lexical spatial items.

6.1 The lateral axis

The lateral axis is horizontal in nature and lies perpendicular to the frontal axis. The common horizontality of the frontal and lateral axes means that there is interconnectivity in terms of how certain spatial properties are conceptualised. Hence, the previous chapter showed that when speakers lexically encode the concept FOREGROUND, they also use gesture to indicate presence along the lateral axis. Moreover, a collective or communal 'front' can be applied to a group of objects which are aligned along a lateral axis. In spite of such interconnectivity however, there are crucial differences which distinguish the lateral axis from the frontal axis. Firstly, an object's left and right can only be ascertained once vertical and frontal properties have been established (Bryant 1998). Secondly, unlike the frontal or vertical axes, the lateral axis is characterised by the frequent symmetry of physical parts at its directional extremes. For example, the left and right sides of intrinsically-oriented entities such as human beings are mirror-like reflections of each other. In contrast to this, fronts and backs, as well as properties at either extremity of the vertical axis, are asymmetrical in nature (Clark 1973; Lyons 1977). A further distinction between the lateral axis and the frontal axis is how English and French speakers attribute spatial properties to a Ground when using a relative frame of reference. In such a spatial context, conferring a front and back distinction typically involves the 180-degree rotation of the viewer's own intrinsically-oriented frontal axis (Levinson 1996: 369–371; 2003b; although see Chapter 5 for an alternative explanation): this results in a mirror-image alignment (*orientation en miroir*; Borillo 1998). However, a speaker's left and right properties do not undergo this 180-degree rotation (see figure 1,chapter 2). Hence, the way in which French and English speakers assign frontal spatial properties when using relative frames of reference differs crucially to how they assign lateral ones.

The non-rotation of left and right when assigning spatial properties possibly reflects the cognitive difficulty of these two directional concepts (Clark 1973). From a developmental perspective, the lateral axis is the most difficult for children to acquire (Piaget and Inhelder in Levinson 2003b). The use of the terms *left* and *right* to designate spatial relationships within a relative frame of reference occurs late in childhood, around the ages of eleven and twelve (Levinson 2003b: 46). Even later in life, adults confuse the left/right distinction (Levinson 2003b: 207). Furthermore, experiments discussed in Bryant (1998: 220–221) show that subjects access the left/right axis at a slower rate than they do the vertical and frontal axes: this indicates that there may be a higher cognitive charge associated with distinguishing lateral direction, as opposed to frontal or vertical direction. Fillmore (1975: 21) explains that recognising left from right is difficult, because there are no easier concepts which can explain these two notions. All of this evidence suggests that distinguishing between left and right is a problematic area of spatial cognition.

In terms of lexical encoding, French and English have few spatial items which express left and right direction. This lexical weakness is most prominently highlighted by the absence of any verbs which encode either direction in French or English[35]. In contrast, numerous verbs encode direction along the frontal and vertical axes: for example *reverse/reculer* and *advance/avancer* for the frontal axis, as well as *ascend/monter* and *lower/baisser* for the vertical axis. An overview of items in both English and French which encode a specific direction along each of the three spatial axes is presented in table 11 below.

---

35 This was an observation made by Daniele van de Vèlde during a paper given by the author at the SILEXA workshop, Université Lille 3, France, January 2008. I thank her for this most productive remark.

Tab. 11: English and French lexical items which encode a specific direction along a spatial axis

Axis	Lexical verbs	Non-verbs
Vertical	ascend, rise, arise, raise, escalate, sprout, mount, scale, (up-)lift, increase, boost, skyrocket, soar, raise, descend, fall, lower, sink, dive, drop, decline, slump	high, up, above, over, low, down, below, beneath, under(neath)
	(re-)monter, augmenter, descendre, baisser, tomber, dégringoler, chuter, s'effondrer, plonger, décroître, (re-)lever, (re-)hausser, soulever, hisser	en haut (de), en bas (de), sous, au-dessous (de), en dessous de, au-dessus de, dessus
Frontal	advance, forward, further, lead, progress, regress, reverse, recoil	in front (of), forward(s), ahead, onward(s), back, backwards, behind
	(s')avancer, progresser, mener, régresser, (se) reculer	devant, en face de, au-devant, à l'avance, en avant, derrière, en arrière, au fond (de)
Lateral	—	All are combinations with *right/left*. e.g *to/on the left (of)*, *to/on the right (of)*. Two exceptions: *port* and *starboard*
	—	All are combinations with *droite/gauche*. e.g *sur la droite (de)*, *sur la gauche (de)* Two exceptions: *bâbord* and *tribord*

As shown in table 11 above, English almost exclusively uses items *right* and *left* to encode a specific direction along the lateral axis. The two exceptions to this are the items *port* and *starboard*, which encode the left- and right-hand sides of a transport vessel. The same is true of French: right and left direction is encoded exclusively by the items *droite* and *gauche* with the exception of *bâbord* (port) and *tribord* (starboard). In contrast, a range of lexical possibilities exists for the two other axes, with the vertical axis having a particularly large range of verbs which encode direction towards each axial extremity.

This lexical deficiency, coupled with the cognitive difficulty of distinguishing between left and right, has potential ramifications for how speakers encode location along the lateral axis. Firstly, as far as the restricted range of left-and right-encoding items is concerned, speakers may make productive use of directionally non-specific lexemes and express direction in gesture. Secondly, given the cognitive difficulty associated with the concepts LEFT and RIGHT, speakers may use gesture to assist spatial conceptualisation. The analysis that follows concentrates on the first of these two questions, by examining how speakers use directionally non-specific items to encode location along the lateral axis. As explained earlier in our work (see Chapter 5), a 'directionally non-specific' item does not encode a particular direction along a spatial axis: for example, *next to*. *Next to* encodes the adjacency of a Figure to a Ground, but does not indicate the direction of the former to the latter. In contrast, items which *do* encode a specific direction along the lateral axis are *to the left* and *to the right*. The second question, which concerns the use of gesture to assist spatial cognition, warrants a full investigation of its own in a separate study. Responding to this question involves more than comparing, for example, whether speakers gesture more when encoding left and right information than they do when encoding front or back information. Other factors, such as the frame of reference used in the encoded directional relationship, need to be considered. Hence, an analysis of how speakers gesture when using left- and right-encoding items will only be addressed briefly in what follows. The point of this brief analysis will be to examine the role of gesture in revealing information about viewpoint, perspective and origo.

As in the preceding chapter, our investigation looks at the data for each language and picture separately. A comparative discussion of results is presented at the end of the chapter, in section 6.6.

6.2 Lounge room scene – English descriptions

This section begins by presenting the lexical items which English speakers used to encode location along the lateral axis in descriptions of the lounge room scene. Table 12 below brings these items together, using the semantic criterion of direction as a category divider. The first three categories are for items which encode left direction, right direction and centre direction. The fourth category accounts for directionally non-specific items, while the fifth presents sequence-encoding items. As in our analyses for the frontal axis (see Chapter 5), distinctions between items are made in order to highlight patterns in the data which are conducive to a clear analysis. For example, speakers made six uses of *to the right of* (column 'right-encoding items', row A) and four uses of the non-Ground introducing *to the right* (column 'right-encoding items', row D). By maintaining these two sub-categories instead of a more generic one that subsumes both variants, a direct comparison can be made between the uses of *to the right of* and the left-encoding equivalent *to the left of* (column 'left-encoding items', row A).

Tab. 12: Lexical items, lateral axis, English descriptions of the lounge room scene

	Left-encoding items	N	Right-encoding items	N	Centre-encoding items	N
A	to the left of	6	to the right of	6	in the middle (of)	7
B	left-hand (modifier)	5	right-hand (modifier)	7		
C	on the left	3	on the right	3		
D	to the left	2	to the right	4		
E	on your left (side)	2				
F	OTHER left of (1) on its left (1) to your left (1)	3				
G			to my right	1		
H			right (modifier)	2		
I	TOTAL	21		23		7
	Directionally non-specific items	N	Sequence-encoding items	N		
J	next to	26	then	5		
K	(in) between	5				
L	OTHER beside (1) closer to (1) on the other side of (1) further across from (1) towards (1) in the middle of[36] (1)	6				
M	TOTAL	37		5		

---

36 This use of *in the middle of* is synonymous with *between*. It is therefore counted as a directionally non-specific item as opposed to one which encodes centre direction.

As far as items encoding left direction are concerned (column 'left-encoding items', table 12), six sub-categories are proposed. The first (row A) is comprised of uses of *to the left of*, which was the most frequently recruited item. The second sub-category is made up of occurrences of the noun phrase *left-hand* when used as a modifier: for example, *left-hand side*. The third and fourth sub-categories account for uses of *on the left* and *to the left* respectively, while the fifth accounts for the two occurrences of *on your left (side)*. The sixth and final sub-category ('OTHER') collates the three remaining items which encode left-directional information. These latter phrases all include the nominal *left*.

Our table presents the different lexical phrases which lexicalise 'right' direction alongside their left-encoding equivalents. Hence, a look at row 'A' shows that there are six occurrences of *to the right of* and *to the left of* alike. Only small differences were noted in the lexical phrases that speakers used to encode left and right direction. These differences are revealed by looking at rows 'E' to 'H': for example, row 'G' shows that there was one use of *to my right*, but no use of the left-encoding equivalent *to my left*.

The first point to make concerning these left- and right-encoding items is that they all contain the lexemes *left* and *right*. This contrasts to the wider range of items which speakers used to encode direction along the frontal axis: in addition to the prepositions *in front of* and *behind*, speakers also recruited *foreground*, *ahead*, and *back* (cf. table 2,chapter 5). The routine use of *left* and *right* therefore highlights the restricted range of lexical items which encode a specific direction along the lateral axis. McCullough (2005: 249) touches upon this issue when he remarks on the many instances of the lexemes *left* and *right* in his own experimental data.

There were seven occurrences of items which encode location at the midpoint of the lateral axis. However, these were all due to one speaker. Hence, the encoding of centre-directional information was not widely noted. We shall not explore this category any further in hat follows.

The most compelling result presented in table 12 is the remarkably productive use which speakers made of directionally non-specific items. Members of this category account for 37 of the 93 (40%) items which encode location along the lateral axis. When combined with the five uses of sequence-encoding items this increases to a total of 42 (45%), which is almost equivalent to the combined number of left- and right-encoding items (total: 44). This contrasts to the results obtained for the frontal axis. In descriptions of the lounge room scene, directionally non-specific items accounted for 17 of the 53 items used (32%; cf. table 2,chapter 5). The table below presents the number of directionally-specific and directionally-non-specific items noted for the frontal and lateral axes. Hence, the row '+ direction' adds the number of front- and back-encoding items for the frontal axis, and the number of left- and right-encoding items for the lateral axis. The row '- direction' presents the number of directionally non-specific items noted for each axis. We do not include 'centre-encoding' or 'sequence-encoding' items in this table, because these were noted for the lateral axis only.

Tab. 13: Number of directionally specific and directionally non-specific items used to express location along the frontal and lateral axes

	Frontal axis	Lateral axis
+ direction	36 (68%)	44 (54%)
- direction	17 (32%)	37 (46%)
TOTAL	53	81

Given the greater use of directionally non-specific items in the lateral axis data, the following question arises: is directional information relating to the lexically-encoded locative relationship expressed at another point in the locative expression? The analysis which follows concentrates on this question, paying particular attention to how speakers use *next to* to encode location. The 26 occurrences of this preposition constitute a total greater than that of items which encode left- (21 examples), right- (23 examples), or centre- (seven examples) directional information.

6.2.1 Encoding location with 'next to'

Next to is a directionally non-specific preposition which encodes the adjacency of a Figure to a Ground. Adjacency and direction are natural semantic partners: this is because if a Figure is *next to* a Ground, it must also be located in a certain direction away from it[37]. On a cognitive level, adjacency and direction go hand-in-hand because determining adjacency requires a mental scanning from one object to another. Adjacency also has to do with proximity, and so relates to the semantic concern of distance. Ashley and Carlson (2007) show that when speakers attend to distance, they concurrently attend to direction. With this in

---

[37] Direction will naturally be contingent on the origo.

mind, it is feasible that when speakers use *next to* to encode adjacency, they also attend to the direction of the Figure in relation to the Ground.

Analysis of our data supports this expectation. 20 of the 26 (77%) uses of *next to* were accompanied by the expression of left/right directional information relating to the encoded relationship of adjacency. Moreover, directional information was contextually inferable in two of the six examples in which speakers did not specify direction. This result suggests a close association between the concerns of lateral adjacency and lateral direction as far as the demands of the current experimental task are concerned.

There were three ways in which speakers expressed directional information relating to the relationship encoded by *next to*: in speech, in gesture, or in both speech and gesture. The 20 examples which feature such expressions of direction are represented in the graph below. These examples are divided up according to whether directional information is expressed in speech, in gesture or in both modalities.

Graph 6: How speakers expression directional information relating to occurrences of *next to*

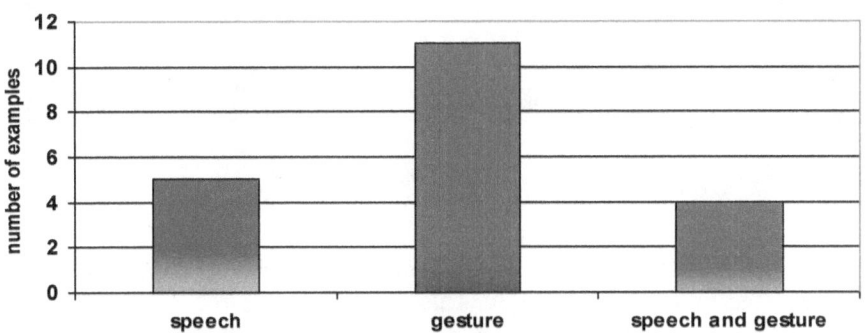

The results show that speakers most frequently used gesture alone to express directional information relating to relationships of adjacency encoded by *next to*. This occurred in 11 (55%) examples, as opposed to speech alone which expressed direction in five (25%) examples, or both speech and gesture which did so in four (20%). As far as the use of speech alone is concerned, the following example shows how the two concerns of lateral adjacency and direction are encoded by separate lexical items.

(124)   **next to** the mirror **to the left** *is a portrait of a boy it looks like* (EngDesc1)

The speaker begins by lexically encoding the relationship of adjacency (*next to*), before immediately specifying the direction of the Figure to the Ground (*to the left*). In addition to the five examples in which speech alone encoded directional information, there were a further four examples in which both speech and gesture did so. Therefore, speech encoded lateral direction in a total of nine examples. As far as the syntactic distribution of distance and directional semantic elements is concerned, in seven of these nine expressions *next to* preceded the direction-encoding phrase (see example 124 above). While nine examples is too small a sample for reliable conclusions to be drawn, this result suggests that there may be a tendency for *next to* to precede the direction-encoding phrase.

As shown in graph 6, the most common way in which speakers expressed directional information concerning the relationship encoded by *next to* was in gesture alone. This occurred in 11 (55%) of the 20 examples, with these 11 examples being produced by seven different speakers.

(125)   *the television <u>is next to the</u> fireplace* (EngDesc8)

The speaker's gesture in example (125) communicates the location of the television to the right of the fireplace. This expression of direction uses a speaker-based origo, such that we understand directional information in terms of the speaker's intrinsic lateral properties. Lateral direction is not concurrently encoded in speech, yet it is pivotal to correctly establishing the television's location in the scene. Speech and gesture are therefore expressing different, complementary strands of information in this example. Notice also that the speaker emphasises this unlexicalised direction through the hand's pronounced trajectory out to the extreme-right periphery of gesture space.

It is not possible to accurately determine whether speakers express adjacency in gesture. This is because potential gestural representations of adjacency are actually representations of proximity: speakers can only represent the idea of adjacency in gesture by suggesting the proximity of the Figure to the Ground.

Proximity and adjacency are not equivalent concepts however, as two objects may be proximate without being adjacent. The only reliable way to express adjacency is to encode it lexically: this explains the remarkably frequent use of *next to* in the data (see table 12). In contrast, while gesture may not be conducive to unambiguous representations of adjacency, it is ideal for expressing direction. This is shown in the following example, in which the speaker uses gesture to highlight directional information at the expense of a representation of proximity.

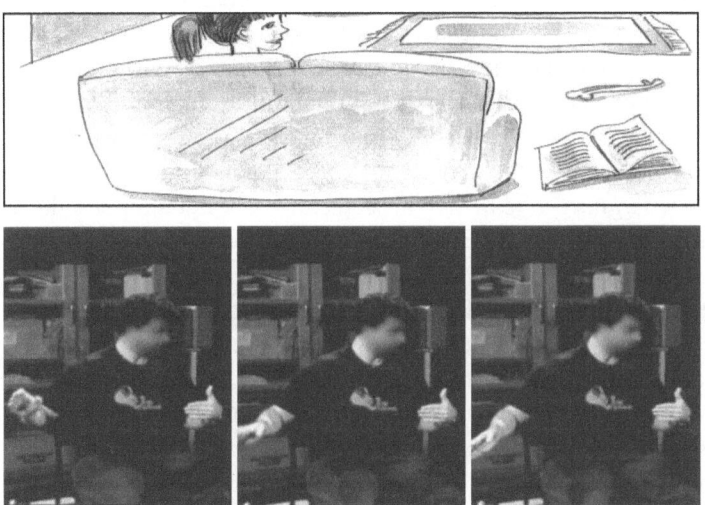

(126)   *laying next to the sofa.. on the floor so immediately to the right of the sofa..
        there is.. a book.. that's open* (EngDesc10)

The speaker begins this locative expression by using *next to* to encode adjacency. The proximity of the Figure to the Ground is subsequently stressed by the use of the intensifier *immediately*, which qualifies the direction-encoding phrase *to the right*. However, this emphasis on proximity is not present in gesture. The speaker's right hand, which represents the book, moves down at the far right of gesture space. In contrast to this, his left hand (which marks the sofa's location) is maintained in a post-stroke hold on the left of gesture space. Clearly, the distance between the two hands expresses neither proximity nor adjacency. Rather, the gestural depiction highlights the direction of the Figure to the Ground by exaggerating the distance between the two objects (see picture extract above). Speech and gesture are thus foregrounding different, complementary spatial ideas which characterise the Figure's location in space.

It has already been established that directional information is central to the expression of object location (Landau and Jackendoff, Vorwerg in Ashley and Carlson 2007). As far as descriptions of the lounge room scene are concerned, the provision of such information is essential: without it, the locative distribution of objects within the scene cannot be known. The fact that speakers most commonly express direction along the lateral axis in gesture alone when using *next to* suggests that they are using gesture to communicate this information to their addressee. If this were not the case, then the gesturally-expressed directional information should also be encoded in speech. However, of the 15 examples in which gesture expresses directional information (see columns two and three in graph 6), speech only encodes this information in four examples (see example 126, above). Hence, in the majority of cases, gesture alone carries the directional charge when *next to* is used. These gestures are not simply indicating the speaker's perspective on a visually-represented locative configuration; rather, they contain pivotal directional information which is not found elsewhere in the locative expression. This reinforces results obtained by Melinger and Levelt (2004). In this study, the authors found that speakers who expressed 'necessary' spatial information in gesture were more likely to omit this information from speech than speakers who did not gesture. According to the authors, this shows that such gestures were performed with the intention to communicate. Our data present a similar story, because the expression of lateral direction is pivotal to successfully describing a Figure's location in our experimental set-up. Such information routinely occurs in gesture alone when speakers encode adjacency with *next to*. It therefore seems that speakers intend these gestures to communicate direction to their addressees.

Finally, it is important to point out that speakers express the correct direction of the Figure to the left or to the right of the Ground. This information is expressed using speaker viewpoint and observer perspective. The gestural expression of left or right is therefore not arbitrary: it is motivated. If speakers were simply using gesture to represent the lexically-encoded relationship of adjacency, it would not matter if directional information were faithfully reproduced. However, the evidence presented here shows that speakers *do* correctly express lateral direction, and that this information is most commonly expressed in gesture alone. This provides further evidence that the relationship between speech and gesture is complementary and non redundant (McNeill 1992, 2005; Kendon 2004). Moreover, the finding that speakers correctly reproduce lateral direction aligns with research by McCullough (2005). McCullough reports that speakers' gestures correctly reproduced lateral information pertaining to object location and motion event paths in 90% of cases in his data. This shows that speakers not only attended to left/right directional information, but also that such information was important enough to be faithfully represented in his study. In another cartoon-based study, Kita and Özyürek (2003) report that speakers regularly expressed the lateral direction of motion events in gesture alone – and did so correctly. The results presented in this chapter therefore align with those obtained by McCullough (2005) and Kita and Özyürek (2003). However, they present the new finding that speakers use gesture to express unlexicalised lateral direction which relates to the use of *next to*. This shows how the information expressed in gesture interacts with the semantics of a spatial preposition to create a finer-grained locative expression.

6.2.2 Why speakers use 'next to' to encode adjacency

There are different ways in which the same Figure/Ground relationship may be conceptualised for linguistic encoding. For instance, prepositional expressions such as *next to* and *beside* encode the adjacency of a Figure to a Ground while others, such as *to the left of*, encode direction instead. While the prepositional expressions *to the right/left of* may be used when a Figure is adjacent to a Ground, any reading of adjacency is due to pragmatic inference rather than to lexical encoding. Hence, it is possible to isolate the direction encoded by these prepositional items from the concern of adjacency, as in the invented example below.

(127) *the dog is the second object* **to the right of** *the sofa*

In (127), *to the right of* encodes purely directional information. The non-adjacency of the Figure to the Ground is revealed by the sequential encoder *second*, which modifies the directional expression. It is nevertheless possible to lexically conflate the concepts of lateral adjacency and direction in English. Both of these concepts are encoded by the prepositional phrases **on** *the right/left of* (Herskovits 1986). In the following example, *on my left* is an alternate realisation of *on the left of me*.

(128) *Joanne sat* **on my left** *at the dinner table*

Yet the use of *on the right/left of* to encode Figure and Ground adjacency is restricted. An analysis of its use with different Figure and Ground objects reveals that as soon as the Ground can be conceptualised as a supporting surface for the Figure, a reading of support also becomes available. Therefore, in terms of grammatical form, two combinations compete for expression: the reading of adjacency encoded by *on the right/left + of*, and the reading of support encoded by *on + the right/left + of*.

(129)   the blanket is on the right of the sofa
(130)   the lamp is on the left of the table

Without further contextual information, examples (129) and (130) are ambiguous between readings of Figure/Ground contact (i.e. the blanket is *on* the sofa; the lamp is *on* the table) and adjacency (i.e. the blanket is *next to* the sofa; the lamp is *next to* the table). However, once the Ground is no longer conceptualised as a supporting surface for the Figure, the reading of adjacency emerges.

(131)   the printer is on the right of the computer

Such restrictions underpinning the use of *on the right/left of* mean that the concepts of LATERAL ADJACENCY and DIRECTION are conflated with some difficulty in English. Examples (129) and (130) represent attempts at using these two prepositional expressions to encode relationships of adjacency in the lounge room scene. Neither, however, is ideal. This explains why speakers instead expressed adjacency and direction in separate communicative units: that is, they used *next to* to encode adjacency, and gesture to express the Figure's location to the left or to the right of the Ground.

Finally, it is important to mention that there was only one use of *next to* to encode location along the frontal axis in descriptions of the lounge room scene (cf. table 2, chapter 5). Instead, relationships of proximity were encoded by *in front of*. Therefore, whereas speakers lexically specified directional information when encoding proximity along the frontal axis, such information most commonly emerged in gesture alone as far as the lateral axis was concerned. This suggests that speakers may make greater use of gesture to communicate direction along the lateral, as opposed to the frontal, axis.

6.2.3 'Between', the lateral axis and gesture

English speakers also recruited the preposition *(in) between* to encode location along the lateral axis. For all five of its occurrences in the data, speakers provided complementary information which showed that the use of the preposition concerned the lateral axis. In two of these five examples this information was expressed in speech only.

(132) and **sort of to the top in the middle** of the.. um whole room there's a.. mirror on the wall.. which is **between** the portrait of the boy and between um the curtains (EngDesc5)

(133) and located next to the like **to.. the left** of the dog and **to the right** of the sofa so **between** the dog and the sofa is a book (EngDesc1)

Example (132) encodes the Figure's location along the vertical axis in *sort of to the top*, and along the lateral axis with *in the middle*. In example (133) the speaker encodes the Figure's location along the lateral axis with the two prepositional phrases *to the left* and *to the right*. In the three remaining examples, gesture alone disambiguates the spatial axis which underpins the use of *(in) between*. The speaker does this by marking the Ground objects' locations along the lateral axis. In each instance, the locations of these Ground objects have been provided at an earlier point in discourse. The use of gesture therefore brings back into focus directional information which is salient to the current locative context, as shown in the following example.

1   2

(134) also in that general area where the ball and the bone and the dog is.. which is kind of between <u>the table with</u> the tablecloth <u>and the</u> sofa.. um there's an open book (EngDesc4)

The use of *between* in (134) serves to clarify the location of *that general area where the ball and the bone and the dog is*. Notably, the speaker does not encode directional information in speech which allows for this *general area* to be located. This, in turn, means that the location of the Figure, the *open book*, is unclear. The speaker's gestures, however, indicate that the table and the tablecloth are on the right-hand side of the picture, while the sofa is over on the left-hand side. The end of the gesture stroke which indicates the table's location is shown in the first still above. The speaker subsequently arcs her hands across to the left, thereby establishing the location of the sofa at the other end of the lateral axis. The end of this stroke phase is represented in the second still. The lexical segments that accompany the two strokes are underlined.

As indicated earlier (see Chapter 5), speakers also use *between* to encode location along the frontal axis. Therefore, in order to clearly communicate location, speakers need to specify the spatial axis that underpins individual uses of this preposition. The speaker in example (134) above does this by using gesture to mark the respective locations of the Ground objects along the lateral axis. In doing so, she provides the unlexicalised information that the two objects are located on the right- and left-hand sides of the picture, respectively.

As far as the internal composition of overall locative expressions is concerned, the gestures which accompany the use of *between* in example (134) are secondary locative expressions: this is because they mark the respective locations of the two lexical Ground objects, which are therefore simultaneously gestural Figures. Both these gestural expressions of location occur within the secondary locative beginning with *which*. The speaker's overall locative expression is a complex of a primary expression ('*also in that general area where the ball and the bone and the dog is* [...] *um there's an open book*'), a secondary locative realised by a relative clause ('*which is kind of between the table with the tablecloth and the sofa*'), and two further secondary locatives (the two gestures expressing the locations of the table and tablecloth, and the sofa). This example highlights the degree to which locative expressions can be a rich semantic complex of interconnected locative propositions. Crucially, within this network are two propositions in which gesture alone carries the locative charge: these are the gestures that establish the locations of the lexical Ground objects along the lateral axis.

6.2.4 The use of 'then' to encode location along the lateral axis

Table 12 records five uses of the sequential item *then* to encode location along the lateral axis. For four of these five uses, speakers provided supplementary information which specified the direction in which this locative sequence progressed. In one instance this was expressed in both speech and gesture. In the other three instances however, it emerged in gesture alone. The latter three examples are all due to the one speaker, and represent the conceptualisation of location as a sequential progression from (the speaker's) left to right.

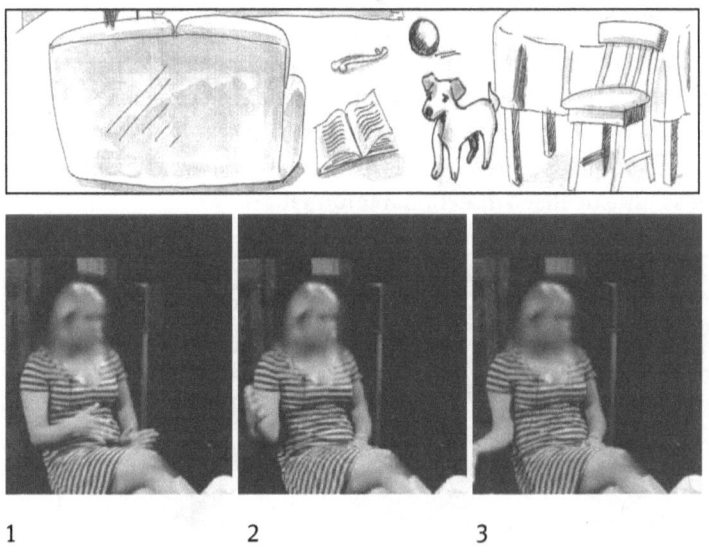

(135) *(and next to the couch there's an open book) and a.. then a dog* (EngDesc2)

Prior to the gesture shown above the speaker uses her right hand, fingers clearly separated and palm facing the left-hand side, to mark the location of the *open book*: this location is shown by the position of the right hand in the first still above. The speaker subsequently executes a large, arc-like trajectory to the right (stills 1–3), her hand moving from the front of her lower torso to the extreme-right periphery (and mostly off camera; see still 3). This establishes the dog's location to the right of the book, using a speaker-based origo. Notably, the gesture foregrounds directional information at the expense of a representation of proximity. This gestural focus on direction potentially arises because distance information is inferable in the lexical expression: the sequential encoder *then* establishes the *dog* as the next locatable object along the relevant spatial axis, and so the proximity of the dog to the book is perhaps implicit. The use of *then* in this example, with its co-occurring gesture, operates in a similar manner to the way in which speakers use *next to*. Both lexical items encode the idea of a progression, the directional colour of which is lexically unspecified. It is gesture which expresses this information, neatly bringing to light the multimodal integration of locative information.

6.2.5 The use of gesture with semantically-similar lexical items

There were six other uses of directionally non-specific items which encoded location along the lateral axis: these are subsumed under the category 'OTHER' (see table 12). One of these items, *beside*, is a synonym for *next to*. The comparable locative semantics of the two prepositions are suggested by the common use of gesture to express unlexicalised directional information.

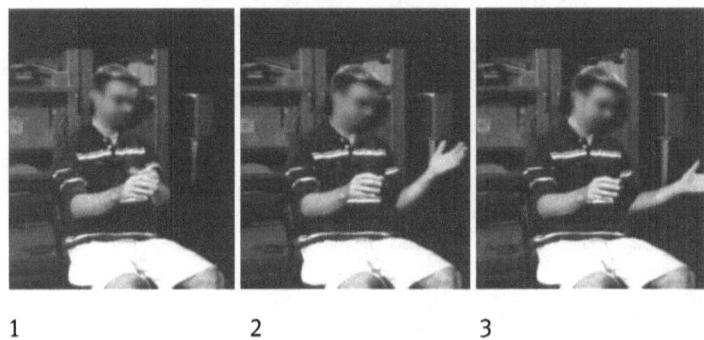

1   2   3

(136)   <u>um and</u> just beside that ball ah is a bone (EngDesc9)

In section 6.2.1 we established that speakers recurrently expressed unlexicalised directional information in gesture pertaining to the relationship encoded by *next to*. This same use of gesture is noted for *beside*, as shown in the example above. The contrast between the lexically-encoded and gesturally-expressed information is particularly pronounced here. That is, the speaker stresses the proximity of the Figure to the Ground through the use of *just* as modifier of *beside*. The speaker's right hand, in a post-stroke hold, marks the location of the Ground (*that ball*), while his left hand arcs out to the far-left periphery. He therefore correctly shows that the bone is located to the left of the ball, using a speaker-based origo. However, the size of the gesture trajectory and the resulting distance between the two hands (see still 3) does not suggest the proximity encoded by *just beside*. Rather, it foregrounds directional information, thereby recalling the directional gestures which accompany occurrences of *next to*. Example (136) suggests that the use of semantically congruous spatial units, such as *beside* and *next to*, triggers parallel uses of locative gestures. This hypothesis may be explored further by looking at the one use of *in the middle of* which has a contextual reading similar to *between*.

1　　　　　　2　　　　　　3　　　　　　4

(137)　　and in the <u>middle of the sofa</u> and the ch- and the table there's a little dog
　　　　　(EngDesc4)

In example (137) the speaker encodes the location of the dog between the sofa and the table using the prepositional phrase *in the middle of*. While uttering *middle*, she begins a gesture which marks the location of the sofa on the left side of her gesture space (stills 1–2). Her hand then rises (still 3), before moving down to mark a location to the right of that associated with the sofa (still 4). This gesture indicates the locations of the two Ground objects along the lateral axis: the sofa is on the left-hand side of the room, while the table is on the right. This marking of the Ground objects' locations echoes the pattern of gestural behaviour noted previously for *between* (cf. section 6.2.3).

Examples (136) and (137) suggest that the locative information expressed in gesture reflects the synonymy of spatial items. Such parity in gestural behaviour highlights how the information expressed in gesture is tied to that encoded in speech: when speakers recruit lexemes with similar semantics, they also execute gestures with similar informational content.

6.2.6 Gesture and the use of other directionally non-specific spatial items

The four remaining spatial items categorised under OTHER in table 12 are *closer to*, *on the other side of*, *further across from* and *towards*. Each encodes the Figure at a separate location to the Ground without specifying the direction of the former to the latter. Once again, this allows for the complementary nature of speech and gesture to emerge. In all four instances, speakers express directional information relating to the lexically-encoded relationship in gesture alone.

(138)   *(the tablecloth is on the table) which is um further across from the tv but in the foreground of the picture..* (EngDesc3)

In example (138) *further across* establishes the physical separation of the Figure and the Ground. However, such information requires directional complementation if the Figure's correct location is to be understood. This complementation emerges in gesture. The speaker's hand pushes out to the right in synchrony with *further across*, thus establishing the location of the tablecloth and the table on the right-hand side of the picture. Speech and gesture therefore attend to different, yet complementary spatial ideas, both of which are pivotal to characterising the Figure/Ground configuration.

The examples presented so far in this chapter have looked at the gestures which accompany occurrences of *next to*, *beside*, *between*, *in the middle of*, *then* and *further across*. The common feature of these examples has been the use of gesture to express salient, unlexicalised directional information. Table 12 counts 42 occurrences of directionally non-specific items in expressions which encode location along the lateral axis: this is inclusive of the five uses of sequence-encoding items. For 35 of these 42 occurrences, speakers supplied salient, unlexicalised directional information concerning the lateral axis in either speech, gesture, or both modalities: this highlights the importance of directional information to expressing location (Landau and Jackendoff 1993, Vorwerg

2003 in Ashley and Carlson 2007). Moreover, gesture *alone* carried the directional charge in 23 (66%) of these 35 examples. This contrasts to speech alone which did so on just seven (20%) occasions, and both speech and gesture which did so on five (14%). These results clearly indicate that speakers made productive use of gesture to express directional information pertaining to relationships lexicalised by directionally non-specific items. The strands of information expressed in speech and gesture combine to create a finer-grained locative expression. This was particularly in evidence for occurrences of *next to* in our data. Graph 7 below summarises our results.

Graph 7: How speakers express directional information concerning the lateral axis for occurrences of directionally non-specific and sequence-encoding items

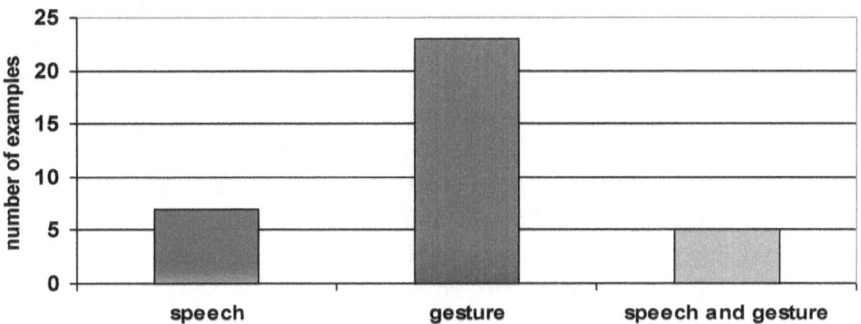

6.2.7 The use of left-encoding items

Table 12 records 21 uses of left-encoding items in the lounge room scene data. Speakers executed representational gestures for nine of these 21 occurrences. These gestures all used the intrinsically-oriented speaker as origo for the gestural expression of direction, as well as speaker viewpoint and observer perspective. In certain examples, information relating to the origo, perspective and viewpoint was not available in the co-occurring speech. This information, which is crucial to understanding the lexically-encoded directional information, emerged in gesture instead.

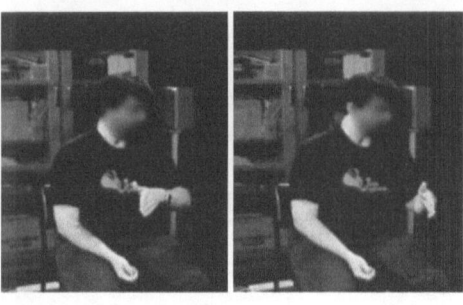

1   2

(139)   *left of the fireplace.. there's a cat.. sitting next to the fireplace just on its left* (EngDesc10)

In example (139), the speaker begins by marking the location of the fireplace in his gesture space: the end of this gesture stroke is shown in still 1. He subsequently moves his hand across to his left: the end of this stroke is shown in still 2. This latter stroke accompanies the Ground-encoding noun phrase *the fireplace*. These two consecutive gestures reveal the use of observer perspective, as the speaker maps the conceptualised locations of the Figure and the Ground onto the gesture space in front of him. There is nothing to indicate that the speaker is using a character perspective here, as the locations of these two gestural markings are consistent with the speaker's view of the scene as an external observer. The directional trajectory of the second gesture reveals the use of a speaker, as opposed to an addressee, viewpoint. Since the addressee is seated opposite the describer, describing left direction from the addressee's viewpoint would necessitate the inversion of the speaker's own left and right properties: this would entail a gesture to the speaker's right. Finally, the speech content of (139) is ambiguous as to whether the speaker is using an intrinsic or a relative frame of reference. Is the speaker expressing location to the intrinsic left of the fireplace (as the phrase *on its left* suggests), or rather to the left of the fireplace as he views the picture (i.e. with a relative frame of reference)? The speaker's gesture reveals the latter to be the case. If the speaker were using an intrinsic frame of reference, he would need to gesture to his right instead: this is because the fireplace is opposite the speaker as he views the picture, and so its intrinsic left is aligned with the speaker's right. This shows furthermore that the origo of the directional information is located at the speaker, as opposed to the fireplace. Hence, the speaker's gesture sheds light on four spatial elements which are pivotal to understanding the lexical expression of direction: these are the use of an observer perspective, a speaker viewpoint, a relative frame of reference, and a speaker-centred origo.

6.2.8 The use of right-encoding items

There were 23 occurrences of right-encoding items in the data (see table 12). For 13 of these, speakers executed representational gestures. Each of these gestures expressed direction from speaker viewpoint, thus echoing the results presented for left-directional gestures above. Such regularity of speaker viewpoint highlights the cognitively complex nature of left/right inversion involved in the use of addressee viewpoint. Speakers' gestures also indicated the use of observer, as opposed to character, perspective in the encoding of lateral direction. The following locative expression provides one example of this.

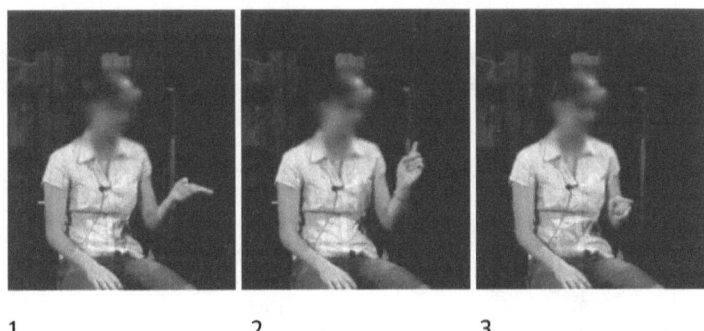

(140)   and to the right of that.. is a window with curtains (EngDesc6)

In (140) the speaker moves her hand to the right of the location associated with the mirror (pronominalised as *that*), thus establishing the Figure's location in gesture space. The stills represent the gesture from the beginning of the preparation phase (still 1) through to the completion of the stroke (still 3). The gesture also shows that direction *to the right* is determined in relation to the speaker's intrinsic lateral properties, and hence that the origo of the directional information is located at the speaker. There is nothing in this gesture to suggest that the speaker conceptualises location from an imagined location within the picture. That is, the direction of the gestural movement is consistent with her orientation as external viewer of the picture, and she does not use an iconic hand form which suggests that the Figure has been viewed from a non-aligned, scene-internal location. As far as frame of reference is concerned, the pronoun *that* refers to 'the mirror'. It is debatable as to whether mirrors have intrinsic left and right properties. Given that they do have an intrinsic front (the reflective surface itself) and a back (the non-reflective side), deriving left and right properties from these distinctions is theoretically possible. However, conceptualising location in terms of these intrinsic left and right properties seems somewhat unlikely. The speaker's gesture expresses direction to the right of the mirror as she observes it, thereby suggesting the use of a relative frame of reference. Her gesture therefore reveals information relating to the viewpoint, perspective, origo and frame of reference which underpins the lexical expression of direction.

6.3 Lounge room scene – French descriptions

This section begins by presenting, in table form, the lexical items which French speakers used to encode location along the lateral axis in descriptions of the lounge room scene. In the same way as for the English-language data, these items are divided up into categories based on the semantic concern of direction.

Tab. 14: Lexical items used to encode location along the lateral axis in French descriptions of the lounge room scene

	Left-encoding items	N	Right-encoding items	N	Centre-encoding items	N
A	*à gauche* ('to the left')	12	*à droite* ('to the right')	10	*au milieu de* ('in the middle of')	5
B	*gauche* [modifier] ('left')	4	*droit* [modifier] ('right')	4	*au milieu* ('in the middle')	4
C	*à gauche de* ('to the left of')	2	*à droite de* ('to the right of')	5	*le milieu* ('the middle')	2
D	OTHER *de gauche* 'of left' [modif] (1) *à ma gauche* 'to my left' (1) *sur ma gauche* 'on my left' (1)	3	*sur la droite (de)* ('on the right (of)')	2	*le centre* ('the centre')	1
E	TOTAL	21		21		12

Tab. 14 (cont'd): Lexical items used to encode location along the lateral axis in French descriptions of the lounge room scene

	Directionally non-specific items (cont'd)	N	Sequence-encoding items (cont'd)	
F	à côté de ('next to')	23	après ('after')	2
G	entre ('between')	7	puis ('then')	1
H	ici ('here')	5		
I	à côté ('next to'/'nearby')	4		
J	vers ('towards')	2		
K	du côté ('on/of the side')	2	N/A	
L	là-bas ('over there')	2		
M	OTHER de l'autre côté 'on the other side' (1) près de (1) 'near' là 'there' (1)	3		
N	TOTAL	48		3

As far as lexical items encoding left direction are concerned, the most commonly noted was the prepositional phrase *à gauche* ('to/on the left'). Similarly, the most frequent right-encoding item was *à droite* ('to/on the right'). However, far more frequent than either left- or right-encoding items were those which did not encode a specific direction at all: there were 48 uses of directionally non-specific items in the lateral axis data, this total exceeding the number of left- and right-encoding items combined. The most commonly recruited item of any category was *à côté de* ('next to'), which occurred 23 times. The lexically similar *à côté* (column 'directionally non-specific items', row I) differs from *à côté de* in two ways. Firstly, it does not introduce a Ground-encoding complement. Secondly, it may also be used to encode simple proximity as opposed to adjacency: an English translation would be the adverb *nearby*. Hence in the following invented example the Figure (*telephone booth*) may be proximate, but not adjacent to, the speaker.

(141) il y a   une cabine téléphonique   à côté
       there is   a telephone booth   nearby

The following sections analyse how French speakers used directionally non-specific items to encode location along the lateral axis. As part of this approach we pay particular attention to whether, and how, speakers express directional information pertaining to the locative relationships encoded by these items.

6.3.1 Encoding location with 'à côté' and 'à côté de'

Just like English *next to*, the French locative preposition *à côté de* encodes the adjacency of a Figure to a Ground. As stated above, the lexically similar *à côté* differs from *à côté de* in two ways. Firstly, it does not introduce a Ground-encoding complement, and secondly, it may encode proximity as opposed to adjacency. However, all four uses of *à côté* in the lounge room scene data describe relationships of Figure/Ground adjacency, with the Ground item being contextually inferable.

The question arises as to whether speakers expressed the direction of the Figure to the Ground along the lateral axis when using these items. There were 23 occurrences of *à côté de* in the lounge room scene data. Two of these have been removed from the analysis which follows because, in both cases, the speaker executes a gesture which is ambiguous as to whether or not it expresses direction along the lateral axis. This reduces the number of items for analysis to 21. 18 (86%) of these occur in expressions which provide lateral directional information. In most cases, this information relates directly to the relationship of adjacency encoded by *à côté de*, and therefore expresses the direction of the Figure in relation to the Ground. However, for five of these occurrences of *à côté de*, the left/right directional information which speakers provide does not relate exclusively to the relationship encoded by the preposition. Instead, this information localises the Figure in relation to the picture as a whole. Example (142) provides one instance of this.

(142) le portrait du jeune garçon..   eum **à gauche**..   en haut..
       the portrait of the young   um **to/on the left**.. up the top..
       boy..

donc **à côté du** miroir..	et au-dessus du canapé	(EngDesc1)
so **next to the** mirror..	and above the sofa	

In this example the speaker localises the portrait of the young boy *à gauche* ('to/on the left'), before subsequently encoding its adjacency to the mirror. The use of the directional encoder *à gauche* localises the portrait in relation to the picture as a whole, and does not specifically relate to the subsequent use of *à côté de*. While the use of *à gauche* may allow us to pragmatically infer the portrait's location to the left of the mirror, there is room for interpretive ambiguity. Hence, we have not included this example in the analysis which follows, nor have we included the other four examples which work in a similar fashion.

To summarise then, 13 (72%) of the 18 left/right directional specifications relate to the Figure/Ground relationship encoded by *à côté de*, while the remaining five (28%) localise the Figure within the broader context of the picture (e.g. example 142 above). We have excluded these five examples from our analysis, therefore leaving us with a total of 13 occurrences of *à côté de*. There are three ways in which speakers may conceivably express directional information in these examples: in speech, in gesture, or in both modalities. The graph below presents out findings as to how this information was expressed.

Graph 8: The expression of left/right directional information pertaining to relationships of adjacency encoded by *à côté de* ('next to')

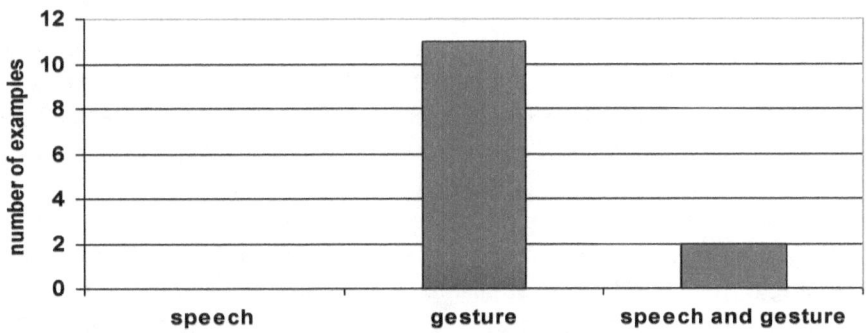

There were 11 (85%) examples in which gesture alone carried the directional charge, and two (15%) in which both speech and gesture did. Hence, speakers most frequently expressed lateral direction pertaining to the relationship of adjacency encoded by *à côté de* in gesture only. These 11 examples were produced by six different speakers, thus showing that a good range of speakers used gesture to express this type of complementary directional information. This echoes the result obtained for *next to* in the English-language data (cf. section 6.2.1). Working on the basis that the information expressed in gesture is tightly linked to lexically-encoded semantic information (McNeill 1992), these uses of gesture to express complementary directional information potentially indicate the similar lexical semantics of *next to* and *à côté de*. One of the examples in which the speaker expresses directional information in gesture alone is shown below.

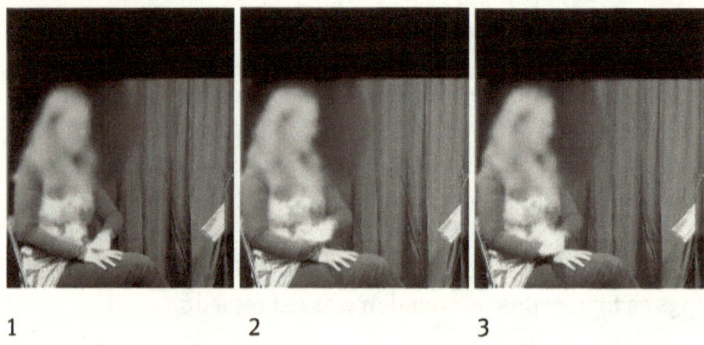

1   2   3

(143)   *et à <u>côté du livre</u>..*   *il y a le chien* (FrenDesc2)
        and <u>next to the book</u>..   there is the dog

The speaker's left hand is initially in a post-stroke hold (still 1), having just marked the location of the *livre* ('book'). Her hand then rises and makes a clear movement to the right, finishing in a location where the left hand extends over the top of the right wrist (still 3). The hand's trajectory along the lateral axis is particularly noticeable when stills 1 and 3 are compared.

In addition to the uses of *à côté de*, there were four occurrences of *à côté*. For three of these four occurrences, speakers supplied directional information relating to the lexicalised relationship of proximity. In each of these three examples, gesture alone carried the directional charge. Moreover, each of these examples was produced by a different speaker.

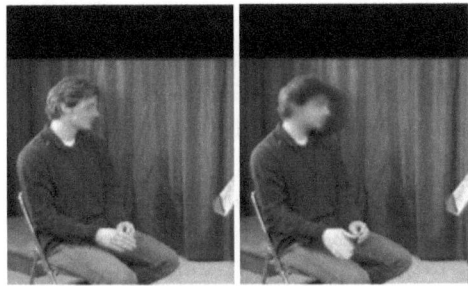

(144) *et un chien* <u>*à côté*</u> (FrenDesc11)
       and a dog   <u>next to (it)</u>

The two stills above capture the start and finish points of a gesture stroke in which the speaker's hand makes a rapid, brushing movement out to the right. This gesture supplies directional information which colours the lexically-encoded relationship of adjacency: the dog is located to the right of the implicit Ground, using speaker viewpoint, observer perspective, and an origo based at the speaker. This information is pivotal because *à côté* could refer to proximity along any horizontal axis radiating out from the Ground. Hence, the co-occurring gesture fine-tunes the semantics of the lexical expression by restricting its directional interpretation.

The role of gesture in communicating unlexicalised lateral direction is clearly revealed when the results for *à côté* and *à côté de* are collectively considered.

Graph 9: The expression of left/right directional information pertaining to relationships of adjacency encoded by *à côté* and *à côté de*

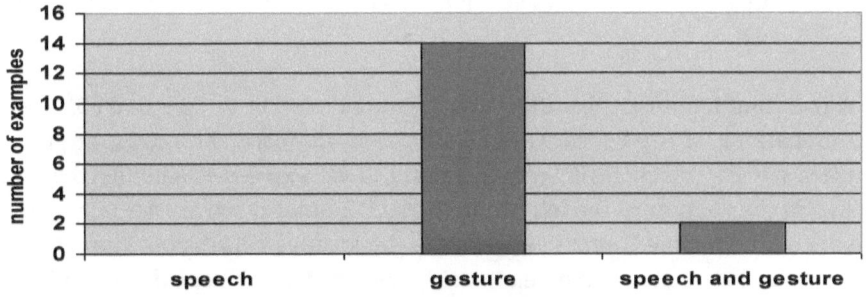

Graph 9 represents the 16 uses of *à côté* and *à côté de* for which speakers supplied directional precision in the locative expression. The results show that speakers used gesture alone to express the direction of the Figure to the Ground on 14 (88%) occasions, and both speech and gesture on two (13%) occasions. The 14 examples in which gesture alone carried the directional charge were produced by seven different speakers, thus showing that this use of gesture was widely attested across our group of describers. The necessity of providing directional information to articulate object location in this experimental task has already been stated. The fact that speakers most often expressed this information in gesture alone strongly suggests that these gestures are intended, in part at least, for the addressee. If this were not the case, then the directional information should also be encoded in speech. However, speech only encodes such information in two (13%) of the 16 examples. It would therefore seem that the expression of left/right directional information in gesture does not simply reflect the speakers' viewpoint on the encoded relationship of adjacency and proximity: rather, it constitutes part of the informational package which the speaker intends for the addressee. This claim could be verified by looking at the interactive segment in which receivers discuss the picture with the describers. The receivers' output could be assessed for the expression of directional information that the describer previously expressed in gesture alone. Such re-expression by the receiver would very likely indicate that they have attended to the directional information in the describer's gestures. Cassell, McNeill and McCullough (1999) provide evidence that listeners do assimilate the information provided in speakers' gestures, thereby leading us to hypothesise that addressees may indeed pick up on directional information that is expressed in gesture alone. Given the space restraints of the present study however, this needs to be the subject of a future investigation.

6.3.2 Establishing the Ground's location in gesture space when using 'à côté de'

A recurrent feature of the directional gestures relating to uses of *à côté de* was the marking of the lexical Ground's location in space. As shown in graph 8, there were 11 instances in which gesture alone expressed whether the Figure was to the right or to the left of the Ground. Two of these are actually gestures which accompanied *entre* ('between') in the locative expression. These gestures nevertheless relate to the relationship encoded by *à côté de*, because they clearly indicate whether the Figure is to the right or to the left of the Ground.

(145) et **à côté de** la table et des chaises.. donc euh **entre** la table
and **next to** the table and the chairs.. so ah **between** the table
et le canapé il y a un chien (FrenDesc6)
and the sofa there is a dog

As the speaker encodes the relationship headed by *entre*, she marks the table's location on the right-hand side of gesture space, and the sofa's location on the left-hand side of gesture space. In doing so, she shows that the Figure (the 'dog') of the relationship encoded by *à côté de* must also be to the left of the table: this is because it is between the table and the sofa. Hence the speaker's gestures, which accompany the use of *entre*, also provide directional precision concerning the relationship of adjacency encoded by *à côté de*.

In Chapter 5, we established that speakers recurrently mark the locations of the lexical Grounds when using *entre*. We will therefore leave the two examples mentioned above aside for the moment, and concentrate on the remaining 11 in which the marking of the Ground's location cannot be attributed to *entre*. It turns out that in eight (73%) of these 11 examples, speakers mark the Ground's location in gesture space. This occurs either as part of the stroke phase, or as a post-stroke hold. The following example illustrates how speakers used post-stroke holds to indicate the location of the lexical Ground in gesture space.

(146) à côté de <u>la cheminée il y a</u>   une télévision (FrenDesc8)
       next to <u>the fireplace there</u> is   a television

The speaker moves his right hand forward and down, expressing the location of the Figure, *une télévision* ('a television'), to the right of the fireplace. The stroke temporally aligns with the Ground-encoding noun phrase (*la cheminée*) and is followed by a second identical gesture shortly after (which is not shown here). Notice how the speaker maintains his left hand in a post-stroke hold: this represents the location of the fireplace. There are two possible reasons for this hold. Firstly, the speaker may use it to highlight the Figure's location to the right of the Ground. A second – and quite different – explanation is that the speaker is using both hands to keep track of his descriptive trajectory through the picture. However, the speaker could mark the current location in his trajectory by using his right-hand alone: there is no need to retain the use of the left-hand to mark the preceding location in space. Irrespective of whether this is the case or not, the post-stroke hold draws attention to the gestural expression of direction. This helps to highlight this information, marking it as salient in the speaker's discourse. Crucially, this directional information is not concurrently available in speech.

The use of gesture to mark the location of the Ground is recurrently noted in our data for both languages (see examples (126), (136), and (139) in this chapter for English). This is a productive device which allows speakers to emphasise directional information. It furthermore suggests that one of gesture's main roles in the expression of location is to represent the location of the lexical Ground. This is a role which is examined more closely in Chapter 8.

6.3.3 'Entre', the lateral axis and gesture

French speakers made seven uses of the preposition *entre* ('between') to express location along the lateral axis (see table 14). Of these seven uses, four were accompanied by gestures. These four gestures all marked the respective locations of the two lexical Ground items in gesture space. As far as gesture execution is concerned, in three of these four instances the gesturing finger or hand moved downward, marking the location associated with each Ground item. In the fourth example however, the speaker executed a looping gesture that connected the locations of the two Ground items in gesture space.

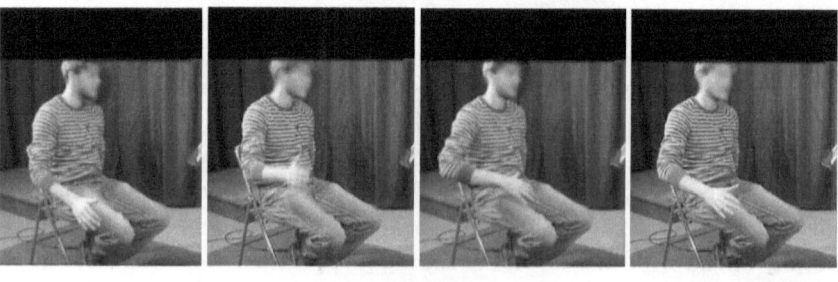

1   2   3   4

(147) [...] *le livre l'os la balle..*   *à mi-chemin entre la télé et le canapé*
[...] the book the bone the ball.. halfway between the tv and the sofa
en fait (FrenDesc10)
in fact

In (147) the use of *entre* is modified by the prepositional phrase *à mi-chemin* ('halfway'), which encodes the distance of the Figure in relation to the two Ground objects. The speaker gesturally indicates the location of the first Ground object, *the television*, by moving his hand up and out to the right (stills 1–2): this establishes its location on the right-hand side of the picture. He then loops his hand back in towards the centre (still 3), thus establishing the sofa's location in the foreground and to the left of the television (using a speaker-based origo). Finally, the speaker moves his hand back out along the diagonal trajectory he has created (still 4), thereby representing the idea of distance encoded by *mi-chemin* ('halfway'). The speaker's gesture conflates distance and directional information within the one continuous motion. Importantly, just as in the other three examples which relate to *entre*, the speaker marks the respective locations of the lexical Ground objects in gesture space. In addition to expressing unlexicalised locative information, this specification of the Ground objects' locations reveals how speakers conceptualise the relationship encoded by *entre*. The following example reinforces this claim.

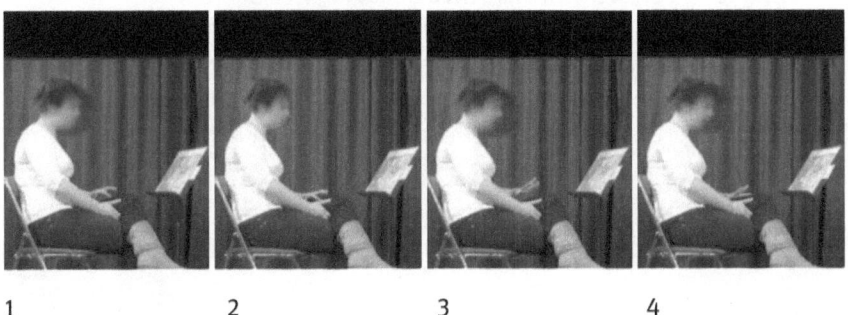

1   2   3   4

(148) [...] *entre le chien..*   *et le canapé* (FrenDesc5)
[...] between the dog.. and the sofa

The speaker in (148) executes two discrete gestures. The first of these is a downward movement of the left index onto the thigh (stills 1 and 2): this represents the location of the dog. The second gesture is the downward movement of the left ring finger, also onto the same thigh (stills 3 and 4): this marks the sofa's location to the left of the dog. Both these gestures are subtle movements which are not seemingly marked for the addressee's attention. Nevertheless, they suggest the speaker's conceptualisation of the lexically-encoded locative relationship in terms of the area marked by the two Ground objects. This conforms to the interpretation of spatial uses of *entre* proposed by Franckel and Paillard (2007: 53): "In the examples where Y is realised by N and N, the localisation space for X is defined as the intermediate space founded by the respective positions of each N." (Translation MT; note that in this quotation the abbreviation 'Y' refers to what we understand as the Ground, 'X' as the Figure, and 'N' stands for noun phrases). In addition to this, example (148) shows that the speaker is processing location along the lateral axis. As indicated in Chapter 5, speakers use *entre* to encode location along the frontal axis as well. When this occurs, they also mark the respective locations of the Ground objects in gesture space. This common pattern of gestural behaviour suggests that speakers conceptualise the relationship encoded by *entre* in terms of Figure/Ground alignment along a spatial axis. The particular axis along which this alignment holds recurrently emerges in gesture alone. This reinforces the particular aptitude of gesture for expressing directional information pertaining to directionally nonspecific items.

6.3.4 The use of gesture with sequence-encoding items

Speakers made three uses of sequence-encoding items in descriptions of the lounge room scene (see table 14). Although highly infrequent, the occurrences of these items nevertheless highlight the role which gesture plays in expressing unlexicalised directional information. Both uses of *après* ('after'), for instance, were complemented by gestures which expressed direction along the lateral axis.

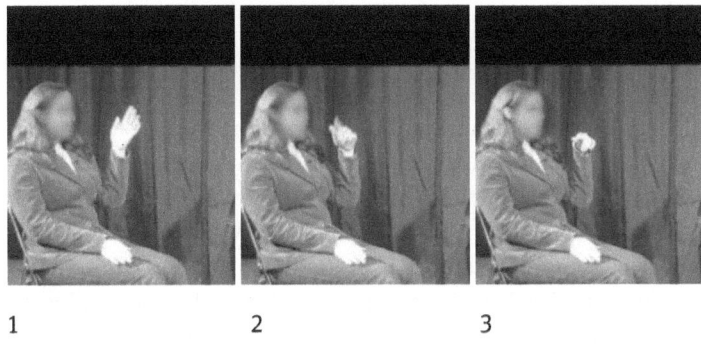

1   2   3

(149)   *après il y a*   <u>*un miroir*</u> (FrenDesc6)
         after there is   <u>a mirror</u>

Prior to example (149) the speaker encodes the location of the portrait *sur* ('on') the wall. As she does so, she uses her left-hand to establish the portrait's location on the left side of the picture. The gesture in (149) continues the unlexicalised expression of lateral direction by establishing the mirror's location to the right of the portrait. Crucially, it provides directional colour for the sequential relationship encoded by *après* ('after'). The salience of this information is highlighted by the fact that the speaker actually executes two gestures which express the mirror's location to the right of the portrait. The first of these gestures, which is not shown here, is a movement of the speaker's flat hand to the right of the location associated with the portrait. The speaker then changes hand form to the extended index of stills 2 and 3 above, and makes a diagonal movement down to the right. Crucially, in both this locative expression as well as the previous one in the speaker's discourse, directional information is expressed in gesture only.

The provision of lateral directional information in gesture also complements the single use of *puis* in the data.

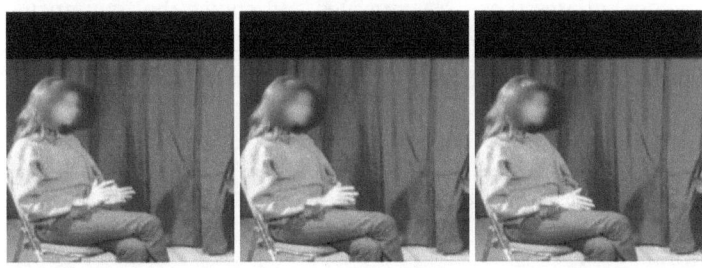

(150) *puis un petit chien* (FrenDesc4)
       then a little dog

In example (150) the speaker moves her right hand down, marking the location of the dog in gesture space; this follows on from a gesture with the left hand which marks the book's location. Each of these gestures expresses directional information using speaker viewpoint, observer perspective, with the origo located at the speaker. Locative progression is signalled by the use of the sequential encoder *puis* ('then'), yet the directional nature of this progression emerges solely in gesture. This once again highlights how gestures frequently carry the directional charge in locative expressions.

6.3.5 The use of gesture with directionally non-specific and sequence-encoding items

The combined consideration of directionally non-specific and sequence-encoding items allows us to better understand the role of gesture in expressing locative information. There were 51 overall uses of these items: 48 belong to the 'directionally non-specific' category, while three belong to the 'sequence-encoding' category. As outlined in section 6.3.1 above, there were two uses of *à côté de* which were accompanied by ambiguous gestures, and a further five in which the expression of lateral direction did not necessarily relate to the encoded relationship of adjacency. We will therefore exclude these seven examples from our analysis. This results in an amended total of 44 occurrences of directionally non-specific and sequence-encoding items. For 36 of these, speakers supplied complementary directional information concerning the lateral axis. This is seen, for example, when speakers use gesture to express the Figure's location to the left or the right of the Ground with *à côté (de)*, or when they express the respective locations of the Ground objects along the lateral axis with *entre*. The graph below collates these 36 examples and shows the frequencies with which speakers used speech, gesture, or both speech and gesture to express such lateral directional information.

Graph 10: How speakers express directional information concerning the lateral axis for occurrences of directionally non-specific and sequence-encoding items

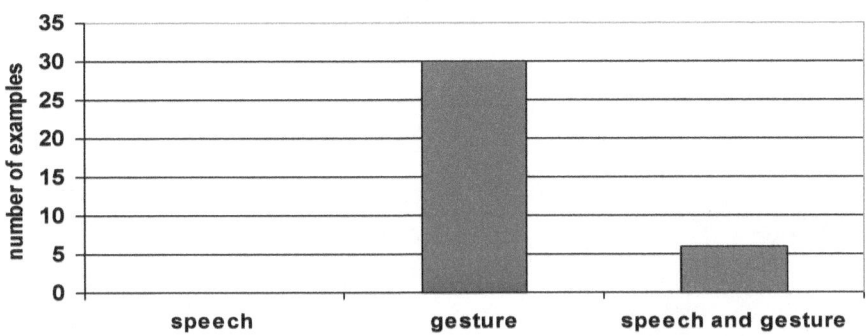

Graph 10 indicates that speakers most frequently used gesture alone to express directional information concerning the lateral axis for directionally non-specific and sequence-encoding items. Gesture carried the directional charge in 30 (83%) examples, while both speech and gesture did so in six (17%). Therefore, our results provide clear evidence that gestures express salient, unlexicalised directional information, and that locative expressions are multimodal constructions. Examples (143)–(147), which are taken from the descriptions of seven different French speakers, show how location is expressed multimodally. Particularly striking is the result that speech alone never expressed this type of complementary directional information. This reflects an overall trend in the French and the English data: speakers favour gesture to express directional information relating to directionally non-specific items (cf. Chapter 5).

6.3.6 The use of left-encoding items

The most commonly recruited left-encoding phrase was *à gauche* ('to the left'). The nominal *gauche* ('left') in this phrase encodes part of the Ground, although the particular object with which this 'left' property is associated (i.e. the speaker or the picture) must be understood in context. This object is either the observer or the picture itself. In most cases this directional property is one and the same, since the left side of a picture is normally understood in terms of the observer's left.

Of the 21 occurrences of left-encoding items, 14[38] were accompanied by representational gestures. Each of these gestures expressed directional information from speaker viewpoint. This shows that speakers comprehensively avoided the 180-degree rotation of lateral properties required for the use of an addressee viewpoint in gesture.

(151)   [...] *dans la partie gauche..*   *de l'image* [...] (FrenDesc3)
        [...] in the part left..   of the picture [...]
        'in the left part.. of the picture'

The gesture above represents left direction in terms of the speaker's intrinsic left-hand side. The speaker therefore conceptualises location from her own point of view, as opposed to that of the addressee seated opposite. Furthermore, in this example, as in the 14 other examples of gestures which express left-directional information, the speaker uses an observer perspective. This same perspective is also present in the co-occurring lexical locative expressions. There are several factors which indicate that the speaker is using observer perspective in these gestural expressions of direction. Firstly, the direction of the gesture trajectory is consistent with the speaker's location as external observer of the picture. Secondly, none of the hand forms used suggests that the Figure has been viewed from a location which is different to that of the external observer. Thirdly, all gestures are executed in the frontal half of the speaker's gesture space, and not behind them. While this alone is insufficient to indicate

---

38 There is a further gesture which is not counted here because it likely constitutes a spatial mismatch. This gesture comprises a movement of the hand to the speaker's right instead of to his left. It is unlikely that this constitutes a use of addressee viewpoint, since the rest of the describer's directional gestures use speaker viewpoint. Rather, the more likely interpretation is that the speaker momentarily confuses his left/right distinction, as can sometimes be the case (Levinson 2003: 207).

that an observer perspective has been used, it provides additional support when considered alongside the two previous statements concerning directional trajectory and hand form.

6.3.7 The use of right-encoding items

Just as the most frequently employed left-encoding phrase was *à gauche* ('to the left'), the most frequently employed right-encoding one was *à droite* ('to the right'). Speakers executed representational gestures for 12 of the 21 occurrences of right-encoding items. In the same way as for the left-encoding phrases, these gestures all expressed direction using speaker viewpoint. All used an observer perspective except for one example, in which the speaker adopted a scene-internal role and hence a character perspective. This perspective was present in both speech and gesture, as shown below.

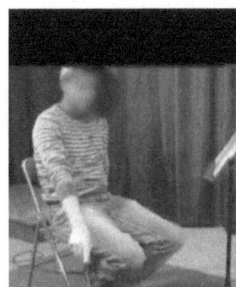 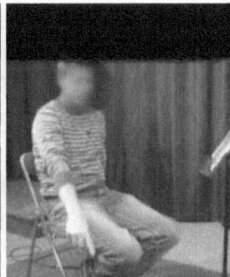 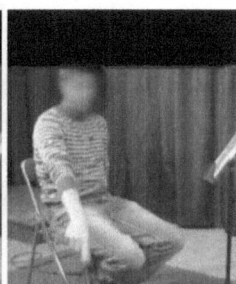

(152) *il y a un os..*   *qui se trouve là..*   *presque à mes pieds..*
      there is a bone..   which is found there..   almost at my feet..
      mais un peu à   *droite du canapé*   (FrenDesc10)
      but a little to   the right of the sofa

In example (152) the speaker imagines himself on the sofa where the lady is seated. This use of character perspective is established earlier in the speaker's discourse and is re-enforced in the current expression thanks to the possessive pronoun *mes* ('my'). As the speaker encodes the location of the Figure ('the bone') to the right of the sofa, he uses his extended index to trace the outline of a circle to the right of his own location in space. This tracing motion completes three full circles in an anti-clockwise direction, and is partially captured in the stills above. The use of character perspective in gesture therefore transforms the physical space surrounding the speaker into the event space, as the speaker imagines himself within the visually-represented scene.

One of the 12 gestures also shows how gesture can clarify the frame of reference underlying a lexical expression of direction.

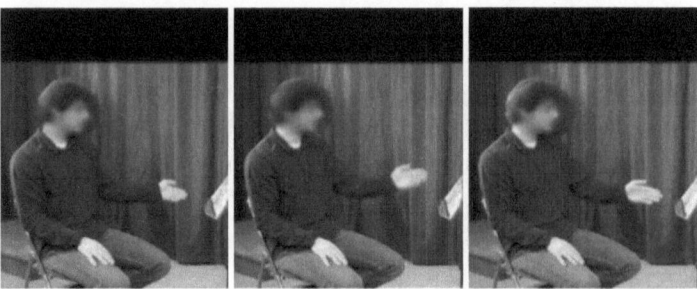

(153) et *à droite* de la cheminée   il y a une télévision (FrenDesc11)
       and to the right of the fireplace   there is a television

In the expression prior to example (153) in discourse, the speaker acknowledges the directional ambiguity which may arise when it is unclear whether an intrinsic or a relative frame of reference is being used. Describing the cat's location to the left of the fireplace, the speaker states *pour nous à gauche de la cheminée* ('for us to the left of the fireplace'). In doing so, he indicates the use of a relative frame of reference with the origo located at the speaker. The continued use of a relative frame of reference is contextually implicit in example (153) above, yet is reinforced by the directional gesture. The movement of the speaker's hand expresses direction to the speaker's right, as opposed to the intrinsic right of the fireplace. This maintains focus on the relative frame of reference, whilst also specifying location from speaker viewpoint and observer perspective.

6.4 Street scene – English descriptions

This section begins by presenting, in table form, the lexical items which English describers used to encode location along the lateral axis in descriptions of the street scene. These items are once again divided up according to the semantic criterion of direction.

Tab. 15: Lexical items used to encode location along the lateral axis in English descriptions of the street scene

	Left-encoding items	N	Right-encoding items	N	Centre-encoding items	N	Directionally non-specific items	N
A	on the left-hand side (of)	16	on the right-hand side (of)	18	in the middle (of)	5	outside (of)	11
B	left (various)	11	right (various)	8	middle (other)	2	opposite	7
C	left-hand (various)	6	right-hand (various)	3	centre	1	next to	2
D	on the left	4	on the right	2			across…from	2
E			on the right side of	6			on the other side of	2
F							OTHER close to (1) just about where (1) between (1) there (1) about the same spot as (1)	5
G	TOTAL	37		37		8		29

There were 37 occurrences of items which encode left direction in the data, and another 37 of items which encode right direction. This similarity in frequency nicely reflects the set-up of the experimental task: speakers were required to describe the locations of six objects on the left-hand side of the road, and another six on the right-hand side. The final two objects ('the bus' and 'the cinema') were located at the centre of the picture's lateral axis. Fittingly, descriptions of these two objects accounted for the eight occurrences of items which encode centre direction.

The street scene is readily conceptualised in terms of left and right halves: this is facilitated by the distinct presence of two rows of shops on each lateral side of the picture. A coarse-grained overview of an object's location can therefore be established by specifying whether the object concerned is on the left- or the right-hand sidewalk. This alleviates the need to make recurrent use of directionally non-specific items to some extent, because the division into lateral halves is so prominent. Nevertheless, there were 29 occurrences of directionally non-specific items. The analysis which follows begins by examining how speakers used gesture with directionally non-specific items, before turning to a discussion of left- and right-encoding items.

6.4.1 The use of directionally non-specific items

6.4.1.1 'Outside (of)'

The most frequently recruited directionally non-specific item was *outside (of)*. *Outside (of)* encodes a basic relationship of exteriority and does not specify reference to any spatial axis. It has been included in this chapter because each of its occurrences in the data describes location along a lateral axis which is parallel to the speaker's as they view the picture. In all examples of *outside (of)*, the speaker encodes location using a scene-external observer perspective.

Outside (of) does not encode reference to any particular surface (i.e. the 'front' or 'back', etc) of a Ground. However, if a Figure is described as being *outside* a building or a shop, the inference is that the Figure is at the building's entrance: this is generally the side understood as the building's 'front'. This is a clear, simple spatial relationship which does not require particular elaboration. With this in mind what information, if any, do speakers express in gesture? Of the 11 locative expressions which encode location with *outside (of)*, three contain locative gestures which relate to the lexically encoded Figure/Ground configuration. These three examples are all due to the one speaker, and in each case the gesture fulfils the same locative function: to establish the location of the Figure/Ground configuration on the left- or the right-hand side of the street.

(154)   and outside <u>the hotel</u>.. *is a phone booth* (EngDesc6)

In example (154) the speaker moves her left hand down as she utters *the hotel*. This gesture is not representational for *outside* as it bears no connection to the idea of exteriority, nor does it suggest the separate locations of the Figure and the Ground. Rather, it expresses unlexicalised directional information concerning the hotel's location along the lateral axis. When this gesturally-expressed information is considered alongside the locative semantics of *outside*, we understand that the Figure (the telephone booth) must also be located on this same side of the street as the hotel. Hence, the consideration of both speech and gesture allows us to understand the locations of the lexical Figure *and* Ground.

The expression which immediately precedes example (154) in the speaker's discourse also sheds light on the complementary interaction of speech and gesture.

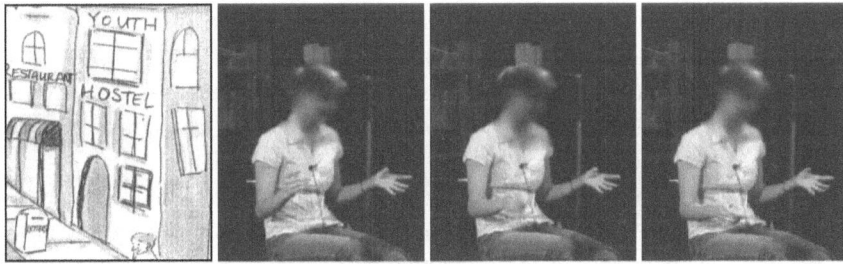

(155)   *outside the youth hostel.. is <u>the letterbox</u>.. yep post office box* (EngDesc6)

In contrast to the hotel and the phone booth, the post-office box and youth hostel are located on the right-hand side of the street. The stills above show how the speaker moves her right hand down to mark the post-office box's location on the right hand side of gesture space. The non-gesturing left-hand remains elevated, as the speaker makes constant use of both hands to mark location on the left- and right-hand sides of gesture space. Note that the speaker changes to this left hand when locating the phone booth in the subsequent expression (see example 154 above): these two gestures clearly serve to indicate location on the right- and left-hand sides of the street respectively. Another point of interest is that the gesture in example (154) occurs with the Ground (*hotel*), whereas the gesture in example (155) occurs with the Figure (*letterbox*). As far as the expression of locative information is concerned, it matters little whether the gesture falls on the Figure- or the Ground-encoding item. This is because the use of *outside* tells us that both items must be located on the same side of the street.

Hence, a gesture which establishes the location of one of these objects on a particular side of the street necessarily applies to the other object as well.

6.4.1.2 'Opposite'

The preposition *opposite* encodes the alignment of two objects along a horizontal spatial axis. These objects may have intrinsic frontal orientations and be positioned so that they are facing each other: hence, two people are *opposite* each other when they are face-to-face. Yet it is not an unfailing requirement that intrinsically-oriented objects face one another in order for *opposite* to be used. For example, two cars may be *opposite* each other in a street even though they are facing in different directions. *Opposite* may also be used to describe the alignment of non-oriented entities along a horizontal axis. Hence, two trees or telegraph poles on either side of a street may be *opposite* each other. The crucial factor underpinning the use of this spatial item seems to be the alignment of the Figure and Ground along a horizontal axis. As far as the street-scene data is concerned, all occurrences of *opposite* encode location along a lateral axis which is parallel to the speaker's as they view the picture: it is for this reason that they have been included in this chapter. Table 15 records seven uses of *opposite*. Two of these uses, both of which describe the same Figure/Ground configuration, occurred in the same locative expression[39]. Six of the seven occurrences of *opposite* were accompanied by gestures. These gestures all fulfil a common locative role: to establish the respective locations of the Figure and the Ground along a lateral axis. The following example brings this to light.

1   2   3

(156)   *the building closest to you.. so <u>opposite the supermarket</u>.. right up in the*

---

39 Both uses were also accompanied by gestures.

foreground.. um is a café (EngDesc9)

The stills above show how the speaker's fingers are bent at the knuckles so that they are nearly perpendicular to his palm. This allows his hands to slice through space, making a pronounced gestural reference to the lateral axis. His left hand, which represents the supermarket, and his right hand, which represents the café, move in to the centre of his gesture space (still 2). Each hand subsequently moves out to its respective lateral side, thereby marking the locations of the café and the supermarket opposite each other (still 3). As stated earlier, *opposite* does not encode reference to a particular horizontal axis. In example (156) the speaker's gesture not only singles out the lateral axis as salient, but it also communicates the unlexicalised locations of the supermarket and the café on the left- and right-hand sides of the street respectively.

Overall, the six gestures which relate to *opposite* appear in five locative expressions (remembering that one expression contains two occurrences of the preposition). The common factor which unites all of these examples is that no speaker lexically encodes the location of the Ground on the left- or the right-hand side of the street. In contrast, gesture expresses this information in all five examples. A highly comparable use of gesture is noted for the two occurrences of *across from* in the data. In both instances, speakers establish the location of the lexical Ground in gesture while leaving this information unencoded in speech.

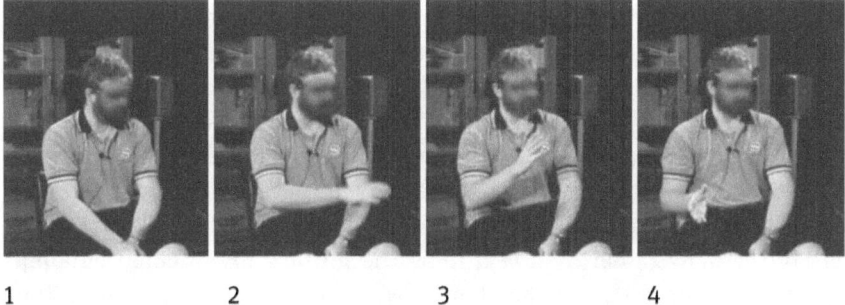

1   2   3   4

(157)   *the um.. post office box the letter box <u>is across the road</u>.. from the trolley and it's on the right hand side* (EngDesc8)

In example (157) the speaker lexically encodes the location of the Figure as *across the road* [...] *on the right hand side*. This naturally implies that the Ground, *the trolley*, is located on the left-hand side of the road. Instead of leaving this piece of information as a contextual inference however, the speaker presents it in gesture: his right hand moves from his lap (still 1) and across to the left-hand side of gesture space (still 2), before arcing over to the right-hand side (stills 3 and 4). This occurs as one continuous, fluid gestural movement. Notice that it expresses the trajectory encoded by *across from*, and pre-empts the lexical encoding of *right hand side*. The establishment of the Ground's location in space is pivotal to the gestural representation of *across from*. It also highlights the role of the Ground in determining the type of locative relationship which it shares with a Figure. For example, if the trolley were on the same side of the road as the post-office box, then the trolley could no longer be said to be *across the road* from it. Instead, the trolley would be *up/down the road* from the post-office box. The location of the Ground therefore plays a crucial role in defining the nature of a locative relationship, and the importance of this role is seemingly reflected in gesture.

6.4.1.3 'Next to'

There were only two occurrences of *next to* in the street-scene data. There are several potential reasons for this. Firstly, the picture is drawn so that the shops are located in sequential fashion along a frontal axis that has its origo at the speaker. This favours the use of sequence-encoding items, such as *then*, to encode location, as well as numerical encoders like *first* and *second* (see Chapter 5). There is less opportunity for speakers to localise objects adjacent to one another along a lateral axis because the picture emphasises adjacency along the frontal axis instead. A second reason is that speakers often encoded location within a framework of motion events (see Chapter 5). Such an emphasis on the dynamic aspect of the spatial domain may therefore work against the recruitment of static locative prepositions like *next to*. Finally, there are many intrinsically-oriented entities in the street scene, and this triggers the use of front-encoding items. For example, it is more natural to describe the car's location as *in front of* the bank rather than *next to* it. The intrinsically oriented buildings along both sides of the street therefore provided ideal reference entities, thus reducing the need for directionally non-specific items. Hence, we noted 29 occurrences of the latter items in descriptions of the street scene, as opposed to 42 occurrences (sequence-encoding items included) in descriptions of the lounge room scene.

As far as the two occurrences of *next to* are concerned, one was accompanied by a gesture which clearly expressed the Figure's location to the right of the Ground. This directional information was expressed in gesture only.

6.4.1.4 Expressing directional information relating to directionally non-specific items

In this section we examine whether speakers supplied directional information relating to directionally non-specific items. Example (156) shows how this type of information may be expressed in gesture alone. In this locative expression, the speaker marks the locations of the Figure and the Ground of the *opposite* relationship on the right- and left-hand sides of gesture space. Examples (154) and (155) also reveal the use of gesture alone to express directional information. The two gestures made by this speaker localise the configurations encoded by *outside (of)* on the left and right-hand sides of the street respectively. In contrast, example (157) shows how left/right directional information pertaining to the relationship encoded by *across from* may be present in both speech (*on the right hand side*) and gesture.

As indicated in table 15, there were 29 uses of directionally non-specific items in the street-scene data. Of these, two occurred with gestures which did not make a clear movement along the lateral axis: they were therefore considered ambiguous and excluded from the following analysis.

Speakers expressed directional information concerning the lateral axis for 23 of the 27 remaining uses of directionally non-specific items. The different ways in which they expressed this information, and the frequency with which they did so, are represented in the graph below.

Graph 11: How speakers express directional information concerning the lateral axis for occurrences of directionally non-specific items

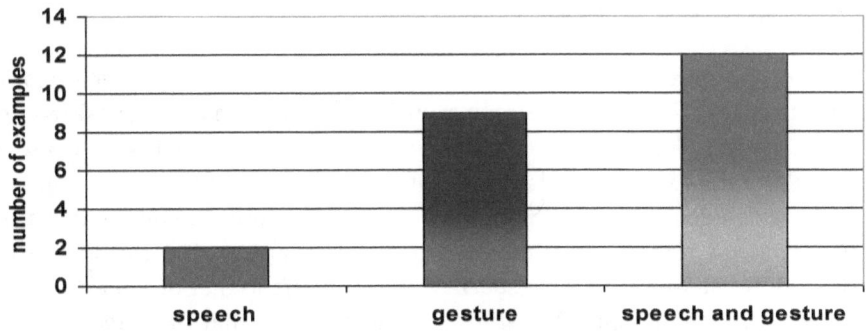

Our results indicate that speakers most frequently used both speech and gesture to express directional information, with 12 (52%) examples of this noted in the

data. The use of gesture alone was also well represented (nine examples; 39%), although the use of speech alone was not (two examples; 9%). This continues the trend which we first noted in our analysis of the frontal axis data: when speakers express directional information relating to directionally non-specific items, they use gesture more frequently than speech.

6.4.2 The use of left-encoding items

Speakers produced representational gestures for 19 of the 37 left-encoding items in the street-scene data. These gestures all share the common property of expressing direction from speaker viewpoint, thus reinforcing speakers' preference for representing direction from their own point of view as opposed to that of their addressee. This is represented in the following example.

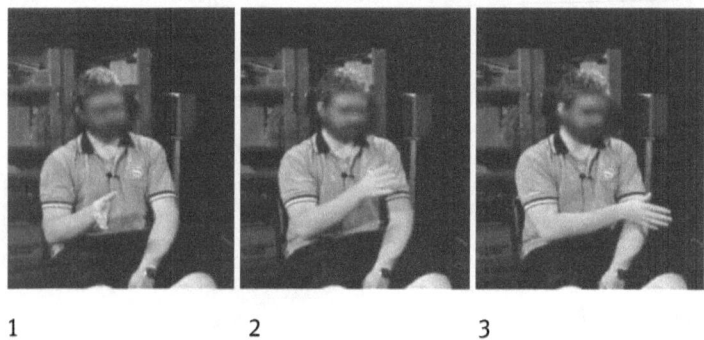

1   2   3

(158)   *off to the left hand side of the bus there's <u>a cat</u>* (EngDesc8)

In (158) the speaker initially marks the location of the bus in the centre of his gesture space. This location is represented by the position of the speaker's right hand in still 1. Following this, he executes a movement to his left as he lexicalises *a cat* (stills 2 and 3). This is congruent with the use of observer perspective in the lexical locative expression. Note also that the form and orientation of the hand do not provide any information which suggests that the Figure and Ground are viewed from a perspective which differs to that of the external observer. Once again, speech/gesture synchrony shows that the directional gesture does not temporally align with its co-expressive lexical partner (i.e. *left hand side*): rather, it synchronises with the Figure-encoding phrase *a cat*. Now, the vast majority of left-encoding items in the street-scene data describe relationships in which the Figure and the Ground share the same location in space.

This is encoded, for instance, by the use of *on* in the left-encoding phrase *on the left-hand side of the street*. This stands in contrast to example (158) above, in which the left-encoding phrase describes the Figure at a location which is separate to that of the Ground. There is one other expression (example 159 below) which encodes a similar locative configuration and which also features a representational gesture for *left*. This gesture, like that in (158), also synchronises with the Figure-encoding noun as opposed to the direction-encoding phrase.

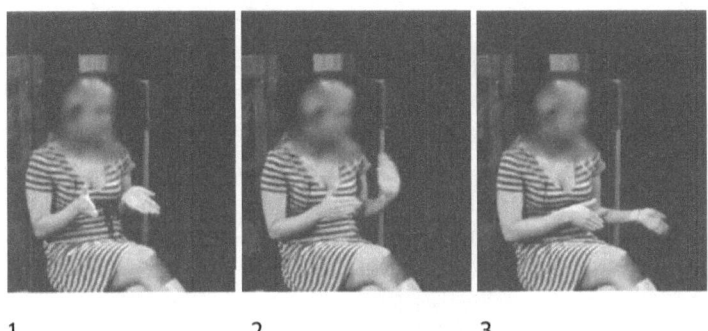

1   2   3

(159) *to the.. um.. the left if you're in the bus to the left of the bus is a <u>trolley</u> on the footpath* (EngDesc2)

In example (159) the speaker begins by delivering an iconic representation of the lexical Ground *bus*. She tilts her two hands, held upright with palms facing each other, straight down the frontal axis: this leads to the gesture form shown in still 1 above. The speaker then holds this gesture in place before crisply shifting orientation so that both hands point out to her left (stills 2-3): this stroke synchronises with the Figure-encoding nominal *trolley*. As in (158), the speaker initially establishes the location of the Ground (*the bus*) in gesture space. This location is maintained even as the speaker lexicalises directional information, and a change in gesture only occurs when the Figure is encoded. As argued earlier, the Ground's location is pivotal to determining the nature of the Figure/Ground locative relationship: this potentially explains the post-stroke hold which precedes the gesture stroke shown above.

An observation which is particular to example (159) is the possible use of different perspectives in speech and gesture. The phrase *if you're in the bus* establishes the use of a character perspective in speech. However, the speaker's gesture does not suggest that the bus surrounds her location in space. Instead, she places the iconic gesture squarely in front of her (still 1). This potentially suggests two things. Firstly, it may represent the part of the bus which extends out in front of the speaker, who therefore conceptualises location from an imagined location within the bus itself: this would mean the use of a scene-internal character perspective. Secondly, the gesture may be an iconic representation of the whole bus, meaning that the speaker is conceptualising location using a scene-external observer perspective. The actual perspective which the speaker adopts is therefore ambiguous, although inconsequential to our understanding of the Figure's location on the left-hand side of the street.

6.4.3 The use of right-encoding items

There were representational gestures for 23 of the 37 right-encoding items in the street scene data. Once again, each of these gestures provided a viewpoint for the lexical expression of right direction. In all cases the viewpoint was the speaker's except for one, example (160), in which the speaker attempted to approximate that of the addressee.

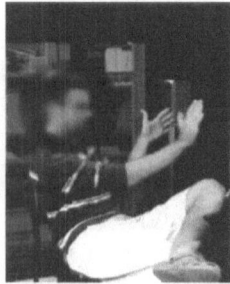

(160) *about halfway down the street.. on the right hand side.. so heading down toward.. on the right hand side* [...] (EngDesc9)

For the first occurrence of *right hand side* in this example, the speaker executes a directional gesture using speaker viewpoint (this gesture is not shown here). For the second occurrence however, he shifts position so that he is facing towards his (original) left: the addressee therefore views him side-on. This is captured in the still above, which shows the speaker's orientation at the start of the gesture stroke phase. Notice how the describer's viewpoint is halfway between that of the canonically-positioned speaker (i.e. as they view the stimulus picture), and that of the addressee. This hybrid viewpoint is an attempt to represent direction from the addressee's point of view. By tailoring his physical orientation to take into account the addressee's location in space, the speaker makes a clearly communicative use of gesture.

For three of the 23 uses of right-encoding spatial items, speakers used a character perspective in speech. This was matched by a congruent representation of directional information in gesture, suggesting that a character perspective was present cross-modally.

1 2 3

(161)   the shopping trolley is located.. to the right of the phone booth on the.. path.. like if you were looking out onto the road.. it'd be <u>located</u> to the right (EngDesc1)

In example (161) the speaker describes the location of the trolley. From an external observer perspective, the trolley is located on the left-hand side of the picture. However, the speaker adopts a scene-internal, character perspective in speech: 'if you were looking out onto the road.. it'd be located to the right'. Her imagined location therefore lies at the telephone booth, with the speaker facing the other side of the street. This character perspective is echoed in gesture, as the speaker gestures out to her right (stills 1–3).

Of the remaining 20 uses of right-encoding items, 17 encoded direction using an observer perspective in speech: this was matched by an observer perspective in gesture. For the three remaining uses it was unclear whether the speaker was using an observer or a character perspective in speech. Although the encoded direction agreed with the speaker's external location as observer of the picture, in previous expressions the speaker had specified their imagined location within the picture. In all three cases, this imagined location aligned with the speaker's position and orientation as external observer of the picture. Hence it could not be established whether the speaker was continuing this imagined, scene-internal location, or whether they had adopted an external observer perspective.

6.5 Street scene – French descriptions

Table 16 below presents the linguistic spatial items which French speakers used in their descriptions of the street scene. Occurrences of items which were ambiguous as to the spatial axis referred to were not included in the analysis. For example, several occurrences of *à côté de* ('next to') potentially referred to either the frontal or lateral axis (possibly both), and so were not counted. Similarly, ambiguous uses of *au niveau de* ('at the level of') and *au milieu de* ('in the middle of') were excluded from the analysis.

Tab. 16: Lexical items used to encode location along the lateral axis in French descriptions of the street scene

	Left-encoding items	N	Right-encoding items	N	Centre-encoding items	N	Directionally non-specific items	N
A	*à gauche* 'to/on the left'	6	*à droite* 'to/on the right'	11	*milieu* 'middle' (nominal)	4	*de l'autre côté de* 'on the other side of'	4
B	*de gauche* 'of left' (modifier)	5	*de droite* 'of right' (modifier)	6			*à côté de* 'next to'	3
C	*gauche* 'left' (modifier)	3	*droit* 'right' (modifier)	2			OTHER *entre* 'between' (1) *sur la même horizontale que* 'on the same horizontal [line] as' (1) *du même côté de* 'on the same side as' (1) *sur*[40] 'aligned with' (1) *près de* 'near' (1)	5
D	*sur la gauche* 'on the left'	3	*droite* 'right' (nominal)	2				

---

[40] *sur* is not used to mean 'on' here. Rather, it is used in the sense of 'aligned with'.

Tab. 16 (cont'd): Lexical items used to encode location along the lateral axis in French descriptions of the street scene

	Left-encoding items (cont'd)	N	Right-encoding items (cont'd)	N	Centre-encoding items (cont'd)	N	Directionally non-specific items (cont'd)	N
E	*à gauche de* 'to/on the left of'	1	*à droite de* 'to/on the right of'	2				
F	TOTAL	18		23		4		12

6.5.1 The use of directionally non-specific items

There were three uses of *à côté de* ('next to') to encode adjacency along the lateral axis. The infrequent use of this preposition here contrasts to its prevalence in descriptions of the lounge room scene. This potentially results from the different spatial layouts of the two pictures. The street scene anchors the speaker's attention on the frontal axis, with the image extending out from the viewer towards the horizon. The buildings which speakers were required to locate are ordered along this frontal axis, thereby facilitating the use of sequence-encoding items (see Chapter 5). Moreover, each of these buildings possesses an intrinsic frontal surface which speakers could use to determine the locations of other objects in the street. Hence, speakers recruited the prepositions *devant* ('in front of') and *en face de* ('in front of') to describe the location of the post-office box in relation to the youth hostel. In contrast, they did not use the directionally non-specific item *à côté de* ('next to') to describe this Figure/Ground configuration, even though the post-office box and the youth hostel are aligned along a lateral axis as the speaker views the picture.

Speakers executed directional gestures for two of the three uses of *à côté de* ('next to'). The first of these gestures is a flick of the speaker's index across to the left and the right, yet it is unclear whether the speaker is expressing the Figure's location to the left or to the right of the Ground. In spite of this ambiguity, the gesture nevertheless suggests that the speaker conceptualises the relationship of adjacency in terms of the lateral axis. In the second example, the speaker provides directional specification for the use of *à côté de* in a somewhat unusual manner.

1 2

(162)   euh la pharmacie elle est au fond..   à côté du du cinéma (FrenDesc2)
        uh the pharmacy it is at the back..   next to the to the cinema

In example (162), the speaker establishes the location of the pharmacy next to the cinema. As she does so she moves her right hand, followed by her left, into the positions shown in still 1 above. At this stage, we are unable to understand which hand represents the cinema, and which hand represents the pharmacy. Immediately following this expression she states that the bakery is next to the pharmacy. While doing this she moves her left hand back along the frontal axis (part of this motion is captured in still 2, above): this shows that the left hand in still 1 must represent the pharmacy, and the right hand the cinema. Hence, it is the speaker's subsequent gesture along the frontal axis which provides directional specification for the relationship of lateral adjacency in (162).

The directionally non-specific phrase *de l'autre côté de* ('on the other side of') occurs four times in the data. On each of these four occasions, speakers use gesture alone to identify whether the side in question is the left- or the right-hand side of the street (from their viewpoint). One particular example of this occurs in the discourse of the speaker who uttered (162). The speaker continues on from (162) by moving her hand back along the frontal axis (still 2) and identifying the shops along the left-hand side of the street. She does not state which side of the street she is describing: this directional information emerges solely in gesture. She then switches sides by saying *de l'autre côté de la rue* ('on the other side of the street'). As she does this, she makes a clear motion with her right hand along the right-hand side of gesture space. In doing so, she provides directional clarification for the use of *l'autre côté* ('the other side').

Another example in which a speaker provides directional complementation in gesture for *l'autre côté* ('the other side') is shown below.

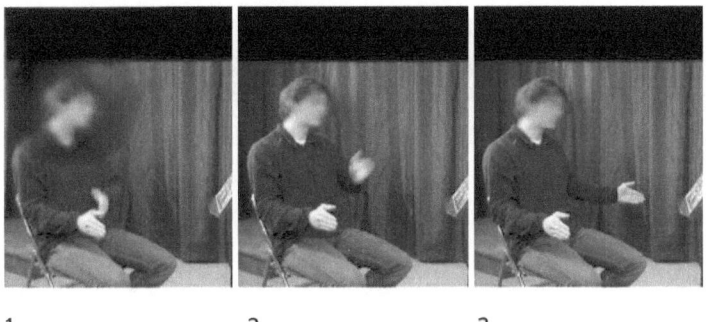

1   2   3

(163)   *et en face de cette boîte à lettres..*   *donc de l'autre <u>côté de la rue</u>..*
        and opposite this post-office box..   so on the other <u>side of the street</u>..
        i' y a le chariot pour faire   *les courses*   (FrenDesc11)
        there's the trolley for doing   the shopping

Prior to executing this gesture the speaker uses a flat form of the right hand, palm facing left, to mark the location of the lexical Ground *boîte à lettres* ('post-office box'). This remains as a post-stroke hold in the stills above, allowing the speaker to keep the unlexicalised location of the Ground in focus. The speaker's left hand then departs from a point close to this location, making a large arc across to the left hand-side of gesture space (see stills 2 and 3 above). In doing so, he uses gesture to identify the side of the street upon which the Figure is located.

The use of gesture alone to express lateral direction reflects a general tendency in this particular speaker's discourse. Prior to example (163), he lexically encodes location on the left- and right-hand sides of the street on just two occasions. On the first occasion, he identifies the shops running along the left-hand side of the street. On the second occasion, he identifies those on the right-hand side of the street. Importantly however, when the speaker subsequently locates other objects in relation to these shops he does not lexically encode their locations on a particular side of the street. Instead, he uses gesture to express this information. Hence, gesture keeps track of the speaker's movements from one side of the lateral axis to the other. The expression of such information is crucial: without it, it would be highly difficult to understand and remember the locations of individual objects in the scene.

There are five items classified under 'other' in the 'directionally non-specific' category of table 16. For four of these five items, speakers provided complementary lateral directional information pertaining to the encoded relationship. Gesture alone carried the directional charge in two of these four examples, one of which is provided below.

(164) [...] *sur la même* horizontale   *que la voiture* [...] (FrenDesc1)
      [...] on the same horizontal (line)   as the car [...]

In example (164) the speaker localises the telephone booth in relation to the car by specifying its location along the same horizontal axis. However, she does not indicate the directional nature of this horizontal axis: this information emerges in gesture alone. The speaker engages her right forearm, extended laterally in front of her, and moves it across to the right, and then to the left. The end of this stroke is shown in the still above. With this gesture the speaker shows that the telephone booth and the car are aligned along a lateral axis which is parallel to that of the viewer. This provides directional refinement for the general, directionally-ambiguous horizontal axis which the speaker encodes in speech.

6.5.1.1 Expressing directional information relating to directionally non-specific items

There were just 12 uses of directionally non-specific items in descriptions of the street scene. While this is not a large number, it is worthwhile pointing out that there were only 18 occurrences of left-encoding items in the data. In fact, the overall number of spatial items in descriptions of the street scene was just 57 (see table 16): this strongly contrasts to the total of 105 noted for descriptions of the lounge room scene (table 14). This difference in frequency is discussed in section 6.6 below. As far as the 12 occurrences of directionally non-specific items are concerned, speakers expressed directional information concerning the lateral axis for ten of these. However, one of the ten examples was somewhat ambiguous in terms of the exact directional information which it expressed and has thus been excluded from the following analysis. The expression of directional information across speech and gesture in the nine remaining examples is represented in the following graph.

Graph 12: How speakers express directional information concerning the lateral axis for occurrences of directionally non-specific items

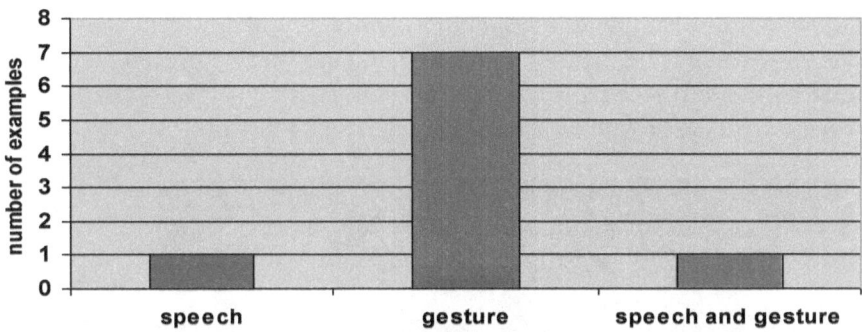

Gesture alone expressed directional information in seven examples, while speech alone and both speech and gesture did so on one occasion each. We cannot hope to draw strong conclusions from these results given the small number of examples under analysis. Nevertheless, these results are consistent with our findings so far: that is, French speakers make very little use of speech alone to provide complementary directional information relating to directionally non-specific items. In contrast, they most commonly use gesture alone to express this information. This suggests that speech and gesture are fulfilling complementary roles in the expression of location by focusing on different aspects of the locative relationship. Three different instances of how the two modalities interact in this manner are highlighted in examples (162)–(164) above.

6.5.2 The use of left-encoding items

There were 18 uses of left-encoding items in descriptions of the street scene. Speakers produced representational gestures for eight of these 18 occurrences. Each of these gestures expressed direction to the left from the speaker's viewpoint. This confirms a tendency noted in earlier sections of our data analysis: speakers express directional information according to how they perceive the picture, not according to how their addressee, seated opposite, would see it. The expression of direction in these gestures is also consistent with speakers' use of observer perspective in the co-occurring lexical expressions. Pivotal to understanding these directional gestures is the consideration of the gestural trajectory in relation to the intrinsically-oriented speaker. These eight gestures all refer to the left-hand side of the street. Streets do not have intrinsic left- or right-hand sides, and so the speaker must attribute this distinction using a relative frame of reference. The feature of gesture which is critical to the expression of direction is the trajectory of the arm or hand in relation to the origo (i.e. the speaker). This leaves the speaker free to use hand form to reflect other salient aspects of the locative relationship. In the example below, the speaker orients his flat hand directly forward along the frontal axis: this possibly suggests the horizontal extension of the Ground object (the footpath) along this axis.

(165)   *euh la pharmacie..*   *elle se trouve sur le trottoir <u>de gauche</u>*
                               (FrenDesc10)
        uh the pharmacy..   it is found on the footpath <u>of left</u>
        'uh the pharmacy.. it is found on the left footpath'

In contrast, when speakers focus uniquely on directional information and do not attend to other features of the locative expression (such as the horizontal extension of the Ground in example (165) above), various flat hand forms emerge. The following stills show the hand orientations of two speakers who use gesture to express direction alone. These represent the end of the stroke phase.

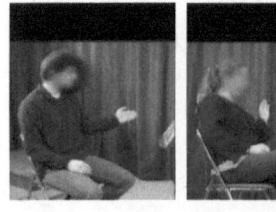

6.5.3 The use of right-encoding items

As detailed in table 16, there were 23 uses of right-encoding items. Speakers executed representational gestures for 14 of these 23 occurrences. These gestures all expressed direction using a speaker viewpoint, once again confirming the trend noted previously. All gestures were executed in the frontal half of the speakers' gesture spaces, and all were congruent with the use of observer perspective in the co-occurring lexical expressions. One potential representational gesture (which would therefore bring the total to 15) was not included in our analysis. This consisted of a movement to the speaker's left instead of to the right. While this may indicate the use of an addressee viewpoint, this is inconsistent with the use of a speaker viewpoint in this describer's other gestural representations of direction.

6.6 Comparison and discussion

As in Chapter 5, this section compares and discusses findings concerning descriptions of the two pictures. We begin by comparing the English descriptions of the lounge room and the street scene. This same process is then observed for the French data. We subsequently provide a comparative discussion of the English and French results for both stimulus pictures.

6.6.1 Comparison of lounge room and street scene descriptions in English

In table 17 below, we recapitulate the frequencies of the different types of spatial items in descriptions of the two pictures.

Tab. 17: The use of different categories of spatial items in English descriptions of the lounge room and street scenes

	Left-encoding	Right-encoding	Centre-encoding	Directionally non-specific	Sequence-encoding	TOTAL
Lounge room	21	23	7	37	5	93
Street	37	37	8	29	·	111
TOTAL	58	60	15	66	5	204

The greater frequency of left- and right-encoding items in street-scene descriptions possibly reflects the division of the street into two lateral halves: this is an easy trigger for the use of *left* and *right* to encode object location. This may also have affected the use of directionally non-specific and sequence encoding items, both of which are less frequent in descriptions of the street scene. Indeed, one important discovery in our analysis of the lounge room scene data was the remarkably frequent use which speakers made of *next to*: 26 occurrences of this item were noted. This contrasts markedly to the street scene data, in which just two occurrences were observed. This difference in result does not necessarily allow us to draw the conclusion that speakers use *next to* more often when describing location at smaller scales of space. Rather, it may be due to the fact that there were many intrinsically-oriented objects in the street scene. Hence, it is more natural to describe the location of the post-office box in relation to the intrinsic front of the youth hostel (i.e. 'the post-office is *in front of* the youth hostel'), than it is to describe its location *next to* the youth hostel. This same line of reasoning holds as far as establishing the location of the car ('in front of the bank'), the telephone booth ('in front of the hotel') and the trolley ('in front of the hotel') is concerned. Nevertheless, the presence of intrinsically-oriented reference objects – and hence the increased use of the intrinsic frame of reference – may be a phenomenon associated with larger types of spaces. That is, as space increases in size, the spatial nature of objects changes (Lautenschütz et al. 2007).

Our analysis also examined whether speakers provided directional information concerning the lateral axis for uses of directionally non-specific items. Such information was expressed for 35 (83%) of the 42 occurrences of these items in the lounge room scene data, and for 23 (85%) of the 27[41] in the street-scene data: these are similar proportions. Overall, speakers made greater use of gesture than speech to express this directional information. Looking across all three categories of 'speech', 'gesture', and 'speech and gesture' for the lounge room scene data, there were 28 examples in which gesture expressed direction and 12 in which speech did so. As far as the street scene is concerned, there were 21 examples in which gesture expressed direction and 14 in which speech did so. Hence, in both descriptive contexts, speakers favoured gesture over speech. The combined results for the two pictures provide the totals in table 18 below.

---

[41] There were 29 uses of directionally non-specific items, but two of these were excluded from the analysis on account of the ambiguous directional gestures which accompanied them (see section 6.4.1.4).

Tab. 18: The use of speech and gesture to express directional information relating to directionally non-specific items: both scenes combined

	Speech	Gesture
Both pictures	26	49
TOTAL	26	49

Therefore, as far as the provision of complementary directional information concerning the lateral axis is concerned, gesture clearly plays a pivotal role.

6.6.2 Comparison of lounge room and street scene descriptions in French

Overall, French speakers made far greater use of spatial items in descriptions of the lounge room scene than they did in descriptions of the street scene. Hence, we noted 105 occurrences of spatial items in descriptions of the former scene, as opposed to just 57 in descriptions of the latter. This is shown in the table below.

Tab. 19: The use of different categories of spatial items in French descriptions of the lounge room and street scenes

	Left-encoding	Right-encoding	Centre-encoding	Directionally non-specific	Sequence-encoding	TOTAL
Lounge room	21	21	12	48	3	105
Street	18	23	4	12	-	57
TOTAL	39	44	16	60	3	162

One reason for this is the far greater use of *à côté de* and *à côté* in descriptions of the lounge room scene. There were 27 occurrences of these items, as opposed to just three in descriptions of the street scene. This is seemingly a consequence of the two different stimulus pictures. The street scene draws the speaker's attention to the salience of the frontal axis as the street runs away from the viewer's perspective. Describers therefore located objects in terms of sequential progressions along this axis, as opposed to adjacency along the lateral axis. Moreover, as we have stated previously, there are many intrinsically-oriented entities in the street scene, leading speakers to encode location in relation to the intrinsic frontal properties of these entities. This explanation is corroborated by our results for the frontal axis (see table 7, chapter 5): there were 116 occurrences of front- and sequence-encoding items. This total is more than double that of all items used to encode location along the lateral axis in descriptions of this same scene (57 occurrences; see table 16 and table 19, above).

Although the street scene clearly proposes a left- and right-hand divide, French speakers did not make highly frequent use of either left- or right-encoding items: there were 18 occurrences of the former, and 23 of the latter. This owes to a particular descriptive technique in which speakers identified a particular side of the street, before expressing the successive location of numerous entities along this particular side. An example of this is as follows.

(166) donc on a le café   sur le trottoir de droite   le café..
      so we have the cafe   on the footpath of   the cafe..
                                 right

      l'auberge de jeunesse..   le restaurant..   la banque et le bar
      the youth hostel..   the restaurant..   the bank and the bar
      'so we have the café on the right footpath the café.. the youth hostel.. the restaurant.. the bank and the bar' (FrenDesc11)

In (166) the speaker signals that he is attending to the right-hand footpath. Just a single use of the direction-encoding phrase *le trottoir de droite* ('the right footpath') is sufficient to establish the locations of five entities (the café, the youth hostel, the restaurant, the bank and the bar) along this particular side of the picture. This type of technique enables speakers to achieve considerable economy in the use of left-and right-encoding items.

The frequent occurrence of directionally non-specific items in descriptions of the lounge room scene enabled us to investigate whether, and how, speakers expressed directional information relating to these items. Our results showed that speakers expressed directional information for 36 (82%) of the 44 occurrences of directionally non-specific and sequence-encoding items. Of these, gesture alone carried the directional charge for 30 (83%), while both speech and gesture did so for six (17%). Therefore, gesture expressed directional information in all 36 examples, while speech did so in just six. This very strongly endorses gesture's role in the expression of location. As far as the street scene was concerned, our sample was limited to just nine examples. Gesture alone carried the directional charge in seven of these examples. As far as the two other examples are concerned, speech alone expressed direction in one, while both speech and gesture did so in the other. Although this is not a large enough number on which to draw conclusions, this nevertheless reflects our results for descriptions of the lounge room scene: that is, speakers most frequently used gesture alone to express directional information relating to the relationships encoded by directionally non-specific items. Looking across all three conditions of speech only, gesture only, and speech and gesture, French speakers overwhelmingly favoured gesture to express directional information relating to directionally non-specific items. The combined results for the two pictures are shown in the table below.

Tab. 20: The use of speech and gesture to express directional information relating to directionally non-specific items: both scenes combined

	Speech	Gesture
Both pictures	8	44
TOTAL	8	44

6.6.3 Comparison of English and French descriptions of the lounge room scene

English and French describers made similar use of spatial items to encode location along the lateral axis. This is reflected in the recapitulative table below.

Tab. 21: Types of linguistic item used to encode location along the lateral axis in descriptions of the lounge room scene

	Left-encoding	Right-encoding	Centre-encoding	Directionally non-specific	Sequence-encoding	TOTAL
English	21	23	7	37	5	93
French	21	21	12	48	3	105

Turning to the individual semantic categories ('left-encoding', 'right-encoding', etc), 'directionally non-specific' items were greater in number than those belonging to any other category: this is true of both English and French. Furthermore, *next to* and *à côté de*, both directionally non-specific encoders of adjacency, were the most commonly-recruited items of any category. Speakers of both languages recurrently complemented the lexicalised relationship of adjacency by expressing the direction of the Figure to the Ground in gesture alone.

English speakers supplied directional information for 35 (83%) of the 42 uses of directionally non-specific and sequence-encoding items, while French speakers did so for 36 (82%) of 44[42] such items. Hence, the two groups behaved in a very similar manner. Moreover, English and French speakers most frequently expressed this directional information in gesture alone. This accounted for 23 (66%) of the 35 examples in the English data, and 30 (83%) of the 36 examples in the French data. The slight increase by the latter group of speakers may partly be explained by the fact that there were eight uses of deictic adverbs in the French data (i.e. *ici* 'here'), whereas none were noted in the English data. The use of such items entails directional explication in gesture (Fricke 2003), and therefore helps to account for the greater use of gesture only in the French data.

The marking of the lexical Ground's location, either as part of a gesture stroke phase or a post-stroke hold, was one way in which French speakers highlighted unlexicalised left/right directional information. A look at the English-language data uncovers this same phenomenon. The gestural marking of the lexical Ground's location was noted in nine (82%) of 11 examples with *next to*: these are the examples in which gesture alone expressed directional information. There is therefore no easy divide between an object's status as a Figure or a Ground, since an object can assume both roles simultaneously across speech and gesture. We think that this finding deserves more research. It is investigated to a larger extent in Chapter 8.

One difference between English and French speakers concerns the representation of distance between the Figure and the Ground. While certain examples revealed how English speakers amplified this distance to highlight directional information (see examples 126, 135 and 136), this phenomenon was not noted in the French data. This is possibly due to different tendencies by English and French speakers in the breaking up of the visual stimulus for analysis. For example, French speakers made greater reference to the foreground and background sections of the picture than English speakers did (see Chapter 5). Establishing reference to such visual properties requires an appreciation of distance in relation to the speaker-based origo. Moreover, earlier analysis (see Chapter 5) showed that French speakers used *en face de* to encode relationships of both proximity and distance. When the latter type of relationship was salient, speak-

---

[42] There were actually 51 uses of these items in the French data. However, as mentioned earlier (see section 6.3.5), we excluded seven ambiguous examples from our data analysis.

ers expressed distance information in the locative expression. These observations suggest that French speakers may potentially be more sensitive to the concern of distance than English speakers.

Both groups of describers made greater use of directionally non-specific items to encode location along the lateral axis than along the frontal axis. In the tables below, we look at the frequency of such items (the totals also including any sequence-encoding items) in both languages. The frequency of these items is compared to those of items which did encode specific directional information: we call this category 'directionally specific'. This bundles the 'front-encoding', 'back-encoding' and 'centre-encoding' categories for the frontal axis; and the 'left-encoding', right-encoding' and 'centre-encoding' ones for the lateral axis.

Tab. 22: English: the use of directionally non-specific and directionally specific items

	Directionally non-specific	Directionally specific	TOTAL
Frontal axis	17	36	53
Lateral axis	42	51	93
TOTAL	59	87	146

Tab. 23: French: the use of directionally non-specific and directionally specific items

	Directionally non-specific	Directionally specific	TOTAL
Frontal axis	10	51	63
Lateral axis	51	54	106
TOTAL	64	105	169

Beginning with the English results (table 22), describers made proportionally greater use of directionally non-specific items when encoding location along the lateral axis (42/93 items; 45%) than along the frontal axis (17/53 items; 32%). The same is true for the French speakers, and to a greater extent: directionally non-specific items accounted for 51/106 items (48%) in the lateral axis data, as opposed to 10/63 items (16%) in the frontal axis data. Part of the reason for the reduced difference in the English data is that English speakers recruited directionally non-specific items to refer to the back of the visually represented lounge room (see section 5.2.3). In contrast, French speakers used back-encoding items to do so. This helps to contribute to a greater difference in the use of directionally non-specific items in the French data for the two axes. Moreover, there were eight occurrences of deictic items in the French data for the lateral axis; in contrast, none were noted for the frontal axis. This, once again, helps to inflate the difference in result for the two axes.

6.6.4 Comparison of English and French descriptions of the street scene

In terms of overall totals, English speakers made far greater use of spatial items to encode location along the lateral axis than French speakers did. There were 111 occurrences of such items in the English descriptions, as opposed to just 57 in the French ones. The lower total for the French data cannot be attributed to just one category of spatial item (i.e. left-encoding items, directionally non-specific items, etc). Rather, French speakers made less use of left-encoding, right-encoding, and directionally non-specific items than English speakers did. The category totals for both languages are given below.

Tab. 24: Frequency of spatial items by category in English and French

	English	French	TOTAL
Left-encoding	37	18	55
Right-encoding	37	23	60
Centre-encoding	8	4	12
Directionally non-specific	29	12	41
TOTAL	111	57	168

Despite the differences in raw frequencies, the number of items in each category as a proportion of the whole is similar across the two languages. Hence, left-encoding items accounted for 33% (37/111) of items in the English data, and 32% (18/57) in the French data. Turning to right-encoding items, these amounted to 33% (37/111) for the English speakers, and to 40% (23/57) for the French speakers. Centre-encoding items accounted for 7% (8/111) of items in the English data, and 7% (4/57) in the French data. Finally, directionally non-specific items comprised 26% (29/111) of the total for English speakers, and 21% (12/57) for the French speakers.

However, the overall difference in raw totals shows that English speakers more frequently encoded lexical reference to object location on the left- and right-hand sides of the street. For example, five English describers specified the location of the post-office box on the right-hand side of the street, as opposed to one French speaker who did so. However, this does not mean that French speakers considered this information unimportant: five French describers presented this information in gesture only, as shown in the following example.

(167) la boîte postale   elle est..   <u>encore</u> avant le..   avant la voiture
       the letter box   it is..   <u>even more</u> before the..   before the car
       (FrenDesc2)

The gestural movement in the stills above indicates that the locative sequence encoded by *avant* ('before') plays out along the frontal axis. However, it is not merely the direction of the stroke in relation to the speaker that carries a locative charge. Notice that the speaker executes the gesture on the right-hand side of gesture space: this represents the Figure's location on the right-hand side of the street. Notably, the speaker does not lexically encode reference to the lateral axis in speech, and this directional information emerges only in gesture. Why does this occur? One likely answer is that gesture operates within three-dimensional space and may therefore express numerous pieces of directional information simultaneously. Hence, speakers may indicate an object's location along a particular spatial axis without concurrently encoding it in speech[43]. This explanation is supported by the fact that French speakers most frequently used gesture alone to provide directional information concerning the lateral axis for directionally non-specific items: this was true for descriptions of the lounge room and street scenes. In contrast, English speakers were more inclined to use *both* speech and gesture to express such information as far as the street scene was concerned.

---

43 This phenomenon is explored further in Chapter 8.

As far as directionally non-specific items are concerned, the different frequencies noted for the two languages owes to the use of *outside (of)* and *opposite* in English. This is because French speakers recruited *en face de* to encode the configurations for which these two English items were used. As explained in Chapter 5, *en face de* encodes reference to a Ground's frontal property: it was therefore included in our analysis of the frontal axis. Hence, we have a situation in which these two English items have been counted in the analysis for the lateral axis, while the French item has been assigned to our analysis of the frontal axis. If we deduct the 18 occurrences of *outside (of)* and *opposite* from the number of directionally non-specific items, we are left with a total of 11. This almost perfectly matches the 12 which were recorded in the French data. Hence, the discrepancy as far as this category is concerned can be traced to the use of *en face de* in French descriptions, and is thus rendered negligible.

7 How speakers gesture when encoding location with *on* and *sur*

This chapter examines how speakers gesture when using the topological prepositions *on* and *sur* ('on') to encode location. These prepositions encode locative configurations in which the Figure is in physical contact with a Ground and/or in which the Ground functions as a supporting surface for the Figure (Conventry and Garrod 2004; Herskovits 1986; Vandeloise 1986; Borillo 1998). The analysis presented here argues that speakers do not express the ideas of contact or locative support in gesture when using these prepositions. Rather, they use gesture to express directional information which establishes the location of the topological configuration in space. As outlined in preceding chapters, speakers recurrently execute directional gestures which relate to direction-encoding items (i.e. *to the left of*), as well as to directionally non-specific ones (i.e. *next to*). The fact that such gestures also relate to locative configurations encoded by *sur* and *on* suggests that gesture's role in communicating location is tightly linked to the expression of directional information.

7.1 A basic overview of topological relationships

Having examined how speakers express the location of objects along the frontal and lateral spatial axes, the focus now shifts to how speakers gesture when encoding topological relationships with *on* and *sur*. Different researchers understand topological relationships differently. For example, Coventry and Garrod (2004) take an approach which not only includes the non-directional prepositions *in*, *on*, and *at*, but also distance-encoding terms like *far* and *beyond*. Borillo (1992, 1998), on the other hand, is more restrictive and does not include distance-encoding terms in her understanding of topology. Instead, topological relationships are viewed as configurations in which "the Figure is found in a location ... which has a certain coincidence with that of the Ground." (Borillo 1998: 32; translation MT). Such locative coincidence emphasises a common, shared location between the Figure and the Ground. This approach to the understanding of topological relationships will be adopted in what follows. More specifically, our analysis will focus on how speakers use two topological prepositions which are comparable in English and French: *on* and *sur*. These prepositions are the object of study in this chapter because they occur with greater frequency in the data than other topological 'pairs', such as *in* and *dans*. The findings reported in this chapter provide a starting point for a larger-scale investigation into how speakers use gesture with topological prepositions in English and French.

The locative relationships encoded by *on* and *sur* are often characterised by the physical contact between Figure and Ground. Such contact, however, is not a necessary condition for the felicitous use of either preposition. After all, a book may be *on* a table even if a tablecloth physically separates the book from the table's surface (Herskovits 1986: 41). Vandeloise (1986: 188), using a spatial scenario provided by Herskovits, shows that French *sur* also allows this same type of physical separation. There is therefore a certain 'tolerance' (Herskovits 1986) in the use of these prepositions – as there is with others also – which allows for minimal deviations from an 'ideal meaning' (Herskovits 1986).

Our two previous chapters focused on how speakers gesture when describing the location of a Figure in relation to a Ground along a particular spatial axis. The results indicated that gestures represent the directional information encoded by co-occurring lexical spatial items (i.e. *to the right/left of*), while also providing information concerning the viewpoint and perspective from which this direction is conceptualised. In addition, locative directional gestures accompany the use of directionally non-specific prepositions such as *next to* and *à côté de*. They also play a pivotal role in expressing location by indicating the salient spatial axis which underpins uses of *between* and *entre*. However, we do not yet know what role gesture plays when speakers use topological prepositions. It is feasible that speakers will gesture differently when encoding location with *on* and *sur*, because these prepositions commonly encode relationships in which the Figure and Ground share a location in space. Hence, there is not the same need to specify the direction of the Figure in relation to the Ground. The possibility exists that speakers will instead focus on the gestural expression of topological information, such as relationships of contact. Work by Arik (2009) has observed how speakers of signed and spoken languages describe topological relationships of Figure/Ground contact. In his experiments, Arik presented participants with images of basic topological configurations, such as a ruler in a measuring cup, and an orange on a mug. He noted that the gesturing hands of English and Turkish speakers remained apart when describing these configurations, meaning that contact was not expressed in gesture. However, Arik's analysis does not specifically focus on how English speakers gesture when using *on*, and he investigates relationships which cannot necessarily be encoded by this preposition (such as a ruler *in* a measuring cup). Hence, we cannot use this study as a firm basis on which to construct a hypothesis. We therefore suggest that speakers may gesturally represent the encoded relationship of contact, because this may be salient information. In contrast, as stated above, given the shared location of the Figure and the Ground in space, it is unlikely that speakers will gesturally represent the direction of the former in relation to the latter.

7.2 Using *on* and *sur* to encode location

In this section, we provide an overview of the semantics of the prepositions *on* and *sur*. We begin with an examination of the former item, before moving on to the latter.

Used in a locative context, English *on* typically encodes two types of relationships. The first of these is the shared location of a Figure with a surface or a line (Herskovits 1986: 49). Such relationships are geometrical in nature and include simple occurrences of Figure/Ground contact, as shown in the following example.

(168)   *the tablecloth is on the table* (EngDesc1)

In (168) the Figure (*the tablecloth*) is understood to be in a relationship of contact with the Ground (*the table*). Such Figure/Ground locative contiguity exists across a range of geometrical configurations, with *on* licensing the use of differently shaped and oriented Ground surfaces. Hence, a light may be *on* a ceiling (an extended surface oriented horizontally) just as a picture may be *on* a wall (an extended surface oriented vertically) or a ring *on* a finger (a cylindrical surface with flexible orientation).

The second type of relationship which *on* encodes is the functional relationship of support (Miller and Johnson-Laird 1976: 382). In such relationships, the Figure may or may not be in physical contact with the Ground. The concern of support nearly always underpins uses of *on* involving three-dimensional objects (Herskovits 1986: 49). Hence, *the tablecloth* in example (168) is physically supported by *the table*, whose uppermost surface also provides a point of contact for the two objects. Physical contact is not, however, a precondition for support. For example, a book can be described as *on* a table even if it is on top of a pile of books and not in direct contact with the table itself (Coventry and Garrod 2004: 88). In such an example there is indirect contact between the Figure and the Ground, with the table also functioning as a surface that supports the book's location in space.

Just as relationships of support do not presuppose strict Figure/Ground contact, neither does such contact presuppose a relationship of support. Hence,

Herskovits (1986) claims that to describe a shadow *on* a wall is to describe the shared location of the shadow with a part, or all, of the wall's visible surface, without conceptualising the wall as a supporting surface for it. Both geometrical and functional concerns therefore underpin the felicitous use of *on*. The relative weight attributed to each of these concerns fluctuates across different Figure/Ground configurations (Coventry and Garrod 2004: 53).

The analysis which follows is concerned with how speakers gesture when using *on* to encode instances of Figure/Ground contact. From a geometric perspective, the Figure and the Ground share a common portion of space. From a functional perspective, the examples also encode situations in which the Ground supports the location of the Figure. Hence, representational gestures for *on* should communicate the ideas of contact and/or support.

Just like *on*, the physical contact of the Figure and the Ground characterises many uses of *sur* (Vandeloise 1986; Borillo 1998). This is shown by the following example from the lounge room scene data.

(169)   *i' y a une nappe*   *sur la table* (FrenDesc6)
        there's a tablecloth   on the table

In another similarity with *on*, *sur* also has strong links to the functional concern of support. This is discussed by both Vandeloise (1986) and Borillo (1998), who describe the functional dynamics of the preposition in terms of a carrier/carried ('porteur/porté') relationship. For instance, the tablecloth in example (169) is not only in contact with the table, it is also supported, or carried, by it. Both geometric concerns (the physical contact of the Figure and the Ground) and functional concerns (the locative support of the Figure by the Ground) therefore underpin its use in this example.

At other times, the weighting given to geometric or functional concerns is subject to variation (Coventry and Garrod 2004: 53). To retake Herskovits' (1986) example of *the shadow on the wall*, the relationship encoded by *on* here could be translated by the French *sur*. As Herskovits points out for *on*, the Figure (*the shadow*) and the Ground (*the wall*) occupy a common location in space but the latter does not function as a support for the former. This means that the equivalent use of *sur* in this context would be motivated by the geometric concern of contiguity as opposed to the functional concern of support.

Despite the crossover between *sur* and *on* in terms of the types of relationships they encode, certain differences exist in the Ground entities which each preposition introduces. This results in an intersection of contexts between the French use of *sur* and the English use of *in* (as opposed to *on*).

(170) *Janette est sur Paris*
    Janette is on Paris
    'Janette is in Paris'

(171) *Janette est sur la photo*
    Janette is on the photo
    'Janette is in the photo'

In example (170) Janette can be *sur* ('on') Paris so long as Paris is conceptualised as a supporting surface; the same conceptualisation holds for the photo in example (171). In contrast, English conceptualises the objects represented by photos as elements within a containing structure: this explains the need for *in* as opposed to *on* in the translation of example (171). Similarly, English conceptualises cities as containers rather than supporting surfaces, thereby explaining the use of *in* as opposed to *on* in the translation of example (170). As far as the data analysis which follows is concerned, these differences matter little: all but one of the uses of *sur* describe relationships of Figure/Ground contiguity that would be translated by *on*. The sole example which diverges from this pattern is a use of *sur l'image* ('on [in] the picture'), which describes the presence of an object in the stimulus picture[44].

In the following sections we investigate how speakers gesture when using *on* in descriptions of both stimulus scenes. We subsequently examine how French speakers gesture when using *sur* in descriptions of these scenes.

7.3 Identifying representational gestures for *on*

According to research into motion event descriptions (McNeill and Duncan 2000; Özyürek et al. 2005), gestures which express Path information usually synchronise with their semantically co-expressive lexical items. It therefore follows that representational gestures for *on* – itself a Path-encoding item – should generally synchronise with *on*'s occurrence in a locative expression. However, McNeill and Duncan (2000) and Stam (2006) point out that Path ges-

---

[44] It is worthwhile mentioning that *sur* is now also used to encode motion events describing progression towards a goal or destination: for example, *Jeanne va sur Paris* (lit: Jeanne is going on/onto Paris, i.e. 'Jeanne is going to Paris'). This results in the translation of *sur* by the English dynamic preposition *to*.

tures can also occur with Ground-encoding noun phrases. Our own data confirm this finding. Furthermore, we also find that Path gestures can synchronise with Figure-encoding noun phrases. Two examples in which the Path gesture synchronises with the Figure- and the Ground-encoding noun phrase are shown below.

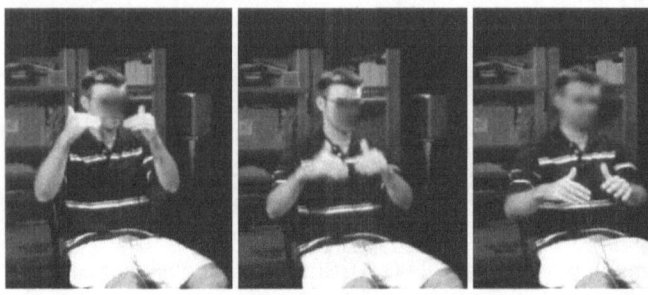

(172)   *there's a television under the window*

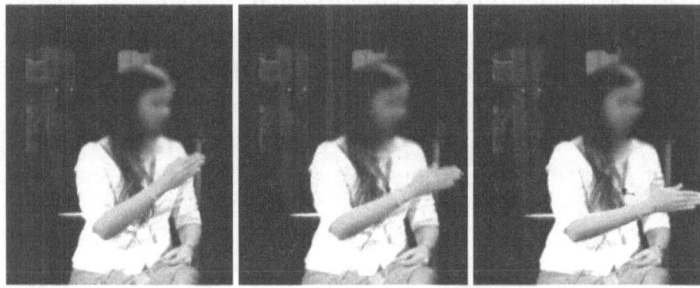

(173)   *and to the left of the fireplace is where the cat is sitting* [...]

Hence, gestures which accompany the lexicalised Figure and Ground should also be taken into account. Such an approach requires caution however, because the lexical Ground may include distance- or direction-encoding items: any co-occurring gestures may therefore relate to these items as opposed to *on*. Consequently, examples containing Grounds such as *the left*, *the far wall* or *the wall at the back* are not included in the analysis which follows. This is a cautionary measure to minimize the influence of any distance- or direction-encoding items on the occurrence of gesture in the *on* phrase.

Gestures accompanying the lexical Figure were taken into account provided that the Figure-encoding item did not relate to multiple Figure/Ground configurations in the expression. In example (174) below, *a window* is the lexical Figure which is not only *next to the mirror fireplace and rug* but also *on the far wall*. Since we already know that representational gestures for spatial items can co-occur with lexical Figures, any gesture accompanying *a window* may feasibly relate to either *next to*, *on* or *far*. The gestures accompanying such multi-relational Figures were therefore excluded from the analysis.

(174)   *next to.. the mirror fireplace and rug you have.. on the far wall a window* (EngDesc8)

In her study of dynamic motion events, Stam (2006) reports that Path-expressing gestures can also synchronise with the verb. However, gestures accompanying the verb were not included in our analysis. This is because locative expressions frequently contain only one lexical verb but multiple non-verb spatial items. For instance, in (174) above the speaker uses the spatial items *next to*, *on* and *far* but just one lexical verb, *have*. It is unlikely that any locative gesture would co-occur with *have* here because it does not encode the most newsworthy locative information in the expression: more detailed locative semantic information is encoded by the spatial items *next to*, *on* and *far*. Nevertheless, if a gesture were to co-occur with *have* it may relate to any of these three spatial items. Hence, a hand movement forward might relate to either *far*, *on*, or to both of these items. It may relate to *far* on account of the distance expressed by the gesture. In contrast, it may refer to *on* because it represents the conceptual placement of the window onto the wall: this placement event leads to the relationship of contact and locative support encoded by *on*. Therefore, for the sake of simplicity and to avoid such ambiguity, gestures accompanying the verb were not included. Moreover, location-encoding verbs may also lexicalise manner of location information (i.e. *lie* and *hang*, see Lemmens 2005). Such verbs, and the gestures which represent them, are not of interest in this study.

7.3.1 Gestures relating to *on* in descriptions of the lounge room scene

Following the criteria outlined above, 35 uses of *on* across 33 (primary and secondary) locative expressions were noted in descriptions of the lounge room scene[45]. The different Ground entities licensed by *on* are presented in the table below.

Tab. 25: Grounds in relationships encoded by *on*

Ground in *on* phrase	N
floor	14
table	7
wall	5
window	4
sofa	3
other side of room	1
cabinet	1
TOTAL	35

Of these 35 Grounds, 34 are entities with extended flat surfaces upon which the Figure is located. The exception to this is the more abstract *other side of the room*. Leaving this example aside for the moment, the 34 remaining Grounds occur in configurations in which the Ground functions as a locative support for the Figure and is in physical contact with it. An example of this is as follows.

(175) *straight ahead in front of you on the floor is the rug* (EngDesc3)

Table 26 below draws together all the gestures which accompany either *on* or relevant Figure- and Ground-encoding lexical items. These gestures can be divided into two semantic categories: those that express directional information pertaining to the location of the Figure/Ground configuration in space, and those that do not.

---

45 Two locative expressions each contained two uses of *on* to describe the same Figure/Ground relationship. Both uses were counted in the two examples. This is because in one example the speaker executed a gesture alongside the Ground-encoding nominal for one use of *on*, but not for the other. The two uses of *on* can therefore be differentiated on the basis of the co-occurring gestural behaviour.

Tab. 26: *On* + gesture

Gesture type	N
+ directional locative information[46]	
a. directional information lexicalised in expression	4
b. directional information unlexicalised in expression	7
sub-total: +directional locative information	*11*
- directional locative information	
d. non-locative gestures	8
sub-total: - directional locative information	*8*
TOTAL	19

The category '+ directional locative information' in table 26 is comprised of gestures which, as the name suggests, express locative directional information. This information establishes the location of the Figure/Ground configuration in relation to the larger containing space of the lounge room. Three of these 11 gestures were post-stroke holds. These holds enabled speakers to maintain focus on directional information which was salient to locating the lexicalised topological configuration in the picture. In the example below we present one of these holds, and describe the strokes which lead up to it. Note that we do not count these strokes in table 26 above. Rather, we count the directional hold which results, because it is this which co-occurs with the *on* phrase.

(176)   *and* <u>next to the</u> <u>book</u> *there's a dog.. sitting on the floor* (EngDesc10)

---

[46] Gestures which were bi-manual post-stroke holds, in which each hand marked the respective locations of two objects, were considered just one gesture. This is because both hands contributed to the expression of directional information.

Before encoding the topological relationship at the end of the expression, the speaker gesturally represents the location of the dog to the right of the book (see still above). He does this by placing his left hand, which represents the book, in front of his torso, before positioning his right hand, which represents the dog, in the far-right periphery of gesture space. The lexical items which accompany these two strokes are underlined in the example. Note that this directional information is unlexicalised in the co-occurring speech segment, and semantically complements the relationship of adjacency encoded by *next to*. Notice also the distance between the speaker's hands: this draws attention to the unlexicalised directional information as opposed to the encoded relationship of adjacency (cf. section 6.2.1). The speaker then holds his hands in place as he encodes the topological configuration with *on*. This allows for two things to occur. Firstly, it establishes the part of the floor upon which the dog is located: it is to the right of the book. Secondly, it anchors the encoded topological configuration within the context of a directional relationship: the dog *on* the floor is located to the right of the book. Gesture complements the lexicalised topological relationship by localising this relationship within the larger space of the picture. Note that the Figure remains the same across the two lexicalised relationships: that is, *the dog* is initially located in relation to *the book*, before being located in relation to *the floor*. This retention of the same entity as Figure does not always occur, however, as the following example shows.

(177)   *(and then there's <u>a table</u>)* with a tablecloth on it (EngDesc2)

In example (177), the speaker establishes the location of the table through the use of the sequential term *then* with a concurrent gesture to the right (the stroke is underlined in the example). The *table* subsequently becomes the Ground of the secondary locative (*with a tablecloth on it*). The speaker's gesture to the right and the ensuing hold (see the still above) mirrors the speaker's gestural behaviour in example (176): salient directional information is held in place as a topological relationship is encoded. However, despite the gestural congruity between the two examples, there are key differences in the lexical encoding of location. In (176) the speaker maintains the Figure of the initial relationship for the topological relationship which follows. In (177) however, the Figure changes from *table* in the primary locative to *tablecloth* in the subsequent secondary locative. The consistent gestural patterns across both examples – in spite of the differences in the attribution of Figure/Ground roles – can be explained by the different relationships of contiguity. In (176), the dog's location only covers a portion of the area occupied by the Ground (*the floor*): it is the dog's location which is of interest, as opposed to that of the entire floor. The speaker therefore uses a hold to retain focus on the previously expressed directional information concerning the dog's location in space. In contrast, (177) introduces a Figure (*table*) which subsequently becomes a Ground. The subsequent topological Figure (*tablecloth*) entirely covers the table's surface. This means that the entire location occupied by the Ground (*table*) is relevant, and so the speaker uses a hold to maintain the previously expressed directional information concerning the table's location. These two examples highlight two different ways in which speakers use holds to express directional information. In (176) the Figure remains the same across the primary and secondary locatives, while in (177) the Figure changes. Nevertheless, the same use of a direction-expressing hold occurs. This is because the gesturally-expressed directional information of the primary locative remains salient to the topological locative expression which follows.

In examples (176) and (177) above, speech encodes a topological relationship while post-stroke holds maintain focus on unlexicalised directional information. Speakers also use gesture strokes to bring back into play directional information lexicalised earlier in an expression.

 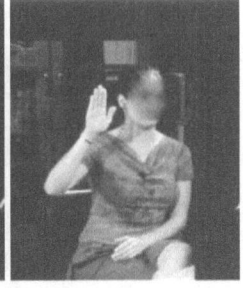

1   2

(178)   *as you walk in <u>it's just it's</u> above the <u>cat it's on the</u> wall* (EngDesc3)

Still 1 above captures the end of the stroke which accompanies the first underlined section in example (178). The pronoun *it* refers to the portrait of the young boy, and the speaker's hand acts as an iconic representation of this object. Her left hand, in a post-stroke hold, iconically represents the door. The speaker suggests the idea of vertical superiority, as encoded by *above*, through the height of her right hand in gesture space. She subsequently begins to retract this hand (this is not shown here) before suddenly re-installing it in its previous elevated location: the end of this stroke is shown in still 2 above. This gesture therefore re-expresses directional information as the speaker encodes the topological relationship with *on*. Hence, it is counted under the category '+directional information' in table 26.

The second category in table 26 '- directional information' is comprised of gestures which do not express any sort of locative information. Examples include beats and Figure/Ground iconics which did not have a locative charge. Given that the present research focuses on how gestures express locative information, these gestures will not be of interest here. This category simply appears in table 26 to show that gestures can be divided into two semantic sub-groups: those which express locative information (this information being directional in nature), and those which do not.

No gestures suggesting the Ground's support of the Figure were identified. The difficulty of manually representing the functional concern of support is obvious. While gestures can readily depict physical properties such as size and shape, an invisible functional idea like support defies easy gestural representation. In contrast, it is easier to envisage a gestural expression of physical contact: the speaker may engage both hands to represent the Figure and Ground respectively, bringing them into contact to iconically depict the spatial relationship. Given that all uses of *on* here encode relationships of Figure/Ground contact (the sole exception being the more abstract *on the other side of the room*), such gestures seem feasible. However, none were noted. This is possibly because the relationships of contact and support in our stimulus picture are very typical: for example, a portrait on a wall, a tablecloth on a table, etc. In contrast, speakers may have behaved differently if these relationships had been more unusual – such as a table on a tablecloth, instead of the inverse. Such unusual Figure/Ground topological pairings may have seemed more newsworthy, hence leading to gestural representations of contact. As it stands however, speakers in our experiment used gesture to communicate the locations of topological configuration in the overall scene. Hence, in example (178), the speaker localises the portrait on the wall at an elevated location along the vertical axis. In example (177), the speaker's post-stroke hold identifies the location of the Figure and the Ground on the right-hand side of the lounge room. Gesture is therefore connected to the expression of directional information along different spatial axes. This connection is further highlighted by the frequent co-occurrence of directional gestures with distance- and direction-encoding lexical items. The following example from the lounge room scene data – which is not included in table 26 because the gestures do not occur with *on* – brings this to light.

(179)   the tablecloth is on the table which is um <u>further across</u> from the tv but in the foreground of the picture.. (EngDesc3)

The speaker begins with a primary locative which encodes a topological relationship, 'the tablecloth is on the table'. No use of gesture occurs. She then uses a secondary locative, introduced by *which*, to encode the location of the primary Ground object (*table*). Her gestures synchronise with the distance-encoding item (*further across*) as well as the directional one (*foreground*; this gesture is not shown here), and in both instances express directional information. This directional information is provided from speaker viewpoint and observer perspective. The speaker's first gesture stroke, shown above, synchronizes with *further across* and is a movement out to the right: it expresses the table's location to the right of the television. This directional information is not encoded in the co-occurring speech segment and it semantically complements the lexical expression of distance. The speaker subsequently encodes the location of the table *in the foreground of the picture*. As she does so, she makes gestural reference to the area just in front of her (this gesture is not shown here). Both of these gestures establish the location of the table, and by extension that of the tablecloth which is *on* it. The topological relationship encoded by *on* is spatially unambiguous. In contrast, the expression of distance (*further across*) requires clarification: the necessary directional information is readily expressed in gesture. The part of gesture space which the speaker singles out as *the foreground* –

that is, the part closest to her along the frontal axis – shows that the speaker is using speaker, as opposed to addressee, viewpoint. Using addressee viewpoint would entail a 180-degree rotation of the spatial scene as the speaker sees it, with the inversion of front and back, and right and left. This gesture therefore shows that the preceding one which accompanies *further across* also needs to be interpreted as a gesture to the right from the speaker's viewpoint. Both these gestures communicate directional information which is pivotal to understanding the location of the table. By extension, this information is also pivotal to understanding the location of the tablecloth which is *on* it.

7.3.2 Gestures relating to *on* in descriptions of the street scene

Using the selection criteria described in section 7.3, 28 uses of *on* were found in descriptions of the street scene. The Ground entities which occur with these uses of *on* are presented in table 27 below.

Tab. 27: Grounds in relationships encoded by *on*

Ground in *on* phrase[47]	N
sidewalk	13
branch	4
other side of the road	2
side of the road	2
(t) intersection	2
road	2
roof	1
post-office box	1
tree	1
TOTAL	28

All 28 of the Ground-encoding entities in table 27 have surfaces upon which the Figure is located. In all examples there is physical contact between the Figure and Ground, with the latter also functioning as a locative support for the former.

---

[47] Synonyms have been collapsed into a single sub-category. For instance, 'sidewalk' covers uses of *sidewalk* as well as *footpath*, *pavement*, and *path*.

(180) *there's a cat to the left of the bus.. on the path* (EngDesc1)

In example (180) the Figure (*cat*) is encoded in a relationship of contact (*on*) with the Ground (*path*). The object *path* also functions as a supporting surface for the cat's location in space.

16 gestures were noted for the 28 uses of *on* following the guidelines specified in section 7.3. These 16 gestures can be differentiated according to whether they express locative directional information or not.

Tab. 28: *On* + gesture

Gesture type	N
+ directional information	
a. directional information lexicalised in expression	5
b. directional information unlexicalised in expression	7
c. some information lexicalised, some information unlexicalised	2
sub-total	14
- directional information	
d. non-locative gestures	2
sub-total	2
TOTAL	16

Of the 16 gestures recorded in table 28 above, 14 communicate directional information pertaining to the location of the Figure/Ground topological configuration in space. Five of these express directional information which partners with a semantically congruent item in the lexical expression, while seven express unlexicalised directional information. Two gestures (row 'c') express two pieces of directional information, one of which is lexicalised, the other not. The example below shows how gesture expresses directional information pertaining to the locations of topological configurations.

(181) and a bird is.. <u>on the branch of</u> a tree.. um just above that cat.. that's on the sidewalk (EngDesc9)

Example (181) establishes the location of the bird in relation to two Grounds: *the branch of a tree* and *that cat*. The latter also functions as the Figure of the secondary locative, *that's on the sidewalk*. The speaker does not lexically encode the location of these relationships on the left- or right-hand side of the street. However, in the preceding expression the speaker describes the location of the tree as *on the left-hand side of the street*. One of gesture's roles in (181) is to maintain focus on this piece of directional information. Therefore, as the speaker lexicalises the bird's location *on the branch of a tree*, he moves his hand around in the area above his left shoulder: this targets the bird's isomorphic location in gesture space. The preceding piece of directional information is thereby held in focus. Following this, the speaker marks the location of the cat in gesture space, expressing its location underneath the bird in the tree. The final frame of the relevant gesture stroke phase is shown below.

Note that the speaker retains his left-hand in a post-stroke hold, keeping the location of the bird in play. The result is a gestural representation of *above* with both hands engaged to represent the lexical Figure (*bird*) and Ground (*cat*) respectively. The speaker then maintains his hands in these respective locations as he encodes the secondary locative *that's on the sidewalk*. In doing so he frames the secondary locative within these directional parameters[48].

Example (181) above highlights two ways in which speakers use gesture to communicate and organise locative information. Firstly, it confirms the observation that speakers use gesture to communicate directional, as opposed to topological, information when using *on*. This is reflected not only by the gesture stroke which accompanies the lexical segment *on the branch of*, but also by the two stroke-holds which accompany *on the sidewalk* in the secondary locative expression. Gesture thereby maintains focus on lateral directional information that was encoded in the preceding expression. Secondly, the speaker shows how gesture can be used to synthesize primary and secondary locatives into a single overall expression. When the speaker switches to the secondary locative *that's on the sidewalk*, he nevertheless retains a gestural presence for the Figure of the primary locative: his left hand remains elevated in gesture space, representing the location of the bird along the vertical axis. Gesture highlights the salience of this information to the secondary topological expression, underscoring the status of primary and secondary locatives as connected parts of a single overall expression.

As noted for the lounge room scene, all gestures with a locative charge in table 28 express directional information pertaining to the location of the Figure/Ground configuration. This highlights the centrality of directional information to the expression of location (Landau and Jackendoff 1993; Vorwerg 2003 in Ashley and Carlson 2007). Furthermore, it shows that directional information plays a pivotal role even when speakers use a non-directional topological preposition like *on* to encode location. This information may be communicated at a prior point in the expression, before re-emerging in gesture when the speaker uses *on*. This was shown in an example from the lounge room scene description (example 178). The same use of gesture also occurs in the following example from a street scene description.

---

48 These two holds (the first which involves just the left hand, the second which involves both hands) account for the two examples in row 'c' (some information lexicalised/some information unlexicalised) of table 28. This is because both gestures contribute to a representation of the spatial unit *above*, while also expressing unlexicalised information concerning the locations of the cat and the bird along the lateral axis.

(182) *just to the right of the bus.. so <u>standing on the sidewalk</u> just about where the bus is.. um there's a lady* (EngDesc9)

The speaker begins by expressing the Figure's location to the right of the bus in speech and in gesture. He then encodes the Figure's location *on the sidewalk*. As he does so, his hand again moves out to the right-hand side of gesture space (see stills above). Notably however, the hand's trajectory to the right is even larger than in the preceding gesture. The speaker therefore highlights direction along the lateral axis in gesture, despite concurrently using *on* to encode a non-directional locative relationship in speech. The relationship of physical contact and support encoded by *on* is not present in the gesture shown above. Instead, the speaker's gesture expresses directional information which allows for this relationship to be located within the larger scene.

When speakers encode location with *on*, the same type of locative information emerges in gesture: this is irrespective of whether speakers are describing the street scene or the lounge room scene. This information is directional in nature and localises the topological configuration within the surrounding spatial scene. Gesture therefore expresses a different piece of locative information to that encoded by the topological preposition.

7.4 Identifying representational gestures for *sur*

Examples from the French language data were obtained by following the criteria outlined in section 7.3 for the English language data. Therefore, expressions in which the Ground featured distance- or direction-encoding terms were excluded from the analysis. This was to reduce the possibility that gestures co-occurring with the prepositional phrase were triggered by the distance- or direction-encoding item(s). Example (183) below, in which the lexical Ground is *le mur du fond* ('the back wall'), was therefore not included.

(183)   donc la fenêtre   est   à droite..   sur le mur *du fond* [...]
        so the window   is   on the right..   on the wall of the back
        'so the window is on the right.. on the back wall'
        (FrenDesc5)

Gestures accompanying the Figure, the Ground and *sur* itself were included in the analysis. Gestures accompanying the Figure were excluded when the Figure-encoding item related to multiple locative relationships. This is the case of *la fenêtre* ('the window') in example (183) above: *la fenêtre* ('the window') is not only *à droite* ('on the right') but also *sur le mur du fond* ('on the back wall'). Finally, as was the case for the English-language data, gestures which solely accompanied the lexical verb were not considered.

7.4.1   Gestures relating to *sur* in descriptions of the lounge room scene

16 uses of *sur* were found following the criteria outlined above. The Ground-encoding complements for these uses of *sur* are presented in table 29 below.

Tab. 29: Grounds in relationships encoded by *sur*

Ground in *sur* phrase	N
table ('table')	7
canapé ('sofa')	4
mur ('wall')	3
sol ('floor')	1
image ('picture')	1
TOTAL	16

Of these 16 configurations encoded by *sur*, 15 describe physical relationships of Figure/Ground contact and support. Amongst these is example (184), in which *sur* describes a relationship of spatial inclusion.

(184)   sur le mur   il y a   une fenêtre..   donc avec les rideaux
        on the wall   there is   a window..   so with the curtains

Windows are not entities which are placed upon a wall's surface. Rather, they fit into the wall's architecture itself and maintain contact with it on all sides. The concerns of support and contact therefore explain the use of *sur* to encode the window's relationship with the wall in (184). Only one use of *sur* does not describe a physical relationship between two objects in the picture. This example locates an entity *sur l'image* ('on the picture'), and so encodes the entity's existence in relation to the picture itself.

12 relevant gestures were found in these examples. These gestures can once again be broken down into the established categories of +/- directional information.

Tab. 30: *Sur* + gesture

Gesture type	N
+ directional information	
a. directional information lexicalised in expression	1
b. directional information unlexicalised in expression[49]	8
sub-total	9
- directional information	
d. non-locative gestures	3
sub-total	3
TOTAL	12

In eight out of the nine examples in which gesture expressed directional information, this information was not encoded in speech. Example (185) below shows one instance of this. The still image below captures the end of the gesture stroke phase.

---

[49] One speaker actually executed two gestures, one after the after, when expressing the location of the portrait on the wall. However, the second of these gestures was a 'repeat' of the first, triggered by a lexical correction. The speaker initially lexicalised the portrait as *une photo* ('a photo'), before correcting herself by saying *enfin un portrait* ('well a portrait'): this is shown in example (185). Therefore, only one gesture was counted.

(185) sur le mur eum..   donc il y a..   <u>il y a une photo</u>
       on the wall um..   so there is..   <u>there is a photo</u>
       enfin un portrait.. *de jeune garcon*   (FrenDesc6)
       well a portrait..   of (a) young boy

The speaker executes this gesture at an elevated position on the left-hand side of her gesture space. In doing so, she provides directional information which enables the portrait, together with the part of the wall which supports it, to be located in terms of the picture as a whole. Speech encodes the topological relationship (*sur*), while gesture expresses direction along the vertical and lateral axes: the portrait is in an elevated position to the left, as you view the picture. The level of locative semantic detail is therefore determined by the information communicated in both speech and gesture.

None of the 12 gestures identified in table 30 represent the contact between the Figure and the Ground, nor do they communicate the idea of the Ground supporting the Figure. Instead, speakers' gestures express directional information which localises the Figure/Ground configuration along one or more spatial axes. The following example shows how a speaker uses gesture to establish the location of the topological configuration along the lateral axis.

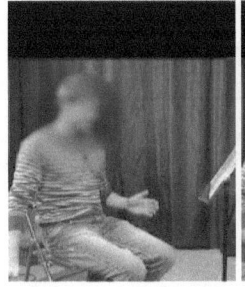 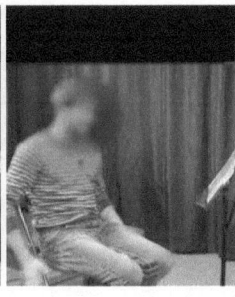 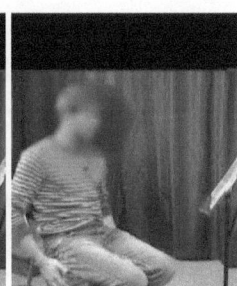

1   2   3

(186) *juste ici comme si j'étais sur le canapé moi*   *il y a le livre* [...]
just here as if I was on the sofa myself   there is the book
(FrenDesc10)

Prior to the gestural movement represented in the stills above, the speaker gestures out to the right (see the location of the right hand in still 1): this provides directional clarification for the deictic item *ici*. The speaker signals the use of a character perspective with *comme si j'étais sur le canapé moi* ('as if I was on the sofa myself'). This provides a spatial context for the interpretation of the preceding gesture to the right. While uttering this, the speaker brings his hands to touch either side of his chair (see stills above). He therefore re-enforces the preceding piece of directional information by showing that the sofa is to the left of the preceding location to the right. This has the effect of negating ambiguity about the direction of the book in relation to the sofa. Notably, the speaker's gesture does not communicate the topological information encoded by *sur*: rather, it focuses on directional information which clarifies the book's location relative to the sofa along the lateral axis. The speaker does not lexically encode any directional information in this example. Rather, the expression of direction falls solely within the domain of gesture, just as the relationship of contact and support is solely encoded in speech.

7.4.2 Gestures relating to *sur* in descriptions of the street scene

There were 24 occurrences of *sur* in descriptions of the street scene. These occurrences were determined following the selection criteria outlined in section 7.4 above. The Ground-encoding complements of *sur* are presented in table 31 below.

Tab. 31: Grounds in relationships encoded by *sur*

Ground in *sur* phrase	N
trottoir ('path')	11
arbre ('tree')	3
branche ('branch')	3
hôtel ('hotel')	3
toit (de l'hôtel) ('roof' 'of the hotel')	2

Tab. 31 (cont'd): Grounds in relationships encoded by *sur*

Ground in *sur* phrase	N
route ('road')	1
restaurant ('restaurant')	1
TOTAL	24

In 23 of these 24 examples the Figure is in direct physical contact with the Ground. The Ground also plays the functional role of providing locative support for the Figure. There were occasional differences in the level of specificity at which the Ground was encoded. Hence, some speakers localised the satellite dish on *le toit* ('the roof') of the hotel, while others took a larger, coarser view of the Ground and used *l'hôtel* ('the hotel') instead. A similar tendency was noted for descriptions of the bird's location: some speakers encoded this in relation to a branch of the tree, while others did so in relation to the tree as a whole. Hence, metonymic processes played a role in how speakers encoded the lexical Ground in these locative expressions.

Only a single use of *sur* which did not encode a relationship of physical contact was noted:

(187)   *donc la voiture se situerait   euh à peu près um..   sur le restaurant*
          so the car would be situated   ah about um..   on the restaurant
        'so the car would be situated roughly in line with the restaurant'

The speaker uses *sur* here to encode the car's alignment with the Ground *le restaurant* ('the restaurant'). This is a use of the preposition which does not encode locative contact or support, but rather the parallel locations of the Figure and the Ground along a spatial axis. The speaker uses gesture to indicate the spatial axis along which this parallelism holds. Her arm, as shown in the still above, is extended laterally in front of her. This orientation of the arm indicates that the locative relationship encoded by *sur* should be interpreted in terms of the lateral axis. Gesture therefore refines the use of *sur* by providing directional information which is unencoded in the lexical expression. This information is pivotal to understanding the location of the car in relation to the restaurant, and the example highlights the complementary nature of speech and gesture in the expression of location.

Relevant gestures can once again be divided into the established sub-categories of '+directional information' and '−directional information', as shown in table 32 below.

Tab. 32: *Sur* + gesture

Gesture type	N
+ directional information	
a. directional information lexicalised in expression	1
b. directional information unlexicalised in expression	7
sub-total	8
- directional information	
d. non-locative gestures	9
sub-total	9
TOTAL	17

A total of 17 gestures are represented in the table above[50]. Nine of these were non-directional gestures which did not express locative information (for example, beats). One locative expression, which contains an example of a directional gesture as well as two non-directional ones, is presented below. Note that we have only underlined the lexical items which accompany the stroke of the directional gesture.

---

[50] An additional gesture was noted but excluded from the analysis due to its questionable status as a direction-expressing gesture. A further movement was ambiguous as to whether it was a gesture or not, and also excluded.

(188)   <u>et sur cet arbre..</u>   *tu as un oiseau*   *sur une branche*
        <u>and on this tree..</u>   you have a bird   on a branch

The speaker raises her left-hand in synchrony with *et sur cet arbre* (see stills above). In doing so, she expresses the location of the bird along the vertical axis. This is therefore a directional gesture, counted under category 'b' in table 32. She subsequently executes two beat gestures. The first of these aligns with the Figure-encoding unit *un oiseau* ('a bird'), the second with the Path- and Ground-encoding units *sur une branche* ('on a branch'). These gestures account for two of the examples in the category '- directional information' in table 31. They are mentioned here because of what they reveal about how speakers express directional information. Although executed on the left-hand side of the speaker's gesture space, they do *not* communicate the unlexicalised location of the bird and the tree on the left-hand side of the road. This is because the speaker uses the left-hand side of gesture space even when describing the locations of objects which are found on the right-hand side of the street. Hence, understanding whether a speaker communicates directional information in gesture requires observing their gesture style throughout their entire discourse. It is only by correctly understanding how an individual speaker uses their gesture space that gestures may reliably be assessed for directional load.

Once again, all location-expressing gestures expressed directional information. This concerned the location of the topological configuration in the overall scene. Speech and gesture therefore played complementary roles in the expression of locative information.

No further commentary will be provided about the gestures which fall under the category '- directional information' in table 32. The essential point to retain by having this category is that there are two types of gestures which accompany the use of *sur*: those which express directional information concerning the location of the topological configuration (category '+ directional information'), and those which do not (category '- directional information').

Looking across the results obtained for the use of *sur* in descriptions of the street scene and the lounge room scene, all location-expressing gestures communicated directional information. In the majority of instances this information was unlexicalised: this was the case for eight out of nine directional gestures in the lounge room scene data, and seven out of eight in the street-scene data. There were no bi-manual representations of the Ground supporting the Figure, nor were there any bi-manual representations of Figure/Ground contact. Moreover, no single-handed gestures representing the ideas of support or contact were noted. This suggests that speakers do not use gesture to represent the relationships of locative contiguity and support encoded by *on* and *sur*. Instead, they use gesture to express directional information concerning the location of the Figure/Ground configuration along one or multiple spatial axes.

7.5 Comparative discussion of English and French results

There was clear comparability in terms of the type of locative information which speakers expressed in gesture when using *sur* and *on*. In contrast, there were twice as many occurrences of *on* as there were of *sur*. This owes to the availability of other prepositions in French to encode Figure/Ground contact, and to the tendency of French speakers to leave pragmatically inferable topological information unlexicalised.

7.5.1 Ground-encoding complements of *on* and *sur*: lounge room scene

There were certain differences in the Ground items which occurred as the complements to *on* and *sur* in descriptions of the lounge room scene. The table below recapitulates the Grounds from the examples used in the data analysis.

Tab. 33: Grounds occurring with *on* and *sur*: lounge room scene

Ground in *on* phrase	N	Ground in *sur* phrase	N
floor	14	*table* ('table')	7
table	7	*canapé* ('sofa')	4
wall	5	*mur* ('wall')	3
window	4	*sol* ('floor')	1
sofa	3	*image* ('picture')	1

Tab. 33 (cont'd): Grounds occurring with *on* and *sur*: lounge room scene

Ground in *on* phrase (cont'd)	N	Ground in *sur* phrase (cont'd)	N
other side of room	1		
cabinet	1		
TOTAL	35		16

The first point to be made is that there was more than double the amount of uses of *on* than there was of *sur*. Part of the reason underlying this is the greater range of prepositions which French speakers can use to encode the contact a Figure has with a surface. Therefore, whereas 14 uses of *floor* occurred as Ground in English, only one use of the noun *sol* ('floor') was noted in French. This is because French speakers also used the prepositional phrase *par terre* (translated literally as 'by earth') to lexicalise a Figure's contact with the floor: five examples of this were noted in the data. Furthermore, one speaker also used the preposition *à* (meaning *on*) to describe the location of a Figure on the floor. These six examples therefore account for part of the difference in frequency between the uses of *on* and *sur*. The second point to be made is that English speakers encoded relationships of contact and support which were unlexicalised by French speakers. For example, only two out of ten French Describers encoded the location of the portrait on the wall, as opposed to six out of ten English Describers who did so. French speakers instead left this topological relationship to be pragmatically inferred.

(189) *au-dessus du chat   il y a   le portrait du jeune garçon* (FrenDesc2)
       above the cat   there is the portrait of the young boy

World knowledge tells us that portraits cannot maintain a location in space without a supporting surface. We also know that portraits are typically found on walls. The speaker in example (189) therefore encodes directional information while leaving the topological relationship to be pragmatically inferred. In contrast, six English speakers lexicalised the portrait *on the wall*, with one speaker doing so twice within the same expression. Four of these seven uses of *on the wall* included the spatial items *back* or *far* as modifiers of *wall*. It is therefore possible that the prepositional phrase headed by *on* occurred as a way of introducing the directional information concerning the wall's location. Example (190) below presents this possibility.

(190) *if you open the door.. of the room.. there's a portrait of the young boy.. at um head height.. on that far wall.. ah it's closest to the door* (EngDesc8)

This explanation, however, cannot account for the other three uses of the prepositional phrase which do not include such directional modifiers. The upshot of this is that English speakers may be more inclined to lexicalise pragmatically-inferable topological relationships than French speakers. This explanation, merely hypothetical at the moment, is given greater weight in the following section.

7.5.2 Alternative strategies to using *on* and *sur*

The tendency of French speakers to leave certain relationships, which would normally be encoded by *sur*, to pragmatic inference is highlighted by other examples in the data. For instance, no French speaker described the location of the curtains *sur* ('on') the window. Instead, six speakers made an implicit locative association between the curtains and the window by using the non spatial preposition *avec* ('with'):

(191) *au-dessus de la télévision..*   *tu as une fenêtre avec des rideaux..*
       above the television..   you have a window with some curtains..
       donc dans la partie droite   (FrenDesc3)
       so in the part right
       'above the television.. you have a window with some curtains.. so in the right part'

In example (191) the speaker lexicalises direction along the vertical and lateral axes but does not encode the topological relationship between the window and the curtains. This is left to be pragmatically inferred thanks to the locative association prompted for by *avec* ('with'). In contrast, four English speakers used *on* to encode the curtains' relationship with the window:

(192) *the window actually has a set of curtains on it so.. that's where the curtains are.. and they're open* (EngDesc4)

This difference between the English and French data may be explained by the type of Ground in play: *wall* and *window* are both vertically oriented objects, and French speakers commonly use *sur* with Grounds of horizontal orientation.

Hence, five French speakers described the tablecloth's location *sur* ('on') the table:

(193) *i' y a   une nappe   sur la table* (FrenDesc6)
      there's   a tablecloth   on the table

Vandeloise (1986) points out that *sur* is required to encode contact between horizontally oriented objects, such as a cup and a table. However, as far as contact between vertically oriented objects is concerned, the preposition *à* can also be used and may even be preferable to *sur* (Vandeloise 1986). Yet there are no examples in which French Describers used *à* to encode the relationship of the curtains to the window, or that of the portrait to the wall: these topological relationships were left to pragmatic inference. French speakers therefore squarely placed the emphasis on directional information when it came to localising the curtains and the portrait.

Just as French speakers used *avec*, so too did English speakers use *with* to prompt for Figure/Ground locative associations, albeit with less frequency. Three such examples of *with* were noted in the lounge room scene data, as opposed to the nine examples of *avec* in the French data.

(194)   and then on the far right.. is the table.. *with the tablecloth* (EngDesc6)

The tendency of French speakers to leave relationships of contact between two vertically oriented objects unlexicalised is also noted in examples describing the location of the mirror. No French speaker used the prepositions *sur* ('on') or *à* ('on') to encode the mirror's relationship with the wall. In contrast, seven French Describers encoded the mirror's location *au-dessus de* ('above') the fireplace, thereby providing vertical directional information. It is worthwhile examining why this relationship along the vertical axis is recurrently encoded, while the topological relationship is not. As sturdy immobile entities, fireplaces make ideal reference objects. Accurately encoding the location of the mirror in relation to the fireplace necessitates referencing the vertical axis unless a basic statement of proximity is sufficient (i.e. *the mirror is near the fireplace*). However, it is insufficient to claim that the expression of vertical directional information is a corollary of using the fireplace as Ground. If speakers fashioned locative relationships on the basis of initially selecting a Ground, then speakers should also select the wall – itself an ideal reference object – and hence describe the mirror's relationship of contact and support with it. This, however, does not occur. Instead, French speakers privilege the lexical encoding of direction. This can be explained by the fact that whereas the topological relationship can be inferred, the directional one cannot. That is, there is no default directional connection between mirrors and fireplaces. In contrast, there is a default association between mirrors and walls: our world knowledge tells us that the former are commonly located upon the latter. The directional information is therefore the newsworthy information, and this explains why it is lexically encoded. An observation which clearly reinforces this explanation is that no French or English speaker describes the sofa's location *on/sur* the floor. This is because the topological relationship of the sofa to the floor is obvious and does not require lexical specification. In contrast, seven English speakers and eight French speakers lexically encode the sofa's location on the left-hand side of the room: this is because there is no default directional relationship between sofas and particular sides of lounge rooms. Selecting a Ground therefore depends on the type of locative information that is salient in context. Whereas many objects have default relationships of contact with other objects, they do not have default directional relationships with them. This means that directional information is often more crucial in the encoding of location. As such, speakers may simply use *with* or *avec* to prompt for topological relationships of contact – or not encode them at all.

The results presented above reveal a contrast between English and French speakers in terms of the lexicalisation of pragmatically inferable locative information. This aligns with how English and French typically lexicalise the semantic feature of Manner (Talmy 2000) for motion events. That is, while English routinely lexicalises the manner in which a motion event takes place (Slobin 1997: 456), French does not (Slobin 1997: 457). This is because such information can be pragmatically inferred from knowledge about the agent in motion and their 'default' mode of displacement.

(195) Jeannie walked into the room

(196) Jeannie est entrée   dans la pièce
       Jeannie entered   into the room
       'Jeannie entered the room'

Therefore, while English speakers commonly specify the manner of motion in a boundary-crossing motion event (example 195), such information is routinely unlexicalised in French (example 196). This stands in contrast to *non* boundary-crossing motion events, for which French lexicalises manner of motion in the main verb (Gullberg et al. 2008). Now, as far as boundary-crossing events are concerned, the lexical encoding of manner information in French normally requires the addition of an adverbial to the main clause. This makes the expression heavier and indicates that manner of motion is particularly salient in context (Slobin 1997: 457). Because of this, manner information is typically unlexicalised and left to pragmatic inferencing. This observation, taken from the related semantic domain of dynamic motion events, provides an explanation as to why French speakers sometimes leave topological information unspecified.

7.5.3 Ground-encoding complements of *sur* and *on*: street scene

There were few differences in the Ground items which occurred as complement to *on* and *sur* in descriptions of the street scene. The table below recapitulates these Ground items, as presented in the preceding data analysis.

Tab. 34: Grounds occurring with *on* and *sur*: street scene

	Ground in *on* phrase[51]	N	Ground in *sur* phrase	N
A	sidewalk	13	trottoir ('sidewalk')	11
B	branch	4	branche ('branch')	3
C	road	2	route ('road')	1
D	side of the road	2	hôtel ('hotel')	3
E	other side of the road	2	toit (de l'hôtel) ('roof' 'of the hotel')	2
F	(t) intersection	2	restaurant ('restaurant')	1
G	tree	1	arbre ('tree')	3
H	post-office box	1		
I	roof	1		
J	TOTAL	28		24

The only difference of note in table 34 is French speakers' use of the hotel and its roof as Ground entities (rows D and E). No use of *hotel* as Ground occurred in the English-language data, and only one use of *roof* was noted. This difference is explained by the fact that English speakers used *on top of*, as opposed to *on*,

---

51 Synonyms have been collapsed into a single sub category. For instance, 'sidewalk' covers uses of *sidewalk* as well as *footpath, pavement, sidewalk* and *path*.

to encode the contact of the satellite dish with the hotel and its roof. Other discrepancies between the two languages are minimal and likely the result of individual variation. For example, one English speaker accounts for both the uses of *side of the road* (the equivalent of which is not found in the French data), and there are only two occurrences of *other side of the road* (the equivalent of which, once again, is not found in the French data).

While most of the Ground entities used across the two languages are flat surfaces, there are certain exceptions. Trees, for instance, have cylindrically shaped trunks and branches. They can also be geometrically conceptualised as bounded volumes (Herskovits 1986), which explains why some English and French speakers used *in* and *dans* to describe the bird's location relative to the tree. The use of *on*, in contrast, reveals a conceptualisation of the tree as a surface which supports the bird and which is in contact with it. The choice of *on* or *in* therefore depends on whether a speaker conceptualises the tree as a volume or a surface.

7.6 General discussion and summary

In her seminal work on English spatial prepositions, Herskovits (1986: 105) remarks that "a locative expression gives us only a constraint on location: if a spider is said to be *on a wall*, it could be anywhere on the wall. We cannot derive a full visual representation, unless we choose to assign a precisely defined default location to the spider." It is true that locative expressions only provide us with constraints on a Figure's location. However, speakers are skilful at providing detailed constraints, and these involve the use of both speech and gesture. As Herskovits writes, if a spider is described as being *on a wall* "it could be anywhere on the wall". However, by attending to a speaker's gestures we can gain a better idea of the spider's precise location on this wall. Consider the following use of French *sur*, which was previously presented as example (185).

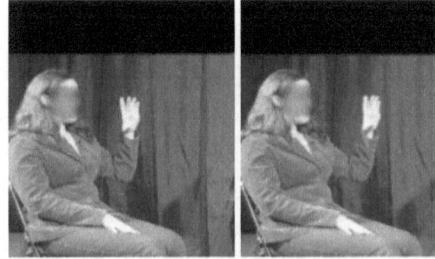

(197) sur le mur eum..   donc il y a..   *il y a une photo*
       on the wall um..   so there is..   there is a photo
       enfin un portrait..   *de jeune garcon*   (FrenDesc6)
       well a portrait..   of (a) young boy

The speaker lexically encodes a topological relationship of contact and support while concurrently expressing the Figure's location along the vertical and lateral axes in gesture. The location of the speaker's hand is crucial to interpreting the directional information: it localises the portrait of the young boy at a superior point along the vertical axis, while also showing that it is on the left-hand side of the wall (using a speaker-based origo). The direction along the lateral axis which gesture expresses is particularly crucial here. While world knowledge tells us that pictures are generally at elevated locations on walls, their locations on particular sides of walls cannot be similarly inferred. Moreover, this information concerning the lateral axis is not available from what precedes in the speaker's discourse. There is thus a division of Path information across speech and gesture: contact is encoded in speech, while vertical and lateral direction is expressed in gesture. The consideration of locative expressions as multi-modal constructions therefore allows us to move closer to the 'full visual representation' of which Herskovits writes.

All locative gestures in this study were of a common type: they expressed directional information. This information concerned the location of the Figure/Ground topological configuration encoded by *on* and *sur*. The uses of *on* and *sur* identified in this study encoded relationships of contact in which the Ground supported the location of the Figure. With this in mind, representational gestures for these prepositions should present the ideas of contact and/or support. No such gestures were noted in the data analysis.

There were several ways in which speakers used gesture to communicate salient directional information about the location of a topological configuration. Firstly, English speakers used post-stroke holds to maintain focus on a piece of previously expressed directional information. This use of post-stroke holds occurred in descriptions of the lounge room scene (examples 176 and 177) as well as of the street scene (example 181). Secondly, English speakers used gesture to re-express a piece of directional information which had previously been presented in the locative expression. Once again, this occurred in descriptions of the lounge room scene (example 178) and in descriptions of the street scene (example 182).

The gestures noted for French describers differed only slightly to those produced by their English-speaking counterparts. For instance, French describers did not make use of post-stroke holds to maintain focus on directional information. They also produced a slightly greater number of gestures which communicated unlexicalised directional information: 15 (88%) of the 17 gestures by French speakers fell into this sub-category, as opposed to 14 (61%) of the 23 produced by English speakers[52].

The common expression of directional information in gesture by both English and French speakers suggests a parallel between *on* and *sur*. As pointed out earlier, there are minimal differences in the two prepositions: one such difference is the slight variation in the Ground entities which each preposition licenses. However, *on* and *sur* are very similar in terms of the geometrical and functional relationships they encode. This similarity goes some way to explaining the parallel gestural behavior of the two groups of speakers. Previous research has shown that the type of information that speakers express in gesture is related to the semantic content of co-occurring lexical spatial items (Kita and Özyürek 2003). The results presented here support this claim by showing that similar spatial lexemes in two different languages occur with gestures which express the same type of informational content.

The final question to be answered is why speakers do not execute representational gestures for *on* and *sur*. There are two possible reasons for this. The first of these is that the relationships of contact and locative support encoded by *on* and *sur* do not normally require clarification: they are generally unambiguous and remain consistent irrespective of changes in viewpoint or perspective. In contrast to this, lexically-encoded directional information requires the use of a viewpoint and a perspective. In Chapters 5 and 6, we showed how gesture expresses viewpoint and thus helps to disambiguate directional information.

Secondly, English and French spatial language sets speakers up to express directional, but not topological, information in gesture. The spatial deictic terms *there* and *là* are clear indications of this. Fricke (2003) points out that *there* "is obligatorily accompanied by a direction-indicating gesture" (p.73). Bühler (1982) agrees with Wegener and Brugmann in understanding deictic words as signals. When used spatially therefore, *there* and *là* are signals which receive directional colour thanks to gestural complementation. In contrast, there are no lexemes in English or French that are obligatorily accompanied by a topology-indicating gesture. The absence of such lexical items suggests that gesture is suited to communicating directional, as opposed to topological, information.

---

52 This total for the English speakers excludes the two gestures in table 28 which contain both lexicalised and unlexicalised directional information.

This, in turn, helps to explain the absence of representational gestures for the prepositions *on* and *sur*.

8 Further findings, and the theoretical application of our results

This chapter is divided into two major subparts. The first part presents a qualitative analysis of further evidence to show that speakers use gesture to express salient unlexicalised locative information. We argue that this occurs in two main ways. Firstly, gestures can express a Figure's location along one or more spatial axes which is/are not referenced in speech: this amounts to the presentation of one or more key strands of directional information in gesture only. Secondly, speakers use gesture to establish the location of the lexical Ground in gesture space. This information is not concurrently encoded in the lexical expression, and reveals the Ground as a 'gestural Figure'. This is a phenomenon that we have touched upon throughout the course of our data analysis (see Chapters 4, 5 and 6). Here we show that the categorisation of an object as a Figure or a Ground is more complicated than it initially seems, and that the two semantic roles are actually intimately related. The second part of the chapter not only builds upon the results presented in the first part, but indeed upon all of the results from our study. Specifically, we show how our findings can be integrated into the theoretical framework of Cognitive Grammar (Langacker 1987), and argue in favour of structural modifications to the 'symbolic assembly' – the core unit of linguistic analysis in this framework – to enable the integration of representational gestures into this theory of language.

8.1 Summary of our approach to analysing static locative relationships

As outlined in Chapter 2, we have structured our analysis of static locative relationships around the semantic criterion of direction. Establishing a Figure's direction in relation to a Ground and an origo (each of which may be manifested by different objects; see Chapter 2) is pivotal to communicating location. The salience of direction is also reflected by our understanding of space in terms of the frontal, lateral, and vertical spatial axes (see Vandeloise 1986; Borillo 1998; Lyons 1977), each of which is associated with two opposite directions: front-back, left-right, and up-down. Hence, we examined how speakers express location along the frontal axis (Chapter 5) and along the lateral axis (Chapter 6). In these two chapters we categorised linguistic spatial items according to whether or not they encoded reference to a specific directional half of a spatial axis. Items which did not do this, such as *next to* and *à côté de*, were labelled 'directionally non-specific' items. We subsequently examined how speakers used these items by looking at whether directional information relating to the lexically-encoded relationship was present elsewhere in the locative expression. This led to the discovery that such information was often expressed in gesture alone. Finally, in a separate chapter, we observed how speakers gestured when encoding location with *on* and *sur*. This revealed that speakers attended to the semantic concern of direction even when using these two non-directional topological items to encode location.

The following sections add to these findings by exploring two further ways in which gestures express unlexicalised locative information. The first of these concerns how speakers establish reference to a Figure's location along one or more spatial axes in gesture alone. This is followed by an investigation of how and why speakers express the location of the lexical Ground in gesture space.

8.2   Referencing different spatial axes in speech and gesture

Our previous chapters have largely focused on how speakers gesture when they do *not* encode specific directional information in a lexical item. In our analysis, we showed that occurrences of such 'directionally non-specific' items are frequently accompanied by gestural expressions of direction. Yet what happens when speakers do encode directional information in speech? In Chapters 5 and 6 we showed that gestures provide unlexicalised information concerning the viewpoint from which directional relationships are encoded. Gesture also represents directional information from a character or observer perspective. Perspective use across speech and gesture is normally consistent, although cross-modal variations are possible (see Chapter 5). The concerns of viewpoint and perspective, however, will not be the focus of what follows. Instead, we will focus on a finding which we have not yet explored in our study: this is the use of gesture to express location along a spatial axis which is different to that referenced in speech. We will examine how this occurs by looking at descriptions of the two stimulus pictures separately.

8.2.1 Different spatial axes in speech and gesture: lounge room scene

As stated above, speakers may represent the same piece of directional information in speech and gesture, with gesture providing additional information concerning viewpoint and perspective. In addition to this however, speakers may also indicate the Figure's location along one or several spatial axes in gesture alone.

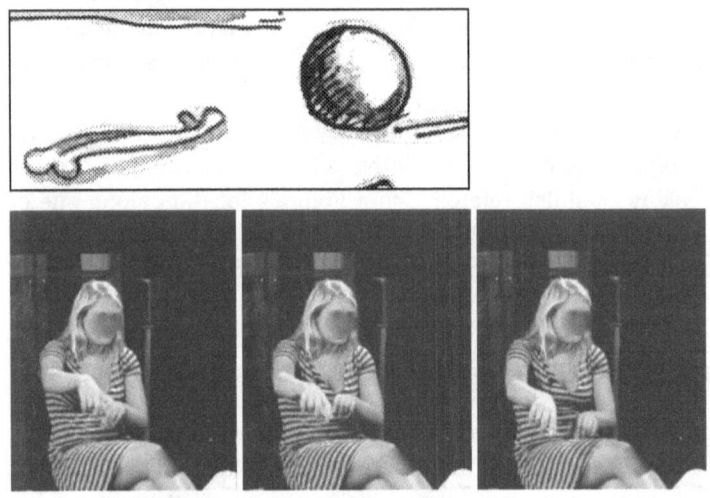

(198) and a ball.. a bit *further in* front (EngDesc3)

In example (198) the speaker locates the ball in relation to a contextually understood Ground (the 'bone'). She encodes location along the frontal axis in speech, describing the ball's location as *a bit further in front* of the bone. Her right index finger traces the round shape of a ball whilst moving forward and to the right (see stills above): this not only represents the directional information encoded by *in front*, but it also shows that the ball is *to the right* of the bone as the speaker views the picture. Gesture accomplishes three tasks here. Firstly, the speaker's index outlines the shape of the ball: this is an iconic representation of the lexical Figure. Secondly, the movement of her hand represents the Figure's location relative to the Ground along the frontal axis. Bones do not have intrinsic frontal surfaces, and so the speaker needs to attribute this property to the Ground using a relative frame of reference. As shown in Chapter 5, speakers do not always use the 180-degree rotation of their own front/back distinction to achieve this. In the current example, the speaker's hand moves forward and away from her location in space. This means that the conceptualised 'front' of the Ground object, the unlexicalised 'bone', does not face the speaker: rather, it faces in the same direction. The speaker has therefore used the process of 'translation' to assign a front/back distinction to the bone, thus breaking with the 180-degree rotational analysis associated with English (Levinson 1996: 369–371, 2003). Thirdly, and most importantly for our current argument, gesture expresses the Figure's location along the lateral axis. The speaker's hand clearly moves out to the right, thus expressing the Figure's location to the right of the bone (using a speaker-based origo). Reference to the lateral axis is not concurrently encoded in speech, nor is it inferable from what precedes in the speaker's discourse. In addition to making an important contribution to expressing the Figure's location, this gesture also reveals that the speaker has construed the Figure's location at a finer degree of detail than her speech would have us believe: that is, she conceptualises the ball's location along both the frontal *and* lateral axes, as opposed to along the frontal axis alone.

Any combination of spatial axes is possible in these speech/gesture directional fusions. Hence, in the following example the speaker references the vertical axis in both speech and gesture, while also referencing the lateral axis in gesture alone.

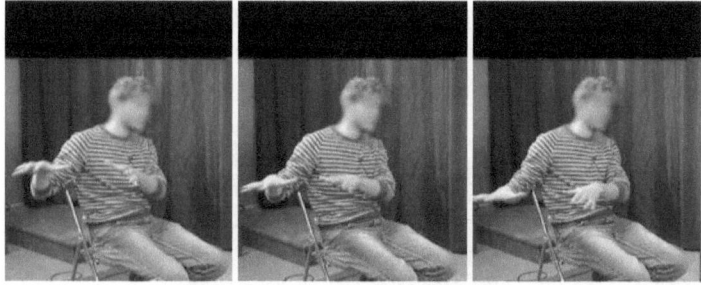

(199)   [...] *elle est vraiment euh..*   *trente centimètres* <u>*au-dessus de la table*</u>
        [...] it is really uh..   thirty centimetres <u>above the table</u>

This example is part of a longer expression which localises the lamp in the lounge room scene. The gesture occurs on the right-hand side of gesture space, and involves the movement of both hands downwards. This movement along the vertical axis semantically coordinates with the spatial item *au-dessus de* ('above')[53]. However, at no point in the expression does the speaker lexically encode the lamp's location along the lateral axis: this information emerges in gesture only. Such propensity for expressing directional information results from gesture's status as a visual-spatial modality. Since it operates within three-dimensional space, gesture can express location along the three spatial axes simultaneously. In spite of this, we cannot state with absolute certainty that the speaker in the current example is expressing the Figure's location along the frontal axis. This is because the gesture occurs within the default region of frontal gesture space, just a short distance in front of the speaker. The same problem occurs when speakers describe the locations of other objects which are located in the foreground of the picture. As far as the lateral axis is concerned, such a problem is not encountered when an object is clearly on the left- or the right-hand side of the picture. However, representing the location of an object in the centre of the picture will intersect with the default, centre-region of gesture space: this makes it difficult to determine whether the speaker intends to express its location along the lateral axis or not. Given these difficulties, we will not provide an overall frequency for these speech/gesture axial fusions. Instead, we will present another example for which such ambiguity does not exist. As far as the lounge room scene is concerned an ideal object is the lamp, which is found on the far right of the picture. As shown in example (199) above, the speaker lexically encodes location along the vertical axis while referencing location along the lateral axis in gesture alone. Two of the remaining nine French describers also use gesture in this way. Turning to the English data, we note that three describers behave in this manner.

---

53 Interestingly, the speaker's hands move down instead of up: this is somewhat striking, given that *au-dessus de* encodes the location of the Figure at a higher point than the Ground along the vertical axis. The potential reasons behind this will not be the focus of the present discussion, however.

(200) *and the light's above the table* (EngDesc3)

In example (200), the speaker uses the preposition *above* to encode the lamp's location along the vertical axis. She maintains her left hand in a post-stroke hold on the right-hand side of gesture space: this represents the location of the Ground object 'the table'. Her right hand rises above this, the index finger and thumb coming together in a pinch-like formation: this iconically represents the cord which connects the lamp to the ceiling. She repeats this motion three times, such that the gesture accompanies the entire length of the lexical locative expression. Notably, the lamp's location on the right-hand side of the room is presented exclusively in gesture. Similarly, gesture alone expresses the table's location along the lateral axis in the previous expression in discourse. Hence on both occasions, the speaker expresses the Figure's location on the right-hand side of the picture in gesture only. This highlights a particularly productive use of gesture to express a strand of directional information which is not encoded in speech.

8.2.2 Different spatial axes in speech and gesture: street scene

As far as the street scene is concerned, the majority of objects which speakers were required to localise were on the right- or the left-hand sides of the street. How speakers expressed object location on these respective sides merits attention. Speakers frequently established cohesion in their discourse by creating the Ground of a locative expression from the Figure of the preceding expression. The following example shows how this occurs.

(201) *the café is the first shop on the right hand side..*
       and that's where there's a a lady out the front of that (EngDesc4)

Example (201) contains two locative expressions: *the café is the first shop on the right hand side*, and *and that's where there's a a lady out the front of that*. The 'café' is the Figure of the first locative expression and subsequently assumes the role of Ground in the second. There is a degree of cohesion between the two expressions thanks to the use of this object in a Figure then a Ground role. Looking more closely at the first expression, the speaker uses sequence-encoding *first* to reference the Figure's location along the frontal axis which extends from the foreground to the background of the picture. In addition to this, she explicitly encodes location along the lateral axis (*right-hand side*). In the second expression, this Figure ('café') becomes the Ground in relation to which a new Figure ('a lady') is localised. However, the speaker does not re-encode reference to the frontal and lateral axes of the preceding expression, although both are salient to establishing the lady's location. At first glance this omission appears logical because the information is contextually inferable: if the café is on the right hand side of the road, then so too must be any object which is *out the front* of it. Furthermore, if the café is the first shop along the road, then an object *out the front* of it will also occupy this same location along the frontal axis. Nevertheless, as stated above, both strands of information are pivotal to understanding the lady's location in the picture. Hence, the speaker uses gesture to maintain focus on them while she encodes the new locative configuration in speech. The following stills show the end points of the two gesture stroke phases executed by the speaker in her locative expression.

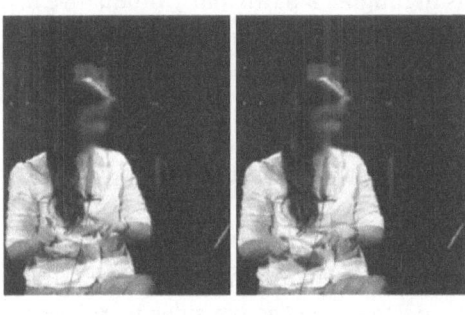

1   2

(202)   <u>and that's</u> where there's <u>a</u> a lady out the front of that (EngDesc4)

The speaker uses her extended index fingers to point to a location on the right-hand side of gesture space (still 1). She maintains the end point of this movement in a post-stroke hold, before subsequently lowering her two hands (still 2). The same hand form is retained across the two gestures, and the same location along the frontal and lateral axes is targeted. Both these gestures maintain focus on the two strands of directional information which were presented in the preceding expression. The directions of the speaker's fingers indicate that the Figure and Ground are located on the right-hand side of the picture. Moreover, her fingers are angled in such a way so as to suggest that these two objects are in the front region of the picture: this brings back into focus the café's status as the *first* shop on the left-hand side of the street. This example reveals the remarkable economy with which gesture expresses directional information: in just one movement, the speaker is able to communicate location along two salient spatial axes. In contrast, multiple spatial items would be required for speech to achieve the same feat. This would necessitate an expression such as the following:

(203) and that's where there's a lady out the front of that.. **on the right-hand side in the foreground / at the front-right of the picture**

The addition of either of the lexical possibilities suggested in bold above renders the locative expression considerably heavier, and fails to capture the economy with which gesture expresses this same information. Since gesture operates in three-dimensional space, it is well-suited to establishing location along multiple axes simultaneously. The speaker in example (202) exploits this potential to maintain focus on salient directional information from the preceding expression. The example below presents a similar use of gesture from the French data.

(204) et sous l'oiseau..   un chat (FrenDesc7)
       and beneath the bird..   a cat

Less than a minute prior to example (204) in discourse, the speaker signals his focus on the left-hand side of the street by saying *les bâtiments de gauche* ('the buildings on the left'). He subsequently names these buildings and indicates their respective locations along the frontal axis in gesture space. Notably, the locations of these buildings along the frontal axis are indicated in gesture alone. He then indicates the locations of other items, such as the telephone booth, along this side of the street. What is particularly noticeable about this stretch of discourse is that the speaker never again mentions that he is establishing location on the 'left' side of the street. However, this information consistently emerges in gesture. Hence, the speaker uses *sous* ('beneath') to describe the cat's location along the vertical axis, while concurrently expressing the cat's location along all three spatial axes in gesture. Looking more closely at this gesture, the downward trajectory of the speaker's hand references the vertical axis and semantically coordinates with *sous*. The hand's location on the left-hand side of gesture space maintains focus on the lateral axis, in a manner similar to that described in example (202). Finally, the gesture expresses the Figure's location in the foreground of the picture. In the discourse which precedes this expression, the speaker associates different parts of his frontal gesture space with different locations along the frontal axis: we therefore come to associate the location of his hand in example (204) with the foreground. So, while the speaker encodes the Figure's location along one spatial axis in speech, he expresses location along all three axes in gesture.

8.2.3 Discussion

Using gesture to express a Figure's location along one or several spatial axes which are not referenced in speech is a particularly productive strategy. This is because it allows speakers to deliver a maximum of directional information by using the joint resources of both communicative modalities. Examples (198)–(204), with the exclusion of (203), show how this occurs.

In previous chapters we examined the role of gesture in expressing unlexicalised directional information relating to the use of directionally non-specific items. We showed how speech and gesture can focus on different semantic aspects of a locative relationship, and that the information expressed in the two modalities combines in a complementary fashion. The use of gesture described above is similar to this, in that it also highlights the complementary nature of the two modalities in the expression of location. However, we are no longer dealing with a situation in which gesture is providing directional character for a directionally non-specific item. Rather, gesture is expressing *additional* directional information to that encoded in speech. This occurs when a speaker wishes to maintain focus on a piece of previously-expressed directional information which has current salience. Hence, in example (202) the English speaker maintains the preceding references to the frontal and lateral axes while she encodes a new locative relationship in speech. The French speaker in example (204) uses gesture in a similar way, maintaining focus on the salient lateral side of the street. In example (200) the describer employs a post-stroke to retain focus on the Ground's location, while also expressing the Figure's location along the same lateral axis in gesture alone. However, speakers may also use gesture to express directional information which has not been expressed previously, and which is not contextually inferable. A clear instance of this occurs in example (198), in which the speaker indicates the Figure's location to the right of the Ground in gesture only.

In addition to the communicative value of these gestures, it is also important to understand what they reveal about a speaker's construal of location. Noyau et al. (2005: 158) propose that "The human mind is able to modulate its representations of a state of affairs, taking different, more or less differentiated, views on it, i.e. identifying a smaller or bigger number of its sub-components." Examples (198)–(204) (excluding 203) show that the analysis of speech alone cannot reveal all of the sub-components which comprise the speaker's construal of an object's location: this is because gestures reveal other strands of directional information which play a part in the speaker's conceptualisation of locative relationships. It is only by looking at speech and gesture together that we are able to understand the full value of a speaker's locative message.

8.3 A different Figure in speech and in gesture

Chapters 5 and 6 revealed that when speakers encode location with *between* and *entre*, they recurrently indicate the locations of the two Ground objects in gesture space. We believe that this finding is important for several reasons. Firstly, it shows that gesture adds a layer of precision by identifying the salient horizontal axis that underpins individual uses of these two prepositions. Secondly, it highlights the centrality of the Ground's location to establishing that of the lexical Figure. Thirdly, it suggests that the lexical Ground is also conceptualised as a Figure. Hence, the Ground is not merely a reference object in relation to which the Figure's location is established, but it is also an object *whose own location is at issue*. The following sections examine the role of the Ground more closely, and investigate why speakers express its location in gesture.

8.3.1 Establishing the location of the lexical Ground

In Chapter 4 we proposed an approach for defining and separating locative expressions in oral discourse. As part of this approach we suggested that there were two sub-types of locative expression. The first of these encodes the location of a Figure which is not currently engaged in a Figure or Ground role. We termed these 'primary locative expressions'.

(205) *there's a cat to the left of the bus.. on the path* (EngDesc1)

In example (205) the speaker encodes the location of a Figure, *a cat*. This object is not simultaneously engaged in another locative expression in discourse, and the speaker does not provide locative information concerning either of the two Ground objects (i.e. *the bus* and *the path*). In contrast, speakers may specify the location of the lexical Ground object(s) of a primary expression: this results in a 'secondary locative expression'. We highlighted two major ways in which this occurs in speech: through the use of relative clauses, and through embedding. These two processes are highlighted in examples (206) – (207) below.

(206) *in front of her to the right like in front of the book* **which is next to the sofa** *there's a bone* (EngDesc2)

(207) *um on top of the hotel* **so that was the second shop** *there's a satellite dish*
(EngDesc3)

In example (206) the speaker introduces a relative clause headed by *which* to specify the location of the lexical Ground, *the book*. She therefore assigns this object a secondary role as Figure that depends on its function as Ground in the primary expression. Example (207) shows how the speaker embeds the clause *so that was the second shop* within the structure of the primary one. These secondary expressions combine with the primary ones to comprise what we have termed 'overall locative expressions'.

In addition to these two linguistic strategies however, we also showed that speakers use gesture to express the Ground's location. In Chapters 5 and 6, we discussed how this occurred when speakers encoded location with *(in) between* and *entre*. Our results showed that speakers used gesture to mark the respective locations of the two Ground objects of relationships encoded by *(in) between* and *entre*. In doing so, they revealed the salient horizontal axis underlying individual occurrences of these items. Hence, in the following example, the speaker's gestures show that the Figure is between two Ground objects which are aligned along the frontal axis.

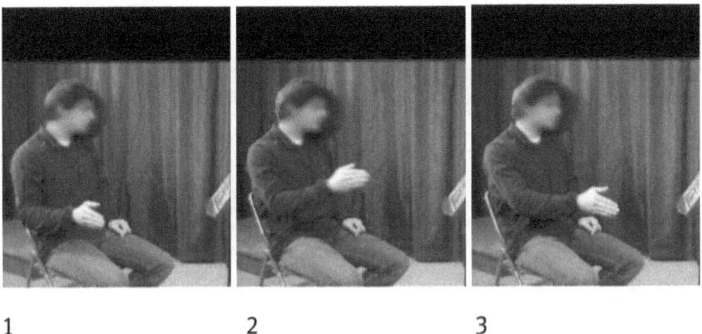

1 2 3

(208) entre le café et l'auberge de jeunesse [...] (FrenDesc11)
between the café and the youth hostel [...]

Still 1 captures the speaker's right hand just after he has marked the location of the first Ground object, 'the café'. Still 2 shows the hand's subsequent movement up and forwards, while still 3 shows how the speaker marks the location of the second Ground object, 'the youth hostel'. These gestures express direction along the frontal axis, with the first gesture indicating that 'the café' is closer to the conceptualised front of the picture than the second Ground, 'the youth hostel'. The table below shows how often speakers executed such Ground-indicating gestures when encoding location with *between* and *entre*. Our totals are inclusive of both the lounge room and street scene data.

Tab. 35: Ground-marking gestures relating to uses of *(in) between* and *entre*

	Ground-marking gestures: *(in) between*		Ground-marking gestures: *entre*	
	Frontal axis	Lateral axis	Frontal axis	Lateral axis
Sub-total	6 (of 10)[54]	3 (of 5)[55]	4 (of 10)	4 (of 7)

---

54 One gesture was ambiguous and so the example was not counted (there were therefore 11 uses of *(in) between*, instead of 10). In another example, the speaker is sequentially locating items along the right-hand side of the street and states the following.
"then there's like a gap between the youth hostel and the café" (EngDesc3)
She marks the location of the cafe, which is the next item to be located in her sequence as well as being a Ground in the *between* relationship. This was counted as a Ground-marking use of the preposition.

Tab. 35 (cont'd): Ground-marking gestures relating to uses of *(in) between* and *entre*

	Ground-marking gestures: *(in) between*	Ground-marking gestures: *entre*
TOTAL	9 (of 15)	8 (of 17)

The table above shows that speakers employed such gestures on roughly half the occasions on which *(in) between* and *entre* were used. In addition to this, we noted Ground-marking gestures for eight (73%) of the 11 relevant occurrences of *à côté de* in the lounge room scene data (see section 6.3.2); a similar result was also found for *next to* (nine of 11 occurrences, 82%; see section 6.6.3). These gestures also accompanied the use of other directionally non-specific items, such as *opposite*. If a Figure is *opposite* a Ground, we know that the two items are aligned along a horizontal axis. However, we do not know the directionality of this axis such as it is perceived by the viewer of the picture. Any gestural representation of this axis requires the speaker to connect the two points associated with the Figure and the Ground in gesture space.

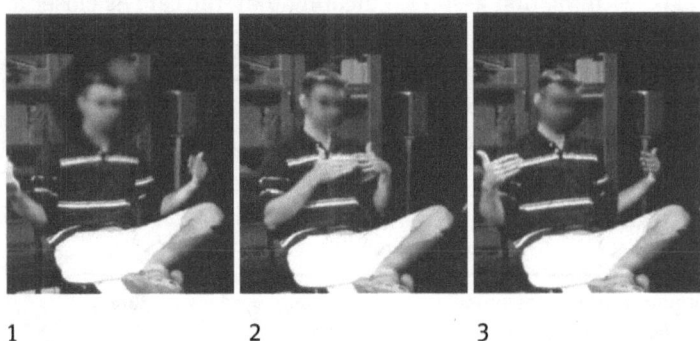

1   2   3

(209) *the building closest to you.. so <u>opposite the supermarket</u>.. right up in the foreground.. um is a café* (EngDesc9)

In example (209) the speaker uses both hands to mark the locations of the Figure and the Ground on the right- and left-hand sides of the street, respectively. He creates prominent reference to the lateral axis (as seen from his viewpoint)

---

55 There were actually six uses of *(in) between*. However one of these referenced a diagonal axis, thus incorporating both the frontal and lateral axes. We have counted this example under the 'frontal axis' subcategory and do not count it again under the 'lateral axis' subcategory.

by moving both hands into the centre of his gesture space (still 2), before subsequently retracting them out to their respective sides (still 3). Establishing reference to the Ground's location is pivotal to gestural representations of *opposite*. The same is true for *across* which, like *opposite*, "describes a horizontally oriented region" (Landau and Jackendoff 1993: 227). There were two uses of *across* in the street scene data, and on both these occasions speakers executed gestures which referenced the locations of the Figure and Ground at their respective points along a lateral axis (as viewed by the speaker). One of these is shown below.

1   2

(210)   *directly across.. almost directly across from the <u>car is a</u> telephone booth* [...] (EngDesc5)

The stills above represent the beginning and end points of a gesture stroke. The speaker's hand begins in an orientation which faces towards the right-hand side of gesture space (still 1). It subsequently moves across (as indicated by the arrow) to finish further left (still 2). The speaker thus manually demonstrates the salience of the lateral axis to this particular occurrence of *across from*, whilst also revealing the locations of the Figure and the Ground on the left- and right-hand sides of the street, respectively.

Ground-marking gestures therefore serve a clear function as far as *between/entre*, *opposite* and *across from* are concerned: they provide axial disambiguation by specifying the particular horizontal axis along which the Figure and Ground lie (as viewed by the speaker). They also specify the locations of the Figure and the Ground along this salient axis. Gesture therefore adds important directional precision to the lexically-encoded locative relationship. Yet these gestures do not occur exclusively with directionally non-specific items. Section 8.3.2 below shows that they also occur with direction-encoding ones as well.

8.3.2 Establishing the location of the lexical Ground when speakers use direction-encoding items

Example (211) below shows how an English speaker accompanies a lexical expression of direction with a gesture which establishes the Ground's location in space.

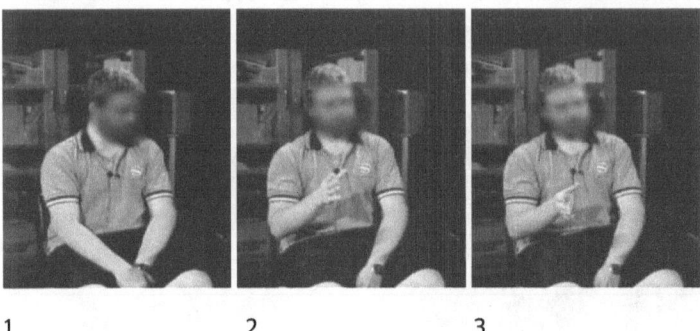

1　　　　　　　　2　　　　　　　　3

(211)　*off to the <u>left hand side</u> of the bus there's a cat* [...] (EngDesc8)

The speaker raises his right hand from its rest position and tilts it down and forward (see stills 1–3): this marks the location of the lexical Ground ('bus') in gesture space. Notably, this gesture stroke accompanies the direction-encoding phrase *left hand side* but it does not express the lexically-encoded directional information: a gestural expression of direction to the left accompanies the Figure-encoding noun phrase *the cat* (this is not shown here). Why then does the speaker mark the location of the lexical Ground in gesture space in example (211)? One explanation is that the gestural expression of direction requires the speaker's hand to begin its directional trajectory at some location. Given that the Figure's location is established in relation to a Ground, it logically follows that this trajectory should begin at the location associated with the Ground. Hence, the speaker marks this location in space before subsequently executing a gesture out to the left. Interestingly, the Ground-marking gesture synchronises with the direction-encoding *left hand side*: this possibly highlights the connection between the Ground's location and the lexicalised directional information.

Speakers do not appear to use these Ground-marking gestures preferentially for any one spatial axis. Rather, they occur when speakers establish location along any of the three spatial axes.

A different Figure in speech and in gesture — 281

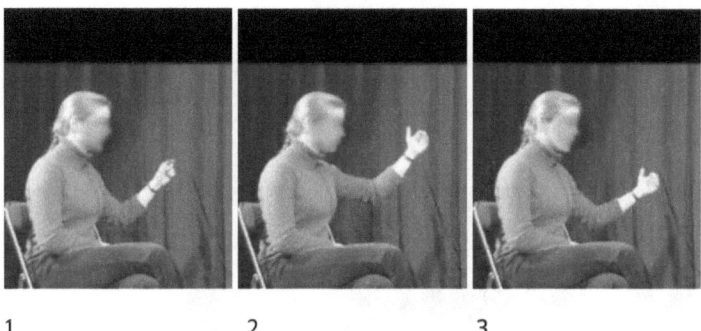

1   2   3

(212)   *le chat il est*   *en <u>dessous du portrait</u> du garçon* (FrenDesc3)
       the cat it is   <u>under the portrait</u> of the boy

The speaker in example (212) begins with a gesture preparation phase in which she raises her hand up and forwards (stills 1–2): this allows her to target the vertically superior location of the Ground ('the portrait of the boy'). As she does this her hand changes from a 'C' formation of the index finger and thumb (still 1) to a form in which her four fingers are in contact and pointing out to the right (compare still 2 with still 1). Retaining this hand form, she subsequently executes the gesture stroke (still 3). This movement downwards semantically coordinates with the spatial item *en sous de* ('under'), which encodes location along the vertical axis. Note that the speaker could have presented this information from the initial, raised location of the hand in still 1. The fact that she moves her hand into a higher location suggests that she is attending to the location of the Ground. Hence, the speaker's gesture does not merely seek to represent direction: it also seeks to identify the location in relation to which this direction is understood.

8.3.3 Why speakers mark the location of the lexical Ground in gesture space

In order to move closer to understanding why speakers mark the location of the lexical Ground in gesture space, we will consider one further example. This example differs from the two presented above as it shows that speakers may mark the location of two different Ground objects which are in two different spatial relationships with the Figure. In what follows, the speaker lexically encodes the location of the Figure ('a portrait of a young boy') in relation to three Ground entities: 'the mirror', 'where the cat's sitting' and 'the back wall'. The modifier 'back' in the latter noun phrase indicates the salient wall's location in the picture. However, the speaker provides information concerning the location of the two other Ground entities in gesture alone.

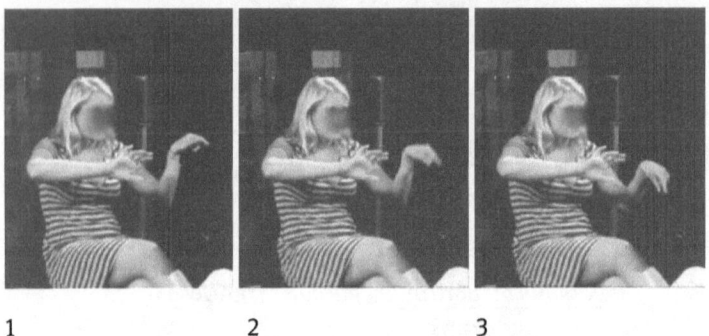

1   2   3

(213)   and then to the left of the mirror above where the <u>cat</u>'s sitting.. on the back wall is a portrait of a young boy (EngDesc2)

In still 1 the speaker's right hand is in a post-stroke hold: this indicates the location of the Ground object 'the mirror'. Her left hand has just moved out left from this location, thereby indicating the Figure's location to the left of the mirror. The speaker then recruits *above* to encode the Figure's location along the vertical axis. As she utters the Ground-encoding noun *cat*, her hand makes a rapid movement downwards (see stills 2 and 3), thus targeting the location associated with the cat. Note that the speaker's hand in still 1, which is at the location associated with the Figure, captures the idea of vertical superiority encoded by *above*. Why then does the speaker subsequently move her hand downwards, thus targeting the cat's location below the portrait? One explanation is as follows. The Ground's location plays a pivotal role in the nature of the locative relationship which a speaker encodes in speech. Hence, if the cat were located further into the foreground of the picture, the portrait would no longer be *above* it (unless, of course, the speaker conceptualised the scene as a two-dimensional space). This suggests that the nature of a locative relationship not only depends on the location of the Figure in relation to the Ground, but also on the location of the Ground in relation to the Figure. Hence, example (213) also includes a post-stroke hold (still 1) which maintains focus on the location of 'the mirror', which is a lexical Ground. In doing so, we have a visual representation not only of the portrait's location to the left of the mirror, but also of the mirror's location to the right of the portrait.

According to Langacker (1987: 233) "Figure/ground organization is pervasive in human cognition." At a basic level, this explains the salience of the

Ground and hence the representation of its location in gesture. In the spatial domain, research has also shown that the Ground's properties can help to determine the reading which we attribute to spatial items in context. Hence, the occurrence of the locative preposition *in* with certain types of Ground objects triggers the boundary-crossing reading typically associated with *into* (Nikitina 2008; Tutton 2009). Yet gestures, such as those in example (213), may not be suggesting the importance of an object in its role as Ground. Rather, they may be suggesting that this Ground *is also a Figure*, and hence that Figure/Ground relationships are not as asymmetrical as we have previously thought them to be. Hence, when a speaker lexically encodes a Figure's location in relation to a Ground, they may also conceptualise the Ground's location in relation to the Figure. Ultimately, the distinction between these two semantic roles may not be as clear-cut as we have been led to believe. The following examples provide instances of how two objects can each play Figure and Ground roles in a lexical locative expression. Note that they are attributable to the one speaker, and do not come from our first-mention data pool (which did not contain any such examples).

(214) *so if you looked at the television.. you would see a bone and a ball offset slightly from each other* [...] (EngDesc8)

The speaker begins by specifying a particular orientation in order to view the forthcoming locative relationship ('so if you look at the television'). He then encodes a locative configuration in which the first object ('a bone') and the second object ('a ball') are localised in relation to one another: 'you would see a bone and a ball offset slightly from each other'. That is, the bone, as the Figure, is slightly offset from the Ground, the ball. However the inverse relationship is also true: the ball, now as Figure, is slightly offset from the Ground, the bone. These dual Figure/Ground roles hold thanks to the use of *each other* to encode a relationship of reciprocity. Yet the use of linguistic items such as *each other* or *one another* is the not the only way to lexicalise these dual Figure/Ground relationships. In the following example, the speaker encodes a locative relationship with *between*.

(215) *you've got um say a metre between.. the sofa and the dog* (EngDesc8)

Clearly, the speaker is not localising the abstract measure of distance *a metre*, even though this is lexicalised as the subject of the *between* relationship. Rather, the relationship of distance works by suggesting that the sofa is a metre away from the dog, and the dog a metre away from the sofa. Hence, the notion of reciprocity is again pivotal to the dual Figure/Ground relationship, although the speaker has used a different lexicalisation strategy to that shown in (214). On the basis of these two examples, we can see that Figure and Ground roles are not always clearly delineated, and that objects may occupy both simultaneously. Hence, an object which is conceptualised as a Ground may also be conceptualised as a Figure, and vice versa. It is telling that we found so many examples of gestural Figures in our data. It suggests that speakers may conceptualise Grounds as Figures far more often than we think, and that the two roles are actually interrelated. Such role reciprocity adds weight to the argument that the lexical Ground is not just a reference object: rather, it is also a Figure whose own location is at issue. As earlier examples have shown, this location is determined relative to that of the lexical Figure, with speakers marking out the respective locations of the lexical Figure and Ground in gesture space. But what of the examples with *between* and *entre* in which the speaker marks out the locations of the two Ground objects, but not that of the lexical Figure? Is the speaker conceptualising the location of the Ground in relation to that of the Figure in such cases? The answer, we believe, is yes: in such cases, the locations of all three objects (the two lexical Grounds and the Figure) must be considered in relation to each other. This leads to the speaker considering them as a linear arrangement, the beginning and end points of which are defined by the respective locations of the two Ground objects. This is why speakers mark out these two locations in gesture space.

Another explanation for gestural Figures lies in the domain of perception. Tversky and Lee (1998) point out that the object a speaker visually perceives as Figure is not necessarily encoded as such in language; rather, it may be lexicalised as the Ground. Hence, it is conceivable that a gestural Figure is actually a perceptual Figure, and that its location achieves expression in gesture because it is salient in the mind of the speaker at the time of utterance encoding.

A third possibility is that gestural Figures reflect speakers' conceptualisations of locative relationships as linear arrangements in space. That is, a locative relationship between a Figure and Ground is conceptualised as a line connecting the two or more objects: this would explain why speakers mark out the locations of the Figure and Ground in gesture space. As mentioned above, it would also provide a reason for the Ground-marking gestures noted for uses of *between* and *entre*: all three objects (lexical Figure included) lie upon the axis created by joining the two plotted points. It would also explain why the speaker in example (213) also gestures downward when encoding location with *above*: she is connecting the location of the Figure with that of the Ground (which is further down the vertical axis). The conceptualisation of location in terms of such linear arrangements also fits in with the idea that the lexical Ground's location is considered in relation to that of the lexical Figure: the creation of such an axis necessarily requires the consideration of both locations with respect to each other. This hypothesis would not, however, apply to 'topological' relationships which, following Borillo (1998), are relationships in which the Figure and Ground share a location in space (for example, *on* and *sur*). In such instances, the common location of the Figure and Ground at a point in space would be salient: it is precisely this location that is often expressed in gesture (see chapter 7 and Tutton 2011).

8.4 Positioning our findings within Cognitive Grammar

Our work up until the present has brought to light the different ways in which speech and gesture partner to form multimodal locative expressions. The question now becomes the following: can these findings be integrated into a theory of language? We believe that the answer to this question is yes, and that an ideal theoretical approach for this purpose is Cognitive Grammar (Langacker 1987; Taylor 2002). There are several reasons for making this choice of framework. First of all, Cognitive Grammar is a usage-based approach to language. Representational gestures, which are created at the moment of utterance production, are necessarily a usage-based phenomenon. Furthermore, they are visible, spatial creations that are therefore particularly well suited to face-to-face interaction, given their communicative potential. Clark (1973) has pointed out that face-to-face interaction is the default context of human interaction. While modern technology has certainly amplified the role of *non* face-to-face settings in how we communicate with others since the time of Clark's publication, the visual and physical co-presence of interacting parties arguably remains the canonical (and most ideal) context for interpersonal communication. The central status of this form of interaction also suggests the potentially crucial role of communicative modalities such as gesture in interaction; indeed, this is a role that should also be considered in accounts of language acquisition and development (as discussed by Kelly 2004). With these factors in mind, usage-based accounts of language need to be open to a view of language that encompasses more than speech alone. Unfortunately, as Cienki (in press) and Cienki and Kok (submitted) have noted, there has been little work on the integration of gesture into Cognitive Grammar up until the present. Based on the results we have presented in the current study, we will propose a clearer way of accommodating gesture within this theoretical framework. More specifically, our proposal will focus on representational gestures. There are two reasons for adopting this particular approach. Firstly, this type of gesture has been the subject of investigation in the current study: it is therefore logical to focus on its integration into a multimodal theory of language. Secondly, representational gestures express semantic information. The basic unit of analysis in Cognitive Grammar, the *symbolic assembly* (Langacker 1987, 2013) or *symbolic unit*[56] (Taylor 2002), is comprised of two poles: a semantic pole and a phonological pole. Crucially, this latter pole may be realized gesturally (cf. Langacker 2008). Hence, the core analytical unit of Cognitive Grammar, the symbolic assembly, posits a link between gesture and semantics. In order to appreciate this more fully, it is necessary to explain the concept of the symbolic assembly in greater depth.

Symbolic assemblies are form-meaning pairings, defined as "the conventionalized association of a phonological structure with a semantic structure" (Taylor 2002: 25). A simple example is the noun *book*, which associates the semantic concept BOOK with the phonetic structure [/bʊk/]. Cognitive Grammar holds that language can be comprehensively explained by referencing these three constitutive elements of symbolic assemblies, i.e. the semantic pole, the phonological pole, and the link between the two (the symbolic relation). These three elements are represented in the image below: S represents the semantic pole, P the phonological pole, and the line connecting the boxes represents the symbolic relation between the two.

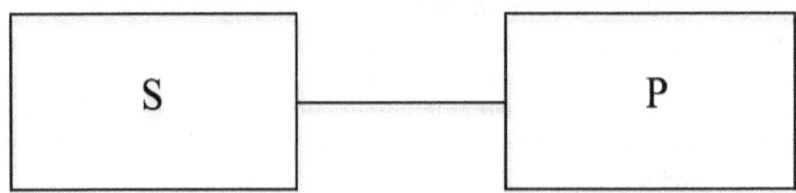

Fig. 8: The components of a symbolic assembly

Given the purported descriptive and analytical potential of these three concepts, it naturally stands to reason that they need to explain a great deal more than just lexical items. Hence, these concepts are used to explain other aspects of

---

56 We will retain the term 'symbolic assembly' in what follows.

language, including abstract notions like NOUN and TRANSITIVE CLAUSE. These more abstract notions are related to more concrete manifestations (e.g. individual examples of nouns) by appealing to the concepts of 'schema' and 'instance'. An instance is a more detailed realization of a schema: hence, the verb *hit* is an instance of the more general symbolic unit (and schema) VERB. Diagrammatically, this relationship may be seen to play out along a vertical axis, with more schematic units positioned higher up and their more specific instantiations lower down. For our current purposes of description we may therefore visualise analysis in Cognitive Grammar as working in multiple directions: horizontally (by analysing the combinatorial relationship of a semantic and a phonological pole via a symbolic relation), and vertically (by arranging symbolic units in terms of their schema/instantiation relationships)[57].

At this point it is logical to ask the following question: if an abstract notion like VERB is indeed a symbolic unit, then what constitutes its phonological pole? Obviously it cannot have any single phonological manifestation, since the notion VERB represents a category as opposed to any particular instantiation of it. One answer to this question is that its phonological pole is maximally schematic. However, as Taylor (2002) shows, lexical categories (such as nouns and verbs) have particular phonological properties associated with them. For example, nouns in English tend to be longer than verbs, and duo-syllabic words with initial stress tend to be nouns, not verbs. Naturally, such patterns do not hold for all members of a category: for example, some nouns are short, while others are very long. However, these recurrent tendencies lead to sub-groups of categories being identified. Hence, Taylor (2002: 184) suggests that the phonological poles of notions like VERB or NOUN may be initially schematic, but then subsequently break down into more specific sub-schemas (based, for example, on variables like stress patterns). We believe that this idea of a schematic, non-fully-specified phonological pole is particularly useful, and we will adopt it in order to show how representational gestures may be integrated into a revised version of the symbolic assembly. This will be discussed in what follows.

---

57 Langacker (2013) actually represents symbolic assemblies vertically, with the semantic pole positioned higher up and connected, via a symbolic relation, to the phonological pole below. We have chosen to adopt a horizontal representation here in order to facilitate a visual contrast between the structure of a symbolic assembly (imagined horizontally), and that of schema/instance relations (imagined vertically).

8.4.1 Adjusting the phonological pole of symbolic assemblies

As stated earlier, the phonological pole of a symbolic assembly does not necessarily equate to a psychological representation of a phonetic form: the term 'phonological' is understood more broadly and includes other modalities capable of entering into a relationship with semantic content, such as gestures. Unfortunately, Langacker does not go into further detail concerning the types of gestures that may constitute phonological structures. Nevertheless, such gestures must participate in established form/meaning pairings: as we saw above, symbolic assemblies are conventionalized associations of phonological and semantic structures. In line with this idea, Cienki and Kok (submitted) have noted that certain gestures are more suited to partaking in symbolic assemblies than others. Specifically, lexicalized gestures, such as signs or emblems, meet the requirement of form conventionalization and are therefore apt candidates for such a role. Taking up the example of these types of gestures, the semantic pole of the assembly would be constituted by a conceptualization, and the phonological pole by a psychological representation of a particular gestural form. In contrast, representational gestures are more difficult to integrate into the symbolic assembly, such as it exists currently, for the following reasons.

– They do not have conventionalised form-meaning pairings, thus contradicting the definition of a symbolic assembly.

– With the exception of representational gestures that are explicitly prompted for by deictic items, they are not usually compulsory elements. Hence, in most cases a representational gesture alone will not be able to fulfill the phonological pole of a symbolic assembly.

– Representational gestures depend on the co-occurrence of a phonological structure in speech (or sign, as far as signed languages are concerned). This is very often a unidirectional dependency: that is, while a representational gesture relies on the presence of a phonological unit in speech, a phonological unit in speech does not tend to rely on a representational gesture[58]. Obviously, given that the current model of the symbolic assembly does not really cater for representational gestures, the nature of this cross-modal dependency is not represented.

---

58 There are, of course, exceptions: certain uses of deictic items like *here* and *there* come to mind.

The first point presented above is discussed by Cienki and Kok (submitted), who state that even though gesticulation (and hence representational gesture) is largely idiosyncratic and lacking in standards of form, it nevertheless possesses certain consistent features. For instance, speakers typically create gesticulations by deploying certain strategies, such as tracing the shape of an object (Müller 1998) or by making their gestures in certain areas of gesture space (typically avoiding the interlocutor's face, for example). With this in mind, it is possible that the part of the phonological pole that caters for representational gestures only specifies a very schematic phonological structure. This lack of specificity does not, however, rule out the feasibility of such a proposal: as discussed earlier, schematic phonological structures have been proposed for units like VERB (see Taylor 2002: 184). Points 2 and 3 above concern how the phonological pole of a symbolic assembly can be structured in order to address issues pertaining to cross-modal dependency. Before addressing these issues of dependency further, a slight detour is in order. It is important to remember that in Cognitive Grammar semantics equates to conceptualization. It therefore follows logically that the semantic pole of a symbolic assembly is an entrenched conceptualisation. If we take up the idea that speech and gesture emerge from a common conceptual point of origin (McNeill 1992, 2005), then we see the need for the phonological pole of a symbolic assembly to cater for both speech and gestural sub-parts. Langacker (2001), as discussed by Cienki (submitted), brings up the example of *that* in utterances like "I want that one", in which the deictic determiner *that* receives stress and is accompanied by a pointing gesture. Langacker (2001: 241) argues that the pointing gesture in this example "is part of the expression's conceptual content". This shows that both speech and gesture connect to the semantic pole of the symbolic assembly, thus resulting in a "complex linguistic sign" (Cienki, in press). Returning now to issues of cross-modal (i.e. speech/gesture) dependency, we see that the two modalities rely on each other in this particular example. That is, the use of *that* requires an accompanying gesture, and the interpretation of the gesture is linked to the spoken content. However, while the use of gesture may be compulsory here, this is not the habitual case as far as representational gestures are concerned: there is no obligation to gesture when encoding location with *next to*, for example. Furthermore, there are symbolic assemblies for which it is hard to imagine any pattern of gestural movement that may plausibly be represented as part of the phonological pole: the preposition *of* and the derivational suffix *–al* are two examples that spring to mind.

The challenge therefore becomes the following: to create a version of the symbolic assembly which reflects the fact that the phonological pole may be comprised of both speech and gestural sub-parts. Furthermore, seeing that Cognitive Grammar is a usage-based account of language, we might want to maximize the usefulness of our proposal by also trying to account for the nature of speech-gesture dependency: for example, by showing that representational gestures depend on the realization of an associated phonological form in speech, but that the phonological realization of a representational gesture is not routinely compulsory when a symbolic assembly is used. To make this challenge more concrete, we will consider the English lexical item *between* – a preposition that has been the object of much discussion in the current work. We posit that the semantic pole of this symbolic assembly is an entrenched conceptualisation concerning the location of one object (the Figure) in relation to at least two others (the Ground objects); the respective locations of these latter objects define the spatial axis along which the Figure is located. As far as the phonological pole is concerned, there is a psychological representation of the phonetic sequence [/bɪˈtwiːn/]. However, as we saw in earlier chapters, *between* is also often accompanied by a particular pattern of gestural behaviour: the marking out of the respective locations of the lexical Ground objects in gesture space. Naturally, the particular locations of these objects are analogical aspects of the conceptual representation and thus differ from one context of occurrence to the next: no definite locations can therefore be stored in long-term memory. However, common to all of these gestures is their specification of the Ground entities' locations along a spatial axis (which is typically, but not exclusively, horizontal in nature), as seen from a particular perspective and viewpoint. We therefore hypothesise that the gestural component of the symbolic assembly *between* is a schematic pattern of motor activity that prompts the speaker to mark out the respective locations of the Ground objects along a salient spatial axis, using a perspective and viewpoint of their choice. We nevertheless need to remember that such gestures are optional (i.e. a speaker may use *between* without gesturing at all), and that their association with the semantic pole of *between* depends on the realization of the phonological representation [/bɪˈtwiːn/]. That is, a speaker marking out the locations of two objects in gesture space does not necessarily refer to the relationship encoded by *between*: this same type of gestural behaviour could apply to many other symbolic units, such as *from* and *to* in a sentence such as 'the road goes from Sydney to Melbourne'.

We therefore propose a reworking of the symbolic assembly in Cognitive Grammar as follows. The semantic pole (S) of the symbolic assembly links to a revised version of the phonological pole (P), which is now made up of two components: P_1 and P_2 (see Figure 9, below). As far as spoken language is concerned, P_1 is the psychological representation of a phonetic structure (such as

[/brˈtwiːn/]), while P_2 is a program of motor activity that concerns the realisation of a representational gesture. The phonological form of P_2 may be schematic or quite specific: the level of specificity depends on the symbolic assembly in question. As far as *between* is concerned, the phonological pattern of P_2 is fairly specific and may be summarized along the following lines: the speaker adopts a viewpoint (unspecified, and hence only schematically represented), perspective (also unspecified and only schematically represented) and enacts a pattern of movement that specifies the salient spatial axis relating to the locative relationship. This axis is most conveniently, but not obligatorily, expressed by marking out the respective locations of the lexical Ground entities in gesture space.

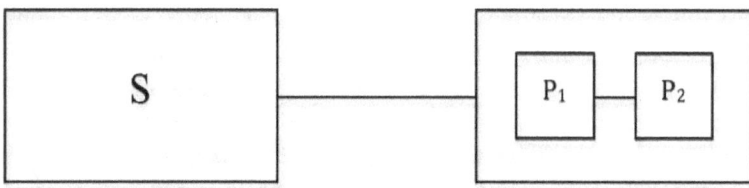

Fig. 9: The components of the revised symbolic assembly (version 1)

Positing such a revised version of the symbolic assembly therefore allows us to capture the recurrent pattern of gestural behaviour that we noted for *between*. However, if we wish this version of the symbolic assembly to be truly usage-based, then we should try, as mentioned earlier, to account for the fact that representational gestures are co-speech gestures: that is, they depend on the realization of P_1 in speech. With this in mind, we propose the revised version below (see Figure 10). The dotted lines around P_2 show, first of all, that there may not be a pattern of motor activity associated with the symbolic assembly (this might be the case, for example, for the preposition *of*). Secondly, the dotted line that connects P_2 with P_1 shows that the physical realisation of the former is not compulsory in a usage event. Note that for some symbolic assemblies, such as uses of deictic terms like *this* and *that* to designate an entity in the speaker's physical environment, the outline of P_2, as well as the line connecting it with P_1, will be solid: the solid outline represents the presence of a stored phonological form, while the solid connecting line indicates its necessary realisation in a usage event.

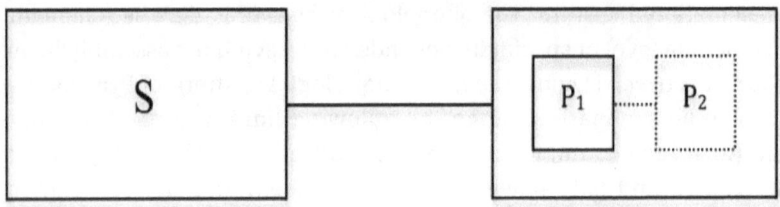

Fig. 10: The components of the revised symbolic assembly (version 2)

How might this revised version work as far as other lexical spatial items are concerned? We suggest that the P_2 of all projective spatial items is similar to an important degree. More specifically, P_2 prompts for a pattern of bodily movement that expresses at least one of the salient spatial axes underlying the use of the symbolic assembly in question. The precise axis or axes will be left unspecified for directionally non-specific items, but will be specified for directionally precise ones (for example, *left* and *right*). This axis is often referenced through the marking out of the locations of the lexical Figure and Ground entities: as discussed earlier in this chapter, this pattern of behaviour plays out for many linguistic spatial items. Our results have shown that speakers use gestures to highlight at least one spatial axis pertaining to the location of the lexicalized Figure. It is for this reason that we suggest that the pattern of gestural movement encoded in P_2 concerns the precision of at least one spatial axis that is salient to the use of the lexical spatial item in context. Results discussed in the earlier part of this chapter have also shown that multiple spatial axes related to the use of a spatial linguistic item might be presented simultaneously: this is perfectly compatible with what is being proposed here. As far as the variables of viewpoint and perspective are concerned, these will only be schematically represented, as a specific choice will be made at the moment of utterance creation.

To summarise, the three compulsory elements of P_2 for symbolic assemblies that encode projective spatial relationships are:
– The choice of a viewpoint
– The choice of a perspective
– The choice of at least one salient spatial axis related to the use of the symbolic assembly in context

As far as the third point is concerned, the spatial axis will typically be expressed in gesture through the marking out of the Figure and Ground's respective locations in gesture space, except in instances where more than one Ground object is used (e.g. *between* and *entre*): in such cases, the locations of the multiple Ground objects will be expressed in gesture. In all cases, we suggest that the pattern of gestural movement chosen by the speaker will be shaped, in part at least, by contextual factors. For example, if the Ground's location has just been marked in gesture, it is feasible that a trajectory along the salient spatial axis to the Figure's conceptualized location may be sufficient. It should be pointed out that the key factor here is the spatial axis itself as opposed to any particular direction along it. Earlier on we saw the example of a speaker gesturing down the vertical axis when encoding location with *above* (see example 213). This downward movement – seemingly at odds with the semantics of *above* – nevertheless allowed her to show the salience of the vertical axis to the conceptualised locative relationship, while also enabling her hand to move into a more optimal location to target the next object of her locative attention. There is therefore flexibility in terms of the direction that a gestural movement may follow along an axis, as well as the particular location (e.g. that of the lexical Figure or the lexical Ground) that a gestural movement ends on. We suggest that the reason for this flexibility is as follows. The Figure and Ground are both part of the profile (i.e. the foregrounded part) of locative relationships (cf. Langacker 2013: 70–71). While the speaker initially targets the location of the entity chosen as the lexical Figure, they may shift their attention during the course of the utterance and focus on the location of the lexical Ground. This reflects the "rather flexible" nature of Figure/Ground organization (Taylor 2002: 10), and echoes Tvery and Lee's (1998) claim that an object which is visually perceived as a Figure will not necessarily assume this role in language. These observations provide two explanations as to why lexical Grounds can become gestural Figures. The crucial role of P_2 in expressing information pertaining to spatial axes is reinforced by our findings concerning how speakers gesture when encoding location with *on* and *sur*. Specifically, our data have revealed that gestures expressing locative information when these two prepositions are used identify the location of the Figure/Ground configuration within the larger containing space, and that this is achieved by expressing its location along one or more spatial axes.

At this point it is important to remember that spatial language is special: speakers tend to gesture more when they talk about space than they do when they talk about other topics because gestures are themselves spatial creations that lend themselves well to the task of spatial description. But how might this revision of the symbolic assembly work for non-spatial symbolic assemblies? If we are going to propose a modification of the symbolic assembly in Cognitive Grammar, then this needs to hold for all symbolic assemblies, not just those that relate to locative spatial items. Let's take a familiar example like *the portrait is on the wall*. It is perfectly feasible that a speaker may choose not to express any locative information in gesture when uttering this locative expression. They may, for example, believe that the location of the lexicalized Figure is perfectly understandable given the discursive context, and instead wish to focus on the iconic properties of the 'portrait'. In such a case, the speaker would activate the P_2 of the 'portrait' – as opposed to that of *on* – thus leading to an iconic representation of this object in gesture. But what might the P_2 content of non-spatial words like *portrait* be? After all, portraits come in all sorts of sizes, and while the variable of shape might be restricted to a certain degree, there is nevertheless room for considerable variation. As pointed out by Cienki and Kok (submitted), Müller (1998) shows that when speakers gesturally represent an object, they do so by using their hands in particular ways: that is, by outlining the shape of the object, by moulding its shape, or by using their hands to embody the object. Müller's important contribution here is to show that there is a restricted palette of options for iconically representing an object (Cienki and Kok, submitted). We therefore believe that this finding should be integrated into the revised version of the symbolic assembly that we are proposing. More specifically, we suggest that the schematic motor programs which constitute the P_2 of a symbolic assembly that refers to an object are comprised of prompts for tracing, moulding or embodying actions. However, in addition to what Müller has suggested, we also posit a fourth schematic motor program: one that indicates a location in space associated with the object. As we showed in chapter 4, speakers can make anaphoric reference to an object by indicating its location in gesture space. This brings into play a different representational process that no longer involves iconicity, but rather indexicality (Bedreslioska et al., 2013). The choice of the motor program for P_2 (i.e. between one that iconically represents the object by means of outlining, moulding or embodying it, and one that indexically references the object by pointing to a location associated with it in gesture space) will be shaped by contextual factors. Specifically, the latter, indexical strategy will be favoured when the entity has already been associated with a location in gesture space, whereas an iconic representation of the object will be more likely to occur the first time it is mentioned in discourse.

9 Conclusion

At the beginning of our study, we specified three broad hypotheses about what we expected to find in our data. These hypotheses were as follows.

– Speakers will use representational gestures when describing locative configurations.
– Speakers will use gesture to express salient, unlexicalised locative information.
– The use of lexical spatial items with similar semantics in English and French will result in the expression of the same locative information in gesture by speakers of the two languages.

As far as the first hypothesis is concerned, our study has shown that speakers do indeed use representational gestures to describe locative configurations. We need only look, for example, at the gestural representations of direction which relate to the use of left- and right-encoding items (see Chapter 6), or those which relate to uses of *in front of* or *en face de* (see Chapter 5). As far as directionally non-specific items are concerned, speakers represent the relationships encoded by *between* and *entre* in terms of the respective locations of the two Ground objects along a salient horizontal axis. This was shown to be an important finding in our study (see Chapters 5, 6, and 8). It also feeds into our second hypothesis: that speakers use gesture to express unlexicalised locative information. The locations of these Ground objects were not concurrently established in speech, thereby highlighting the role of gesture in presenting complementary, salient locative information. Speakers' use of *between* and *entre* also showed that these two spatial items, which have similar semantics, were accompanied by the same types of location-expressing gestures. This, in turn, provides support for our third hypothesis: that spatial items with similar semantics cross-linguistically will result in the expression of the same information in gesture by speakers of English and French. Additional support for this hypothesis comes from gestures which express directional information relating to lexicalised relationships of adjacency (i.e. *à côté de* and *next to*), and to topological relationships of contact (i.e. *on* and *sur*).

In what follows, we will present the major findings from our work. These findings validate the three hypotheses listed above, and also highlight our contributions to the literature on space and gesture.

9.1 The framework of our investigation, and main findings

9.1.1 Laying the foundations

Chapter 1 began by establishing the aim of our investigation: to understand how English and French speakers use speech and gesture to express the nature of static locative relationships. By 'nature' we mean the 'Path' (Talmy 2000) component of such expressions. We identified the major studies on locative expressions in the literature and showed that there was no precedent for the investigation which we were proposing. Hence, our study allowed great scope for previously unreported findings to emerge.

Chapter 2 laid the theoretical foundations for our work. We began by identifying Talmy's (2000) four main semantic components of Motion events: Figure, Ground, Path, and Motion. As far as dynamic motion events are concerned, we showed that English and French are typologically different languages in Talmy's verb-/satellite-framed typology: that is, French encodes Path in the verb, while English does so in satellites. A crucial feature of this typology is that dynamic motion and static location are treated alike as 'Motion' events. However, neither English nor French conforms to a verb- or satellite-framed typological pattern as far as the expression of static location is concerned: this is because both languages use prepositions to encode Path (Lemmens and Slobin 2008), and prepositions are not satellites (Talmy 2000: 102). Hence, static location and dynamic motion events cannot truly be subsumed under the same umbrella in Talmy's typology. Following this, we established that our investigation would focus on the two horizontal spatial axes (i.e. the frontal axis and the lateral axis), and that we would use the semantic criterion of direction to categorise lexical items. We understood direction as the endpoints of each spatial axis: that is, left and right for the lateral axis; front and back for the frontal axis; and up and down for the vertical axis. Both English and French have linguistic items which specifically encode each of these directions. We termed these 'directionally-specific items' (e.g. *to the left of/à gauche de*; *behind/derrière*). Both languages also have spatial items which generalise across multiple directions: we termed these 'directionally non-specific items' (e.g. *next to/à côté de*; *towards/vers*). This categorical distinction was particularly evident in the ensuing chapters, which focused largely on whether, and how, speakers expressed directional information relating to directionally non-specific items.

The final section of Chapter 2 established the main areas of the spatial domain which had received attention by gesture researchers. This allowed us to position our work within a larger body of literature, and to highlight the individual nature of our study.

9.1.2 Methodology

Chapter 3 outlined the development of our main experiments. The pilot study revealed the need to fine-tune our experimental protocol and to devise a better-adapted stimulus picture. We ultimately designed two pictures to use in the main experiments, since spatial language shifts across scales of space (Lautenshütz et al. 2007). These pictures were of a lounge room and a street scene respectively. Following initial transcription in Word, we analysed our data in Elan. This involved identifying, amongst other things, lexicalised semantic content as well as form-based features of gestural expression. One particular contribution of our coding strategy was the development of a series of labels[59] which specify the main information expressed by gestures in locative discourse. We believe that this system could be used as a tool in future research on the topic.

9.1.3 Defining and separating static locative expressions in oral discourse

In Chapter 4 we addressed the question of how static locative expressions should be defined and separated in oral discourse. We argued that a functional approach to this problem was preferable to a grammatically-based one: that is, locative expressions should not be defined in terms of prepositions, nor should they be separated on the basis of clauses or prepositional phrases. Rather, we should consider locative expressions as the uninterrupted stretch of discourse that localises a Figure. There were three main reasons for adopting this approach. First of all, lexical categories other than prepositions can express locative information: for example, nouns and adverbs. This means that a definition centred on a particular grammatical category is best avoided. Secondly, the expression of a Figure's location can build across successive phrases and clauses. The directional information expressed in one phrase or clause may be modified in the one that follows, thereby suggesting that both should be considered as related parts of a semantic whole. Thirdly, dividing locative expres-

---

[59] A complete list of these labels is provided in Appendix E - Gesture code for transcriptions in Elan.

sions on the basis of grammatical concerns is an approach which may be suited to speech, but it is ill-adapted to gesture. We demonstrated this conviction with an example in which a pointing gesture alone carried the entire locative charge. In this example, the only element present in speech was the Figure-encoding noun 'cat'. Our argumentation therefore showed that the most ideal way to consider multimodal locative expressions was to take a functional approach to the data.

We subsequently suggested that there were two sub-types of static locative expressions: primary locatives and secondary locatives. The key feature differentiating the two is the notion of dependency. Secondary locatives create a Figure from an object which is already engaged in a Figure or a Ground role, while primary locatives do not. Examples of secondary locatives include gestures which establish the location of the Ground in gesture space, and speech segments which lexically encode the Ground's location. When both a primary locative and its related secondary parts are collectively considered this comprises an 'overall locative expression'. We took these overall locative expressions into account when analysing the first mention of target objects in a speaker's discourse. Overall therefore, Chapter 4 presented a new system for the analysis of static locative expressions in oral discourse.

9.1.4 Describing location along the frontal axis

Chapter 5 explored how describers expressed location along the frontal axis. Our first major finding was that English speakers do not always apply 180-degree rotation to attribute frontal surfaces to objects when relative frames of reference are used. Instead, when multiple objects are aligned along a lateral axis, speakers can conceptually transfer the intrinsic front of one object onto the one(s) beside it: this involves the translation, as opposed to the 180-degree rotation, of spatial properties. We believe that this is an important finding for the literature on spatial language, and that further research is required to investigate how and why speakers attribute frontal properties in this way.

Our analysis also revealed that speakers use different perspectives in speech and gesture. Although not common in the data, such cross-modal conflations highlight the ability of speakers to hold different conceptualisations of object location simultaneously. As far as spatial conceptualisation is concerned, our analysis also revealed that both English and French speakers represented extension along the lateral axis in gesture when describing the foregrounds of the stimulus pictures. Hence, while the concept FOREGROUND focuses attention on the primacy of the frontal axis, gestures revealed that speakers also attended to extension along the lateral axis.

Several new insights emerged from our study relating to how speakers used individual spatial items to encode location along the frontal axis. One of these concerned the French item *en face de*, which translates into English as both *in front of* and *opposite*. The crucial factor which distinguishes between these two readings of *en face de* is the interpretation of distance: *opposite* encodes greater distance between the Figure and Ground than *in front of* does. Our results showed that speakers signalled interpretations of *en face de* as *opposite* by expressing distance information in speech, in gesture, or in both modalities. This pattern of behaviour was noted in descriptions of both pictures. However, the type of relationship which *en face de* encoded in the two spatial scenes changed: while it most commonly encoded relationships of distance in the lounge room scene (hence translating as *opposite*), it most frequently encoded relationships of proximity in the street scene (hence translating as *in front of*). We suggested that this was due to the use of *en face de* to encode location in relation to buildings in the latter scene. The French lexeme *face* can mean the 'front' of a building, and so *en face de* was recurrently used when objects were located out the front of buildings. This therefore meant that speakers used *en face de* to encode relations of proximity as opposed to relations of distance, thus contrasting to what we had observed in descriptions of the lounge room scene.

Chapter 5 also showed that speakers of both languages recruited sequence-encoding items to specify location. Moreover, they made greater use of gesture than speech to express the directional progression of these lexically-encoded sequences. This was particularly noticeable in the French data: there were 23 examples in which speakers expressed the direction of lexicalised sequences, and in 18 (78%) of these they provided this information in gesture alone.

As far as the category of directionally non-specific items is concerned, we noticed a particular pattern of gestural behaviour when speakers encoded location with *between* and *entre*. This was the marking of the Ground objects' locations in gesture space. This pattern of gestural behaviour revealed three things: firstly, that speakers conceptualised location in terms of the area bounded by the two Ground objects (cf. Landau and Jackendoff 1993; Franckel and Paillard 2007); secondly, that gesture identified the salient horizontal axis along which the locative relationship played out; and thirdly, that these lexical Grounds were simultaneously gestural Figures. This third finding was addressed in greater depth in Chapter 8, and will be discussed again shortly.

9.1.5 Describing location along the lateral axis

We began Chapter 6 by stating that there are no lexical verbs in either English or French which encode left or right direction. Moreover, we showed that there are only two lexemes in each language which are recurrently used to encode this information: *left* and *right* in English; and *droite* and *gauche* in French. This stands in contrast to the wider range of lexical possibilities available to encode direction along the frontal and vertical axes (see table 11). Our analysis of English spatial items in descriptions of the lounge room scene subsequently revealed that the most frequently-recruited item was *next to*. *Next to* is a directionally non-specific item and does not encode whether the Figure is to the right or to the left of the Ground. Our analysis showed that speakers most frequently expressed this salient directional information in gesture alone. This pattern of behaviour was not just limited to *next to*: speakers most frequently provided directional precision for all directionally non-specific items in gesture only. This result clearly highlights the complementary nature of speech and gesture in the expression of location along the lateral axis. Importantly, we found this same result for directionally non-specific items in the French data. Moreover, just like English speakers, French speakers recurrently expressed Figure/Ground adjacency in speech: this involved the use of *à côté (de)* ('next to'). Once again, speakers most frequently expressed the direction of the Figure to the Ground exclusively in gesture. Hence, as far as descriptions of the lounge room scene are concerned, there were important parallels between the English and French data.

Moving on to the street-scene descriptions, both English and French speakers made proportionally less use of directionally non-specific items than they did in descriptions of the lounge room scene. This resulted from the division of the street scene into prominent left and right halves, which thereby favoured the use of left- and right-encoding items. As far as these items were concerned, speakers' gestural representations of the lexicalised directional information expressed location from a particular viewpoint and perspective. This was, in fact, the role of gesture when representing any lexical expression of direction (whether this be left or right, front or back). In such examples, speakers nearly always expressed direction using speaker viewpoint and observer perspective. Gesture sometimes also expressed location along another spatial axis simultaneously: these directional 'fusions' were addressed separately in Chapter 8.

9.1.6 How speakers gesture when encoding location with *on* and *sur*

Chapter 7 signalled a break from our focus on the spatial axes. Instead, we examined gestures relating to occurrences of *on* and *sur*. We sought to investigate whether speakers represented the topological ideas of contact and support in gesture, as opposed to direction along one or more spatial axes. *On* and *sur* typically encode relationships in which the Figure is in contact with the Ground, and/or in which the Ground functions as a supporting surface for the Figure. While these conditions of contact and support can coexist in locative configurations, just one is sufficient to license the use of either preposition. Hence, *on* and *sur* can encode support which does not involve Figure/Ground physical contact, just as they can encode physical contact which does not involve support (Herskovits 1986; Coventry and Garrod 2004). Nevertheless, in 100 of the 103 overall examples that we analysed, these two conditions of contact and support were satisfied.

Our data analysis began by looking at English descriptions of the lounge room scene. We discovered that gestures could be divided into two different categories: those which expressed directional information concerning the location of the topological configuration, and those which did not (pragmatic gestures, etc). Our results therefore showed that all location-expressing gestures were of the same nature: they established the direction of the Figure/Ground configuration along one or multiple spatial axes. We followed this up with an analysis of the English street-scene data, and found the same result. Our analysis also revealed that speakers used post-stroke holds to retain focus on previously-expressed directional information which helped to localise the topological configuration in space.

Turning to the French descriptions, we observed that gestures could once again be separated into two categories according to whether or not they expressed locative directional information: this was true for descriptions of both the lounge room and street scenes. As for English speakers, directional information was most frequently expressed in gesture alone. However, there were twice as many occurrences of *on* in the English data as there were of *sur* in the French data. We argued that this was due to two factors. The first of these was the availability of other spatial items to encode relationships of contact and support in French: for example, the use of *par* in the phrase *par terre* ('on the ground'). The second factor was the greater tendency of French speakers to leave topological information which was pragmatically inferable unlexicalised. This tendency aligns with how French speakers encode dynamic motion events. As a verb-framed language, French does not express manner-of-motion information when it is the agent's default mode of displacement: this is because it can be contextually inferred. In contrast English, as a satellite-framed language, typically encodes such information (Slobin 1997). Thus, the different frequencies of *on* and *sur* reflect different patterns of attention to contextually inferable information.

Our analysis did not uncover any contact- or support-expressing gestures in either the English or French descriptions. We argued that this owes, in part at least, to the propensity of gesture for expressing directional information. This propensity is exploited by deictic items such as *here* and *ici*, which are obligatorily accompanied by direction-expressing gestures (Fricke 2003).

9.1.7 Other ways in which gesture expresses unlexicalised locative information

Our final chapter of data analysis was a qualitative investigation of two ways in which speakers express unlexicalised locative information, and a discussion of how our findings could be accommodated within Cognitive Grammar. As far as the first half of the chapter is concerned, the first finding discussed was the use of gesture to express additional directional information to that encoded in speech. This use of speech and gesture highlights how speakers engage the two modalities to enable a fine-grained presentation of the Figure's location in three-dimensional space. We noted that the unlexicalised directional information which gesture presents may be new in the speaker's discourse, and hence highly salient to determining the Figure's location. We also recognised that such gestures may be deployed as a discursive strategy to maintain focus on recently expressed directional information. This information, which has usually helped to establish the location of the previous Figure in discourse, is nevertheless salient to localising the new lexical Figure. We observed this use of gesture across English and French data sets, and in descriptions of both the lounge room and street scenes.

Our second subject of analysis was a trend which had consistently appeared throughout the course of our investigation: this was the use of the gesture to express the location of the lexical Ground. We initially noted this tendency when speakers encoded location with *between* and *entre*, but further analysis revealed that it also occurred with other spatial items. This included directionally non-specific items, such as *opposite* and *across from*, as well as direction-encoding ones. We argued that such 'gestural Figures' show that different Figures can surface in the speech and gesture modalities. By attending to gesture, we are therefore able to identify more accurately the objects which a speaker conceptualises in this semantic role. Furthermore, we suggested that the roles of Figure and Ground are not as clearly delineated as the literature leads us to believe. By drawing on linguistic examples which showed that both roles can simultaneously apply to both objects in a locative expression, we provided evidence for the non-asymmetry of Figure and Ground roles. We believe that this is a discovery which merits further investigation in a study of its own.

Taking into account all of the results that had been presented throughout the course of this investigation, we then showed how our findings were compatible with the view of language that underlies Cognitive Grammar. Drawing on Langacker's key concept of the symbolic assembly, we suggested a modification to the phonological pole of this assembly in order to account for the occurrence of co-speech representational gestures. We applied our modification of the symbolic assembly to spatial items that encode projective spatial relationships (for example, *between*), and in doing so sought to show just what the content of the gestural pole (labelled P_2) would be for such items. This revised approach to the symbolic assembly needs to be explored more widely in future research, and in relation to a wider range of linguistic data, in order to critically assess the viability of the changes proposed here.

9.2 Overall conclusions

Our study has shown that speakers make productive use of gesture to express the nature of static locative relationships. This information is directional in nature, although the concern of distance may also be represented (for example, when encoding location with *en face de*). Importantly, speakers use gesture to express directional information relating to directionally non-specific (including sequence-encoding) items. Notably, they make greater use of gesture than speech to express this type of complementary directional information.

Our results also indicated that speakers express the same information in gesture when using semantically similar lexical items. Therefore, speakers of English and French express the direction of the Figure to the Ground in gesture when encoding location with *next to* and *à côté de*. Moreover, gesture provides disambiguation as to the salient horizontal axis that underpins individual occurrences of *between* and *entre*. The pivotal role of gesture in expressing direction is highlighted by the lack of contact- and support-expressing gestures when speakers encode location with *on* and *sur*. Instead, gesture establishes the location of the topological configuration along one or more spatial axes.

Our study has therefore shown that gestures are an integral part of locative expressions, and that speech and gesture must be collectively considered in order to understand how speakers conceptualise and express location. Such a multimodal approach to the domain requires a suitably adapted analytical framework. We have argued that this necessitates understanding locative expressions on the basis of functional, as opposed to grammatical, criteria. Furthermore, we have devised a new approach to defining and separating static locative expressions that may be adopted as an analytical tool in future related studies.

9.3 Theoretical implications of results

The results presented in this study have clear implications for the fields of gesture studies and spatial language. Firstly, as far as gestures studies is concerned, our data clearly show that speakers' gestures express salient, unlexicalised spatial information. This provides support for Kendon's (2004) view that utterances are comprised of both speech and gesture components: certain strands of information emerge in speech, while others appear in gesture. It furthermore provides support for models of speech and gesture production in which a speaker's communicative intention is unpacked through both speech and gesture (e.g. McNeill 1992, 2005; de Ruiter 2000, 2007). By expressing unlexicalised spatial information, gesture also allows us a view of how speakers understand spatial concepts. Hence, we showed that the direction-expressing gestures which accompany uses of *next to* and *à côté (de)* suggest that speakers conceptualise relationships of adjacency in terms of the direction of the Figure relative to the Ground. This pattern of attending to directional information when encoding relationships of proximity aligns with findings reported by Ashley and Carlson (2007). Furthermore, our results showed that speakers express the same type of semantic information in gesture when using lexical items with similar semantics. This supports the view that the information which we express in gesture is regulated, to some degree, by the features of a scene or event encoded by the language we speak (Kita and Özyürek 2003).

As far as the domain of spatial language is concerned, our results clearly show that any study which seeks to examine how speakers express locative relationships cannot ignore gesture. Despite the wealth of literature on the lexical semantics of location-encoding items in English and French, linguists have so far ignored the possibility that speakers may use gestures in recurrent, principled ways when these items are used. Our study has identified recurrent patterns of gesture use for a range of spatial items, including *next to* and *à côté de*, *between* and *entre*, and *sur* and *on*. This suggests that the spatial relationships encoded by these items can be better understood by attending to the gestures that speakers make when they use them.

9.4 Future research

The findings presented in this book have identified several pertinent areas for future research. Firstly, building on our study of *on* and *sur*, we suggest that an investigation into how speakers gesture when encoding location with *in* and *dans* be carried out. Based on our results for *on* and *sur*, we hypothesise that speakers' gestures will express directional information relating to the location of the lexicalised Figure/Ground topological configuration in space.

Secondly, our study showed that speakers used *en face de* to encode relationships of proximity and distance. Speakers signalled the latter reading by expressing distance information in speech, in gesture, or in both modalities. Further research is required to understand whether the default reading of *en face de* as a relationship of proximity or distance fluctuates according to the type of space described. In addition, the role of gesture in signalling a reading of distance should be investigated more closely.

Thirdly, our investigation highlighted the fact that gesture recurrently marks the Ground's location in gesture space. There are several different factors which motivate this behaviour. Firstly, as far as *between* and *entre* are concerned, these gestures mark the boundaries of the area which surrounds the Figure. Secondly, as far as directional items like *to the right of* are concerned, the initial marking of the Ground's location allows for a clearer representation of directional information. Thirdly, and most importantly, these Ground-marking gestures allow the speaker to present the lexical Ground as a gestural Figure. This latter point deserves substantial investigation, as it may potentially alter our understanding of Figure and Ground roles in the expression of location. In order to investigate this, a larger quantitative study of how and when this gestural marking of location occurs is required.

Related to the study of gestural Figures is the use of post-stroke holds in the expression of directional information. At numerous points in our study we noted that speakers retained a physical presence for the location of the lexical Ground while establishing the Figure's location in gesture space. We hypothesise that these post-stroke holds play a pivotal role in a speaker's communication of directional information. However, further study is required to determine the frequency of these holds, and to examine whether they tend to occur when particular spatial items are recruited.

Next, the ways in which speakers use speech and gesture to express location along the vertical axis need to be explored. At first glance, there appears to be a substantial range of verbs and other spatial items which encode direction along this axis (see table 11): this leads us to believe that speakers' use of directionally non-specific items may be quite restricted. With this in mind, what role will gesture play in expressing unlexicalised locative information?

Finally, our data set also features an interactive segment between the describer and receiver for each picture. It therefore remains to be seen how participants use speech and gesture in this highly interactive context. Results should be compared to those which we have presented in this book. By undertaking such a comparative analysis we will be able to better understand whether, and how, the roles of speech and gesture change when speakers collaborate to express object location.

Appendix A

Shown below is the stimulus picture of the lounge room scene. On the following page are the four different versions of this picture which receivers were shown. Receivers were required to identify the picture which their partner had described to them.

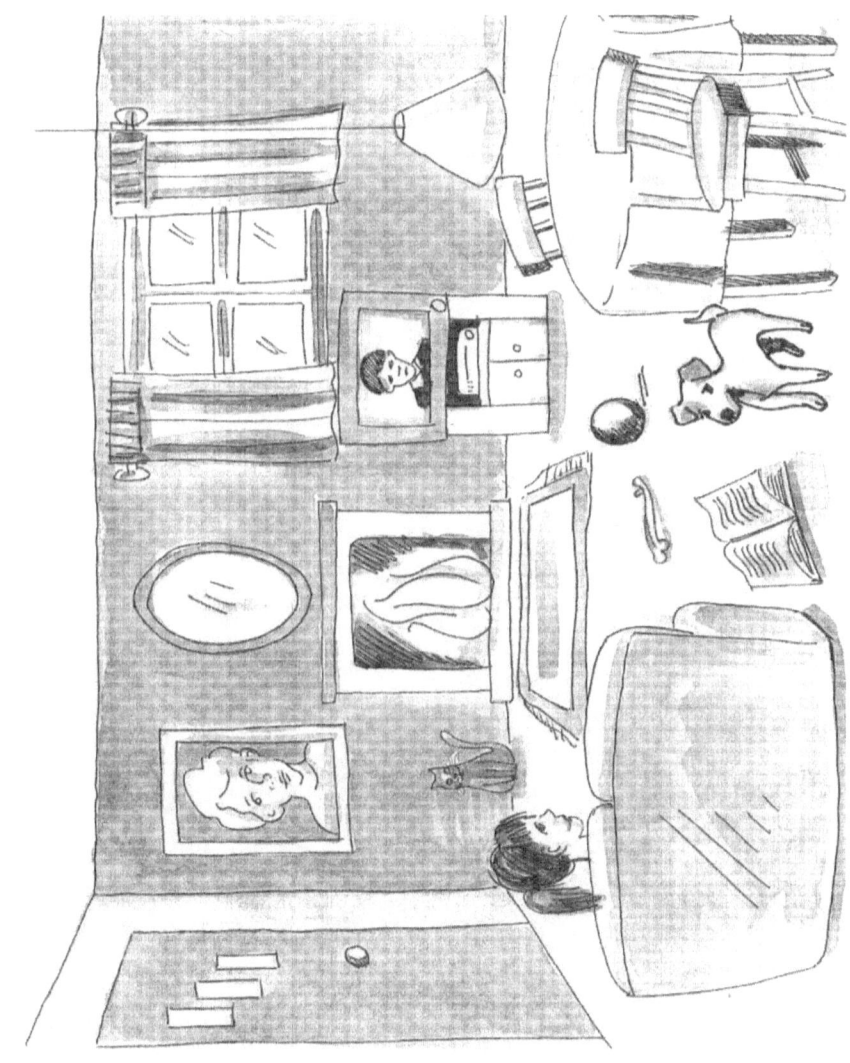

Versions of the lounge room scene shown to receivers. The correct picture is number 4. The other pictures differ in their positioning of the ball or the bone.

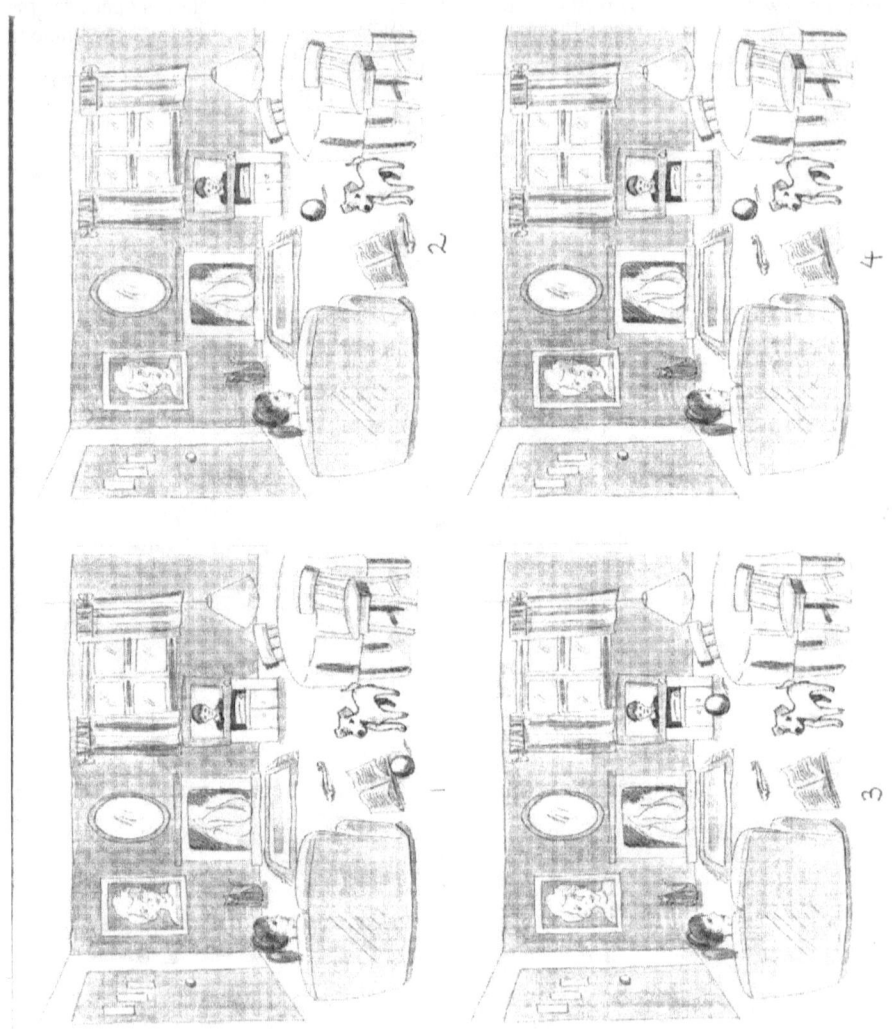

Appendix B

Shown below is the stimulus picture of the street scene. On the following page are the four different versions of this picture which receivers were shown. Receivers were required to identify the picture which their partner had described to them.

Versions of the street scene shown to receivers. The correct picture is number 2. The other pictures differ in their positioning of the satellite dish or the post-office box.

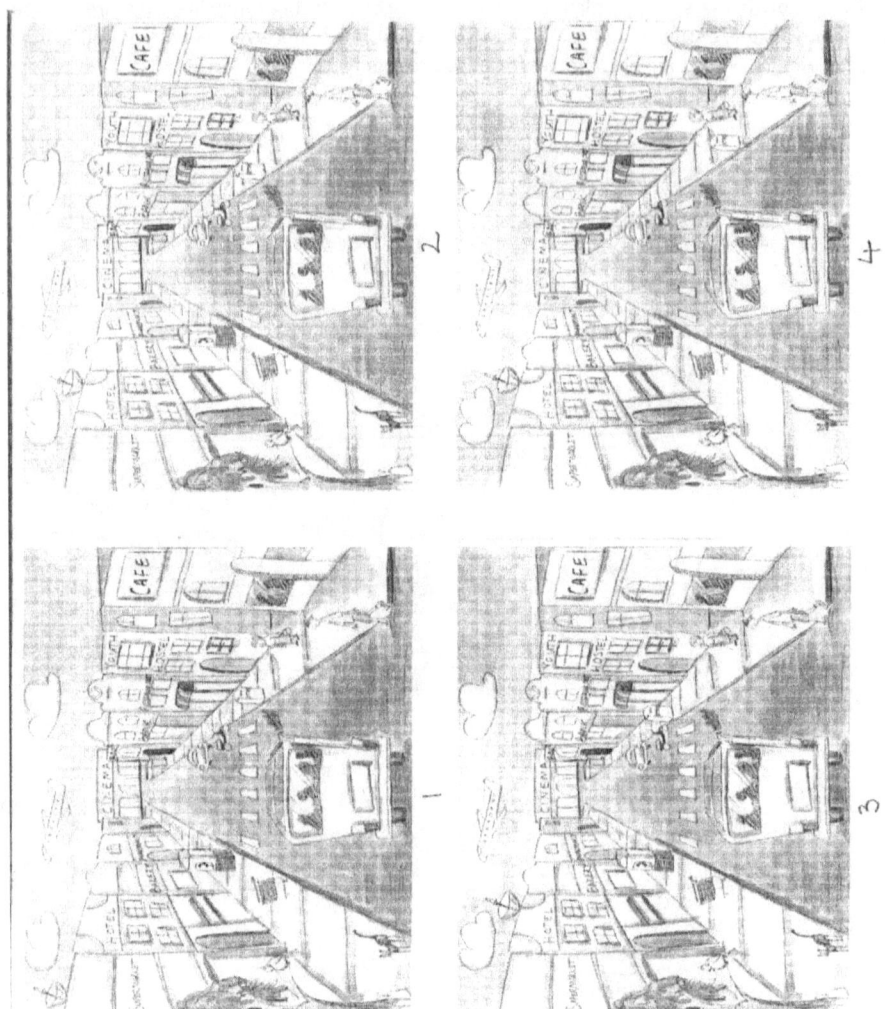

Appendix C

This section presents the instructions sheets for the describer and the receiver in our main experiment.

Instruction sheet: English describer

<u>AIM OF ACTIVITY:</u>

For one person, (the *describer*), to describe a picture in enough detail so that his/her partner, (the *receiver*), can correctly identify the picture from several alternate versions of it.

Describer:

You are going to be presented with two pictures, one at a time. Next to each of these pictures will be a list of 14 items.

Describe the first picture to your partner. In your description, you must specify the location of the fourteen items on the list. Your partner needs to have a very clear idea of where these items are located.

You have 5 minutes to complete your description. This is ample time to undertake this task without any need to rush. You will be told when 5 minutes are up. When you have finished your description, tell your partner he/she can now ask you questions about the picture.

Your partner then has up to 5 minutes to ask you questions about this first picture. After this, he/she will be presented with four different versions of the picture, and will have to select the one you described. Each of the three incorrect versions will have just one of the 14 items in the wrong location. Your partner will then hand the pictures over to you, and you will need to tell your partner if he/she has chosen the correct one by comparing the four versions to the picture you described.

Once this process is complete, you will be presented with the second picture. The procedure for this second picture is exactly the same as for the first one. That is, you will have 5 minutes to describe it, and you must clearly describe the location of the 14 listed items. Your partner will then have up to 5 minutes to ask you questions, before having to choose the picture you described from four alternate versions. You will once again let your partner know if he/she chose the correct one.

Relax! Be as expressive as you want to be! Body language is fine. Your partner needs to understand where those 14 items are located!

Instruction sheet: English receiver

AIM OF ACTIVITY:

For one person, (the *describer*), to describe a picture in enough detail so that his/her partner, (the *receiver*), can correctly identify the picture from several alternate versions of it.

Receiver:

Your partner (the describer) is going to describe two pictures to you. These pictures will be described one at a time.

You will be given a list of fourteen items. Your partner will describe the location of these fourteen items in his/her description.

Your task is to have a clear understanding of where each of these 14 items is located. You are not allowed to take notes or draw.

Do not interrupt your partner until he/she has finished his/her description. You then have up to 5 minutes to ask him/her any questions you may have about the picture and the location of the 14 items. You will be told when 5 minutes are up.

You will then be presented with four versions of the picture, and will need to identify the one which was described to you. Each of the three incorrect versions will have one of the 14 items in the wrong location - so make sure you fully understand where each of the items is located. Once you have made your choice, give the pictures to the describer. Ask him/her to tell you if you chose the correct one.

Once this process is complete, the describer will be presented with the second picture, and you will be given another list. The procedure for this second picture is exactly the same as for the first one. That is, you will listen to your partner's description, without interrupting him/her. After his/her description is complete, you will have up to 5 minutes to ask questions. You will then be presented with four versions of the picture, and will need to identify the one which was described to you. Again, each of the three incorrect versions will have just one of the 14 items in the wrong location. Once you have made your choice, give the pictures to the describer. Ask him/her to tell you if you chose the correct one.

Relax! Be as expressive as you want to be! Body language is fine. Make sure you figure out where those fourteen items are located!

Instruction sheet: French describer

BUT DE LA TACHE :

Le *descripteur* devra décrire une image de façon suffisamment détaillée pour que son/sa partenaire (le *récepteur*) puisse identifier cette image parmi les versions différentes qui lui seront présentées.

Descripteur :

On va vous présenter deux images, l'une après l'autre. A côté de chaque image vous trouverez une liste de 14 objets.

Décrivez la première image à votre partenaire. Dans votre description, il faut préciser la localisation des quatorze objets sur la liste. Il faut que votre partenaire comprenne de façon précise où se trouvent ces objets.

Vous avez 5 minutes pour faire votre description. Cela vous donne suffisamment de temps pour entreprendre la tâche sans vous presser. On vous dira quand les 5 minutes seront écoulées. Quand vous aurez terminé votre description, dites à votre partenaire qu'il/elle peut maintenant vous poser des questions sur l'image.

Votre partenaire aura alors 5 minutes pour vous poser des questions sur cette image. Ensuite, on lui présentera quatre versions différentes de l'image ; il/elle devra identifier celle que vous avez décrite. Trois versions, incorrectes, auront un seul des quatorze objets à la mauvaise place. Ensuite, votre partenaire vous remettra les images et vous devrez lui dire s'il/elle a choisi la bonne en comparant ces quatre versions à l'image que vous avez décrite.

Une fois ce processus terminé, on vous présentera la deuxième image. Le processus est exactement le même que pour la première. A nouveau, vous aurez 5 minutes pour faire votre description. Il faudra décrire avec clarté la localisation des quatorze objets sur la liste. Ensuite votre partenaire aura 5 minutes pour vous poser des questions avant de devoir choisir l'image que vous avez décrite parmi quatre versions différentes. Encore une fois, vous direz à votre partenaire s'il/elle a choisi la bonne image ou pas.

Détendez-vous ! Soyez aussi expressif que vous le désirez ! Le langage corporel est tout à fait accepté. Votre partenaire a besoin de comprendre où se trouvent ces 14 objets !

Instruction sheet: French receiver

BUT DE LA TÂCHE :

Le *descripteur* devra décrire une image de façon suffisamment détaillée pour que son/sa partenaire (le *récepteur*) puisse identifier cette image parmi les plusieurs versions différentes qui lui seront présentées.

Récepteur:

Votre partenaire (le descripteur) va vous décrire deux images. Il/elle décrira ces images l'une après l'autre.

On va vous donner une liste de quatorze objets. Votre partenaire va vous décrire la localisation de ces quatorze objets dans sa description.

Votre tâche consiste à bien comprendre où se trouve chacun de ces 14 objets. Vous n'êtes pas autorisé(e) à prendre des notes ou à dessiner.

N'interrompez pas votre partenaire avant la fin de sa description. Vous aurez ensuite 5 minutes pour lui poser toutes les questions que vous voulez sur l'image et la localisation des 14 objets. On vous dira quand les 5 minutes seront écoulées.

Ensuite on vous présentera quatre versions de l'image et vous devrez identifier celle qui vous a été décrite. Trois versions auront un des 14 objets à la mauvaise place – assurez-vous donc de comprendre précisément où se trouve chacun des objets. Quand vous aurez fait votre choix, donnez les images au descripteur. Demandez-lui de vous dire si vous avez choisi la bonne.

Une fois ce processus terminé on présentera la deuxième image au descripteur et on vous donnera une autre liste. Le protocole est exactement le même que pour la première image. C'est-à-dire, vous écouterez la description de votre partenaire sans l'interrompre. Une fois qu'il/elle aura terminé sa description vous aurez 5 minutes pour poser des questions. Ensuite, on vous présentera quatre versions de l'image et vous devrez identifier celle qui vous a été décrite. À nouveau, trois des versions n'auront qu'un seul des 14 objets à la mauvaise place. Une fois que vous aurez fait votre choix, donnez les images au descripteur. Demandez-lui de vous dire si vous avez choisi la bonne.

Détendez-vous ! Soyez aussi expressif que vous le désirez ! Le langage corporel est tout à fait accepté. Assurez-vous de comprendre où se trouvent ces quatorze objets !

Appendix D

Below is the transcription, in Word, of the lounge room scene description provided by English describer 9. The extract which we provide here ends with the beginning of the receiver's question time.

TRANSCRIPTION KEY
There is minimal punctuation in these transcriptions.

-	incomplete word
[/]	utterance interrupted by another speaker
..	pause – less than three seconds
....	pause – more than three seconds
[X]	incomprehensible – no more than 3 words
[XXX]	incomprehensible – more than 3 words
{ }	utterance between parentheses is uttered at the same time as another speaker's utterance
/...,.../	when more than one interpretation is possible, these are placed between sloping lines, and separated by a comma.
D	Describer
R	Receiver
I	Investigator

D: ok.. so the picture is of a of a room.. a lounge room in a house.. um.. it's looking towards the window and so there's a window ah on the the top right hand.. corner of of the picture.. ah there's a door over on the left and a fireplace in the middle.. ok so it's looking towards a wall.. ah in the the foreground of the picture so closest to to you.. um there's a couch over on the left hand side with a girl sitting on it.. looking out towards the other wall um on the other side of the room is a table and chairs.. um round table and chairs with ah a lamp.. over the table.. in between.. um the couch and the table.. um there's a book and a a small dog.. ah so in the for- the foreground of the picture the very closest to you.. um the couch with a girl on it.. ah do I need to tell you about the girl.. no um.. there's a couch.. book dog.. and table.. ok

R: [*laughs*]

D: um.. ah on the far wall.. um just next to the.. ah the door.. ah hanging on the wall is a a picture of a boy.. um it's a a square picture of a boy um underneath that picture is a cat.. um looking back towards the girl.. um.. next to those those two.. ah is a fireplace with a rug in front of it.. um so pretty much directly in front of the couch.. is.. ah a fireplace with a rug in front.. ah and a mirror just above the fireplace.. ah moving across where the window is.. ah there's a television under the window.. um.. and ah the television's it's on a cabinet and has a dvd player in the.. in the cabinet.. in front of a television.. so.. kinda between the television and the small dog

R: [*laughs*]

D: ah is a ball.. um so just above the dog.. is a ball

R: mmm hmm

D: um and just beside that ball ah is a bone.. ok.. so um.. that's kinda in the the middle of the floor looking.. kinda coming across the picture there's the couch with the girl on it.. um the very foreground has the book and the dog.. uh and in the middle.. is.. the bone and the ball.. and then there's a table and the tablecloth and the chairs.. over on the right hand side of the picture.. um.. now what do I need to tell you about.. um.. ok so.. ah with the table.. over on the the right hand side in the foreground.. um it's got the tablecloth on it.. surprisingly enough.. ah and there there's /ah,a/ a light that sort of one of those lights that hangs from the ceiling and ah the lampshade.. over it.. um…. how about I.. run through it quickly.. and then ah you can ask me any questions you want.. about it

R: good

D: um so the foreground of the picture

R: [*nods then laughs*]

D: there's a sofa.. with a girl sitting on it.. ah there's a book.. on the floor.. and and a small dog.. um and they're between the the sofa.. and the table and chairs.. um on the far wall.. so the wall that you're looking towards.. there's a a portrait of a.. a boy.. hanging on the wall.. and the cat.. is sitting just underneath that.. um just next to them is the fireplace the fireplace has a rug in front of it.. ah and a mirror.. over the top of it.. um.. and then across under the underneath the window is the television.. with a dvd player.. on the.. um.. the tv stand.. um in the middle of the floor.. in front of a television is a ball.. and next to the ball is a bone.. um.. how about you you can ask me any {questions if you like}
R: {*laughs*}ok um.. is it like quite like.. does it remind you of anything the picture like is it like

Appendix E

Below are the labels used to classify gestures on the parent tier 'gesture' in Elan. These labels allow the rapid identification of gestures which express different types of spatial information.

ICON-OBJ: Iconic gesture (physical object).
REP-SPACE: Gesture represents the locative semantic of a linguistic spatial item in the locative expression.
REP-OBJECT: Form is not iconic for object, but represents it nevertheless (i.e. C-fingers for dvd player, in dyad 9, just after 2:06; or C-fingers for the cat, FrenDesc8, 1:01 – 1:02).
REP-ACTION: Rarely used. Gesture re-enacts a physical action.
GEST-FIGURE: Object is presented as a Figure in gesture only.
SPATIAL/PREPOSITIONAL MISMATCH: Speaker gestures opposite of lexically encoded locative semantic (i.e. gesturing 'above' but saying 'below').
METAPHORICAL: Metaphorical gesture.
POINT-LOC: Gesture points at conceptualised location of object in gesture space.
POINT-LOC pic: Points at or towards object on picture (not location as mapped onto gesture space), or picture (without really being able to tell whether an object is being pointed to or not.)
MARK-LOC: Gesture marks location of entity in gesture space
(note: speakers can mark the location of entities in gesture space to show their relation to each other, without such gestural markings representing isomorphic location in gesture space. e.g. dyad 6, gesture 54).
PLACE-OBJ: Gesture places conceptualised object in gesture space.
HOLD-OBJ: New category created when coding dyad 8. Hand seems to hold the entity being described.
INDICATE DISTANCE: Rarely used. Gesture indicates the distance encoded by lexical item in the locative expression. For example, this type of gesture is produced by EngDesc8 when he presents the idea of one metre.
DEICTIC TERM: Used when a gesture provides specification of location for a deictic lexical item, such as *here* and *there*.
UNLEX-LOC NEW: Gesture provides new locative information about a referent (or referents), which has not been previously communicated in the speaker's discourse. Once presented, if repeated in subsequent gestures in the utterance, these further occasions will also be coded as 'unlex-loc new'.
UNLEX-LOC ANAPH: Gesture provides locative information about a referent (or referents). This information is unlexicalised in the current locative expression, although it has previously been lexicalised in the speaker's discourse.
UNLEX-LOC CONTEXT: Gesture expresses locative information which is unencoded in the co-occurring linguistic expression but which is inferable from context (i.e. gesture 8, dyad 8). The locative information may be contextually available because it has been expressed prior, or because the locative information is deductible from information known about another item: i.e. Dyad 2, when the speaker talks about a shop "down from" the post-office box: since it is already know that the post-office box is on the LHS of the street, it is therefore pragmatically inferable that the shop is also on this side of the street.

LOC-CONTEXT: Gesturally-expressed locative information which is also expressed, in either speech or gesture, at another point in locative utterance.

REFINE-LOC: Gesture refines the locative semantic of a co-occurring spatial term: i.e. for *next to* or *à côté de*.

AXIAL FUSION: Gesture expresses information pertaining to a spatial axis not referenced in the concurrent linguistic expression. Speech may reference another spatial axis or none at all (for example, a topological locative relationship may be encoded in speech instead).

REFERENCE-SELF: Gesture references the speaker (often used when reference is made to the foreground of the picture).

DELIMITATION: Gesture of delimitation (C-fingers, etc) for an abstract concept (non-physical object): i.e. 'middle of the foreground' (EngDesc3).

PRESENTATION: Gesture of presentation.

ENUMERATION: Counting gesture. Physical properties: extended digit(s) pressing down on other extended digit(s)/hand.

CRANK: crank gesture.

OUTCOME: The *aboutissement* of a locative process. Ring finger may be used to represent this (see dyad 9).

DISC-MARK: Discourse marker. Used to describe two types of gestures: a) pragmatic gestures whose role is to highlight one or more co-occurring lexical item(s) as salient; and b) gestures which mark prosodic features of language, such as stressed syllables.

This category includes gestures known in the literature as "beats" (McNeill 1992).

LEXICAL SEARCH: Possible word search gesture.

PANTOMIME: Very rare. Speaker re-enacts physical action.

COMMENT: Very rare. Speaker uses hand movement to signal the provision of further information about a lexicalised locative relationship.

OTHER PRAGMATIC: Other type of pragmatic gesture. This category is very rarely used, and codes pragmatic gestures whose occurrence is too infrequent to merit the creation of another gesture sub-category.

STROKE-HOLD: Rare type of gesture; see McNeill (2005).

Appendix F

This appendix draws together the spatial items which located a Figure for a second or subsequent time as part of an overall locative expression in our 'first-mention' data set. The tables below provide this data by language and picture.

Tab. 36: English descriptions: lounge room scene

Frontal axis	N	Lateral axis	N	*On*	N
far	1	next to	2	on	0
TOTAL	1	TOTAL	2	TOTAL	0

Tab. 37: French descriptions: lounge room scene

Frontal axis	N	Lateral axis	N	*Sur*	N
en face de 'in front of'/'opposite'	2	ici 'here'	1	sur 'on'	1
devant 'in front of'	1				
dans le fond de 'in the background of'	1				
TOTAL	4	TOTAL	1	TOTAL	1

Tab. 38: English descriptions: street scene

Frontal axis	N	Lateral axis	N	*On*	N
in front	1	on the left-hand side of	2	on	1
second	1	on the left-hand side	1		
closest to	1	on the right-hand side	1		
far	1				
TOTAL	4	TOTAL	4	TOTAL	1

Tab. 39: French descriptions: street scene

Frontal axis	N	Lateral axis	N	*Sur*	N
premier 'first'	1	NIL	0	NIL	0
TOTAL	1	TOTAL	0	TOTAL	0

References

Alibali, Martha. 2005. Gesture in Spatial Cognition: Expressing, Communicating, and Thinking about Spatial Information. *Spatial Cognition & Computation: An Interdisciplinary Journal* 5(4). 307–331.
Alibali, Martha, Dana Heath and Heather Myers. 2001. Effects of visibility between speaker and listener on gesture production: some gestures are meant to be seen. *Journal of Memory and Language* 44. 169–188.
Ameka, Felix, and Stephen Levinson. 2007. Introduction. The typology and semantics of locative predicates: posturals, positionals, and other beasts. *Linguistics* 45(5/6). 847– 871.
Arik, Engin. 2009. *Spatial Language: Insights from Sign and Spoken Languages*. Indiana: Purdue University doctoral dissertation.
Ashley, Aaron, & Laura Carlson. 2007. Encoding direction when interpreting proximal terms. *Language and Cognitive Processes* 22(7). 1021–1024.
Bavelas, Janet, Jennifer Gerwing, Chantelle Sutton & Danielle Prevost. 2008. Gesturing on the telephone: Independent effects of dialogue and visibility. *Journal of Memory and Language* 58(2). 495–520.
Beattie, Geoffrey, & Heather Shovelton. 1999. Mapping the range of information contained in the iconic hand gestures that accompany spontaneous speech. *Journal of Language and Social Psychology* 18(4). 438–462.
Beattie, Geoffrey, & Heather Shovelton. 2002. An experimental investigation of some propeties of individual iconic gestures that mediate their communicative power. *British Journal of Psychology* 93. 179–192.
Beattie, Geoffrey, & Heather Shovelton. 2006. When size really matters: How a single semantic feature is represented in the speech and gesture modalities. *Gesture* 6(1). 63–84.
Beavers, John, Beth Levin & Shiao Tham. 2010. The typology of motion expressions revisited. *Journal of Linguistics* 46. 331–377.
Bennett, David. 1975. *Spatial and Temporal Uses of English Prepositions: An Essay in Stratificational Semantics*. London: Longman Group Limited.
Berthonneau, Anne-Marie. 1993. *Avant/après*. De l'espace au temps [*Before/after*. From space to time]. In Anne-Marie Berthonneau & Pierre Cadiot (eds.), *Les prépositions : méthodes d'analyse* [Prepositions: analytical methods], 41–109. Lille: Presses Universitaires de Lille.
Borillo, Andrée. 1992. Quelques marqueurs de la deixis spatiale [A few spatial-deictic markers]. In Mary-Annick Morel & Laurent Danon-Boileau (eds.), *La deixis: colloque en Sorbonne 8-9 juin 1990* [Deixis: a conference at the Sorbonne, 8-9 June, 1990], 245–256. Paris: Presses Universitaires de France.
Borillo, Andrée. 1998. *L'espace et son expression en français* [Space and its expression in French]. Gap/Paris: Editions Ophrys.
Bressem, J. 2013. A linguistic perspective on the notation of form features in gestures. In Cornelia Müller, Alan Cienki, Ellen Fricke, Silva Ladewig, David McNeill & Sedinya Teßendorf (eds.), *Body – Language – Communication: An International Handbook on Multimodality in Human Interaction. Volume 1.* (Handbooks of Linguistics and Communication Science 38.1), 1079–1098. Berlin & Boston: De Gruyter Mouton.
Brown, Amanda. 2007. *Crosslinguistic influence in first and second languages: convergence in speech and gesture*. Nijmegen: MPI Series in Psycholinguistics (47).

Brown, Penelope, & Stephen Levinson. 2000. Frames of spatial reference and their acquisition in Tenejapan Tzeltal. In Larry Nucci, Geoffrey Saxe & Elliot Turiel (eds.), *Culture, thought, and development*, 167–197. Mahwah, NJ: Erlbaum.

Bryant, David. 1998. Human Spatial Concepts Reflect Regularities of the Physical World and Human Body. In Patrick Olivier & Klaus-Peter Gapp (eds.), *Representation and Processing of Spatial Relations*, 215–230. Mahwah, NJ & London: Erlbaum.

Bühler, Karl. 1982. The Deictic Field of Language and Deictic Words. In Robert Jarvella & Wolfgang Klein (eds.), *Speech, Place, and Action*, 9–30. New York: John Wiley & Sons Ltd.

Calbris, Geneviève. 2004. Déixis représentative [Representative deixis]. In Cornelia Müller & Roland Posner (eds.), *The semantics and pragmatics of everyday gestures*, 145–156. Berlin: Weidler.

Carlson, Laura, & Eric Covey. 2005. How far is *near*? Inferring distance from spatial descriptions. *Language and Cognitive Processes* 20. 617–631.

Carlson-Radvansky, Laura, & David Irwin. 1993. Frames of Reference in Vision and Language: Where Is Above? *Cognition* 46. 223–244.

Cassell, Justine, David McNeill & Karl-Eric McCullough. 1999. Speech-Gesture Mismatches: Evidence for One Underlying Representation of Linguistic and Non-Linguistic Information. *Pragmatics and Cognition* 7(1). 1–33.

Chu, Mingyuan, & Sotaro Kita. 2008. The relationship between co-thought gestures and co-speech gestures. Paper presented at the Language, Communication and Cognition conference, University of Brighton, 4–7 August.

Cienki, Alan. In press. *Ten Lectures on Spoken Language and Gesture from the Perspective of Cognitive Linguistics: Issues of Dynamicity and Multimodality*. Beijing: Foreign Language Teaching and Research Press.

Cienki, Alan, & Kasper Kok. Submitted. Gesture and Cognitive Grammar: points of convergence, advances and challenges.

Clark, Herbert. 1973. Space, Time, Semantics, and the Child. In Timothy Moore (ed.), *Cognitive Development and the Acquisition of Language*, 27–63. New York: Academic Press.

Costello, Fintan & John Kelleher. 2006. Spatial Prepositions in Context: The Semantics of *near* in the Presence of Distractor Objects. In Boban Arsenijevic, Tim Baldwin & Beata Trawinski (eds.), *Proceedings of the Third ACL-SIGSEM Workshop on Prepositions*, 1–8. Stroudsburg, PA: Association for Computational Linguistics.

Coventry, Kenny, & Simon Garrod. 2004. *Saying, Seeing, and Acting: the Psychological Semantics of Spatial Prepositions (Essays in Cognitive Psychology)*. Hove/New York: Psychology Press.

Debrelioska, Sandra, Asli Özyürek, Marianne Gullberg & Pamela Perniss. 2013. Gestural Viewpoint Signals Referent Accessibility. *Discourse Processes* 50(7). 431–456.

De Ruiter, Jan-Peter. 2000. The production of gesture and speech. In David McNeill (ed.), *Language and Gesture*, 284–311. Cambridge: Cambridge University Press.

De Ruiter, Jan-Peter. 2007. Postcards from the mind: The relationship between speech, imagistic gesture, and thought. *Gesture* 7(1). 21–38.

De Saussure, Ferdinand. 1995 [1916]. *Cours de linguistique générale*. Paris: Éditions Payot & Rivages.

Eberle, Sarah. 2013. *Locative Expressions in Signed Languages: A Cross-Linguistic Comparison*. North Dakota: University of North Dakota MA thesis.

Efron, David. 1972. *Gesture, Race and Culture*. The Hague: De Gruyter Mouton.

Ekman, Paul, & Wallace Friesen. 1981 [1969]. The Repertoire of Nonverbal Behavior: Categories, Origins, Usage and Coding. In Adam Kendon (ed.), *Nonverbal Communication, Interaction, and Gesture*, 57–105. The Hague: De Gruyter Mouton.

Emmorey, Karen, Barbara Tversky & Holly Taylor. 2000. Using space to describe space: Perspective in speech, sign, and gesture. *Journal of Spatial Cognition and Computation* 2. 157–180.

Emmorey, Karen, & Shannon Casey. 2001. Gesture, thought and spatial language. *Gesture* 1(1). 35–50.

Enfield, Nick. 2001. '*Lip-Pointing*': A Discussion of Form and Function with Reference to Data from Laos. *Gesture* 1(2). 185–211.

Fillmore, Charles. 1975. *Santa Cruz Lectures On Deixis 1971*. Indiana: Indiana University Linguistics Club.

Franckel, Jean-Jacques, & Denis Paillard. 2007. *Grammaire des prepositions: Tome 1* [The grammar of prepositions: volume 1]. Paris: Éditions Ophrys.

Fricke, Ellen. 2003. *Origo*, pointing, and conceptualization – what gestures reveal about the nature of the *origo* in face-to-face interaction. In Friedrich Lenz (ed.), *Deictic Conceptualisation of Space, Time and Person*, 69–93. Amsterdam/Philadelphia: John Benjamins.

Galhano-Rodrigues, Isabel. 2007. How do feet gesticulate? Paper presented at the 3rd conference of the International Society for Gesture Studies, Northwestern University, Chicago, 18–21 June.

Goldin-Meadow, Susan. 2003. Thought before Language: Do we Think Ergative? In Dedre Gentner & Susan Goldin-Meadow (eds.), *Language in mind: Advances in the study of language and thought*, 493–522. Cambridge, MA: MIT Press.

Goldin-Meadow, Susan. 2005. The two faces of gesture: language and thought. *Gesture* 5. 239–255.

Grinevald, Colette. 2006. The expression of static location in a typological perspective. In Maya Hickmann & Stéphane Robert (eds.), *Space in Languages: Linguistic Systems and Cognitive Categories*, 29–58. Amsterdam/Philadelphia: John Benjamins.

Gullberg, Marianne. 2006. Some reasons for studying gesture and second language acquisition (Hommage à Adam Kendon). *International Review of Applied Linguistics* 44(2). 103–124.

Gullberg, Marianne, Henriette Hendriks & Maya Hickmann. 2008. Learning to talk and gesture about motion in French. *First Language* 28(2). 200–236.

Gullberg, Marianne. 2011. Language-specific encoding of placement events in gestures. In Jürgen Bohnemeyer & Eric Pederson (eds.), *Event Representations in Language and Cognition*, 166–188. Cambridge: Cambridge University Press.

Hadar, Uri, & Brian Butterworth. 1997. Iconic Gestures, Imagery, and Word Retrieval in Speech. *Semiotica* 115 (1-2). 147–172.

Hendriks, Henriette, Marzena Watorek & Patrizia Giuliano. 2004. L'expression de la localisation et du mouvement dans les descriptions et les récits en L1 et L2 [The expression of localisation and movement in descriptions and storytellings in first and second languages]. *Langage* 155. 106–126.

Herskovits, Annette. 1986. *Language and Spatial Cognition: An Interdisciplinary Study of the Prepositions in English*. Cambridge: Cambridge University Press.

Hickmann, Maya, & Henriette Hendriks. 2006. Static and dynamic location in French and in English. *First Language* 26(1). 103–135.

Hill, Clifford. 1982. Up/Down, Front/Back, Left/Right: A Contrastive Study of Hausa and English. In Jürgen Weissenborn & Wolfgang Klein (eds.), *Here and there. Cross-linguistic studies on deixis and demonstration*, 13–42. Amsterdam: John Benjamins.

Holler, Judith, & Geoffrey Beattie. 2002. A micro-analytic investigation of how iconic gestures and speech represent core semantic features in talk. *Semiotica* 142. 31–69.

Holler, Judith, Heather Shovelton & Geoffrey Beattie. 2009. Do iconic hand gestures really contribute to the communication of semantic information in a face-to-face context? *Journal of Nonverbal Behaviour* 33. 73–88.

Hörberg, Thomas. 2007. *Influences of Form and Function on Spatial Relations: Establishing functional and geometric influences on projective prepositions in Swedish*. Stockholm: Stockholm University MA thesis.

Hostetter, Autumn, & Martha Alibali. 2007. Raise your hand if you're spatial: Relations between verbal and spatial skills and gesture production. *Gesture* 7(1). 73–95.

Hostetter, Autumn, Martha Alibali & Sotaro Kita. 2007. I see it in my hands' eye: Representational gestures reflect conceptual demands. *Language and Cognitive Processes* 22(3). 313–336.

Huddleston, Rodney, & Geoffrey Pullum. 2005. *A Student's Introduction to English Grammar*. Cambridge: Cambridge University Press.

Kelly, Barbara. 2004. The development of constructions through gesture use. In Eve Clark (ed.), *Proceedings of the 2004 Stanford Child Language Research Forum: Constructions and Acquisiton*, 30–39. http://cslipublications.stanford.edu/CLRF/2004/CLRF-2004-toc.html (accessed 8 July 2015).

Kemmerer, David, & Daniel Tranel. 2000. A double dissociation between linguistic and perceptual representations of spatial relationships. *Cognitive Neuropsychology* 17(5). 393–414.

Kendon, Adam. 1980. Gesticulation and Speech: Two Aspects of the Process of Utterance. In Mary Key (ed.), *The Relationship of Verbal and Nonverbal Communication*, 207–227. The Hague: De Gruyter.

Kendon, Adam. 1981. Current Issues in the Study of "Nonverbal Communication". In Adam Kendon (ed.), *Nonverbal Communication, Interaction, and Gesture: Selections from Semiotica*, 1–53. The Hague: De Gruyter.

Kendon, Adam. 1988. How gestures can become like words. In Fernando Poyatos (ed.), *Cross-Cultural Perspectives in Nonverbal Communication*, 131–141. New York: C. J. Hogrefe.

Kendon, Adam. 1994. Do Gestures Communicate?: A Review. *Research on Language and Social Interaction* 27(3). 175–200.

Kendon, Adam. 1996. An Agenda for Gesture Studies. *The Semiotic Review of Books* 7(3). 7–12.

Kendon, Adam. 1997. Gesture. *Annual Review of Anthropology* 26. 109–128.

Kendon, Adam. 2000. Language and gesture: unity or duality? In David McNeill (ed.), *Language and Gesture*, 47–63. Cambridge: Cambridge University Press.

Kendon, Adam, & Laura Versante. 2003. Point by Hand in "Neapolitan". In Sotaro Kita (ed.), *Pointing: Where Language, Culture, and Cognition Meet*, 109–137. New Jersey/London: Erlbaum.

Kendon, Adam. 2004. *Gesture: Visible Action as Utterance*. Cambridge: Cambridge University Press.

Kita, Sotaro. 2000. How representational gestures help speaking. In David McNeill (ed.), *Language and gesture*, 162–185. Cambridge: Cambridge University Press.

Kita, Sotaro. 2003. Pointing: A Foundational Building Block of Human Communication. In Sotaro Kita (ed.), *Pointing: Where Language, Culture, and Cognition Meet*, 1–8. New Jersey/London: Erlbaum.

Kita, Sotaro, & Asli Özyürek. 2003. What does cross-linguistic variation in semantic coordination of speech and gesture reveal?: Evidence for an interface representation of spatial thinking and speaking. *Journal of Memory and Language* 48. 16–32.

Kita, Sotaro. 2009. Cross-cultural variation of speech-accompanying gesture: A review. *Language and Cognitive Processes* 24(2). 145–167.

Kita, Sotaro, & Thomas Davies. 2009. Competing conceptual representations trigger co-speech representational gestures. *Language and Cognitive Processes* 24(5). 761–775.

Kopecka, Anetta. 2004. *Etude typologique de l'expression de l'espace : localisation et déplacement en français et en polonais* [A typological study of the expression of space: localisation and displacement in French and Polish]. Lyon: University of Lyon (Lumière 2) doctoral dissertation.

Kopecka, Anetta & Stéphanie Pourcel. 2005. Motion expressions in French: typological diversity. *Durham & Newcastle Working Papers in Linguistics* 11. 139–153.

Kopecka, Anetta. 2006. The semantic structure of motion verbs in French: Typological perspectives. In Maya Hickmann & Stéphane Robert (eds.), *Space in languages: Linguistic systems and cognitive categories*, 83–101. Amsterdam/Philadelphia: John Benjamins.

Krauss, Robert, Yihsiu Chen & Purnima Chawla. 1996. Nonverbal behaviour and nonverbal communication: what do conversational hand gestures tell us? In Mark Zanna (ed.), *Advances in Experimental Social Psychology*, 389–450. San Diego, CA: Academic Press.

Krauss, Robert, Yihsiu Chen & Rebecca Gottesman. 2000. Lexical gestures and lexical access: a process model. In David McNeill (ed.), *Language and gesture*, 261–283. Cambridge: Cambridge University Press.

Landau, Barbara and Ray Jackendoff. 1993. "What" and "Where" in Spatial Language and Spatial Cognition. *Behavioral and Brain Sciences* 16. 217–265.

Landau, Barbara. 2003. Axes and Direction in Spatial Language and Spatial Cognition. In Emile van der Zee & Jon Slack (eds.), *Representing direction in language and space*, 18–38. Oxford: Oxford University Press.

Langacker, Ronald. 1987. *The Foundations of Cognitive Grammar: Volume I: Theoretical Prerequisites*. Stanford: Stanford University Press.

Langacker, Ronald. 2001. Discourse in cognitive grammar. *Cognitive linguistics* 12(2). 143–188.

Langacker, Ronald. 2008. *Cognitive grammar: A Basic Introduction*. Oxford: Oxford University Press.

Langacker, Ronald. 2013. *Essentials of Cognitive Grammar*. Oxford: Oxford University Press.

Lautenschütz, Anna-Katharina, Clare Davies, Martin Raubal, Angela Schwering & Eric Pederson. 2007. The Influence of Scale, Context and Spatial Preposition in Linguistic Topology. In: Thomas Barkowsky, Markus Knauff, Gérard Ligozat & Daniel Montello (eds.), *Spatial Cognition V, Reasoning, Action, Interaction, Volume 5*, 439–452. Berlin, Heidelberg: Springer-Verlag.

Lemmens, Maarten. 2005. Motion and location: toward a cognitive typology. In Geneviève Girard-Gillet (ed.), *Parcours linguistiques : domaine anglais* [CIEREC Travaux 122] [Linguistic paths: the English domain], pp. 223–244. Saint-Etienne: Publications de l'Université St.-Etienne.

Lemmens, Maarten & Dan Slobin. 2008. Positie- en bewegingswerkwoorden in het Nederlands, het Engels en het Frans [Position- and movement verbs in Dutch, English and French]. In

Philippe Hiligsmann (ed.), Verslagen en mededelingen van de Handelingen van de Koninklijke Academie voor Taal- en letterkunde [Reports and communications of the Activities of the Royal Academy for Linguistics and Literature] 118.1, pp. 17–32. Ghent: KANTL.

Levinson, Stephen. 1992. Primer for the field investigation of spatial description and conception. *Pragmatics* 2(1). 5–47.

Levinson, Stephen. 1996. Language and Space. *Annual Review of Anthropology* 25. 353–382.

Levinson, Stephen. 2003a. Language and mind: Let's get the issues straight! In Dedre Gentner & Susan Goldin-Meadow (eds.), *Language in Mind: Advances in the study of language and cognition*, 25–46. Cambridge, MA: MIT Press.

Levinson, Stephen. 2003b. *Space in Language and Cognition: Explorations in Cognitive Diversity*. Cambridge: Cambridge University Press.

Levinson, Stephen & Sergio Meira. 2003. 'Natural concepts' in the spatial topological domain – adpositional meanings in crosslinguistic perspective: An exercise in semantic typology. *Language* 79(3). 485–516.

Lyons, John. 1977. *Semantics: Volume 2*. Cambridge: Cambridge University Press.

Max Planck Institute for Psycholinguistics. 1998 Annual Report. Nijmegen: Max Planck Institute for Psycholinguistics.

McCullough, Karl-Erik. 2005. *Using Gestures in Speaking: Self-generating indexical fields*. Chicago: University of Chicago doctoral dissertation.

McNeill, David. 1992. *Hand and mind. What the hands reveal about thought*. Chicago: University of Chicago Press.

McNeill, David. 2000a. Analogic/analytic representations and cross-linguistic differences in thinking for speaking. *Cognitive Linguistics* 11. 43–60.

McNeill, David. 2000b. Catchments and contexts: non-modular factors in speech and gesture production. In David McNeill (ed.), *Language and gesture*, 312–328. Cambridge: Cambridge University Press.

McNeill, David & Susan Duncan. 2000. Growth points in thinking-for-speaking. In David McNeill (ed.), *Language and gesture*, 141–161. Cambridge: Cambridge University Press.

McNeill, David. 2005. *Gesture and thought*. Chicago: University of Chicago Press.

Melinger, Alissa, & Willem Levelt. 2004. Gesture and the communicative intention of the speaker. *Gesture* 4(2). 119–141.

Miller, George & Philip Johnson-Laird. 1976. *Language and Perception*. Cambridge: Cambridge University Press.

Montello, Daniel. 1993. Scale and multiple psychologies of space. In Andrew Frank & Irene Campari (eds.), *Spatial information theory: A theoretical basis for GIS*, 312–321. Berlin: Springer-Verlag.

Morris, Desmond, Peter Collett, Peter Marsh & Marie O'Shaughnessy. 1977. *Gestures, their origins and distribution*. London: Jonathan Cape.

Müller, Cornelia. 1998. Iconicity and gesture. In Serge Santi, Isabelle Guaïtella, Christian Cave & Gabrielle Konopczynski (eds.), *Oralité et Gestualité: Communication multimodale, interaction*, 321–328. Paris: L'Harmattan.

Müller, Cornelia. 2004. Forms and uses of the Palm Up Open Hand: A case of a gesture family? In Cornelia Müller & Roland Posner (eds.), *The Semantics and Pragmatics of Everyday Gestures*, 233–256. Berlin: Weidler.

Müller, Cornelia. 2007. From form to meaning: Gestural modes of representation. Talk given at the MGA workshop, European University Viadrina Frankfurt (Oder), 18–21 October.

Nikitina, Tatiana. 2008. Pragmatic factors and variation in the expression of spatial goals: The case of *into* vs. *in*. In Anna Asbury, Jakub Dotlačil, Berit Gehrke & Rick Nouwen (eds.), *Syntax and semantics of spatial P*, 175–196. Amsterdam: John Benjamins.

Noyau, Colette, Cristina de Lorenzo, Maria Kihlstedt, Urszula Paprocka, Gema Sanz Espinar, & Ricarda Schneider. 2011. Two dimensions of the representation of complex event structures: granularity and condensation. Towards a typology of textual production in L1 and L2. In Henriette Hendriks (ed.), *The Structure of Learner Varieties*, 157–202. Berlin: de Gruyter.

Özyürek, Asli, Sotaro Kita, Shanley Allen, Reyhan Furman & Amananda Brown. 2005. How does linguistic framing of events influence co-speech gestures? Insights from crosslinguistic variations and similarities. *Gesture* 5 (1/2). 219–240.

Özyürek, Asli, Sotaro Kita, Shanley Allen, Amanda Brown, Reyhan Furman, & Tomoko Ishizuka. 2008. Development of Cross-Linguistic Variation in Speech and Gesture: Motion Events in English and Turkish. *Developmental Psychology* 44. 1040–1054.

Özyürek, Asli, Inge Zwitserlood & Pamela Perniss. 2010. Locative expressions in signed languages: A view from Turkish Sign Language (TID). *Linguistics* 48(5). 1111–1145.

Perniss, Pamela. 2007. *Space and Iconicity in German Sign Language (DGS)*. Nijmegen: MPI Series in Psycholinguistics (45).

Poggi, Isabelle. 2004. The Italian gestionary. Meaning representation, ambiguity, and context. In Cornelia Müller & Roland Posner (eds.), *The Semantics and Pragmatics of Everyday Gestures*, 73–88. Berlin: Weidler.

Rauscher, Frances, Robert Krauss & Yihsiu Chen. 1996. Gesture, Speech and Lexical Access: The Role of Lexical Movements in Speech Production. *Psychological Science* 7(4). 226–231.

Schober, Michael. 1998. How Addressees Affect Spatial Perspective Choice in Dialogue. In Patrick Oliver & Klaus-Peter Gapp (eds.), *Representation and Processing of Spatial Expressions*, 231–245. Mahwah NJ: Lawrence Erlbaum Associates.

Sinha, Chris & Tania Kuteva. 1995. Distributed Spatial Semantics. *Nordic Journal of Linguistics* 18. 167–199.

Slobin, Dan. 1997. Mind, Code, and Text. In Joan Bybee, John Haiman & Sandra Thompson (eds.), *Essays on Language Function and Language Type*, 437–465. Amsterdam/Philadelphia: John Benjamins.

Slobin, Dan. 2004. The many ways to search for a frog: linguistic typology and the expression of motion events. In Sven Stromqvist & Ludo Verhoeven (eds.), *Relating events in narrative: topological & contextual perspectives*, 219–257. Mahwah, NJ: LEA Publishers.

Slobin, Dan. 2006. What makes manner of motion salient? Explorations in linguistic typology, discourse, and cognition. In Maya Hickmann & Stéphane Robert (eds.), *Space in languages: Linguistic systems and cognitive categories*, 59-81. Amsterdam/Philadelphia: John Benjamins.

Stam, Gale. 2006. Thinking for Speaking about Motion: L1 and L2 Speech and Gesture. *IRAL* 44(2). 145–171.

Striegnitz, Kristina, Paul Tepper, Andrew Lovett & Justine Cassell. 2009. Knowledge Representation for Generating Locating Gestures in Route Directions. In Kenny Coventry, Thora Tenbrink & John Bateman (eds.), *Spatial Language and Dialogue*, 147–165. Oxford: Oxford University Press.

Svorou, Soteria. 1986. On the Evolutionary Paths of Locative Expressions. *Proceedings of the Berkeley Linguistics Society* 12. 515–527.

Tabensky, Alexis. 2001. Gesture and Speech Rephrasings in Conversation. *Gesture* 1(2). 213-236.

Talmy, Leonard. 1991. Path to realization: A typology of event conflation. *Proceedings of the Berkeley Linguistics Society* 17. 480–519.

Talmy, Leonard. 2000. *Toward a Cognitive Semantics*. Cambridge MA: MIT Press.

Taylor, John. 2002. *Cognitive Grammar*. Oxford: Oxford University Press.

Tutton, Mark. 2007. A speech/gesture interface: encoding static, locative relationships in verbal discourse. In Robyn Loughnane, Cara Penry Williams & Jana Verhoeven (eds.), *In Between Wor(l)ds: Transformation and Translation*, 223–234. Melbourne: School of Languages, University of Melbourne.

Tutton, Mark. 2009. When *In* Means *Into*: Towards an Understanding of Boundary-crossing *In*. *Journal of English Linguistics* 37(1). 5–27.

Tutton, Mark. 2011. How Speakers Gesture When Encoding Location with English *on* and French *sur*. *Journal of Pragmatics* 43. 3431–3454.

Tutton, M. 2013. Granularity, Space and Motion-Framed Location. In Emile van der Zee & Mila Vulchanova (eds.), *Motion Encoding in Spatial Language*, 149-165. Oxford: Oxford University Press.

Tversky, Barbara, & Paul Lee. 1998. How Space Structures Language. In Christian Freksa, Christopher Habel & Karl Wender (eds.), *Spatial Cognition: An interdisciplinary approach to representation and processing of spatial knowledge*, 157–175. Berlin: Springer-Verlag.

Tversky, Barbara, Julie Heiser, Paul Lee & Marie-Paule Daniel. 2009. Explanations in Gesture, Diagram, and Word. In Kenny Coventry, Thora Tenbrink & John Bateman (eds.), *Spatial Language and Dialogue*, 119–131. Oxford: Oxford University Press.

Tyler, Andrea & Vyvyan Evans. 2003. *The semantics of English prepositions*. Cambridge: Cambridge University Press.

Vandeloise, Claude. 1986. *L'espace en français*. Paris: Éditions du Seuil.

Vandeloise, Claude. 2006. Are there spatial prepositions? In Maya Hickmann & Stéphane Robert (eds.), *Space in Languages: Linguistic systems and cognitive categories*, 139–154. Amsterdam/Philadelphia: John Benjamins.

Watson, Matthew. 2006. *Reference frame selection and representation in dialogue and monologue*. Edinburgh: University of Edinburgh doctoral dissertation.

Index

à côté (de)   148–49, 187–94, 198, 214, 215–16, 223, 225, 232, 267, 278, 295, 300, 303, 304
across   182, 207–8, 209, 243–44, 279, 302
after   134–35, 156
American Sign Language   3, 45
Amerindian languages   3
après   149–51, 158, 196–97
Australian Sign Language (ASQ)   3
Austrian Sign Language   3, 45
avant   149–51, 158, 229

background   226
basic locative construction   2, 3, 16
– general verb languages   16
– multi-verb languages   16
– postural verb languages   16
before   156
beside   180–81
between   104–7, 156, 159, 177–78, 232, 275, 276–78, 279, 283–84, 284, 290, 291, 295, 299, 302, 303, 305

cardinal directions   21
Catalan Sign Language (CSC)   3
close(r)/closest to   104, 125
Cognitive Grammar   7, 266, 285–94, 302, 303
core schema   14
Croatian   3, 45
Croatian Sign Language   3, 45
crossmodal spatial language hypothesis   3, 4

deixis   17, 25
devant   111–15, 141–42, 145, 158, 159, 161, 215
directionally non-specific spatial items   19, 90
directionally specific spatial items   18
down   128–31, 156, 157

ELAN   58, 62
en face de   111–15, 141–45, 158, 159, 161, 215, 226, 230, 295, 299, 303, 305

entre   118–19, 147–48, 159, 193, 194–96, 232, 275, 276–78, 279, 284, 295, 299, 302, 303, 305
Estonian Sign Language (ESO)   3

far   102–3, 231, 237
Figure   1, 4, 6, 11, 15, 43, 68, 78, 296
– Gestural Figure   1, 8, 79, 78–81, 83, 85, 106, 266, 293, 302, 305
foreground   146, 159, 226, 243, 298
– gestural depiction   101, 109–11
frames of reference   10, 17, 19, 29, 46
– absolute   17, 19, 21
– intrinsic   17, 19, 29, 53, 184
– relative   17, 19, 20, 29, 53, 165, 184, 185, 202, 220
frontal axis   5, 7, 18, 87–163, 166, 266, 269, 270, 271–74, 274, 296, 298–99, 300
– description   87–89

geometric shapes (describing)   43
German Sign Language (DGS)   3, 22
gesture   29, 30, 83
– and syntax   44
– beats   34, 37, 38, 255
– cohesives   34, 38
– deictics   33, 36, 37, 46
– emblems   30, 31, 288
– gesticulations   6, 30, 32, 33, 289
– iconics   33, 34, 38, 44, 45
– Kendon's continuum   30
– metaphorics   33, 36, 38
– palm-up-open-hand (PUOH) gesture   32, 33
– pantomime   30, 31
– pointing   36, 37, 38
– pragmatic gestures   31, 32
– representational gesture   5, 38, 40, 41, 43, 46, 47, 285, 288, 289, 290, 291, 295
– representational spatial gesture   36, 38
– signs   30, 31, 288
– speech-linked gestures   30, 31
Ground   1, 4, 6, 8, 11, 15, 18, 20, 43, 68, 78, 85, 96–98, 296
– Gestural Ground   80

Hausa 21, 88, 93
horizontal spatial relations 17

in front of 91–98, 122–27, 157, 222, 295, 299
in the middle of 181
instance 287

Japanese 43

language acquisition 165, 285
lateral axis 5, 7, 18, 164–230, 248, 251, 254, 258, 263, 266, 269, 270–71, 271–74, 274, 278, 279, 296, 298, 299, 300
– description 164–67
linguistic iconicity 34
– onomatopoeia 34
Location 68
locative relationships 12
– change of localisation 12
– dynamic general localisation 12
– static general localisation 12, 13

manner fog 44
Manner of location 15, 16
mental rotation task 43
metonymy 253
Motion 11, 68, 296
motion (semantic domain) 4
Motion events 11, 13, 14, 16, 24, 28, 43, 51, 134, 175, 296
– core schema 13
– Manner 14, 260–61

next to 167, 170–76, 188, 190, 208, 222, 225, 226, 232, 237, 239–40, 267, 278, 289, 295, 300, 303, 304
Nigerian Sign Language (NSl) 3

on 231–48, 256–65, 267, 285, 293, 295, 301–2, 303, 305
opposite 206–7, 209, 230, 278–79, 279, 299, 302
origo 6, 10, 17, 19, 25, 26, 29, 36, 88, 96–98, 156, 157, 183, 184, 185–86, 191, 195, 198, 202, 220, 266, 269
outside (of) 125, 204–6, 209, 230

past 131–32, 156
Path 6, 11, 15, 68, 78, 235, 236, 237, 296
pauses 78
perception
– visual 284, 293
perspective 6, 10, 17, 22, 24, 29, 42, 183, 184, 185–86, 191, 198, 200–201, 201–2, 202, 210, 211–12, 213, 220, 264, 267, 268, 292, 298, 300
– dual perspectives in speech and gesture 98–100
– route perspective 22
– survey perspective 22
placement events 43
Polish 3
posture 29
profile 293

relative clause 79, 82
relative position 44, 45, 46
rotation of spatial properties 20, 21, 88, 95, 106, 160, 165, 268, 269, 298
– mirror order 20, 165
– translation 21, 88, 93, 95, 269, 298
route descriptions 46

satellite 13, 14, 15, 296
scale of space 5, 21, 51
schema 287
sequence-encoding items 119
sign
– linguistic 34
size (object) 44, 45
Spanish 44
spatial cognition 6, 41, 42, 47, 165
spatial skill 43
speech & gesture production 39, 304
– growth point theory 39
– lexical access 39, 40, 42
– Sketch Model 39
speech fluency 6
static locative expression
– definition 68–75, 76, 78, 298
– functional & grammatical concerns 71–74, 298, 304
– overall locative expression 83–85, 298

– primary locative expression   81–82, 275, 298
– secondary locative expression   83, 85, 276, 298
static locative relationships   266
– basic concepts   11
– definition   1
– sub-types   26, 27
sur   197, 231–35, 248–65, 267, 285, 293, 295, 301–2, 303, 305
Swedish   69
symbolic assembly   8, 266, 286–94, 303

Thai Sign Language (TSQ)   3
then   179–80
time (semantic domain)   4
topology   2, 7, 11, 17, 26, 28, 46, 53, 231–33, 240, 241, 242, 231–65, 267, 285, 295, 301–2, 303, 305
Turkish   3, 43, 44, 45

Turkish Sign Language (TID)   3, 45

up   128–31, 156, 157

verb-framed/satellite-framed typology   13, 28, 296
– equipollently-framed languages   14
verbs
– locative   3
– placement   43
– posture   2
vertical axis   18, 166, 258, 259, 263, 266, 269, 270, 271, 274, 281, 282, 296, 300, 306
vertical spatial relations   17
viewpoint   6, 10, 17, 22, 23, 24, 29, 35, 45, 183, 184, 185–86, 191, 198, 200, 201, 202, 212–13, 219, 221, 264, 267, 268, 292, 300
visibility (interlocutor)   40

www.ingramcontent.com/pod-product-compliance
Lightning Source LLC
Chambersburg PA
CBHW030605230426
43661CB00053B/1854